Popular Religion in Russia

This book dispels the widely held view that paganism survived in Russia along-side Orthodox Christianity, demonstrating that 'double belief', *dvoeverie*, is in fact an academic myth. Scholars, citing the medieval origins of the term, have often portrayed Russian Christianity as uniquely muddied by paganism, with 'double-believing' Christians consciously or unconsciously preserving pagan traditions even into the twentieth century. It shows how the concept of *dvoeverie* arose with nineteenth-century scholars obsessed with the Russian 'folk' and was perpetuated as a propaganda tool in the Soviet period, colouring our perception of both popular faith in Russia and medieval Russian culture for over a century. It surveys the wide variety of uses of the term from the eleventh to the seventeenth century, and contrasts them to its use in modern historiography, concluding that our modern interpretation of *dvoeverie* would not have been recognized by medieval clerics, and that 'double belief' is a modern academic construct. Furthermore, it offers a brief foray into medieval Orthodoxy via the mind of the believer, through the language and literature of the period. If clerics didn't use the word *dvoeverie* to identify acts as unorthodox, which words did they use, and what can these words tell us about popular faith? Was the populace of Rus really more resistant to Christianization than its European counterparts? What was it about popular culture that alarmed the clergy of medieval Rus, and were their concerns so very different from those of Western European clergymen, or the clergy of other neophyte peoples?

Stella Rock is Senior Research Fellow in History at the University of Sussex. Her publications on Russian Orthodoxy span the medieval and post-Soviet periods, and her research interests focus on popular faith (in the broadest sense) and the relationship between religious and national identity.

D1598490

Routledge Studies in the History of Russia and Eastern Europe

Popular Religion in Russia

'Double belief' and the making
of an academic myth

Stella Rock

Routledge
Taylor & Francis Group

LONDON AND NEW YORK

First published 2007
by Routledge
2 Park Square, Milton Park, Abingdon, Oxon, OX14 4RN

Simultaneously published in the USA and Canada
by Routledge
270 Madison Ave, New York NY 10016

*Routledge is an imprint of the Taylor & Francis Group,
an informa business*

Transferred to Digital Printing 2009

© 2007 Stella Rock

Typeset in Times New Roman, Kliment and Method by
Graphicraft Limited, Hong Kong

All rights reserved. No part of this book may be reprinted or
reproduced or utilized in any form or by any electronic,
mechanical, or other means, now known or hereafter
invented, including photocopying and recording, or in any
information storage or retrieval system, without permission in
writing from the publishers.

British Library Cataloguing in Publication Data
A catalogue record for this book is available from the British Library

Library of Congress Cataloging in Publication Data
 Popular religion in Russia : double belief and the making of an
 academic myth / Stella Rock.
 p. cm. — (Routledge studies in the history of Russia and eastern
 Europe series; 10)
 Includes bibliographical references and index.
 ISBN 978-0-415-31771-9 (hardback : alk. paper) 1. Russia—
 Religion. I. Rock, Stella.
 BL980.R8P67 2007
 200.947—dc22
 2007007861

ISBN 10: 0-415-31771-1 (hbk)
ISBN 10: 0-415-54535-8 (pbk)
ISBN 10: 0-203-59228-X (ebk)

ISBN 13: 978-0-415-31771-9 (hbk)
ISBN 13: 978-0-415-54535-8 (pbk)
ISBN 13: 978-0-203-59228-1 (ebk)

In memory of Thomas

Contents

List of abbreviations

BLDR	*Biblioteka literatury Drevnei Rusi*
CUP	Cambridge University Press
GBL	Rossiiskaia gosudarstvennaia biblioteka (formerly Lenin Library)
GIM	Gosudarstvennyi istoricheskii muzei
HLEUL	Harvard Library of Early Ukrainian Literature
HUS	*Harvard Ukrainian Studies*
KJV	King James Version
MERSH	*Modern Encyclopedia of Russian and Soviet History*
OED	*Oxford English Dictionary*
OUP	Oxford University Press
PLDR	*Pamiatniki literatury Drevnei Rusi*
PSRL	*Polnoe sobranie russkikh letopisei*
RAN	Rossiiskaia akademiia nauk
RFV	*Russkii filologicheskii vestnik*
RGADA	Rossiiskii gosudarstvennyi arkhiv drevnikh aktov
RIB	*Russkaia istoricheskaia biblioteka*
TODRL	*Trudy otdela Drevnerusskoi literatury*
TsGALI	Tsentral'nyi gosudarstvennyi arkhiv literatury i iskusstva

Acknowledgements

It is thanks to a three-year studentship from the British Academy that my DPhil thesis, which forms the basis of this book, was written. I was also supported by travel grants from the British Academy and the University of Sussex, and a scholarship to attend the Medieval Slavic Summer Institute at the Hilandar Research Library, Ohio State University, which proved invaluable. I am deeply grateful to all the staff there – in particular to Mary Allen Johnson ('Pasha') – for constant support and encouragement.

I should like to express my thanks to those specialists who have helped in general or in specific matters during the research for and writing of this book, in particular Robin Milner-Gulland, Eve Levin, Simon Franklin, William Ryan, Bernadette Filotas and Peter Burke, who all read and commented on the book manuscript in its entirety or in part. Eve Levin's help in reshaping a dry thesis into a book deserves a special mention – she is a truly generous scholar – as does the erudition and encouragement of Daniel Collins, which saved me from despair when tackling many a convoluted text.

Vladimir Bersenev, Iuri Lesman and Irina Levinskaia were unstinting in their support, and I am also grateful to Maria Korogodina, Aleksei V. Chernetsov, Gregory Freeze, Dmitrii Bulanin, Daniel Kaiser, Ia. N. Shchapov, Oleg Panchenko, Anatolii A. Turilov, Francis J. Thomson, Muriel Heppell, Beryl Williams and the late Fr Sergei Hackel. Jonathan Mitchell and Jeffrey Pratt offered useful insights from the field of anthropology. My editor at Routledge, Peter Sowden, deserves special thanks for his unfailing patience and kindness while awaiting the final manuscript. Thanks are also due to the resourceful staff of Interlibrary Requests at the University of Sussex; Kit Condill and the wonderful Slavic Reference Service at the University of Illinois at Urbana-Champaign; David Howells at the Taylor Institution Library, Oxford; Denis Reidy at the British Library and the librarians at the St Petersburg Spiritual Academy. I also found the help of the staff at the archives of the State Historical Museum (especially Elena Serebriakova) and the Saltykov-Shchedrin Library archive in St Petersburg invaluable. My thanks to the staff at the Institute of Russian Language, Moscow; to Liudmila Kozlova of the DAR Language School, St Petersburg; to the Association for Women in Slavic Studies mentoring service and Christine Worobec in particular, and to the various correspondents of

H-Russia Net, the Medieval Religion mailing list and Medieval Slavic Mailing List who responded to queries about individual books, texts and authors. Special thanks to Daniel Collins, Persephone Liulio, Vassiliki Dimitropoulou, Vassiliki Roupa and Gavin Ashenden for help with the Greek originals. Needless to say, I take full responsibility for any errors or other failings of this book.

Finally, my thanks to friends and family who helped in innumerable ways; especially Matthew Platts, Maureen Radford, Susan Vaughan, Natalia Tronenko and Olga Soboleva. Thanks are also due to Bettina Weichert, Sandra Reddin, Edik Sukhanov, Fr Kevin Ward, Fr Tom Daly and Jonathan Aves, and not least to my daughter Mary, who has stoically travelled around Russia and endured long hours of boredom at home.

Preface

When I set out on the trail of *dvoeverie*, or 'double belief' as it is usually translated, I was puzzled by historiographical application of this term to popular belief in Russia, and the frequent references to its medieval origins. It was my intention to identify those groups of Christians attacked by Church scribes as 'double-believers', and analyze as far as possible the practices they were engaged in that earned them this curious rebuke. The interest for me lay in why particular groups and practices might be singled out for such condemnation – was it a question of the identity of the practitioners (their gender, perhaps, or ethnicity) or the nature of the practices? I turned first to the medieval texts such as the polemics collected by Gal'kovskii and Tikhonravov, expecting to find a plethora of pagan rituals or practitioners castigated as 'double-believing'. However, the obvious material related to paganism or unorthodox beliefs and behaviours did not provide more than one incidence of the term *dvoeverie*, and the texts I subsequently gathered that did contain the word used it in surprisingly diverse and sometimes entirely unexpected contexts. It was an alarming process of discovery, and led me to produce a very different kind of book from the one I'd planned to write.

Included within the study of medieval uses of the term are such lexical derivatives as *dvoverstvo, dvoverstvuyetsia, dvovertsi*, and most of the texts considered are cited in published historical dictionaries or listed in the unpublished card catalogue of the Institute of Russian Language, Moscow.[1] The examples discussed do not bear out the modern use of the term, and the huge semantic gap between the modern use of the term and early uses suggests that the limited number of extant examples I have found may well be the full quota. However, I acknowledge the possibility that there are omissions, since it is an impossible task to search the entire canon of medieval Slavic texts and write up the results while still of able mind and body. Or at least, for this researcher it is.

A large number of the examples discussed appear in translations of Byzantine sources, and I have made no attempt to analyze the original material other than to identify it where possible, and record the Greek word translated as *dvoeverie* where the source material is known and accessible. Anything more is properly a task for a Byzantine specialist, and falls outside the scope of this work, since we are concerned with how Russian clerics would have used and understood the term. I have tried to indicate the extent to which each text containing the word appears to have been disseminated, and the context in which it would have been used – in other words, who was the audience? – while keeping specialist detail about manuscript redactions to a minimum, indicating further reading where available.

This study is by no means intended to offer a complete answer to the problem of *dvoeverie* as a historical or cultural concept; it is rather an attempt to analyze the wide variety of uses of the term from the eleventh to the seventeenth century, in contrast to its use in modern historiography. While I had to spend far more time than I would have liked thinking about issues of translation and textual transmission, this study also offers a brief foray into medieval belief via the mind of the believer, through the language and literature of the period. If clerics didn't use the word 'double-belief' to identify acts as unorthodox, what words did they use, and what can these words tell us about popular faith and culture? What did medieval clerics mean when they called something or someone 'pagan'? Was the populace of Rus really more resistant to Christianization than their European neighbours? What was it about popular culture that alarmed the clergy in medieval Rus, and were their concerns so very different from those of Western European clergy, or the clergy of other neophyte peoples? In terms of the historiographical content of Chapter 4, which addresses the latter two questions, I am aware that I am skating through territory familiar to historians of Western European belief. However, the historiography of Russian Orthodoxy has often portrayed Russian Christianity as uniquely muddied by paganism, and a (perhaps foolhardy) venture into modern debates about the nature of pre-Reformation faith in Western Europe seemed a necessary addition to my original research.

Finally, a few words on presentation. When citing from a published text, I have reproduced as accurately as possible the format used by the publisher and indicated any differences from the published text in a footnote. When citing from an unpublished manuscript, I have inserted my own word divisions where there are none and indicated them with the '/' sign. Again, I have attempted to reproduce the lettering used in the manuscripts as accurately as possible given the limitations of PC fonts. In transliterating Russian and Greek, I have used the Library of Congress system.

Where adequate English translations of major historical works exist, I have used and cited these. With regard to my own translations (particularly in Chapter 2 in which some fairly opaque texts are discussed), I have often translated literally, to reflect the complexity of the texts and any mistakes made by the Slavic translators and copyists, since the comprehensibility of these texts to their medieval readers is significant. In citing from the Bible, I have used the King James translation (for no reason except that the language has particular resonance for me), and in Church Slavonic, the Bible of Elizabeth.

The form in which proper names are rendered is necessarily somewhat arbitrary. Individuals whose lives and careers were normally passed in Russia are given their Russian names – e.g. Feodosii rather than Theodosius, Metropolitan

Ioann II not Metropolitan John II; individuals outside of the Russian sphere such as Theophylact of Ochrid are named in accordance with standard English usage. Where certain spellings have become accepted convention – Vladimir rather than Volodimir, Olga rather than Ol'ga, I have used these. As regards the vexed question of Russia or Rus', Russian, Rus'ian, or Ruthenian and other such geographical and political definitions, for reasons of simplicity I have opted to use Rus or Kievan Rus (with soft sign omitted) in reference to the period preceding the Tatar-Mongol invasions of the thirteenth century,[2] and Russian as the adjectival form referring both to Rus and Russia (except where quoting from an author who uses other terms). I am sure that this will displease many finer scholars, but geographical and political boundaries are rarely respected in the transmission of ideas, and this book is concerned with the concept of Russian double-belief. The exact origin of many of the texts surveyed is uncertain, but their influence as discussed is decidedly within the sphere of Russian culture.

Introduction

The New Age movement gaining ground in the West also found a resonance in the former Soviet Union, where it shared similarities with some indigenous sects and movements influenced by extrasensory perception, hypnotism, and other phenomena, dating back for centuries: a new manifestation, in some ways, of the *dvoeverie* ... which had persisted after the adoption of Christianity in Kievan Rus'.[1]

Jane Ellis, 1998

The concept of *dvoeverie*, usually translated as 'double belief', 'ditheism' or 'dual faith',[2] has coloured our perception of both popular faith in Russia and medieval Russian culture for over a century. Since the *glasnost'* policy of the Gorbachev administration opened up serious scholarship of Christianity in Soviet Russia, the term *dvoeverie* has come under increasing scrutiny. Does it refer to a 'syncretic' faith in which Christian and pagan elements have influenced each other and merged together, or perhaps a covert or overt resistance to Christianity maintained by the peasantry, resulting in two independent and self-contained belief-systems? Currently, there is no clear agreement on what it actually means among scholars, a problem aggravated by the politically motivated use of the term by some Soviet academics. Contemporary historians in the West, in particular those specializing in popular culture and 'lived Orthodoxy', are finding it an unwieldy tool for the close study of folk belief and ritual, imposing as it does over a hundred years of value judgements of varying kinds on the faith, identity and religious allegiance of the Russian peasantry. Russian scholars have also had to wrestle with the additional implications of their predecessors' overtly atheistic approach to Orthodox Church history.

As a concept, *dvoeverie* has been immensely important for Russian cultural and historical studies, and its persistence and ubiquity have encouraged an unhelpful preoccupation with identifying latent paganism in Russian culture and spirituality. Applied to the conversion period, the later medieval and early modern period when Christianity was well established, and even to modern popular culture, it has become at worst a code word for the stubborn 'ignorance' or 'resistance' of the Russian peasantry and parish clergy, simultaneously a value judgement made by Western historians and a tool of Soviet atheist propaganda. At best, it remains a clumsy indicator of the complexity of popular faith and the processes of Christianization in medieval Russia.

While there has been a gradual move towards an understanding of religious belief within the mental framework of the period under study, very little work has been done on the concept of *dvoeverie* as it was understood by those first employing the term. Picked seemingly at random from one sermon usually dated to the eleventh century, which condemns idol-worshippers 'living in double-belief', other uses of the term spread across seven centuries are generally ignored, and although several thought-provoking articles have touched upon the subject, no systematic study of the changing meaning and varied uses of the word in the medieval or pre-Petrine period has been carried out either by Western or Russian scholars.

This book is an attempt to unpick the academic myth of *dvoeverie*. Did Russia experience a unique survival of paganism as many scholars have suggested? Why have so many scholars, from such a variety of conceptual frameworks and over a period of more than a century, found such a theory plausible? Given that the term *dvoeverie* has become the shorthand for this alleged phenomenon, an investigation focused around the use of that term is a convenient means of approaching these problems.[3] As Le Goff observed some years ago,

> Historians doubtless do not yet attach sufficient importance to words. The clerics of the Middle Ages knew better: whether realists or nominalists, they knew that words and things are as closely connected as soul and body.[4]

The problem with words

The problems of terminology are multiple. Contemporary scholarship now acknowledges that we cannot treat Christianity as monolithic,[5] but if we are to study the many variations of Christianity across time and space, and across social and ethnic groupings, we need a terminology that will convey our findings clearly. 'Defining terms' is really the main focus of this book. Margarita Mazo has observed,

> I find the term *dvoeverie* poorly grounded, since it did not originate in an understanding of the beliefs of the Russian peasants as they existed in actual practice, but in the theological bias of those who coined the term . . . it is important to make a distinction between the Church, with its rituals and clergy, and religion as a theoretical and theological doctrine. It is essential to distinguish *religion* from *faith* as a basic, primary, and practical body of beliefs. Faith was a syncretic entity in which village sorcery and Orthodox worships were dynamically fused into one indivisible creed.[6]

It is important to distinguish the structures of the Church from religion, and theoretical, doctrinal religion from faith and practice, and equally important to ensure that the words and concepts we use in historical studies are not weighed down with our 'theological bias', our personal values and judgements. In this book, I have used 'faith' to indicate the body of beliefs and associated rituals held by a recognizably distinct group of individuals – in most cases Orthodox Christians. This does not reflect theological understanding or use of the term, but resembles rather its use in modern historiography.

Following Peter Burke,[7] I have used 'popular culture' to indicate rituals and traditions prevalent among ordinary people (as opposed to the governing nobility, clergy and monastics) although – in some instances – the gentry and lower clergy might participate in it. These rituals and traditions may, or may not, have held some spiritual significance, but for the most part they were not prescribed by the Church. There is a huge debate over the legitimacy and usefulness of dividing medieval society into 'popular' and 'élite' or 'learned', which is as yet unresolved.[8] Mindful of all the issues raised by Natalie Zemon Davis,[9] in the context of this work 'popular' still offers a useful shorthand to distinguish those whom the sermons, penitentials and other corrective or prescriptive texts were aimed at (the laity and lower clergy) and those who were responsible for enforcing the views of their clerical authors (the higher clergy and, to a lesser extent, the ruling class). This does not mean, of course, that the behaviours castigated in these texts were the exclusive prerogative of the laity and lower clergy – drunkenness and inappropriate revelry were certainly embraced by the secular élites, most famously by Ivan IV and Peter the Great, and accusations of sorcery and heresy were levelled at nobles and senior clerics as at peasants – but some manner of indicating the difference between the minority teachers and guardians of the Orthodox faith and the majority who were the target of reforms and teaching is required.

It is worth observing that the division between the lower and higher clergy is more marked in the Orthodox Church than in the Catholic, at least since the thirteenth century when Catholic priests became routinely celibate.[10] Orthodox parish clergy ('white clergy') marry, unless destined for the higher echelons of the Church as monastic 'black clergy', and are therefore arguably closer to their parishioners in terms of lifestyle than Catholic priests.[11] That said, the Tridentine church was still struggling to 'erect secure boundaries between clergy and laity' in sixteenth-century Western Europe, as Inquisition records demonstrate – unmarried parish priests might still operate within kinship groups, for example.[12]

'Religion' I have taken to mean an institutionalized system of doctrines and dogmas that purports to organize the beliefs and rituals of faith. In this schema, the paganism practised on the territory of Kievan Rus would not constitute a religion, since despite Prince Vladimir's efforts to establish an 'official pantheon' in the tenth century, the fragmented evidence that remains suggests that there was no widespread formal structure of gods and mythology, and probably no priesthood.[13] The inhabitants of early Rus, it seems, populated nature with various spirits, practised ancestor worship, and in some parts, at some times, worshipped various idols or natural phenomena. One could, however, talk about various pagan 'faiths', common to groups (agricultural, warrior or merchant), which involved a shared belief in the efficacy of certain rituals (sacrificing to springs and lakes, swearing oaths on weapons or in the name of a god of cattle, for example).

An essential concept for this work is that of 'Christian', or rather 'Orthodox Christian', because in most of the examples of the use of the term *dvoeverie* (from the medieval to the modern period) that address the matter of religious belief, the religion in question is Orthodox Christianity. Similarly, in almost every historian's use of the term, one of the two religions referred to is Russian Orthodoxy.

While most Christian confessions would accept the Nicene Creed as a summary of Christian beliefs, differences in styles of worship and emphasis on different aspects of the Christian tradition have developed over the centuries. The introduction to *Contemporary Heresies and Sects in Russia*, published in 1995 apparently under the editorship of the late Metropolitan Ioann of St Petersburg, warns that Russia is under threat of 'spiritual colonisation' by 'occultism, Catholicism, Protestant heresies and sects' such as AUM and the Moonies.[14] While Metropolitan Ioann is hardly the standard authority on these questions, the approach promoted by this volume highlights the issue at stake: there remain beliefs and practices which divide the major denominations of Christianity in seemingly irresolvable fashion, and hinder a general consensus on what is 'properly' Christian.

For some believers, anything that is not clearly supported by textual evidence from the accepted canon of the New Testament is not 'Christian'. Not all Christians would accept the Dormition or Assumption as a Christian belief, for example, supported as it is by material from the Apocrypha. Rogation Sunday, with the 'beating of the bounds' and blessing of the fields, appears positively pagan to a fundamentalist Protestant. The commandment prohibiting graven images encourages some Christians to consider Orthodox icon veneration and/or the Roman Catholic practice of lighting candles before religious statues, carrying them in procession and clothing or decorating them, as forms of idolatry. In contemporary Belfast, the word 'Christian' among some lay people means a fundamentalist Protestant who doesn't smoke, drink or swear, and the term is used in a pejorative fashion by church-going Catholics and non-practising Protestants alike. To fundamentalist Protestants in Belfast as in the US, a Christian is someone who has undergone a personal conversion experience.

This selection of examples may be an over-simplification of an incredibly complex pattern of beliefs, but it serves to demonstrate the fact that even today, the word 'Christian' is loaded with implications and associations. Christianity must be self-defining in a sense, since none of us (and more pertinently, no historian) can know the mind of God and ascertain exactly what it was He did intend. We must let each Church under scrutiny define its own Christianity, otherwise we run the risk of entering inadvertently into a denominational polemic that is of no benefit to historical studies.

'*Православность*' (*pravovernost'*, 'right belief'), or '*православие*' (*pravoslavie*, 'orthodoxy', literally 'right worship'), defines itself by identifying what is wrong belief and wrong worship, and for pre-modern (and some modern) Russian Orthodox clerics the need to be clear on what was orthodox, what was correct, was an important spiritual drive. Generalizations have been made about the ritualism of the Russian clergy,[15] stressing the importance of fine detail and canonical exactitude in penitential literature, and it is tempting to see in the great Church schism of the seventeenth century an obsessive and incomprehensible desire for exactness in matters of faith. However, if we approach the study of pre-modern belief from the point of view of 'enlightened', post-Vatican II theology (or even post-Reformation theology) we will inevitably fail to understand it. To understand belief one must enter into the mind of the believer, leaving behind one's cultural baggage. While archaeological evidence, church art and architecture all help the historian make the mental leap, the language and literature of a period are crucial. We need to identify what appeared to constitute 'real' or 'true' Christianity during the period within which we are working, and to understand the mutual influences of faith and society. With all that said, whichever terms we use, we will find ourselves making exceptions, and trying to fix boundaries between categories in an often anachronistic fashion. The boundaries of orthodox faith are neither constant nor consistent, and we must be ever mindful of that.

In any given period, it is the guardians of faith, the higher clergy and theologians within a given denomination, who define 'correct' or 'orthodox' Christianity, often with the support of the State.[16] When conflict arises, a Church Council is required to decide which party has the correct interpretation, the 'truth', on its side. Further down the ecclesiastical ladder, priests will appeal to their bishops for guidance in matters of the faith, and the laity to their parish priests and other clerics to whom they have access. Extant church texts (and perhaps to some extent church art and architecture) are our only guide to what constituted orthodox Christian behaviour and belief during the period under analysis.

The question of what constitutes a Christian is slightly more complex. As Fletcher has pointed out, 'being Christian' has meant different things to different people, as has 'conversion',[17] and while we have evidence of forced baptism and mass baptisms in many times and places, we also have the testimony of clerics such as the eighth-century Northumbrian scholar Alcuin, who worried that the baptism of the unfortunate Saxons without proper instruction was redundant, 'for it is not possible for the body properly to receive the sacrament of baptism unless the soul has previously received the truth of the faith into itself'.[18] Although in the early church a person might be referred to as a Christian while preparing to be baptized, baptism is the point at which a neophyte puts off his or her old identity and becomes a 'new man' (Colossians 3:9–11).[19] Van Engen has suggested that 'Christendom' (*Christianitas*) was 'the term used by medieval folk at every level to identify their religious culture', but although medieval folk implicitly acknowledged a difference between those who were simply baptized and those who were fervent believers, at one level Christendom was 'the society of the baptised'.[20]

Clearly, a baptized individual 'belonged' to the Orthodox Church during the period under study, since legal documents from the earliest years of Christian Rus address the status and treatment of the baptized differently from the non-orthodox or unbaptized, and attempted to limit the relations between them. 'А с некрещеным или иноязычьником или от нашего языка некрещен будеть, ни ясти, ни пити с ним, дондеже крестится; а ведаа кто ясть и пиеть, да будеть митрополиту в вине' 'Do not eat or drink with those who are not baptized or with a foreigner or [with anyone] from our own people if he be not baptized, until he is baptized. And whoever knowingly eats and drinks [with unbaptized persons] will be guilty before the Metropolitan' thunders the eleventh-century *Statute of Iaroslav*.[21] Similarly, those who ate with excommunicated individuals were to find themselves excommunicated.

In baptism an individual came to belong to the family of the Orthodox, and remained so unless excommunicated. The 1649 Law Code instructs that those who steal adult or child Tatars from Astrakhan or Siberia must return them to their people unless they have been baptized:

А будет они тех Татар и Татарченков крестят: и на них за тех Татар и за Татарченков доправити против тамошние продажи большую цену, и отдати тем людем, у кого они тех Татар и Татарченков украдут, или отымут, а тем новокрещенным Татарам быти у них.

If they baptized those adult and child Tatars: extract from them a large sum for those adult and child Tatars corresponding to the local sale price, and give [the money] to those people from whom they have stolen or taken away those adult and child Tatars. The newly baptized Tatars shall remain their property.[22]

These unfortunate neophytes had one protection thanks to their Christian status – they could not be sold on: 'по тому что по Государеву указу крещеных людей никому продавати не велено' 'because it has been ordered by the Sovereign's decree that no one shall sell baptized people'.[23]

Baptized Orthodox could appeal to the Church courts for protection and compensation. Their perceived Christian or unchristian behaviour could influence the result of that appeal,[24] but the Church had the right (by canon law), indeed the duty, to intervene in matters related to the family, faith and sexual morality. Certain categories of people 'belonged' to the Church in terms of judgement and punishment:

А се церковные люди: игумен, поп, дьякон, дети их, попадия, и кто в клиросе, игуменья, чернець, черница, проскурница, паломник, лечець, прощеник, задушьныи человек, стороник, слепець, хромець, манастыреве, болнице, гостинници, странноприимнице. То люди церковные богаделные, митрополит или пискуп ведаеть межи ими суд, или обида, или котора, или вражда, или задница.

And these are church people: abbot, priest, deacon, their children, priest's wife, and whoever is in the choir, abbess, monk, nun, the woman who bakes the Eucharist bread, pilgrim, physician, freed [debt] slave, manumitted slave, wanderer, the blind and the lame; [also all church people in] monasteries, hospitals, inns [and] refuges for wanderers and pilgrims. They are church people, those who do God's work. The Metropolitan or bishop holds jurisdiction [in disputes] between them, whether [it be a case of] insult, or quarrel, or physical harm or inheritance.[25]

Finally, once baptized, an individual belonged to the family of the Orthodox even if he or she might prefer not to. Even as late as 1905 apostasy – abandonment of the Orthodox faith for another faith or denomination – was an offence punishable by law in Russia.[26] Baptized Orthodox 'belonged' to the church not only in theological terms, but also legally, and the State's treatment of those newly baptized converts from Islam or paganism who reverted to their former faiths indicates that 'baptism alone usually determined religious status'.[27]

As Daniel Kaiser has observed, Orthodoxy regulated the lives of Muscovites in early modern Russia 'in every sphere of activity': churches defined communities, time was regulated by the Orthodox calendar, and the significant events of birth, marriage and death were accompanied by Orthodox ritual.[28] The further back in time one goes, however, the more difficult it is to assess the role the Church as an institution played in individuals' lives, since parish records were kept systematically only from the eighteenth century onwards.[29] With no certain knowledge of what contact individuals in isolated rural communities had with the Church, the question arises as to whether a baptized individual during this early period, who may have lived out his or her entire life with little access to the sacraments, without reference to the Bible or canon law and with little or no understanding of the doctrines of Orthodox Christianity, constitutes a Christian. In the context of this work the answer must be yes, as both the Church and the State accepted baptism as the determining factor, and we have very little evidence that reveals the self-definition of individuals, or what the popular conception of Christian identity was.[30]

One source of evidence we do have for the self-perception of laypeople is the birchbark documents they wrote from the eleventh to the fifteenth century. As Eve Levin has pointed out, almost 90 per cent of the documents make no reference to religion, but are concerned with the prosaic matters of commercial and domestic life. From those that do, Levin deduces that by the late twelfth century Christian identity was 'clearly manifest' among the urban population, that by the thirteenth century those engaged in agriculture were using the Orthodox calendar, and by the late fourteenth century, peasants were calling themselves Christians, 'indicating their full assimilation of Christian identity'.[31] Supplicatory prayers found in parish service books and miscellanies also reflect a firm Christian identity among the laity in Muscovite Russia, with the petitioner identified as 'servant of God'.[32] Jennifer Anderson, working with petitions and court records from the seventeenth century, concludes that 'Muscovites had a clear Christian identity, even if their vision of Christian morality did not exactly correspond to that of the institutional Church'.[33]

Numerous scholars have explored the process of the Christianization of Rus, and the question of just how 'Christian' the populace of Russia was in the medieval period, particularly since the great surge of interest in the subject sparked by the millennium celebrations of the 'baptism of Rus' in 1988. It is important to bear in mind that Rus, like Scandinavia and the Baltic region, was Christianized comparatively late, and therefore by the twelfth century had had far more limited exposure to Christian ideas and culture than, say, France. Later Christianizations, and Latin America is a case in point, also tend to be better documented. But although more evidence of missionaries' struggles with the pre-Christian beliefs of their neophyte communities may survive, it does not necessarily follow that the struggles were greater than those of earlier missionaries in other lands. These issues will be explored further in Chapter 4, but it is worth observing that until fairly recently, the general consensus among lay historians of Russia has been that

> we may say with confidence that the introduction of Christianity in 988, lacking in any sufficiently solid social and political soil, did not bring about a radical change in the consciousness of the society during the entire course of ancient Russian history.[34]

While the rural peasantry are unlikely to have undergone a radical cultural change in the first centuries of Christianization, clearly this statement is not accurate. For Ilarion, Metropolitan of Kiev, writing in the eleventh century, the citizens of Kiev could proudly define themselves as Christians:

> И уже не идолослужителе зовемся, нъ христиании, не еще безнадеж-ници, нъ уповающе въ жизнь вѣчную. И уже не капище сътонино съграждаемь, нъ Христовы церкви зиждемь; уже не закалаемь бѣсомъ другъ друга, нъ Христос за ны закалаемь бываеть и дробимъ въ жертву Богу и Отьцю.[35]

> Now we are called Christians, no longer idolaters; no longer the hopeless, but longing with hope for eternal life. No longer do we build pagan shrines, for now we construct Christ's churches. No longer do we slay one another as offerings for demons, for now Christ is ever slain and segmented for us as an offering to God and the Father.[36]

Within the boundaries of Kiev, swiftly followed by Novgorod and other major towns, the urban population witnessed the public and dramatic destruction of their pagan idols and the building of masonry and wooden churches, followed by spectacular cathedrals.[37] The spiritual or psychological impact of this work must surely have constituted a radical change in the fabric of society and the consciousness of those who participated in the transformation:

Виждь же и градъ, величьством сиающь, виждь церкви цвѣтущи, виждь христианьство растуще, виждь град, иконами святыихъ освѣщаемь и блистающеся, и тимианомъ обухаемь, и хвалами божественами и пѣнии святыими оглашаемь.[38]

Behold also the city, shining in splendour! Behold churches blossoming! Behold Christianity growing! Behold the glittering city, illumined with icons of saints and scented with incense, resounding with praises and songs to the Lord![39]

While Ilarion certainly had an obligation to celebrate the triumph of Christianity, since his position as a high-ranking cleric made him responsible for its success, this joyous sermon is as valid a source as early sermons bemoaning the continued practice of idol-worship or belief in witchcraft. It describes one facet, or perception, of Rus society, a facet that is reflected in the reports of foreign visitors to early Kiev. Adam of Bremen, for example, who died in 1074, considered Kiev 'aemula sceptri Constantinopolitani, clarissimum decus Greciae',[40] 'rival of the sceptre of Constantinople, the brightest ornament of Greece'.[41] It is impossible to measure the extent to which individual citizens of Kiev felt themselves part of the Orthodox world, but we can say that the élite, the clerics and courtiers, certainly participated in the conversion process, although the *Primary Chronicle* records the protest of the mothers from the 'best people', who wept when their children were taken away to be educated in the new faith 'as if for the dead'.[42] Taking into account the significant number of monasteries founded in the pre-Mongol period,[43] and the (doubtless exaggerated) 'more than four hundred churches' recorded as existing in Kiev in the early eleventh century by the chronicler Thietmar of Merseburg (975–1018),[44] one can also safely assume that there was a demand for church service and services among at least a significant proportion of the ordinary, urban population.

Finds of church artefacts dating from the eleventh to thirteenth centuries in urban areas indicate that manifestations of Christianity were at least visible to the population of major towns, and from the mid-twelfth century onwards Christian artefacts can be found in graves even in remote rural areas.[45] We have no way of demonstrating how many ordinary citizens participated willingly (or unwillingly) in church rituals after the period of enforced baptisms and the educational programme of Vladimir's reign, nor of assessing the depth of their personal faith, but sermons would not have been composed or copied if their authors had no hope of being heard at least by the clerics (and, perhaps, princes) responsible for these souls.[46] To suggest, then, that during the 'entire course of ancient Russian history' the populace experienced no radical change is untenable. Christianity altered the visual landscape and, one can assume, the interior landscape of those who witnessed this alteration and development.

As a secondary consideration, some remark should be made about what we mean by 'the Church'. Theologians define the Church as the sum of those faithful living and deceased – that is, all believers; but for historians, the Church usually means the institutionalized elements – decision-making bodies, e.g. local and general councils, clerical leaders and officials. This approach has been challenged by Vera Shevzov, who points out that *tserkov'* (church) was

> used to refer broadly to the community of Christians – their collective identity proper – as well as to the church building. More important, on the basis of its own historical roots, *tserkov'*, or 'church', like 'nation', can be viewed in terms of a community continually in the making, shaped by all persons who see themselves as belonging to it.[47]

Shevzov favours use of this broader definition of 'church' since it encourages a more holistic approach, which recognizes the communal dynamics shaping Orthodoxy and acknowledges that local diversity did not preclude a sense of unity and belonging. This approach essentially advocates that we accept the self-definition of ordinary Christians who viewed themselves as part of the Church, and did not perceive the faith as having official and popular variants. In the study of late Imperial Orthodoxy this is a workable, creative approach that aims to avoid the pitfalls of distinguishing 'lived Orthodoxy' from 'prescribed', or 'popular' from 'élite'. However, in the context of a study of clerical condemnations of paganism, we need a definition that recognizes the status of those who spoke as representatives of the Orthodox Church in presenting opinions on correct and incorrect religious behaviours. Although lay people influenced the Orthodox faith – in, for example, their promotion of local relics and icons – and may have had some sway in local clerical appointments and parish affairs, they nevertheless recognized the authority of the clergy and appealed to church representatives to offer authoritative judgements on issues of morality and spirituality.[48]

In the context of this study, I have chosen to define 'the Russian Orthodox Church', or for that matter 'the Roman Catholic Church', at any given moment in history, as a body made up of identifiably affiliated individuals and groups (e.g. bishops, monks, parish clergy) who may or may not agree upon spiritual matters, and who may or may not be influenced by external considerations such as politics or personal gain. I use the term 'church' unqualified to distinguish between the laity and those individuals recognisably affiliated to the Church by occupation – primarily the clergy – and where possible qualified, indicating what dissent or difference there might be between groups and individuals within this wider definition. While generalizations can and sometimes must be made about the actions, beliefs and intentions of 'the church', one cannot presume that the church as a unity of individuals, communities and ranks was of one static (or even consistent) and unified mind, as the Arian and Iconoclast controversies demonstrate.

Again, we must be mindful of the distinction between 'the Orthodox Church' and 'the Orthodox faith' – the faith being the primary body of beliefs and rituals accepted by Orthodox Christians. Which beliefs and rituals are legitimate components of that faith, and which are not (and are therefore 'unorthodox') is the crux of the *dvoeverie* debate in modern scholarship. To overcome scruples about displaying prejudice and judgemental attitudes, or simply to better reflect the matter under scrutiny, some recent scholars of popular faith have chosen terms which overcome the division of beliefs into Orthodox and unorthodox, such as 'folk Christianity' (*narodnoe khristianstvo*)[49] and 'everyday Orthodoxy' (*bytovoe pravoslavie*)[50] to describe beliefs and rituals practised by Christian communities and individuals, but perhaps unsanctioned, disapproved of or opposed by the Church. In this book I will often use the term 'popular unortho-doxy', which acknowledges the fact that the higher clergy of the Russian Orthodox Church accepted certain elements of popular belief and made them Orthodox (for example, the adoption of the local veneration of saints on a national scale), and clearly prohibited other elements – such as the leaving of cauls on the altar.

It is examples such as the leaving of prohibited objects in the sanctuary, which implies the participation or at least connivance of the parish priest, which make this such an interesting but complex field of study. Clergy (parish priests and religious) were accused of inappropriate behaviours and beliefs, and of participating in unorthodox practices, Europe-wide. We can rarely be sure about the intentions or self-perception of the practitioners, but if acting in union with their parish priest, they may well have thought they were behaving as an Orthodox Christian should.

We can be sure in many cases of the higher clergy's perception of these behaviours, and where they condemn them, there we have unorthodoxy. This division into Orthodox and unorthodox is not entirely straightforward (as might be expected), since clerics did not always agree on what was acceptable and what was not, but where differences of opinion are known, they are noted. I am not, of course, suggesting 'popular unorthodoxy' as a synonym for 'popular belief' or 'lived Orthodoxy' – the latter are far broader terms which incorporate the prescribed, the prohibited and a huge spectrum of practices in between; it is, however, primarily those elements of popular faith rejected by the Church that the double-belief debate focuses on. Those elements of belief that were acceptable to the Church we hear far less about – such is the nature of our sources – although increasingly researchers are revealing lived Orthodoxy in its multiple regional variations,[51] an academic trend in evidence in the study of medieval and early modern faith in Western Europe.[52]

Having considered the definitions of terms associated with 'right worship', we now turn our attention to 'wrong worship', the main focus of this work. Which words medieval Russian clerics chose to castigate unorthodoxy is the subject of the following chapter, but some broad observations about terms used in the body of this work should be made at this point. As well as 'double-belief', 'superstition' is a label which occurs frequently in the his-toriography of Russian popular belief. I have tried to avoid this, preferring the more neutral 'unorthodox practices'. There is already substantial literature on the term 'superstition' which need not be repeated here;[53] suffice to note that the Russian *sueverie* (*суеверие*) does not appear before the seventeenth century in primary source descriptions of unorthodox practices.[54] More important for this work is the concept of 'pagan', or 'paganism', for which there is more than one word in the Russian language. The contemporary Russian term is *iazychnik, iazychestvo* (язычник, язычество) while the obsolete term *pogan', poganyi* (погань, поганый) implies both 'non-Christian' and 'uncleanliness'. There is a great deal of primary source material which reveals the Orthodox fear of contact with pagan uncleanliness.[55] The eleventh-century Metropolitan Ioann II, for example, in his *Canonical Answers* warns believers against the dangers of eating with non-Christians:

> А йже [ꙗдать] с поганъіми не вѣдаю, молитву творити на ꙋскверненьѐ токмо, й тако приймати достойть.[56]

> And whoever [eats] with pagans unknowingly, must pray only [for purification] against the defilement, and so be brought to be acceptable.

Even sharing food unwittingly with pagans could soil the believer, and defiled individuals were not acceptable within the community of the Orthodox until they had purified themselves with the necessary prayers.

Modern scholars tend to use the term 'pagan' to describe participation in rituals related to pre-Christian cults, although it has been used by historian and medieval cleric alike to cover a multitude of sins – idolatry, heresy, witchcraft and magic, even dancing and drunken debauchery. Early Christian writers throughout Christendom perceived pagan gods as demons, and magic of all types as the work of demons, thereby creating a logical link between magic and paganism. Richard Kieckhefer observes that

> By distinguishing sharply between Christianity (which alone was true religion) and paganism (which had magical reliance on demons at its heart), early Christian writers in effect introduced a distinction between religion and magic which had not previously been made and which was not easily understood except from a Christian viewpoint. It was a short step from saying that paganism was inauthentic religion to maintaining that it was no religion at all but mere idolatry and magic.[57]

Kieckhefer's observation holds true of the sources discussed in this work. Many clerical writers in medieval Russia associated magical rituals with paganism because of their diabolical origins, and demonized figures from the pagan past, thereby setting them within the Christian worldview. William Ryan provides a useful summary of the various definitions of magic (and their shortcomings) in the introduction to his seminal work on magic in Russia, which I will not duplicate here.[58]

Although in terms of what is 'Christian', self-definition is the ideal, with 'paganism' we are on trickier ground. If Christianity is a diverse, fragmented, regionalized, contradictory affair, paganism is even more so. As Carole Cusack observes of the Germanic conversions, 'there was no clash between systematic philosophies, between Christianity and paganism . . . Paganism is a Christian construct . . . There was significant religious variation even among the Germanic peoples; some of whom were in contact with Celtic and Roman religions as well as with Christianity'.[59] Our primary problem is that we have almost no access to the minds of those accused of paganism in Russia, and we view them through the filter of their detractors' Christianity. Although clerics set the boundaries of their particular versions of Christianity, they cannot be trusted to usefully define anything that falls outside these boundaries.[60] A definition of pagan that is wide enough to include idolatry, astrology, dancing, drunkenness, divination and witchcraft ignores the issue of chronological variations in meaning.

A contemporary analogy is the problematic approach of various funda-mentalist Christian groups to Hallowe'en: while the vast majority of families who celebrate Hallowe'en with apple-bobbing, 'trick or treating' and scary masks are in no way involved in pagan worship, accusations of paganism have increas-ingly been levelled at the festival since the late 1980s.[61] Ronald Hutton observes that since Hallowe'en is a Christian feast of the dead, maintained as such by the Roman Catholic Church,

> [t]o describe it as fundamentally unchristian is therefore either ill-informed or disingenuous. Such an attitude could most sympathetically be portrayed as a logical development of radical Protestant hostility to the holy days of All Saints and All Souls; having abolished the medieval rites associated with them and attempted to remove the feast altogether, evangelical Protestants are historically quite consistent in trying to eradicate any traditions surviv-ing from them. If so many of those traditions now seem divorced from Christianity, this is precisely because of the success of the earlier reformers in driving them out of the churches and away from clerics.[62]

Accusations of paganism have often been levelled at Roman Catholics by Protestant writers. The *Oxford English Dictionary* cites a text of 1550, for example, which denounces 'the pagan Papists'. The origin of 'pagan' was the Latin *paganus*, 'villager', 'civilian', and since the Christians called themselves *milites*, 'enrolled soldiers of Christ', all those not enrolled were civilians or *paganis*. Peter Brown has observed that Christianity was first an urban reli-gion,[63] so the contrast implicit in *paganus* may also reflect this early divide. In Christian language pagan meant 'heathen' as opposed to Christian or Jewish, but the *OED* also notes that in earlier use the term practically equalled non-Christian, 'so including Muslims and, sometimes, Jews', or a person who does not worship the true (Christian) God, or who worships nature, which is closer to the understanding of the term in contemporary scholarship.[64]

Within the context of this book I have used the term 'pagan' to indicate pre-Christian beliefs, except where I am citing the clerical perspective. Eve Levin points out that 'The Russian state always contained substantial populations of unassimilated Finno-Ugric, Baltic, Iranian, and Turkic peoples, who had not yet adopted Christianity' and the researcher should be aware that incidents of 'pagan resistance' often involved non-Russians.[65] Scandinavian and Greco-Roman paganism also influenced the peoples of Rus, but identifying the ethnic origin of particular rituals is a difficult (and ideologically dubious) task. The complex system of influences that affect belief and culture, and the manner in which beliefs are transmitted and then modified tends to result in multi-layered, syncretic rituals that draw upon many diverse sources.[66] Robin Milner-Gulland has advised caution in using the term 'paganism', with its Graeco-Roman connotations, when discussing ancient Slavic beliefs, and suggests that researchers should cease 'thinking of the pre-Christian belief system (which is anyhow not altogether "systematic") as a religion in the conventional sense'. As he points out, there was only a very brief period in Russian history when a pagan religion was propagated. This was the decade in which Vladimir attempted to establish a pantheon of idols, before he opted to introduce one of the monotheistic world religions – in the event, Christianity. Milner-Gulland interprets the essential components of this pre-Christian belief as 'incarnations of natural powers or personifications of feelings, aspects of "forces" or "force"', indicating the lack of hierarchy and organizational structure and offering a useful summary of some of these natural powers and forces.[67]

Early English use of the term 'pagan' to mean anyone not worshipping Christ is reflected in early Russian usage. *Погань*, *поганый* were used flexibly, often simply as derogatory terms highlighting the wrong-headedness of one's enemies. The twelfth-century *Igor Tale*, if one is to accept its validity as a historical source,[68] reproaches the Russian princes for bringing the pagan Lithuanians into the Russian land by their sedition: 'Вы бо своими крамолами начясте наводити поганыя на землю Рускую'.[69] In the fourteenth-century *Zadonshchina*, which reflects much of the *Igor Tale*, the author celebrates the destruction of the pagan (*поганые*) Tatars, who were Muslims by this point, while the allies in this 1380 battle – the Lithuanians – are described only as 'brave', 'храбры', despite the fact that they were still predominantly pagan during this period.[70] The Lithuanian rulers toyed with both Eastern and Western Christianity for tactical and political reasons throughout the thirteenth and fourteenth centuries, sometimes converting and subsequently reverting to paganism, but did not finally accept Roman Catholicism until 1385. The deciding factor was the marriage of Grand Duke Iagailo of Lithuania to Yadwiga, heiress to the Polish crown. The last state funeral celebrated in grand pagan style occurred in 1382.[71]

Sreznevskii demonstrates clearly that *поганый* also meant simply 'not Orthodox' and sometimes 'foreign' (*inozemnyi*, *иноземный*; *chuzhezemnyi*, *чужеземный*) in a pejorative sense, often in reference to Northern Europeans and Latins: 'Начаша поганая Латына силу дѣяти на Псковичехъ', 'the pagan Latins began to exercise force upon the Pskovians'; 'Пособи Богъ князю Данилью . . . надъ погаными Нѣмцѣ',[72] 'God helped Prince Danilo . . . against the pagan Germans'; 'Болгарѣ и Жидовѣ и всѧ погань',[73] 'Bulgars and Jews and all pagans'. *Poganyi* is also glossed as 'not Orthodox' in a fifteenth-century penitential, indicating that the clerical reader might not immediately understand who was covered by the term.[74] As we have seen with the English Catholic 'pagans', this is neither an Eastern Orthodox nor a Slavic phenomenon – denouncing one's enemies (whether spiritual or territorial) as pagan was considered an effective insult in Western Europe as well as Eastern.

The term 'unbeliever' (*nevernyi, неверный*), seems to be a synonym for pagan, but is perhaps more appropriately translated as 'infidel'. The *OED* definition of infidel closest to the Russian use of *неверный* is an 'unbeliever', 'an adherent of a religion opposed to Christianity; especially a Muhammadan, a Saracen (the earliest sense in English); also (more rarely) applied to a Jew, or a pagan'.[75] In the anonymous song *The Return of Patriarch Filaret to Moscow*, collected by Richard James in 1619–20, Filaret is described as returning 'from the land of the Infidel, from Lithuania',[76] 'из неверной земли, из Литовской', in contrast to the 'земля свято-русская',[77] 'the holy Russian land'. Lithuania was, when the song was composed and recorded, Roman Catholic and allied with Poland. As enemies of the Russian people, the Lithuanian Latins were enemies of the bearers of the true faith. These examples are indications of a connection between 'Russian' and 'right worship'. 'Foreign' implied, as we have seen, 'pagan' or 'infidel', and this link is conceptualized in the word *inoverets, иноверец*, 'other' or 'foreign believer'.

Heretics, *krivovertsy, кривоверцы*, sometimes *eretiki, еретики*, unlike pagans and infidels, retain belief in Christ while deviating from the doctrine of the Orthodox Church. Heretics do not deliberately separate themselves from the body of the Church (as schismatics do), but choose to believe only part of the faith of that Church which designates them as heretics. This they may do from ignorance and lack of education, or wilfully, as a result of spiritual pride or material objectives. In the pre-Petrine period under scrutiny, the Orthodox Church viewed both the Roman Catholic and the Protestant churches as heretical, although relations between them varied with time and place. As the above examples indicate, in the period under study they were often seen as outside the pale of Christianity altogether. The word '*еретик*' (*eretik*, heretic) often refers to specific heresies of the early Church,[78] while *кривоверный* (*krivovernyi*, literally 'crooked believing') is used to castigate Orthodox Russians entertaining unholy ideas, as we shall see in Chapter 2. Finally, it is worth remarking that these pejorative terms for the non-Orthodox were often treated as synonyms or used interchangeably by medieval Slavic scribes, with little reference to theological niceties.

1 Christian idol-worshippers and 'pagan survivals'

> **Dvoeverie.** The technical term for the intermingling of pagan traditions with a superficial Christianity. In its extreme form, *dvoeverie*, (literally, 'double faith') is what a medieval Russian document (the 'Sermon of a Lover of Christ') defines as 'when people who are baptised in Christ believe at the same time in Perun, Volos and other pagan gods'. More often, however, it is an unwitting practice of primitive folk customs while fulfilling the obligatory rites of the Orthodox Church. . . . ['The Questions of the Priest Kirik to Archbishop Nifont of Novgorod' (twelfth century), the decrees of the Stoglav Council of 1551 and the works of St Tikhon, Bishop of Zadonsk (eighteenth century)] as well as the occasional preserved sermon, give us considerable insight into the non-Christian folk religion of Russia in various periods . . . For all the strength of the Church's denunciations some of these 'double faith' practices still persist today in the Russian countryside.[1]
>
> *The Modern Encyclopedia of Russian and Soviet History*, 1979

The above citation offers a classic definition of *dvoeverie*, and is a good example of the sort of scholarship that has promoted the myth of double-belief in academia. Scholars from the nineteenth century onwards have used the term to describe the preservation of pagan elements by Orthodox Christian communities, generally citing or referring to the same medieval and early modern texts, leading to a widespread perception that Russian clerics invented the term *dvoeverie* to describe 'in their own words' the addiction of their flocks to 'pagan practices'.[2]

This chapter will explore the key texts offered as evidence of double-belief from the *Sermon of the Christlover*, which pre-dates the Mongol invasions of the thirteenth century, to the eighteenth-century sermon of Bishop Tikhon Zadonskii on the festival of Iarilo. The *Christlover*, the most frequently cited sermon in the historiography of double-belief, contains the word *dvoeverie* within the characteristic framework of idol-worship by Christians, and the first section of this chapter is an attempt to unravel the meaning of the word as used in this context. Secondly, this chapter will compare the language of the *Christlover* with other sermons and texts in which the Church wrestles with popular unorthodoxy, asking whether this medieval and early modern textual evidence legitimizes modern historiographical usage of the term, and exploring medieval clerical terminology and concepts of unorthodoxy. Finally, it addresses the issue of whether these texts offer real evidence of the witting or unwitting preservation of 'primitive folk customs' by medieval Russian Christians.

The Sermon of the Christlover

The earliest redaction of the *Sermon of a Christlover and Zealot for the Right Faith* (Слꙛ нѣкоє хꙛлюбца. ревнителѧ по правой вѣре)[3] was discovered in 1847,[4] together with a number of other texts discussed below, in a late fourteenth-century manuscript collection known as the *Paisievskii sbornik.*[5] The *Christlover* sermon was first published in 1861, attracting a great deal of attention, and given that academic use of the term dates from the second half of the nineteenth century, this find doubtless launched the concept of double-belief in modern scholarship.[6]

The *Christlover* sermon was fairly widely disseminated in the medieval and early modern period in both monastic literature and private reading compilations for the educated laity, and is cited in many other sermons on paganism. The date of this sermon's composition is by no means certain,[7] and authorship is also disputed. Some scholars attribute this sermon to Feodosii Pecherskii, the eleventh-century abbot of the Kievan Caves Monastery,[8] and see it as written for the monastic community; others have strongly argued that it was intended for the edification of parish priests.[9] What can be said with some degree of certainty is that this is an original Rus composition, rather than a translation from Greek, which dates from the pre-Mongol period.

The key phrase in this sermon, 'во двоевѣрно живущих' (usually translated as 'double-believingly living' or 'living in double-belief'),[10] has served as primary evidence that Christian communities preserved pagan beliefs and rituals in medieval Rus, and that this phenomenon was named double-belief by the medieval churchmen who expended great effort and many words in trying to combat it:

> *Dvoeverie* as a concept has a long history. It was already mentioned in one of the earliest monuments of Russian written culture: 'Slovo nekoego khristoliubtsia' [the Sermon of the Christlover]. The struggle of the Christian church for dominance in Russian villages is documented in chronicles, in the *Stoglav*, in numerous decrees and orders of Russian tsars, and so on.[11]

Even a scholar who does *not* advocate use of the term *dvoeverie* in the study of popular culture cites the *Christlover* as evidence of the medieval origin of the concept, and implies its existence in other pre-modern texts. As will be discussed in Chapter 3, this approach has been reflected in the work of a great many academics.

The key passage appears at the very beginning of the sermon, and reads as follows:

гакѡ҃ і́льга ѳезвитѧнинъ. ꙁаклавъı ѝѥрѣа жерца і́дольскиѧ учисломъ. т҃. и ре҃. ревнуѧ поревновах. по г҃ѣ вседержители. та҃ и се́і не мога терпѣти хр҃тьıанъ во двоевѣрнѡ [variant: Рум. Муз. № 181: двовѣрнъı̏ живуще] живущиѝ. і̏ вѣрують в перуна і̏ в хорса. і̏ в мокошь. і̏ в сима. і̏ ве рьгла. і̏ въ вилъı. нх же учислѡ г҃. ѳ҃. сестрѣнниць. г҃ать невѣгла̃. і̏ мнѧ҃ бн҃ами. і̏ та покладъıвахуть имъ теревъı. і̏ куръı ѝмъ рѣжю҃ і̏ ѡ҃гневѣ. молать. ꙁовуще ѥ́го сварожичемъ.[12]

As Il'ia Fezvitianin, having slaughtered the priests, the idolatrous sacrificers 300 in number, and said 'zealously I showed zeal for the Lord God Almighty', thus also he [God?] cannot endure Christians living in double-belief [double-believingly living]. And they believe in Perun and in Khors, and in Mokosh, and in *Sim*, and in *R'gl*, and in the *vily*, of whom number 3.9[13] [variant 30] sisters. The uneducated say [this], and consider [them] goddesses, and therefore offer them sacrifices and cut cockerels for them and pray to the fire, calling it Svarozhich [son of Svarog?].

This passage immediately introduces a number of the complexities faced by the researcher who would seek to find in this and other early sermons evidence of Slavic pagan survivals – principally the problem of identifying potential textual sources of the paganism described. The 'Il'ia' referred to is the Old Testament prophet Elijah the Tishbite,[14] who slew the prophets of Baal because he was 'jealous for the Lord God of Hosts'.[15] The Biblical Elijah asks the children of Israel: 'докѡлѣ въı хра́млете на ѻбѣ плеснѣ ва́шъı',[16] literally 'how long do you limp on both your feet?' This is usually translated as 'how long halt ye between two opinions?' and refers to their turning away from God to follow the prophets of Baal and 'the prophets of the groves' who 'eat at Jezebel's table'. The unknown Christlover, or possibly a later editor, has chosen the prophet Elijah and his idol-worshipping enemies apparently as a metaphor for Kievan Christians wavering between the Christian God and their earlier idols. The concept of 'wavering between two opinions' implicit in the choice of this Biblical passage suggests that 'двоевѣрно' here is used in the sense that it is used in many of the works discussed in the following chapter, meaning 'in doubt', 'hesitatingly', 'uncertainly'. The Israelites more than once doubted God's power, abandoned him for idols, and then returned again when convinced by a miracle.[17]

    It has been suggested that early Russian literature is 'dominated' by the Biblical model of a two-fold message – a historical message and a spiritual message:

To make sure the reader would not concentrate on the historical message alone and miss the spiritual sense of the written message – which, unfortunately, seems to be the case with most of our current interpretations of Orthodox Slavic texts – particular compositional devices were employed . . . A thematic clue consisted of scriptural references occurring in a compositionally marked place, namely, at the beginning of the exposition or direct narrative.[18]

Our 'thematic clue' to the spiritual message is clear – the wavering Israelites who cannot choose between God and the idol of Baal. The list of pagan deities that replaces Baal is thought by many scholars to be a later insertion into the text, probably based on the *Primary Chronicle* entry – or perhaps a common source – which tells us that in the year 980,

> Vladimir then began to reign alone in Kiev, and he set up idols on the hills outside the castle with the hall: one of Perun made of wood with a head of silver and a mustache of gold, and others of Khors, Dazh'bog, Stribog, Simar'gl, and Mokosh.[19]

In the *Christlover*, 'Simar'gl' has been corrupted into '*Sim*' and '*R'gl*',[20] and the mysterious *vily* have appeared, of whom more will be learned later in this chapter. Under the year 1114, the *Primary Chronicle* cites an unnamed chronicle on 'the god Svarog' of the Egyptians, and his son Dazh'bog, the Sun.[21] This is probably the Byzantine *Chronicle* of John Malalas, the Slavonic translation of which contains glosses naming the deities Hephaestus and Helios as Svarog and Dazh'bog respectively.[22]

Various scholars have identified Old and New Testament references in the *Christlover*,[23] (the latter generally indicated in the text by the phrase 'Paul said'), in particular those from I Corinthians, in which Paul addresses the young Christian community of Corinth with the words:

> But I say, that the things which the Gentiles sacrifice, they sacrifice to devils, and not to God: and I would not that ye should have fellowship with devils. Ye cannot drink of the cup of the Lord, and the cup of devils: ye cannot be partakers of the Lord's table, and of the table of devils. Do we provoke the Lord to jealousy?[24]

The comparable passage in the *Christlover* reads:

> рҿ же павелъ то оубо требъı кладȣ̑ страны бҍсомъ. а не бȳ. не велю̑ вамъ ѿвҿщнѣмъ бъıти бҍсомъ. ї не можете бо пнти ѵаши гн҃а. ї не можете бо прнѵаститн̑ трапеꙗ̑ гн҃н. да не разъгнҍваёмъ бꙗ҃.[25]

The dependence of the *Christlover* sermon on I Corinthians is considerable. In 10:1–4 Paul describes the 'fathers . . . baptised unto Moses in the cloud and in the sea', drinking from the 'spiritual Rock' that was Christ, with whom God was not pleased 'for they were overthrown in the wilderness'. This Pauline passage reflects the apparent 'confusion' between the new and old, the idolatrous Israelites and the baptized Christians (the 'fathers' both travelled under a cloud and through the sea with Moses, and drank from the rock that is Christ) that has been identified in the *Christlover* as evidence of the sermonizer's neophyte and poorly catechized status. Observing that early Russian scribes were not only semi-literate but also inadequately versed in the Bible, Anichkov suggests that the original author mistook Elijah for a New Testament figure, thus explaining his anachronistic condemnation of *Christians* 'living in double-belief'. His supporting evidence for this supposition consists of a reference to unspecified Slavic texts in which this confusion of Old Testament prophets with the followers of the apostle Paul occurs.[26] He concludes that the later scribe(s), more familiar with Bible texts, could not understand such a construction and therefore inserted a sentence (based on their reading of other sources) to explain the passage. Knowing that Elijah had wrestled with the prophets of Baal, they added in the pagan idols listed in the *Primary Chronicle* and other literary sources to clarify the message.

However, the Pauline passage uses a similar symbolic discourse, applying the narrative of the old to instruct the new. New Christians should flee the idolatry that some of their Israelite forefathers fell into:

> Neither be ye idolaters, as were some of them; as it is written, the people sat down to eat and drink, and rose up to play. Neither let us commit fornication, as some of them committed, and fell in one day three and twenty thousand.
>
> (I Corinthians 10:7–8)

The *Christlover* renders this:

> ї бъіша слѹги кѹмирѡ̃. гакож бо пишѐ сѣдоша бо лю̃ѐ пити гасти. не в законъ но в оу҆по҆ї бъіша пьгани. ї восташа и҆гра̃ · · и҆ того дн̃и погибе и҆хъ. к̃. ї х̃. за своѐ неистовоѐ пьганьство.[27]

and became servants of idols. As it is written, the people sat down to drink and eat. Not lawfully but in ecstacy [they] became drunk, and stood up to play – and on that day perished 20 and 600 people from their unclean drunkenness.

In his letter to Corinth, Paul acknowledges that eating meat offered to idols can do neither good nor harm for 'we know that an idol is nothing in the world' (8:4), but he advises those 'with knowledge' to avoid eating sacrificial offerings lest those less firm in faith be led astray. I Corinthians 10 also gives instructions on the correct behaviour for those attending pagan feasts, suggesting that for a Christian to eat meat offered to idols harms the idol-worshipper by failing to demonstrate the falsity of his act (10:27–29). Some commentators have argued that the *Christlover* is addressed exclusively to priests and scribes who don't conform to canon law, particularly with regard to meals, and who are therefore 'servants of devils and idols'.[28] The priests are singled out for condemnation because they are not ignorant, but enlightened, and the following passage of the sermon may well be a creative reworking of both canonical prohibitions on clerical participation in dancing and drunkenness at celebrations, and similar passages from Corinthians:

> ї чесновитѡ̃. бг̃мъ же его твора̃. егда же оу҆ кого бѹде̃ пиръ. тогда же кладѹ̃ въ вдра ї в чаши и҆ пью̃ ѿ ї҆долѣхъ своіхъ. веселащи̃ не

ХУЖЬШН СҮ ёретнковъ нн жндовъ. їже в вѣре ї во крцнны та твора.
не токмо невѣжн. но ї вѣжн. попове ї кннжннцн. аще не твора
того вѣжн да пьють ї гада моленое то брашно. аще не пьють нн
гада да внда дѣаннга ïхъ ѕлага. аще не вндать да слышать. ї не
хотать йхъ пооучнтн.[29]

And garlic they make into a god. When someone has a feast, then they
put [garlic] in pails [or 'containers'] and in cups and drink to their idols,
making merry, such are not [*sic*] worse than heretics or Jews.[30] Even in
faith and in baptism such [things] do not only the ignorant, but also the
enlightened, priests and bookmen. And if the enlightened do not do this,
then they drink and eat food that has been prayed over; if they do not drink
or eat, then they see their evil actions; if they do not see, then they hear,
and do not wish to teach them.

The belief that garlic had apotropaic powers was fairly widespread in the ancient
world, and since garlic-worship among Egyptians is mentioned in the *Chronicle
of George Harmartolos*, this is perhaps evidence of literary paganism.[31]

It is probable that the references to idolatry in the *Christlover* are, for the
most part, Biblical references and citations from the chronicles available at
the time, rather than first-hand accounts of contemporary Russian paganism.
The language of both the New and the Old Testament provides plenty of
material on idolatrous and impious behaviour, including feasting, drunkenness
and playing, and if there was a lost prototype, as has been suggested, it may
have consisted of a reworking of I Corinthians 10, with explanatory references
to the idolatrous Israelites of the Elijah story and without any mention of Slavic
paganism. This supposition is supported by Anichkov's detailed textual analysis
of three extant manuscripts of the sermon,[32] which dismisses the references
to pagan beliefs and ritual (including the crucial sentence listing the gods
worshipped by the double-believing Christians) as later, gradual insertions into
the text conveying no real information about Slavic paganism.[33]

Longer, clearer and more complicated manuscript redactions are generally
later versions of a text, where scribes have attempted to add educated clarifica-
tions or explanations of something that they could not understand. Redactions of
the *Christlover* follow this general rule, with later versions of the sermon significantly expanding upon the pagan passages of the *Paisievskii* text. Anichkov
sees some references to idolatry (for example the discussion of obscene wedding
rituals which appears in the late fifteenth-century *Novgorodskii Sofiiskii Sobor*
text) as general efforts to strengthen the denunciatory nature of the sermons.[34]
Mansikka, while accepting in the main Anichkov's arguments about later textual
insertions, suggests that the phallic rituals discussed in this passage may well
be genuine observations of popular practices condemned by the Church:[35]

тогда кладꙋть въ вѣдра. й въ уашѣ. й пьютъ веселащеса. ѿ йдолѣхъ
свойхъ й ёгда же оу кого йхъ боудеть бракъ н творать съ боубьны. н
съ сопѣльмн. н съ многыìмн уюдесы бѣсовьскыìмн й йноже сего горѣѐ

ёсть. оустроньвьше срамотоу моужьскоую. й въкрадъıвающе въ вѣдра.
й въ чашѣ й пьютъ. й вынемьше ѿсморкъıваютъ. й ѿблизъıваю̃. й
цѣлоуютъ. не хоужьше соуть жидовъ. й еретикъ. й болгаръ.[36]

Then they put [garlic] in pails and in cups, and drink, making merry over
their idols and when someone has a wedding and they create [music] with
tambourines and with reed-pipes, and with many devilish wonders, and
there is something worse than this. Preparing the male private parts [a
phallus][37] and slipping [it] into pails and cups, and they drink, and having
taken [it] out they sniff, and smack their lips, and kiss.[38] They are not [*sic*]
worse than Jews and heretics and Bulgars.[39]

A more significant passage in terms of the double-belief debate is the Christlover's
complaint that not only do the Christians eat the unclean food of idolaters, but
they also mix Christian actions with pagan:

не тако̃ зло творѡ̃ просто но ї мѣшаемъ. нѣкии чистъıꙗ мл̃твъı. со
проклатъıмъ моленье̃ їдольскй. їже става̃ лише кутьꙗ. ины трапезъı.
законнаго обѣда. їже нарицает̃ безаконнаꙗ трапеза. мѣнимаꙗ родоу ї
рожаннца̃. ї въ прогнѣванье бу̃ . . .[40]

Not thus is evil done simply, but also we mix. Some [mix] pure prayers
with accursed idolatrous prayer, they put in addition to *kut'ia* [ritual food,
a type of porridge],[41] [and] other dishes of lawful food, that which is called
unlawful food,[42] dedicated to *rod* and *rozhanitsy*, even to the angering of
God . . .

The later Novgorodian manuscript again expands on this 'mixing', naming
the pure prayers as the Troparion (a special hymn) of the Mother of God.[43]
The ritual feast is identified as honouring the *rozhanitsy*, commonly held to be
spirits of birth or fate, who are mentioned in a number of the texts explored in
this chapter. If indeed *rozhanitsy* are related to birth, as the name implies, this
connection with Mary would be a logical one in the minds of neophyte Slavs,
since the figure of the Mother of God has traditionally been appealed to by
believers concerned with matters of fertility and childbirth.[44]

Such transference is evidenced in the earliest sources. In Epiphanius' list
of fourth-century heresies, for example, included in the *Kormchaia kniga* (the
Helmsman's Book, a compendium based around the Slavonic translation of
the Byzantine *Nomocanon*),[45] he notes that Collyridian women offer the Mother
of God cakes and drink at a shrine where their ancestors had worshipped
Ashtaroth, the pagan goddess of heaven. Jeremiah (7:18) also records women
preparing cakes for this pagan 'queen of heaven', so the Collyridian women
may have been preserving not only the sacred place, but the ritual also.[46]

More pertinently, a prohibition on the heating of celebratory porridge (as
would be done for ordinary mothers) in honour of the childbirth of the Mother
of God on the Monday after Christmas Day is found in canon 79 of the Council
in Trullo:[47]

As we confess the divine birth of the Virgin to be without any childbed, since it came to pass without seed, and as we preach this to the entire flock, so we subject to correction those who through ignorance do anything which is inconsistent therewith. Whencefore since some on the day after the Holy Nativity of Christ our God are seen cooking σεμίδαλῖν [*semidalin*],[48] and distributing it to each other, on pretext of doing honour to the *puerperia* of the spotless Virgin Maternity, we decree that henceforth nothing of the kind be done by the faithful. For this is not honouring the Virgin (who above thought and speech bare in the flesh the incomprehensible Word) when we define and describe, from ordinary things and from such as occur with ourselves, her ineffable parturition. If therefore anyone henceforth be discovered doing any such thing, if he be a cleric let him be deposed, if a layman let him be cut off.[49]

The canons of this synod, often called the Quinisext Council (convened by the Byzantine Emperor Justinian II in AD 691–2), would have been familiar to the Russian clerical elite via the *Kormchaia kniga*. Tikhonravov cites a similar prohibition from a fourteenth-century South Slav manuscript, purporting to be from the rules of the fourth-century Council of Laodicea:

Sorrow, sorrow to people that do this which is hated by God, and angers Him. Who out of foolishness are doing unseemly and indecent [things], thinking they honour the Mother of God, they put up a feast of flour bread, and cheese, and fill cups with good wine, and they do [this] now to the Nativity and give each other to eat and drink, and think that they do good, and thus give praise to the blessed virgin, while it is dishonourable and worthy of blame . . .[50]

This prohibition is repeated in various pentitentials,[51] and seems like a plausible source for the 'unlawful' feasts in the *Christlover*, as it is very similar to the 'second table' set up for *rozhanitsy* mentioned in a number of Slavic manuscripts. In the *Questions of Kirik*, a twelfth-century Novgorodian text discussed further in the following chapter, the priest Kirik asks Bishop Nifont what should be done with parishioners who 'prepare bread, and cheese and mead for *rod* and *rozhanitsa*'. The bishop replies 'Strongly forbid them, somewhere it is said, sorrow to those who drink to *rozhanitsa*!'[52] It seems conceivable that rather than '*rod*' representing here a specific deity and *rozhanitsa* (singular in this text) meaning 'spirit of birth' or 'fate', they might instead be translated as 'childbirth' and 'a woman giving birth' respectively, as Bishop Nifont, recalling the canonical prohibitions on special meals in honour of the Nativity, applies the same rule to popular celebrations of ordinary births.[53]

There is another Biblical precedent for the *rozhanitsy* feast, however, in Isaiah 65:11, where the Lord complains about those faithless Israelites who have turned away from Him to 'prepare a table for Gad' and 'furnish a drink offering for Meni', the deities of fortune or destiny thus honoured by the Hebrews in Babylonia. In various thirteenth-century manuscripts Gad – the δαίμων (*daimōn*, demon) of the Septuagint – is replaced by *rozhanitsy*, or *rod* and *rozhanitsy*, and Meni – τύχη (*tychē*, fortune) in the Septuagint – is replaced by 'devils'.[54]

The participation of priests in feasts for the *rozhanitsy* has been interpreted by some as a form of creative proselytism, an attempt to instil Christian meaning in pagan rituals and thereby transform them into something harmless:

> It is also possible to see the ways such creativity took place: condemned by the scribe-monk, 'the priests serving their bellies', 'adding the troparion of the Nativity of the Virgin to the feast of *rozhanitsy*', have thereby themselves done, consciously or unconsciously, a great deal for the elucidation of the dogmatic and moral foundations of Orthodoxy to the people.[55]

Musin views the activities of the clerics in this sermon as evidence of common missionary behaviour, sanctioning the transformation of pagan rite and symbol into Christian. Such a theory leaves one wondering why the sermonizer found the practice so objectionable, if it was indeed widespread in Rus. However, the superimposing of Christian beliefs and ritual onto some particularly significant pagan festivals had clerical support and success in many other instances. The most obvious is perhaps Christmas, which was celebrated around the time of the Winter Solstice and eventually spread into a twelve-day festal season (which also covered the Roman Calendae) ending with the Epiphany.[56] The accommodation of certain elements of pagan practice was an accepted missionary strategy (at least in some times and places), and will be discussed further in Chapter 4.

An alternative interpretation to that of proselytism is offered by Gal'kovskii, who attributes the priests' behaviour primarily to indifference: 'The clergy often looked indifferently on survivals of old pagan ritual, and not infrequently even themselves made use of "prayed over" ritual food and drink'.[57] If the sin of the clergy was sloth or lack of zeal, the sin of the double-believing flock was ignorance. According to Gal'kovskii, the 'double-believers' have little understanding of either Christianity or paganism:

> Of course, the people, those praying to Perun, Khors, Mokosh, making offerings to Rod and the Rozhanitsy, were bad Christians, as they did not know Christianity, although they were baptized. But they were even worse pagans, since the meaning of paganism was completely lost to them.[58]

Gal'kovskii manages to conclude this from the fact that the *Christlover* does not explain the intricacies of the pagan cult, which is an unconvincing argument, the more so since he begins his book with the explanation that we have little evidence of pagan beliefs because the clergy did not have the incentive to dwell on pagan survivals. Instead, they were 'busy with the positive side of life, aspiring to explain and strengthen Christian beliefs in the consciousness of the Russian people'.[59] If one is to take the whole sermon at face value, as an accurate reflection of the practices of the time, the author surely would not need to explain the details of the cult to the lax priests and idolatrous flocks; his intention would simply be to unambiguously condemn and correct.

The *Sermon of the Christlover* clearly encompasses two of the main modern interpretations of the term *dvoeverie*, if one ignores the strong possibility that the references to pagan beliefs and rituals are garbled versions of Biblical passages and literary paganism and do not relate to contemporary Russian belief in any way. The text can be interpreted as offering evidence of both pagan/Christian syncretism (the *rozhanitsy* feasts combined with hymns to the Mother of God), and of the continued, separate and distinct worship of pagan figures by Christians reluctant to commit themselves solely to the one God.

There does not appear to be any other reference to *dvoeverie* in Gal'kovskii's unrivalled collection of early anti-pagan polemics, and this may be a unique context for use of the word. The balance of evidence suggests that we should not unquestioningly accept the modern translation of double-belief, however. It is entirely plausible that 'хрестьян двоеверно живущих', as the Biblical context implies, means 'Christians doubtingly [or waveringly] living', in other words 'Christians living in doubt' – as Elijah's Israelites doubted the power of God.

A more satisfying translation would be 'Christians hypocritically [or insincerely] living', an interpretation of the word as used in the Studite text (discussed in the following chapter) with regard to oaths taken insincerely, for example. For this there is some textual evidence:

Да не во лжю буде рекли крещающе Ѿрицаемъ сотоны ї всѣхъ дѣлъ ёго й всѣхъ айглъ ёго. ї всего студа ёго. да ѿвѣщахомъ хвн.[60]

Let us not in falsehood have said: in baptism we renounce Satan and all his works, and all his angels, and all his shame, let us promise ourselves to Christ.

The author or compiler implies that Christians who serve both devils and God, who eat at the Lord's table and the table of idols are false, insincere Christians. However, since the Biblical text of III Kings 18:21 favours the former interpretation, this is probably the stronger possibility.

Gal'kovskii and Tikhonravov between them have published most of the anti-pagan polemics cited by scholars of medieval double-belief. Tikhonravov's collection appeared in 1862 and published various redactions of the *Sermon of the Christlover*, the *Sermon of St Gregory on how firstly the pagans were heathens*, and the *Sermon of St John Chrysostom on how firstly the pagans believed in idols*.[61] Gal'kovskii's 1913 collection expands greatly on this selection, publishing thirty-five such polemics.

The significance of these sermons lies primarily in the negative evidence they offer. If *dvoeverie* was a medieval concept, a term created by Russian Orthodox clerics specifically to struggle against 'pagan survivals', creative accommodation, or rebellious Christians preserving the traditions of their forefathers, one would expect it to appear often in these early sermons and in later texts addressing unorthodox practices identified by the Church as 'pagan'. While there is a great deal of interesting and complex material in these tracts, the word *dvoeverie* does not appear to be used by the scribes to describe it, and in most instances it is by no means clear that it is indeed contemporary Russian beliefs and rituals which are under scrutiny by the authors.

The Sermon of St Gregory on how firstly the pagans were heathens

The *Sermon of St Gregory, devised with commentary on it, On how firstly the pagans were heathens, worshipped idols and brought them sacrifices, and even now do this* (Сло́ ста́ григорьꙗ. їзобрѣтено в толъцѣ ѿ томъ. како первое погани сꙋще ꙗзыци. кланꙗлисꙗ їдоломъ. ї требы им клали. то ї нꙑ творꙗ̑.) is often cited as a polemic against *dvoeverie*.[62]

The age of this sermon is also disputed, with Rybakov dating it to the beginning of the twelfth century,[63] and Gal'kovskii suggesting the end of the thirteenth or the beginning of the fourteenth century.[64] It is a reworking of those parts of St Gregory the Theologian's sermon *On the Epiphany* (Oration 39, also called the *Oration on the Holy Lights*) concerned with classical paganism, and much of the original was simply misunderstood or mistranslated by the copyists, who tried to make sense of things utterly outside their experience and knowledge. It has been suggested that this sermon must have seemed to the Byzantine missionaries a most appropriate source for teaching the neophyte Slavs about the evils of paganism,[65] and Anichkov surmises that the compiler of our sermon was working from an early south Slavic translation of Gregory's oration, and commenting on or interpreting it, as the full title implies. He describes the possible translations from which our compiler could have worked as barely comprehensible:

> Our Russian scribe not only knew nothing from other sources, but even the very sermon of Gregory the Theologian that he had in his hands was an extremely bad South Slavic translation, word for word and barely literate. Reading it, it seems to me that not only is it impossible to understand it now without the Greek context, but that never was any real sense made of it.[66]

The *Sermon* may well be a copy of parts of an earlier, poorly translated south Slavic version with additional commentary, or simply a bad translation of parts of Gregory's original, with commentary. The *Kirillo-Belozerskii* redaction ends with the endearing postscript, 'this is a great sermon and for our laziness we have written little down',[67] and the following extract from passages of the *Oration* used by the Slavic compiler go some way to explaining why he managed to copy so little of it:

We are not concerned in these mysteries with birth of Zeus and thefts of the Cretan Tyrant . . . Nor are we concerned with Phrygian mutilations and flutes and Corybantes, and all the ravings of men concerning Rhea, consecrating people to the mother of the gods, and being initiated into such ceremonies as befit the mother of such gods as these. Nor have we any carrying away of the Maiden, nor wandering of Demeter, nor her intimacy with Celei and Triptolemi and Dragons; nor her doings and sufferings . . . for I am ashamed to bring into daylight that ceremony of the night, and to make a sacred mystery of obscenity. Eleusis knows these things, and so do those who are eyewitnesses of what is there guarded by silence, and well worthy of it. Nor is our commemoration one of Dionysus, and the thigh that travailed with an incomplete birth, as before a head had travailed with another; nor of the hermaphrodite god, nor a chorus of the drunken and enervated host; nor of the folly of the Thebans which honours him; nor the thunderbolt of Semele which they adore. Nor is it the harlot mysteries of Aphrodite, who, as they themselves admit, was basely born and basely honoured; nor have we here Phalli and Ithyphalli, shameful both in form and action; nor Taurian massacres of strangers; nor blood of Laconian youths shed upon the altars, as they scourged themselves with the whips; and in this case alone use their courage badly, who honour a goddess, and her a virgin. For these same people both honour effeminacy, and worship boldness.

And where will you place the butchery of Pelops, which feasted hungry gods, that bitter and inhuman hospitality? Where the horrible and dark spectres of Hecate, and the underground puerilities and sorceries of Trophonius, or the babblings of the Dodonaean Oak, or the trickeries of the Delphian tripod, or the prophetic draught of Castalia, which could prophesy anything, except their own being brought to silence? Nor is it the sacrificial art of Magi, and their entrail forebodings, nor the Chaldaean astronomy and horoscopes, comparing our lives with the movements of the heavenly bodies, which cannot know even what they are themselves, or shall be. Nor are these Thracian orgies, from which the word Worship is said to be derived; nor rites and mysteries of Orpheus, whom the Greeks admired so much for his wisdom that they devised for him a lyre which draws all things by its music. Nor the tortures of Mithras which it is just that those who can endure to be initiated into such things should suffer; nor the manglings of Osiris, another calamity honoured by the Egyptians; nor the ill-fortunes of Isis and the goats more venerable than the Mendesians, and the stall of Apis, the calf that luxuriated in the folly of the Memphites, nor all those honours with which they outrage the Nile, while themselves proclaiming it in song to be the Giver of fruits and corn, and the measurer of happiness by its cubit.[68]

The paucity of classical education and Greek literacy among the medieval Slavs is well documented,[69] and the generally poor standard of translations was acknowledged in the sixteenth century by the ill-fated invitation of Maxim 'the Greek' to Moscow to correct and retranslate the many flawed religious texts in circulation, and again a century later, in Patriarch Nikon's reformation of corrupt liturgical texts. Unsurprisingly then, the translator/scribe struggles with this vast catalogue of devilish activities, inserting apparently Slavic extras such as the revering of Mokosh, and interesting translations such as родопочитанїа, literally the 'reading of *rod*' ('fate' or 'birth') for 'horoscopes'.[70]

The text continues independently of the *Oration*, to address

Ѿкудꙋ̈ ізвыкоша ѐлени класти требы. артемидꙋ. ї артемидѣ. рекше родꙋ ї роженицѣ. тацнїже їꙋптане. такӧ и до словѣнъ доїде. се слов. ї ти начаша требы класти родꙋ ї рожаницꙗ̈. преже перꙋна бѷ̈ їхъ. а нереже того клали требꙋ. оꙋпирё ї берегинꙗ̈. по стӧмъ кре́щеный перꙋна Ѿринꙋша. а по хꙋ̈ бѷ̈ ꙗша но ї ноне по оꙋкраїнамъ молꙗтъ̈ ѐмꙋ проклꙗтомꙋ бꙋ̈ перꙋнꙋ. ї хорсꙋ. ї мокоши. ї вилꙋ. ї то творꙗ̈ Ѿтаі. сего не могꙋтъ̈ лишити. проклꙗтаго ставленьꙗ. в. ꙗ трꙗпезы нареченъ̈ꙗа родꙋ ї рожаницꙗ̈. (на) великꙋ прелесть вѣрнъ̈ꙗ кртьꙗаном. и на хꙋлꙋ стӧмꙋ кр҃щнью. и на гнѣвъ бѷ̈.[71]

Whence the Hellenes became accustomed to offer sacrifices to Artemid and Artemis, that is to say *rod* and *rozhanitsa*, and so also the Egyptians, thus also to the Slavs this came. These Slavs also began to hold rites to *rod* and *rozhanitsy*, at first Perun was their god and before that they held rites to *upiry* [vampires?][72] and *bereginy* [river-bank spirits?]. By holy baptism they rejected Perun, and accepted Christ as God. But now also on the outskirts they pray to him, to the accursed god Perun, and Khors, and Mokosh, and *vily*,[73] and this they do in secret and they cannot give this up. They put up the accursed second table calling upon *rod* and *rozhanitsy*, to the great temptation of believing Christians, and to the abuse of holy baptism, and to the anger of God.

This *Paisievskii* redaction suggests that *rod* and *rozhanitsy* are *'Artemid'* (*sic*; Apollo) and Artemis, a goddess associated with childbirth, usefully demonstrating the scribe's unfamiliarity with both Slavic and Greek paganism.[74] The similarity to the earlier *Christlover* sermon is immediately apparent, as are several Biblical motifs. The Israelites are accused of secret idol-worship in II Kings 17:

And the children of Israel did secretly those things that were not right against the Lord their God . . . And they set them up images and groves in every high hill, and under every green tree . . . And they left the commandments of the Lord their God and made them molten images, even two calves, and made a grove, and worshipped all the host of heaven, and served Baal. And they caused their sons and daughters to pass through the fire, and used divination and enchantments, and sold themselves to evil in the sight of the Lord, to provoke him to anger.[75]

Later in the *Sermon of St Gregory* the apparently Slavic worship of *vily* is curiously correlated with another false god of the Old Testament, 'the idol killed by Daniel the prophet in Babylon'.[76] This is a reference to the idol Bel (*Вил* in the Slavonic, *Vil*) in Daniel 14, who was given over to Daniel along with his priests and temple for destruction. In the Biblical story, the priests of Bel leave out food for the idol, seal up the temple doors, and enter through a hole in the floor to consume the food and 'prove' Bel's existence. Daniel scatters ash on the temple floor, which in the morning reveals the nocturnal visitation of the priests and their families.

The manner in which Daniel reveals the falsity of the idol is reminiscent of a bathhouse ritual discussed in both the *Chudovskii* redaction of this *Sermon of St Gregory*,[77] a sermon attributed to St John Chrysostom (see below),[78] and in the sermon О постѣ к невѣжамь в понедѣлокь в не̃, *On the Fast [addressed] to the Ignorant on Monday [of] the Second Week*. All three texts castigate Christians who leave food in the bathhouse for the dead,[79] and scatter ashes on the floor to show up the footprints of visiting spirits. In the sermon *On the Fast*, the preparation of these feasts for the *navii* happens on Holy Thursday, during the Great Fast of Lent, when strict abstinence from meat and dairy products must be observed:

въ стый великии четвертокъ повѣдаютъ мрътвымъ мѧса и млеко и ѧица. и мылница топѧ. и на печь льютъ. и попе̃ посредѣ сыплю слада ради и глютъ мыйтесѧ. и чехли вѣшаю и оубрѹси. и велѧт сѧ терти. бѣси же смиюсѧ злооумию й. И вълѣзте мыютсѧ и порплютсѧ в попели тѹ. гако и коѹри слѣ свой показаю на попелѣ на прелщеніе имь. и трѹтсѧ чехлы и оубржсы тѣми. и проходѧ топившеи мовници. и глѧдаютъ на попелѣ слѣда. и егѹ видѧтъ на попели слѣ и глютъ приходили. к намь навьѧ мытсѧ.[80]

On Holy Thursday [people] offer to the dead meat and milk and eggs, heat the bath and pour [water] on the stove, and ashes amidst they scatter for the footprints,[81] and say 'wash yourselves'. And undergarments [or 'linen'] and towels they hang up and order them to rub themselves. The devils laugh at their evil-mindedness. And they enter to wash themselves and wallow in the ashes, and they show [or 'leave'] in the ashes footprints like cockerels', for the temptation [of the people], and they use those linen and towels. And [the people] come to the heated bathhouse, and look in the ashes for footprints, and when they see in the ashes footprints, they say 'there came to us the *navii* [spirits of the dead][82] to wash themselves'.

Rybakov, who has done a great deal of imaginative work on the overlap of Christian and pagan festivals in Russia, sees the main sin according to the author of this sermon as the timing of the feast for the dead.[83] As we will see from other texts, inappropriate behaviour on holy days or their eves was a common cause of clerical complaint.

This surprising similarity between a Biblical tale and an apparently unorthodox medieval custom gives some indication of the complex system of influences faced by researchers in the field of medieval religiosity. Is this similarity coincidental, or did the Slavic sermonizer associate or confuse a practice he had witnessed or heard about with a Biblical text familiar to him? The converse is also possible – that the neophyte Slavs heard the tale of Daniel and incorporated elements of it into their native rituals. The frequent use of Biblical references, not always attributed, in these sermons is a potential source of confusion for the researcher, since what may appear as an eyewitness account of medieval paganism might equally be a Biblical motif representing the iniquity of unorthodox behaviour, or at the very least an observation made through the prism of Holy Scripture.

It is significant that these visiting spirits, the *navii*, are identified by the sermonizer(s) as devils who lead the people astray. In many of the works the clerical authors reinforce the teaching that pagan gods or forces are demonic; they put these practices in a Christian context. This is apparent not only in denunciatory sermons, but in apocryphal works such as *The Descent of the Virgin into Hell*. In this tale, the archangel Michael tells the Mother of God that 'they made gods out of the devils Troyan, Khors, Veles, and Perun, and they worshipped these evil devils'.[84] For many of these authors and compilers it is not a matter of two beliefs or faiths, but of one faith that encompasses the true God and his opposing force – Satan, with all his minions. It is doubtful whether these medieval sermonizers accorded paganism the status of a faith at all; like their much later counterparts they perceived pagan belief through the prism of Christian tradition, as simply the lies and temptations of the devil, swallowed by the weak, uneducated and foolish.[85]

The later *Chudovskii* redaction of the *Sermon of St Gregory* is considered more interesting since (as with later redactions of the *Christlover*) it includes many apparently local details not listed in the earlier redactions: for example prayer under the corn-drying bin and stables; fires, baths and food prepared for the dead; and the 'going to the water' of brides. The earlier mentioned rituals of thunder and lightning worship, *rod* and *rozhanitsy* worship, the initial honouring of Perun, *upiry* and *bereginy*, and the accusation that 'even now in the outskirts they pray to the damned Perun, Khors and Mokosh, the *vily*, and they do it in secret and can not give up the accursed celebration of the second feast of *rod* and *rozhanitsy*', also appear in this redaction. While recognizing that some of the apparently Slavic gods catalogued by sermonizers are questionable, 'the product of "scholarly" erudition rather than of personal observation', Fedotov – along with many other scholars – sees this accusation of secret prayers to Perun as 'concrete evidence' of double-belief, an addiction to pagan practices.[86]

Again, there are challenges for the researcher who would pick out of this later catalogue evidence of medieval Slavic unorthodoxy. Praying under the corn-drying bin is listed as one of the offences that Church courts are to judge in the *Statute of Vladimir*, as are praying in a copse of trees and praying by the water.[87] Probably these offences entered the *Statute* via the translated *Nomocanon* or *Kormchaia kniga*, which the *Statute* makes reference to. The *Capitula* negotiated by Charlemagne and his son Pippin I with Italian bishops also contains a reference to a ritual or prayer conducted 'beneath the bread-trough', in a very confusingly worded clause:

> Concerning those wicked men who honour [or keep – *colunt*] the *brunaticus*, and who burn candles beneath the *maida*, and make vows concerning their own men: that each should indeed remove them from such iniquity. But if they want to offer bread to the church, let them do so in a natural fashion, not with an admixture of any of that wickedness.[88]

While it has been suggested that *maida* was related to the ancient Gaulish custom of placing wood or wax models of human limbs at the crossroads, a more probable meaning is bread-trough from the Latin *magis, -idis*, as in the modern Italian *madia* (kneading-trough, bread-bin).[89] This apparent similarity could mean that this is evidence of literary paganism, probably transmitted via canonical prohibitions, or that prayer under the bread-trough was a phenomenon common to both cultures.

Doubtless this sermon began life as a straightforward (if poor) translation of the *Oration on the Epiphany*, and was supplemented by later scribes with apparently Slavic details mainly copied from the *Christlover* sermon, chronicles and other texts. The word *dvoeverie* does not appear in any of the published redactions, despite the frequent citation of this sermon as evidence of medieval double-belief.

The Sermon of St John Chrysostom on how firstly the heathens believed in idols

The full title of this sermon is Слѡ́ стго ѡ҇ца нашего. иѡ҇ златооустаго. Архиеппа костантина града. о томь како пьрвое погании вѣровали въ идолы. И требы имъ клали. И имена имъ нарекали. ѧже и нынѣ мнози тако творать. и въ кртьꙗньстве. соуще. а не вѣдають что есть кртьꙗньство, the *Sermon of our holy father John Chrysostom, Archbishop of Constantinople, about how firstly the pagans believed in idols and offered them sacrifices, and gave them names. Then and nowadays many do this, and are living in Christianity but not knowing what Christianity is.*

For the compiler of this sermon, these errant Christians were acting in ignorance, not knowing what constitutes true Christianity, and he begins his polemic with a passage which Fedotov identifies as from Romans 1:21–27 'on the origin of idolatry'.[90] It is not an exact quotation, and oddly excludes the verse most relevant to idol-worship (v.23), while including the passage on women reversing the natural order of things, and men leaving women aside and turning to each other lustfully, and 'doing evil things'. This reversion of God's appointed order is a result of their failure to glorify God as God, and 'worshipping and serving the creature more than the Creator', for which sin God gives them up to their unclean desires. The guilty in this sermon are clearly the priests, who

> не хотѧще нхъ пооучнтн. Молчаннемь ѕаграднша оуста своѧ. На пагоубоу малооумнъıмъ. оугоднаѧ нмъ творѧть. уревоу работають а не боу. ѧкоже н аплъ глть. нмже въ урово н слава. въ студѣ лнца нхъ.[91]

do not want to teach them. With silence they barred their mouths to the perdition of the weak-minded. They do what is pleasing to them, serving their belly and not God.[92] As the apostle said: 'for those for whom God is the belly and who glory in the shame of their face'.[93]

Because of these harsh words, Fedotov interprets this as another anti-clerical sermon, prevalent in fourteenth- and fifteenth-century collections possibly as a result of Strigolnik influence,[94] a reforming movement subsequently declared heretical. However, he notes that the sermons originate in the earlier period, which indicates a continuous concern:

> the sermons against popular paganism, mostly stemming also from the pre-Mongol times, . . . are full of denunciations of unworthy priests. The preacher sees in the clerical vices, their indolence, their greed, the greatest obstacle in the campaign against paganism.[95]

The contents of this sermon are markedly similar to the *Sermon of St Gregory* and the *Christlover*, implying shared origins. The compiler offers a familiar but expanded list of unorthodox practices such as thunder and lightning worship, worship of the sun, moon, Perun, Khors, *vily* and Mokosh, *upiry* and *bereginy*, the mysterious 39 sisters,[96] Svarozhich, Artemis, the worship of fire, stones, rivers, at springs, in the courtyard, and the customs of jumping through fire, offering milk, meat, butter and eggs to demons, heating the bathhouse and sprinkling ashes for their footprints, believing in Stribog and Dazh'bog, and Pereplut (about whom nothing is known, although Rybakov indulges in a great deal of speculation about possible connections with rain and agriculture), divination by stars and by the voices of birds, witchcraft, and sorcery. These latter three are the subject of many canonical prohibitions and while they may have been common behaviours in medieval Russia, the source of this prohibition is almost certainly textual (probably the *Kormchaia kniga*) rather than any spontaneous outburst of clerical frustration.

Tikhonravov, who offers little analysis of his collected sermons, does attempt to justify this sermon and others as evidence of Slavic paganism despite their probable Greek roots:

> The sermon's citation of John Chrysostom cannot serve as grounds to repudiate the characteristic accounts of Slavic superstition in the sermon:

on the one hand similar quotations were the usual way in our old literature to sanctify the importance of the composition; on the other, if in the works of John Chrysostom there also is a sermon of such content; then our entry represents it in a completely altered form and adapted to Slavic beliefs and rituals.[97]

It is clear, however, that much of the pagan content of this sermon is not conclusively of Slavic origin. More importantly for our purposes, this sermon does not contain the word *dvoeverie*, and the main thrust of the polemic is again against inadequate priests who have failed in their role as teachers and examples of Christian living.

The sermons of St Serapion Vladimirskii

The sermons of St Serapion, abbot of the Kievan Caves Monastery until 1274 and subsequently Bishop of Vladimir until his death in 1275, are often cited as evidence of the medieval polemic against *dvoeverie*. The five sermons commonly attributed to him contain no use of the term *dvoeverie*, although in two of his sermons he does attack the belief in and persecution of *volkhvy*, in this context 'witches' or 'sorcerers'.[98]

Podskalsky cites in particular sermon five, Слⷪ҇ бл҃жнаго Серапиѡ҃на ѡ мⷶловѣрьï or *Sermon of Blessed Serapion on those of little faith*, in his demonstration of *dvoeverie* as one of the 'principal themes that . . . can be discovered in the literature that originated in Kiev'.[99] In both this sermon, and in sermon four, Serapion accuses his flock of maintaining pagan customs:

Аⷩ҇е еще поганьскⷶ ѡбычаіа держитⷷ: волхво(ва)нию вѣрꙋⷷ ï пожигаⷷ ѡгнⷷ невинъіıа чл҃вкъ.[100]

You are still holding to a pagan custom: you believe in witchcraft and burn innocent people with fire.

In sermon four, the 'pagan' custom referred to by Serapion would appear to be the burning of individuals, rather than the belief in witchcraft, but his argument is complex. He argues that if witches have the power to affect the elements, causing famine, then the people should worship them. It is, however, God who permits famine, in order to punish the people for their sins.

In Serapion's view, God permits witches and demons to operate within the world, for they can harm only the gullible, those who are not firm in the Christian faith. Serapion castigates those who, because of their lack of faith in God, fear witches and act in 'senseless' and 'pagan' ways – judging people by casting them into water (a 'dead' element) and then killing them.

The gravity of this sin, addressed again in sermon five, is magnified by the fact that his congregation are turning on their own co-religionists, Christian against Christian:

Поганїи̇ бо, закона бж҃їа не вѣдуще, не оу̇биваю̇ ѐдиновѣрнꙑ̇ своі̇хъ,
ни ѿграбляютъ . . . а мꙑ творимъ вѣрнии, во і̇ма бж҃їе кр҃цꙁни
ѐсмꙑ и̇, заповѣди ѐго слꙑшаще, всегда неправдꙑ ѐсмꙑ и̇сполнени і̇
зависти, немꙁрдꙑꙗ; бра́ю свою̇ ѿграбляѐмъ, оу̇биваѐмъ, въ погань
прода́ѐмъ.[101]

The pagans, not keeping the laws of God, do not kill one of their own
faith, nor rob [him] . . . but we having faith, being baptized in the name of
God and having heard his commandments, are always committing wrong
and in the power of [it], merciless; our own brother we rob, kill, sell to
the pagans.

Serapion's concern over 'those of little faith' relates rather to the general
sinfulness than to any preservation of pre-Christian tradition:

Лучши, бра́га, престанемъ ѿ зла; лишимъ всѣхъ дѣлъ злꙑ̀: разбо́,
грабленѐ, пьꙗньства, прелюбодѣ́и̇ства, скупост, лихвꙑ, ѿбидꙑ, татбꙑ,
лжива послушьства, гнѣва, ꙗрости, злопоминанѐ, лжи, клеветꙑ,
рѣзои̇манѐ.[102]

It is better brothers, that we desist from evil; [let us] deprive ourselves of
all evil-doing: robbery, pillage, drunkenness, adultery, miserliness, usury,
insult, thieving, bearing false witness, anger, rage, bearing grudges, lies,
slander, money-lending.

Doubtless as a result of the shock of the waves of Tatar-Mongol invasion
experienced during his lifetime,[103] the idea that human sinfulness brings divine
punishment is a common theme in Serapion's writings. The only pagans in
the writings of Serapion are those to whom the Christian Russians sell their
brothers.[104]

Metropolitan Kirill II's *Pravilo* and the *Canonical Answers* of Metropolitan Ioann II

John Fennell is one of a number of writers who have cited the *Pravilo* of
Metropolitan Kirill from the 1274 Council of Vladimir in a discussion of
dvoeverie that deals with the problematical issue of 'pagan games'. That
Fennell himself had reservations about how 'pagan' these celebrations actually
were can be gleaned from his ambivalence:

Was *dvoeverie* just a natural reaction to a rigorist attitude of the Church to
what had been for so long the simple pleasures of the people – dancing,
singing, acting and music – as well as the less reputable aspects of popular recreation – fornication, promiscuity, bawdry and carousing? Probably
not, for we have little evidence to show that the Church was in any way
successful in coping effectively with the problem.[105]

The concept of 'pagan games' deserves a monograph of its own. As we will discuss in Chapter 3, other scholars have concluded that *dvoeverie* was in part the result of a natural reaction to the prohibition of games and amusements, which brought the new Christians into conflict with the Church. Anichkov's understandable scepticism about the early written sources leads him to conclude that in these denunciations of games and feasts is found possibly the *only* evidence of Slavic pagan behaviour to be gleaned from these sermons,[106] not a conclusion shared by very many scholars.[107]

The plentiful written evidence for these apparently widespread events, or rather for clerical perception of these 'games', repeats the same complaints about raucous and lewd behaviour, the flouting of the prohibitions against musical instruments and *skomorokhi* (itinerant minstrels),[108] dancing, drunkenness and violence, and all of these usually in close proximity to holy Orthodox festivals:

> Пакъ же оу҆вѣдѣхомъ бесовьскаꙗ ꙗ҆ще дьржаще о҆бычаꙗ треклатыхъ ꙗ҆елинъ, въ божествьныꙗ҆ праздьникы позоры нѣкакъ бесовьскыꙗ҆ творити, съ свистаниꙗ҆емь й съ кличемь й въплемь, съзывающе нѣкы скарѣдныꙗ҆ пьꙗ҆ница, й бьющеса дрьколѣꙗ҆емь до самыꙗ҆ смерти, й възимающе о҆ о҆убиваꙗ҆емыхъ порты.[109]

> Again we see devilish rituals of the thrice-accursed Hellenes still being held, on Godly festival days some devilish infamy is done, with whistling, with screaming and yelling, summoning some abominable drunkards, and beating one another with staves until death, and taking the trousers from those who are killed.

> И се слышахомъ: вь суботу вечеръ сбираються вкупь мужи и жены, и играють и пляшуть бестудно, и скверну дѣють въ нощь святаго въскресенія, яко Дионусовъ праздникъ празднують нечестивіи елини, вкупѣ мужи и жены, яко и кони вискають и ржуть, и скверну дѣють. И нынѣ да останутся того;[110]

> And this we hear: on Saturday evening men and women gather together, and play and dance shamelessly, and engage in vice on the night of Holy Sunday, like the Dionysian festival celebrated by the dishonourable Hellenes, men and women together, like horses gambolling and neighing, and doing filthy things. And even now it remains so.

Metropolitan Kirill's complaints are echoed in other sources, and bear a marked resemblance to the explanation of the chronicler for the pagan invasion of Polovcians in 1068:

> By these and other similar customs the devil deceives us, and he alienated us from God by all manner of craft, through trumpets and clowns [*skomorokhi*], through harps [*gusli*] and pagan festivals [*rusalii*].[111] For we

behold the playgrounds worn bare by the footsteps of a great multitude, who jostle each other while they make a spectacle of a thing invented by the devil. The churches still stand; but when the hour of prayer is come, few worshippers are found in the church, for this reason we shall suffer at the hand of God all sorts of chastisement and the incursion of our foes, and at the command of God we shall endure punishment for our sins.[112]

This, Cross points out, is an extract from the sermon *On the Punishments of God*, attributed to Feodosii Pecherskii, which itself has textual precedents including a sermon by Gregory the Theologian.[113] Similar passages are to be found in the sixteenth-century *Stoglav* and Tikhon Zadonskii's eighteenth-century sermons, which may indicate common textual sources. It also perhaps tells us more about human nature than paganism, and a fair amount about the mind-set of Russian clerics. Drunkenness, obscenity and revelry were considered unchristian, and therefore pagan, but there are also Biblical precedents that connect drunkenness with idol worship (Daniel 5:1–4; I Peter 4:3 for example).[114] A slightly lighter approach is taken by the eleventh-century *Statute of Iaroslav*, which rules that a woman could be divorced for going to the games (*khoditi po igritsam*) without her husband's permission, and refusing to stop when found out, which implies that it may have been acceptable to attend with him, and for him to attend alone.[115]

Golubinskii, among others, cites the eleventh-century *Canonical Answers* of Metropolitan Ioann II as providing evidence of the 'official' nature of double-belief.[116] These *Canonical Answers*, written by the Greek metropolitan in answer to questions from the monk Iakov, also offer advice on 'devilish games', and provide further evidence that these behaviours were not exclusively the preserve of the laity. Feasting and drunkenness *within* monasteries are castigated by the Metropolitan,[117] but clerics are also advised that they should not participate in games, folk dances or music at worldly feasts, because doing so would desecrate them, bring great temptation and, somewhat bizarrely, bad digestion.[118] This reflects a number of canonical rulings, including those of the Council of Laodicea such as canon 53: 'That Christians who go to weddings ought not to use wanton or theatrical dances but to dine or sup as becomes Christians'.[119] The Greek βαλλίζειν ἠ ὀρχεῖσθαι (*ballixein ē orcheisthai*) is translated in the *Kormchaia kniga* as 'играти или плясати', 'play or dance',[120] although βαλλίζειν is to clap one's hands and make noise.[121] Canon 54 of the same Council states that clerics must leave weddings or banquets before the plays begin, an order repeated by Canon 24 of the Council of Trullo (Quinisext Council), also incorporated in the *Kormchaia kniga*, which declares:

No one who is on the priestly catalogue nor any monk is allowed to take part in horse-races or to assist at theatrical representations. But if any clergyman be called to a marriage, as soon as the games begin let him rise up and go out, for so it is ordered by the doctrine of our fathers. And if anyone shall be convicted of this let him cease therefrom or be deposed.[122]

Russian penitentials also reflect a concern that clerics were participating in inappropriate pastimes: one late fifteenth-century manuscript asks monks whether they sang 'devilish songs' or 'played *gusli* [a musical instrument] or chess'. Priests were also asked whether they had been dancing, singing, and playing dice, chess or musical instruments.[123]

Tempting though it is to further explore the reasoning for the designation of 'devilish' or 'unlawful' games as 'pagan', this is unfortunately beyond the scope of this work. One should bear in mind that the Slavs inherited from Byzantium a wealth of prohibitions against plays and theatrical events, horse-racing, prize-fighting and other public games, playing dice, cards and other pastimes, dancing and other 'lewd' amusements. Senior clerics such as Metropolitan Ioann were applying these rules, written in entirely different circumstances, to situations about which they may have known very little, and therefore we must exercise caution before accepting their writings as eyewitness testimony. There is, however, some later evidence that points to the use of dice for sorcery and divination, and gambling with dice was a concern of the Muscovite government as well as the Church.[124] Again, while Metropolitan Ioann observes that those who sacrifice to 'devils, bogs and wells' are 'strange (or "foreign") to our faith' (*chiuzhim byti nasheia very*),[125] neither Metropolitan Kirill nor Metropolitan Ioann accuses their unruly flock of double-belief.

Stoglav

The text of the *Stoglav*, or *One Hundred Chapters*, records the rulings made by a Church Council convened in Moscow in 1551 in an attempt to regulate the Orthodox faith and organizational structure of the Church. Headed by Metropolitan Makarii and composed of two archbishops, seven bishops and various black and white clergy,[126] the Council addressed questions presented to them in the name of Tsar Ivan IV, but possibly drafted by a cleric.[127] A great deal of the text is concerned with establishing the 'correct' forms of piety and Orthodox culture, and as such, has led some historians to conclude that

> *Stoglav* statements regarding superstition, paganism and heresy confirm the standard interpretation that the Muscovite populace practised a 'double faith' of Christian and popular elements.[128]

The *Stoglav* contains numerous references to practices that were condemned by the Church as unacceptable, although practices which might be described as popular unorthodoxy make up only a small proportion of the text and are mostly listed in chapters 41, 92 and 93. The majority of the *Stoglav* is concerned with issues of church discipline and order, such as the status of widowed priests, incorrect liturgical behaviour, unlicensed begging and monastic laxity.

Chapter 41 is apparently composed of 32 questions from the Tsar with simultaneous Synodal answers, around a third of which could be characterized as addressing issues of popular unorthodoxy. The leaving of cauls and soap on the altar,[129] apparently with the connivance of the parish priest, is prohibited, as is the priest's placing of salt beneath the altar during Easter season and subsequent distribution of it for curative purposes.[130] Consulting sorcerers, indulging in astrology and reading magical or heretical books are also condemned,[131] and several questions address the problem of rowdy, lewd, violent or otherwise unchristian behaviour at weddings and festivals, and by roaming bands of minstrels or *skomorokhi*,[132] and the less specific sins of lewd dancing, drunkenness and inappropriate behaviour on the eve of Church festivals. Inappropriate behaviour at church festivals makes up the bulk of the complaints: graveside rituals on Trinity Sunday involving excessive lamenting followed by excessive merry-making;[133] crying and scandalous language at Radunitsa, burning straw and calling on the dead on Maundy Thursday;[134] going into groves for 'devilish amusements' on the first Monday of Peter's fast.[135] That this was a widespread concern is further evidenced in texts such as the seventeenth-century penitential directed at villagers ('Вопрос поселяном') which asks about 'going to the forest' on Maundy Thursday, and gathering 'herbs and roots' at Christmas, for example.[136]

'Devilish' behaviour on the eves of significant feasts is a recurrent theme, and question 24 of chapter 41 is worth citing in full:

Въспро*с* 24. Русал(ь)и о Иване дни и в навечерии Р(о)ж(е)*с*тва Х(ри)*с*(то)ва, и Кр(е)щения сходят*ц*а мужи и жены, и д(ѣ)в(и)ци на нощное плещование и на безчин*н*ый гово*р*, и на бесо*в*ские пѣсни, и на плясание, и на скакание, и на б(о)гомерские дѣла. И бывае*т* отроко*м* осквернение и д(ѣ)вам ра*с*тлѣние. И егда нощь мимо ходя*т*, тогда *от*ходят к рѣцѣ с великим кричание*м*, аки бесни, и умываю*т*ца водою. И егда начну*т* заутренюю звонити, тогда отходя*т* в домы своя и падаю*т*, аки м(е)ртви, *от* велико*г*(о) клопотания.[137]

Question 24. At the Rusalii for [St] John's day and on the Eves of Christmas, and of Epiphany men and women gather together, and maidens, for night games [splashing?][138] and for improper conversations, and devilish songs, and for dancing and skipping, and for impious acts. And there happens defilement by lads and seduction by maidens. And when the night has passed, then they go to the river with a great cry, like devils, and wash themselves with water. And when the morning [bells] start to ring, then they go to their homes and fall, like the dead, from the great noise.

The council answers that such 'ancient Hellenic devilry' is rejected by the church canons and that Orthodox Christians are forbidden to do such things – on holy days they should be busy worshipping God. Similar complaints are made in chapter 92 ('An answer about the games of Hellenic devilry'), which observes that:

Still many of the unintelligent, simple men of orthodox Christians in the towns and villages do Hellenic devilry, various games and clapping (*pleskanie*)[139] before the festival of the Nativity of John the Forerunner; and in the night of the same festival and all the day and until night men and women, and children in houses and on the streets go about, and by water (*po vodam*) make noise (*glum*)[140] with all games and all jesting (*skomrashestvy*) and satanic songs, and dances and *gusli*, and . . . unclean apparitions/representations, and also drunkenness. They do similar on the days and the eve of Christmas, and on the eve of St Basil the Great's [feast], and on the eve of Epiphany.[141]

In picking apart these accusations, there seem to be two potential categories of offence. Drunkenness, lewdness, and rowdy, jovial and 'improper' behaviour on the eve of a holy day are straightforward sins that are 'pagan' only insofar as they are unchristian responses to Christian feasts. The burning of straw and 'devilish games' (perhaps including 'splashing') possibly belong to a different type of behaviour identified by the clerical hierarchy as 'Hellenic devilry' because they were believed to be of some magical significance, either by participants or by their clerical accusers.

In his assessment of double-belief in the eleventh to the thirteenth century, Rybakov refers to the *Stoglav*, and specifically to chapter 93, as providing evidence of 'pagan survivals in Russian daily life'.[142] This chapter – 'an answer about the aforementioned Hellenic devilry and sorcery and witchcraft' – begins:

Правило 61 и 62 с(вя)таго Шестаго събора с(вя)тых от(е)цъ возбраняетъ к волхвомъ ходити и запрещаетъ православнымъ хр(и)стианомъ поганских еллиньских скверныхъ обычаевъ и игръ, и плесаниа, и плесканиа, и над делвами, сирѣчь над бочками, и над корчагами квасъ призывающе и грохочюще, и прочихъ неподобныхъ дѣлъ творити.[143]

Rule 61 and 62 of the holy sixth council of holy fathers prohibits going to sorcerers and forbids by Orthodox Christians [the practice of] pagan Hellene foul customs and games, and dancing [or 'braiding'?], and clapping [or 'splashing'?], and invoking over *delvi*, that is to say over casks, and over earthenware pots [for] *kvas* and crashing, and doing other unseemly things.

This curious 'clapping' and 'invoking over casks for *kvas*' must refer to the prohibition in canon 62 of the Council in Trullo (held in 692 as a supplement to the Fifth and Sixth Councils, which did not make any canons, and which is sometimes referred to as the Sixth Council in Greek Orthodox sources),[144] on invoking 'the name of the execrable Bacchus when they squeeze out the wine in the presses' or 'causing a laugh' when pouring wine into jars.[145] It is possible that the *Stoglav* authors were citing Russian customs ('braiding' and 'splashing') associated with local celebrations of feasts prohibited by canon 62, particularly the January Kalends (or *Koliada* as it is translated in the *Kormchaia kniga*) and the 'first day of March' (which would sometimes correspond with *Maslenitsa*, the pre-Lenten carnival). It seems more likely, however, that плесании (braiding) is a corruption of плясание (dancing), since there is a strong prohibition on 'the public dances of women, which may do much harm and mischief' and 'dances given in the name of those falsely called gods by the Greeks' in the Trullan canon.[146]

Chapters 41, 92 and 93 cite canon law so liberally that it is difficult to interpret these passages as accurately reflecting Muscovite 'popular faith' in the sixteenth century, as Kollmann recognizes.[147] Specifically, canons 42 and 43 of the Apostolic Canons, canons 53 and 54 of the Council at Laodicea, canons 60 and 61 of the Council at Carthage, and canons 24, 50, 51 of the Council at Trullo or Quinisext Council feature, in addition to rules 61 and 62 cited above.[148] Various commentators have identified textual antecedents such as the *Izmaragd*, *Kormchaia kniga*, the *Statute of Vladimir* and Biblical texts, and the repetition of similar material in the household guidance manual of the same period, the *Domostroi*:

> Ruling No. 61 of the Sixth Ecumenical Council, on wizards and sorcerers: If you encounter sorcerers, so-called wise men, magi, or others of this ilk or those who frequent them, punish them according to the commandment of the holy fathers, the ruling in the canon . . . If you have any of those they call cloud-dispatchers, spell-casters, makers of talismans, or sorcerers living among you, who do not abjure their destructive pagan deeds, throw them out of the church altogether, as the holy commandments enjoin.[149]

Canonical prohibitions such as these would have been familiar to clerics and some of their flocks through penitentials and texts such as the *Kormchaia kniga*, Theodore Balsamon's commentaries on the Nomocanons, the *Questions of Kirik* and the *Canonical Answers* of Ioann II. These activities are seen through the prism of canonical prohibitions, and it is not only the clerical recorders of these customs who may have been influenced by their Christian textual heritage. Given the longevity of these particular prohibitions in Russian clerical life, it is, as William Ryan observes, difficult to judge 'how far the recitation of such lists actually encouraged beliefs and practices that had not hitherto existed, just as the preconceptions of inquisitors and judges appear to have prompted the evidential detail in many witchcraft trial confessions in Western Europe'.[150]

The language of clerical denunciation in the *Stoglav*, as in other texts, conflates magic, astrology, drunkenness and dancing with 'paganism', but none of these actions actually calls forth the rebuke of *dvoeverie*. 'Pagan', 'Hellene', 'diabolical', 'impious' and 'heretical' are the epithets of choice, and anachronistic references to Dionysus should alert the researcher to the perils of accepting all of these 'pagan' activities at face value.[151]

A late postscript: Tikhon Zadonskii's Sermon on the Abolition of the Annual Festival, which was called Iarilo

Listed in various encyclopedias as evidence of the continued existence of double-belief, this is a late eighteenth-century sermon of St Tikhon Zadonskii on the

Voronezh area celebrations in honour of Iarilo. As such, it might almost appear in our modern historiographical uses section, as evidence of the educated élite approach to popular belief, but as a clerical condemnation which is frequently cited as evidence of *dvoeverie*, it appears as a late postscript to this chapter.

This sermon is a fascinating work, offering insights into not only the popular festivals of the Voronezh region but into the mind of a representative of the Orthodox hierarchy of the eighteenth century. Tikhon was born in the Novgorod region in 1724, and became Bishop of Voronezh in 1763. His sermon on the festival of Iarilo indicates that this festival was unknown to him before he was informed of it and chose to witness it with his own eyes. His interpretation of the celebrations is complex:

Я, желая лучше удостовѣриться, подлинно ли такъ, какъ мнѣ донесено, самъ на тое мѣсто поѣхалъ и увидѣлъ, что точно такъ, какъ въ слухъ мнѣ дошло: увидѣлъ, что множество мужей и женъ, старыхъ и младыхъ, и малыхъ дѣтей изъ всего города на то мѣсто собралося; между симъ множествомъ народа иныхъ увидѣлъ почти безчувственно пияныхъ; между иными ссоры, между иными драки увидѣлъ, иныхъ раненыхъ, иныхъ окровавленныхъ усмотрѣлъ; примѣтилъ и плясанія женъ пияныхъ съ скверными пѣснями; а посредѣ всего сего беззаконнаго безумныхъ людей торжества стоитъ кабакъ въ палаткѣ.[152]

I, desiring better to attest if it was genuinely so, as reported to me, went myself to that place and saw that it was exactly as it had come to my hearing; I saw that a multitude of men and women, old and young, and little children from the whole town had gathered at that place; among this multitude of people I saw others almost insensibly drunk; among others arguments, among others I saw fights, others wounded, others I saw covered in blood; I also noticed drunk women dancing with foul songs; and in the midst of all of this lawless celebration of senseless people stood a tavern in a tent.

Tikhon objects to these rough festivities not simply because they encourage drunkenness, violence and lewd behaviour, but because of the timing of them, on the day on which the Church has ordered 'genuine Christians to start the fast; in that period in which the holy Church has not [yet] had time to celebrate Pentecost' – probably the period between Easter Sunday and Pentecost. Pentecost in the Eastern Orthodox Church is also Trinity Sunday, and the week preceding this is the much-discussed *Rusal'naia* week,[153] containing the festivities of *Semik* and the welcoming and banishing of the *rusalki*, apparently female water/wood spirits associated with Spring and the unclean dead.[154]

A great deal has been written about the double-belief in evidence in the calendrical festivities of the Russian peasant, and much specifically on the Spring rituals intended to ensure the healthy growth of the newly sprouted crops. Iarilo festivities, which were celebrated at different times in different places, apparently involved the ritual destruction of an effigy (by drowning, tearing apart or burying ceremonially), were fertility related, and resembled the rituals at *Kupalo*, the midsummer feast of the Nativity of St John the Baptist.[155]

Notably it is Tikhon himself who fills in the details about the pagan heritage of the festival – the implication is that the people themselves were not in any way worshipping Iarilo at this time:

> Изъ всѣхъ обстоятельствъ праздника сего видно, что древній нѣкакій былъ идолъ, прозываемый именемъ *Ярило*, который въ сихъ странахъ за бога почитаемъ былъ, пока еще не было хрістіанскаго благочестія. А иныи праздникъ сей, какъ я отъ здѣшнихъ старыхъ людей слышу, называютъ *игрищемъ*.[156]

From all circumstances of this festival we see that there was some sort of ancient idol, named *Iarilo*, which in these lands was honoured as a god, before there was Christian piety. But this other festival, as I hear from local old people, they call *games/spectacles*.

These old locals also tell Tikhon that it is a celebration dating from long ago, that more people attend every year and have come to expect it as an annual event, and dress up for it in their best clothes, that the celebration lasts for a few days over a Christian festival. Tikhon is not deflected:

> Но какъ бы сей праздникъ ни назывался, или когда бы ни начинался, или сколько бы дней ни продолжался, однакожъ точно я вамъ объявляю, что сей праздникъ есть бѣсовскій, смердящій, издаетъ запахъ идолонеистовства; понеже праздникъ хрістіанскій состоитъ въ томъ, чтобъ въ церковь Божію входить и имя Божіе славословить.[157]

No matter what this festival is called, or when it starts, or how many days it lasts, I declare to you regardless that this festival is devilish, stinking, emits the smell of idolatry; because a Christian festival consists of this, that is going to the Church of God and praising the name of God.

Since Tikhon feels the need to reinforce the unchristian nature of the festival to his Voronezh audience, one assumes that the protagonists did not see it as pagan, and needed to have the idolatrous roots explained to them. Tikhon does not use the word *dvoeverie* at any point in the sermon, but it is clear that later historians could identify their own interpretation of the phenomenon here: no matter that the people called the feast by a different name, no matter that it coincided with a Christian season and was probably perceived as an integral part of those Christian festivities – the ignorant masses had unwittingly preserved a pagan festival.

Tikhon's explanation of why the festival is idolatrous is slightly more complex than this, however. A Christian feast consists of church-going and praising God. This festival is full of obscene language, lewd dancing, drunkenness and violence – therefore it is 'devilish'. 'А гдѣ праздникъ бѣсовскій, тамо приносится бѣсу жертва, тамо бѣсъ почитается', 'and where [there is] a devilish festival, there devils are brought sacrifices, there devils are revered' and Christ is injured, the name of God is abused.[158] Tikhon is not specifically describing idol-worship, although he believes that the festival originally involved something of this kind. He is more concerned with the scandalous incongruity of these wild revels on days of Christian solemnity. How is it possible, he asks, to sing both praises to God and diabolical songs? If, he argues, the people maintain these traditions indiscriminately, then they are not worthy to be called Christian. Moreover, this local festival is a source of shame and an object of criticism by spiritual rivals: 'Lutherans, Calvinists and Papists' all look on and mock.

Tikhon certainly is suggesting that this festival is of pagan origin, and smacks of idol-worship. He is not directly accusing his listeners of paganism in any real sense, however, merely trying to point out to them that this behaviour is not worthy of Christians. Riotous behaviour is hardly an infallible indicator of a pagan belief-system, although as we have seen such behaviour was often rebuked as pagan – meaning unchristian – no doubt influenced by early Church canonical descriptions of Greco-Roman festivities. Tikhon gives us little evidence of anything other than carnival-type behaviour in this sermon, and the term *dvoeverie* is again not to be found, confirming dictionary evidence that it had fallen into disuse in the eighteenth century.

Conclusion

What can these sources tell us about Russian piety or Orthodox culture in the medieval period? These early texts are addressed to Christians, and frequently to pastors of the Church, in an attempt to tackle the ignorance of the people and the laxness of the clergy who fail to combat this ignorance and allow the neophyte population to persist in various 'pagan', sinful and unorthodox behaviours. Evidence in the manuscripts relating to the idols themselves is untrustworthy – the compilers of these tracts sometimes translate the names of Greek gods into Slavonic, thereby creating a fictional native equivalent that we cannot verify, and sometimes insert 'explanatory' phrases from earlier texts which are anachronistic or confused. Some sermons are clearly describing cults and ritual behaviours unknown in Rus – the translator of the *Sermon of St Gregory* for instance, misunderstood descriptions of the orgiastic mutilations by the Phrygians for wild dancing and instrument playing by 'Fragians' (Franks, or perhaps Western Europeans).[159]

The obvious interdependence of these texts also makes approaching them as sources of evidence for popular Slavic belief or paganism a rather risky affair – clearly any similarities in content cannot be taken as proof of the prevalence of the activities listed in medieval Russia, as multiple eyewitness reports, since the likelihood is that they share the same written sources, which often are not Russian in origin.

Several historians suggest that the reports of various rites and rituals – such as those conducted at feasts, weddings and commemorations of the dead – are more reliable than those that name pagan gods, as the sermonizers stress their eyewitness status.[160] Most of the behaviours described are common across the centuries – dancing, drunkenness, instrumental music, bawdy songs – but this does not indicate a perverse stubbornness of the populace in defying the Church's attempts to Christianize them. Rather it is an indication of the continual struggle of clerical representatives to define correct Christianity and maintain appropriately Christian behaviour, based on their understanding of Biblical prohibitions and early Church sources.

It is difficult to distinguish whether the diverse activities discussed in this chapter are cited, paraphrased or recalled from these sources; or are simply reflecting behaviours that we know were common to much of European society and that tell us more about human nature than pre-Christian cultures; or survivals of ritual actions specific to the Slavs; or a combination of these, reflecting the transmission of 'paganism' from literary sources to popular culture. The tone and much of the content of these texts is reflected in written sources Europe-wide, as we shall explore further in Chapter 4.

While it is clear that the term *dvoeverie* was used neither commonly nor consistently in condemnations of unorthodox beliefs and practices, the question arises as to whether there is evidence of the *concept* of double-belief in these medieval and pre-modern texts. The balance of evidence suggests that there was no clear concept in the period from the eleventh to the seventeenth century, not only because the term is so notably absent in comparison with 'idolatrous', 'demonic', and so on, but because the texts mostly indicate that clerics perceived their flocks as ignorant, needing to be firmly told that their behaviour was idolatrous or 'serving the devil'. Of course, this rather depends on one's definition of double-belief, and so we have come full circle. One who held to the view that double-belief was unconscious might be able to interpret the written sources as evidence of this. However, since we cannot point to two distinct and consciously held belief-systems in the majority of these instances, and since most sermonizers viewed paganism as the forces of Satan rather than a distinct 'faith', there is little evidence to support the idea of any such medieval concept.

The *Sermon of the Christlover* is an extraordinary text which has not yet been satisfactorily studied, particularly within the context of the compilations in which it appears, and it is even more extraordinary that the modern understanding of double-belief appears to have sprung from this one text that itself raises so many questions. We do not know when the insertion (if indeed it is an insertion) about Christians believing in Perun and other gods was added. We do not know how many times the sermon was recopied and added to between (if Anichkov's dating of the 'lost original' is correct) the mid-eleventh and fourteenth centuries, and most importantly, we do not know conclusively that our modern translation of 'living in double-belief' or 'double-believingly living' is correct. To uncritically cite this one phrase as evidence of a phenomenon or concept particular to medieval Russia is, in my opinion, unsupportable. If these early texts, written almost exclusively by clerics, can be approached without prejudice, setting aside modern judgements on what constitutes 'good' or 'pure' Christianity and accepting the criteria formulated by the Church hierarchy of the time,[161] we may better understand them. If we can learn to read the word *dvoeverie* without imposing on it our modern understanding (or perhaps our modern confusion), we may be able to unravel its meaning and significance in the sphere of medieval Russia.

2   Heretics, doubters and 'wrong-believing'

A literature of sermons and canonical rules which is preserved from the eleventh to the seventeenth centuries aimed at one purpose: the uprooting of pagan survivals in Christian society . . .

What these sermons and canons fight against is, in their own words, the 'double faith'; they accuse the Christian of being addicted to pagan practices and superstitions.[1]

G. P. Fedotov, 1946

As we have seen, medieval clerics found a wealth of words to condemn those aspects of popular piety that were unsanctioned or opposed by the Church. In their own words, what they were fighting against was the devil, 'demonic' or 'unlawful' customs, 'Hellenic', 'idolatrous', 'pagan', even 'Jewish' practices. Later, 'superstition'(*суеверие, sueverie*) became the usual term used by clergy in the eighteenth and nineteenth centuries to describe unorthodox practices. At no time does *dvoeverie* appear to have rivalled these epithets.

We turn now to the medieval sources in which the word *dvoeverie* or its lexical derivatives appear in other contexts. These texts cast new light on the meaning of the word as used in the pre-Petrine period, and do not reflect modern historiographical usage of the term. The majority of these sources are Slavonic translations of Greek works, and it is most probable that *dvoeverie* first entered the Russian language as a calque from the Greek. As Fält has observed, 'the overwhelming majority of early Slavonic compounds (ninety per cent) are based on Greek prototypes. In nearly all such cases we are dealing with calques'.[2] Calques were particularly common in abstract vocabulary, for example διψυχία, *dipsychia*, 'doubt' is rendered *дъводушие, dvodushie* in Old Church Slavonic.[3] It has also been observed that many Slavic translations are largely incomprehensible without reference to the Greek sources,[4] and this has been borne out by texts discussed in this chapter. Mistranslations, misunderstandings relating to a lack of Greek philosophical vocabulary or knowledge of the classical world (see 'Peripatetic' later for a classic example), later scribal errors during textual transmission, and the absence of Slavonic equivalents for Greek abstract vocabulary all compound to render these texts anything but transparent.[5]

Francis Thomson's remark that 'the key to a correct understanding of the evolution of Old Russian culture lies in establishing precisely which aspects of Byzantine culture were assimilated and hence served as the source of original East Slav creativity', could just as easily summarize the task faced by the researcher of the term *dvoeverie*.[6] The key to understanding the lexical development of the word lies in establishing as accurately as possible which Slavonic translations introduced the term into the religious lexicon of Old Russian, and hence served as the source for later native interpretations and creative uses of the word.

There has been a great deal of debate about the quantity and quality of Byzantine material available in Rus in the medieval period. One of the difficulties faced when tracing the origins of a word that appears to have begun its working life as a calque or loan word is that discovering the first uses of the word, and arranging them in any kind of chronological order, requires an accepted corpus of translated works, accurately dated.[7] The problem is complicated by the fact that many of the works that contain the word exist only in manuscript redactions that are, or may be, copies of much earlier translations, often within compilations containing materials of diverse origin and date.

If the problem of conclusively identifying and dating a translated source is overcome, the date of the entry into clerical vocabulary of that particular meaning cannot be taken for granted. The linguistic ability of the translator and his comprehensibility to his audience need to be considered, for a text is an act of communication, and a word has no meaning unless it is heard and understood.

Many of the texts discussed in this section are almost incomprehensible to the modern reader without reference to the Greek original, partly because in many cases the translator and/or later scribes misunderstood what they were reading, and partly because of a feature of early Slavonic that Thomson describes as 'lack of a fixed terminology'.[8] The same Greek word may be translated in various ways, and, in the case of *dvoeverie*, the same Slavonic word may be used to translate various Greek terms. William Veder has also noted the 'idiolectical use' of Church Slavonic words by scribes and translators – using the example of вещь, *veshch'*, which in one text might mean 'sin' throughout, in others 'matter', 'action', 'fault' or 'mistake'.[9] Such diversity of use would have caused problems for the medieval reader as it does for the modern scholar, problems that were compounded by the fact that scribes and readers struggled to comprehend texts without access to the Greek sources.

Most early translations attempted to reproduce the Greek originals word for word, to preserve as far as possible the form as well as the content of the text. When translators could not find a Slavic word that adequately rendered the Greek, they tended to make one up, attempting to reflect the Greek structure of the word. Thomson observes that

> in many cases calques were coined to fill the gaps and many of these became completely assimilated . . . but many were only coined for the occasion by the translator and it is doubtful whether they would be completely comprehensible.[10]

Veder explains the word-for-word translations as a result of poor literacy, seeing the freer translations as evidence of more literate translators. It is possible too that the medieval belief in the spiritual efficacy of words correctly repeated made translators particularly anxious to literally reproduce the Greek content and form, often at the expense of style and, sometimes, clarity. Monastic humility, and perhaps most importantly the fear of inadvertently committing a heresy to paper by misrepresenting the sacred original, was also an incentive to reproduce a holy work (any spiritual treatise, not simply Biblical texts) as exactly as possible, as the preface to a Slavic translation of the Gospels reveals:

> We have attempted to use precise terms, fearful of adding to the Gospel. And if something, however slight, is found added anywhere, let the reader understand that this was done out of necessity and not out of arrogance or daring. For nobody is so bold and forgetful of himself as to dare add or take away a word.[11]

The Prologue to the Slavic translation of *John Damascene Fons Cognitionis* by the Bulgarian Exarch Ioann also begins with a meditation on the perils of translation, with Ioann expressing the fear that he might misinterpret the Holy Fathers and his translations thus prove to be to the detriment rather than the benefit of believers.[12] He ends with a plea asking for forgiveness for imprecise translations, since Greek cannot always be rendered literally when translated.[13]

The lack of Greek originals and perhaps the lack of literacy in the Greek language may have made the work of scribes and readers difficult, but we may surmise that they approached their respective tasks with solemnity, and laboured diligently to understand and reproduce the content of their original material. Cultural attitudes to reading, writing and translation go some way to explaining the prevalence of calques and clumsy word-for-word renditions of Greek source material.

Fedotov has usefully summarized the spirit of the fourteenth- and fifteenth-century literate community, emphasizing the stress placed on the careful and laborious reading of all spiritual writings, whether Scripture or didactic works. He quotes chapter two of the (unpublished) *Izmaragd*, one of the most popular collections of this period:

> When you read books do it attentively and heed with all your heart, read the words twice, not only turning over the pages; read without sloth in order to acquire the fruits of salvation, and the fear of God will dwell in you.[14]

This attitude was not confined to the later period, but appears to have been a constant ideal in medieval Russian culture. As Riccardo Picchio points out, the sermon *On the Reading of Books* in the *Izbornik* (*Miscellany*) *of 1076* 'contains one of the oldest, if not *the* oldest, literary manifesto of Orthodox Slavic civilization':[15]

Ѥгда ѹьтеши кннгъı, не тъштнсѧ бързо нштнстн до дроугъна главнзнъı, нъ поразоумѣн, ѹьто гаютъ кннгъı н словеса та, н трншьдъı обраштаѩсѧ о ѥднной главнзнѣ.[16]

When you read books, do not be anxious to go through the pages quickly in order to get to another chapter, but understand what these books and letters mean, turning back even three times in a single chapter.[17]

This ideal of diligent reading has particular significance for this work, for as Picchio observes,

> this text states that careful reading is important because it enables the reader to 'continuously learn the words of the books' . . . One can interpret this statement as the formulation of a particular Christian theory of imitation concerning the language of literature. The readers of sacred books would assimilate the books' language . . . and combine the learning with the imitation of a selected corpus of exemplary works.[18]

We may approach our texts with the knowledge that reading and writing were both considered acts of devotion, to be undertaken with appropriate care and attention, and that the readers of these texts would have attempted to 'assimilate the books' language'. As a foundation on which native compositions were built, these early, translated works are bound to have influenced the choice of vocabulary that contemporary and subsequent sermonizers made.

Dvoeverie in translation

Dispute, controversy, difference

The earliest translated works were those prepared by the Cyril-Methodian mission to fulfil the liturgical needs of the neophyte Slavs. According to the *Vita and Life of Our Blessed Teacher Constantine the Philosopher, the First Preceptor of the Slavic People*, Constantine (Cyril) first translated St John's Gospel – or at least part of it: 'And right away Constantine composed letters and began to write the language of the Gospel, that is: "In the beginning was the Word, and the Word was with God, and the Word was God" and so forth'[19] – the first reading of the *Aprakos*, celebrating the beginning of the ecclesiastical year, and certainly the most fitting Biblical verse for the first exercise of a new alphabet.

The *Commemoration and Vita of Our Blessed Father and Teacher Methodius, Archbishop of Moravia*, tells us that Methodius

> first took two priests from among his disciples, who were excellent scribes, and translated quickly from the Greek into Slavic – in six months, beginning with the month of March to the twenty-sixth day of the month of October – all the Scriptures in full, save Maccabees . . . For previously he

had translated with the Philosopher only the Psalter, the Gospels together with the Apostolos, and selected church liturgies. And then he translated the *Nomocanon*, that is, the rule of the law, and the writings of the Fathers.[20]

Dvoeverie makes its appearance more than once in later redactions of the nomocanon, and we can surmise that in this translated nomocanon, completed during the ninth-century Moravian mission, was perhaps found the first use of the term *dvoeverie*.

Dvoeverie appears meaning 'dispute' or 'controversy' in chapter 57 of the *Collectio 93 Capitulorum*, in the redaction of the nomocanon known as the *Efremovskaia Kormchaia kniga* (so-called because the scribe Efrem left marginalia encouraging himself in his work, such as 'Efrem you sinner, don't be lazy').[21] The oldest manuscript of the *Efremovskaia Kormchaia* dates from the twelfth century, and is a translation of the Byzantine *Syntagma of Fourteen Titles* without commentaries, with supplements.[22] The relevant passage reads:

Аще нѣции прпⷣбнии епⷭ҇пи· того же събора· двовѣрик нѣкок межю собою имоуть· или црⷦ҇ъвьнѣмь правьдьнѣмь· или о инѣхъ къиихъ вещьхъ· пьрвѣк митрополитъ ихъ· съ инѣми отъ свокго събора· епⷭ҇пъ· вещь да соудить· и аще не прѣвоудеть къиижьдо коньць· въ соудимъиихъ· тъгда прѣблаженъии патриархъ· того строганига межю ими да оуслъишать· и тако да повелить· гаже црⷦ҇вьнъиимъ канономъ и законоу подобакть· ни кдинои же части по соудоу кго· противоу глⷶти могоуции.[23]

If some of the venerable bishops of that Council have a certain *disagreement* between themselves, either by means of an ecclesiastical lawsuit or about any other matters, first let their Metropolitan with other bishops from his Council judge the matter, and if there is not any end [resolution, decision] in the things being judged, then let the most blessed Patriarch of that region between them hear [it] out, and thus let [him] command which [matters] by Church canons and laws as is fitting. Not one of the parties after his judgement may speak against [it].

This is a complete article relating to disputes among bishops, and not related to paganism in any way. The Greek in this context is ἀμφισβήτησιν, *amphisbētēsin* (accusative of ἀμφισβήτησις) meaning 'dispute' or 'controversy'.[24] While *dvoeverie* is undoubtedly a calque, it is not a calque of this word.[25] The Greek is composed of ἀμφι(σ)- meaning 'on both/two sides' and -βήτησις from βαίνω meaning 'go, walk'.

The second lexical derivative of *dvoeverie* in the translated nomocanon appears in a text titled *The Great Writer ['Bookman'] of Antioch, concerning Kalends, Nones and Ides*, believed to be an extract from the work of the sixth-century Constantinople astronomer Rhetorius, known in Russia as early as the eleventh century.[26] This extract seems to be entirely concerned with the

Roman calendar and the means of calculating leap years by the moon and sun calendars,[27] and the word is used in the context of being 'in two minds', 'causing argument' (the interpretation given by the Russian Academy· of Sciences historical dictionary) and 'controversial':

'слнчьноє по животнынмъ двовѣрьств8еться ѿ многыихъ'.[28]

'The solar [passage] through the animals [constellations] is understood differently by many' is one possible interpretation of this passage, although William Ryan suggests the more satisfying translation 'the sun's [passage] through the zodiac is understood differently by different people', noting that живот/ животноє is the usual Old Church Slavonic/Old Russian word for a sign of the zodiac, and is a slight mistranslation.[29] Without access to the Greek original, we do not know what Greek construction was translated as *dvover's̓tvuet's̓ia*, but the implication is 'disputed'.

That *вера*, *vera* originally meant to hold firmly to a particular line of thought rather than belief in the religious sense seems plausible, and it is probable that this use of the word is the root from which later uses grew. Dictionary evidence suggests that this may be the case: two of the early meanings of *вера* are πίστις, *pistis*, trust or faith, confidence or assurance (in something); and γνῶσις, *gnōsis*, seeking to know, enquiry, investigation, result of an investigation, knowledge, decision.[30] Dvornik also makes the interesting point that 'Like the Iranians, [the Slavs] had a special religious term – *věra* (faith) – for the choice between good and evil, which recalls the Indo-Iranian *var*, meaning "choice"'.[31]

A further lexical derivative of *dvoeverie* appears in Beneshevich's published *Kormchaia kniga* under the heading *Epiphanius Bishop of Cyprus, On Heresies: 83 (Chapter VII from John the Tritheite)* [John Philoponus, a sixth-century Alexandrian].[32] However, the text cited below, from chapter seven of John the Tritheite's *Arbiter*, does not appear in other versions of *The Panarion* (Epifanius' work on heresy),[33] and the actual source is St John of Damascus' *On Heresies* (Book Two of his *Fount of Knowledge*).[34]

This passage is particularly opaque, and the RAN dictionary of Old Russian from the XI–XIV centuries does not suggest a possible meaning for this particular use of the word. While Sreznevskii identifies the verb as 'двовѣровати = дъвовѣровати' from the Greek διαφέρουσιν, *diapherousin*, he also inserts a question mark.

Да сице рекоу о писании· ѿ невѣжь нѣкъиихъ съ|ложеник· на нιаже обоихъ того же приобьщивъшеса кстьства дъвовѣроують· и скоро реции ιаже нераздѣльнаιа нарицати· ѿ ходαщαаго дроуга· въ нихъже обьщиихъ родовъ и образъ· съконьчавакться раздѣлкник·[35]

Let me speak thus about the writing, by certain ignoramuses a composition, by them of both partaking of that nature *disagree* [among themselves], and briefly speaking [the things] which undivided they name, from the walking friend, in which of the common families and types ends the division.

Daniel Collins has proposed the following reading for this odd passage, noting that the use of дъвовѣроуютъ is 'an extraordinary translation', and suggesting that the translator may have failed to understand the Greek and taken the subject of διαφέρουσιν to be the 'ignoramuses' mutually *disagreeing*:

> Let me speak in this way about the writing: [it is] a compilation by certain ignoramuses, according to whom they, sharing the same nature, *differ* from one another, and to speak briefly, which [they] of the Peripatetic School like to call atoms,[36] in which the division of common categories and species culminates.[37]

This is a plausible explanation, since as we have seen, in the same *Kormchaia* the term is used to mean 'dispute', and the Greek in this context is διαφέρω, *diapherŏ*, which means both 'maintain on the contrary' and 'differ [from one another]'.[38]

That Methodius included the nomocanon among the initial corpus of texts to be transmitted to the neophyte Slavs gives an indication of its importance in Byzantine, and subsequently in Slavic Christian life. The ecclesiastical *Statute of Vladimir* records use of the nomocanon in the Kievan court:

> По том, разверзъше греческыи номоканон и обретохом в немь, оже не подобаетъ сих судов и тяжь князю судити.

> Then, having opened the Greek nomocanon we discovered in it that the prince ought not to hold jurisdiction over these cases.[39]

According to Richard Hellie, the *Statute of Vladimir* was probably compiled in Kiev before 1011,[40] which would indicate that the nomocanon was accessible to the literate élite in the early eleventh century, even perhaps in the late tenth century, almost certainly in translation. However, Hellie's dating of the Statute is not authoritative, and the *Statute of Vladimir* lists the first Russian metropolitan as Michael, who headed the Russian Church from 1130 to 1145.[41] Other scholars have pointed out that in the earliest period of Christianization, it may have been Byzantine clerics rather than Slavonic translations of Byzantine texts that were consulted on points of Church law.[42] While it seems possible that part of the *Statute* at least originates from Vladimir's reign, and that Vladimir was in possession of a copy of the Greek nomocanon translated as part of the Methodian mission,[43] Simon Franklin also notes that the 'Methodian' translation of the nomocanon (which replicated the *Synagoge of Fifty Titles*) does not appear in Russian manuscript until the late thirteenth- or early fourteenth-century *Ustiug kormchaia*, while the earlier manuscript redaction, the *Efremovskaia kormchaia*, reproduces a different Byzantine nomocanon, the *Syntagma of Fourteen Titles*.[44]

There is some disagreement about the origin and provenance of this oldest manuscript redaction, the *Efremovskaia*. Some scholars consider it to be of Bulgarian origin, prepared in the reign of Boris (852–889) or the early tenth century, although Bulgarian scribes under Iaroslav I (1019–1054) could have copied it in Kiev.[45] The handwriting in the earliest Russian copy has been dated to the twelfth or possibly eleventh century,[46] while Žužek suggests that the language is even older, typical of the very first translations of the Greek collections into Slavonic.[47]

The audience for a work that outlined canonical law and Byzantine imperial law relating to Church matters was naturally limited – it would have been used primarily as a reference work for clerics with some degree of authority, and law-makers such as Vladimir, Iaroslav and their advisers, rather than as material intended for individual or communal spiritual study. The *Kormchaia kniga* was revised in the thirteenth century by Metropolitan Kirill II,[48] and exists in several different redactions extant in a number of manuscripts. For the purposes of this work, the provenance of the original works included in the *Kormchaia kniga* is of lesser importance. What is significant is that these meanings of *dvoeverie* and lexical derivatives – 'dispute', 'controversy', 'to be in two minds', 'to differ' – were probably circulating in Kievan clerical circles from the eleventh century.

A much later example of *dvoeverie* which seems to correspond with the meanings of 'dissension' or 'dispute' is attributed by Sreznevskii to *The Life of St John the Theologian*, from the sixteenth-century *Great Reading Menology* (sometimes called the *Great Menaion* or *Menologion*) compiled by Metropolitan Makarii. Sreznevskii gives the sentence 'Боудоу(т) двовѣрства и распря многы' (*Жит. Iо. Бог. XXI*) in his *Materialy*,[49] without offering the Greek. However, all redactions of the *Life* that I have consulted replace 'двовѣрства' (*dvoverstva*) with 'двостаиства' (*dvostaistva*).

In the published version of the *Uspenskii* redaction of the *Great Menology*, the reading for 26 September is *The tale of the holy and all-praised Apostle and Evangelist John the Theologian, on his life and passing away. Written by his disciple Prokhor*. The passage which resembles Sreznevskii's citation reads:

> Рече же игѣмонъ к ней: да вѣжь, жено, юко мрьзость есть вѣра хрис-тіаньская не ток'мо царю, но и м'ногимъ человѣкомъ; аще убо крещуся и буду убо строя домъ, помощ'никъ отцу твоему и своему дому, Іоану и пріая всѣмъ вѣрующимъ во Христа, быти имуть мятежи и разлученіа, будутъ двостаиства и распря многы; всѣмъ же събрав'шимъся в'купѣ о семь, погибнемъ, и пож'гутъ ны огнемь, или идуть къ царю обадять, и царь мучити ны имать;[50]

> The hegemon said to her: Know, wife, that the Christian faith is an abomination not only to the king, but also to many people; thus if I am baptised and build a house, [as] a helper to your father and my own house, to John and caring for all those who believe in Christ, there will be revolts and separations, there will be *dissensions* and many quarrels; to all having assembled together about this, we will perish, and they will burn us by fire, or they will go to the emperor [and] slander [us], and the emperor will torture us;

The text agrees almost exactly at this point with the *Sofiiskii* redaction of the *Great Menology* held in manuscript in the State Public Library, St Petersburg. Under both 26 September (the anniversary of the saint)[51] and 8 May (the celebration of his miracles)[52] in the *Sofiiskii* redaction, the phrase 'Боудоу(т) двовѣрства и распря многы' is also replaced by 'будуть двостаиства и распря многы':

н/всѣмгъ/вѣроуюцримгъ/во/йма/хрисптиво/боудѣтъ/двойства/й/распра/ мнѡгы/йпѡгыбнемгъ, всѣм/же/собравшимса/ѡ/семгъ[53]

and

боудѣтъ/двостайства. и/распра/многы/всѣмгъ/же/собравшимса.[54]

It is, however, possible that the *Tsarskii* redaction may contain 'двовѣрства' for 'двостаиства',[55] although the published *Uspenskii* redaction of the *Great Menology* offers footnotes with variations from other redactions, and none are offered for this passage.[56]

The Greek text published in *Acta Joannis* by Theodor Zahn (a fifth-century Orthodox revision of the original Gnostic Acts) includes the phrase: 'there will be dissension and many divisions/schisms'.[57] The word which the translator has rendered *двостаиства* is διχοστασίαι, *dichostasiai*, 'dissensions', 'seditions', from the verb διχοστατέω, *dichostateō*, 'stand apart', 'disagree', 'feel doubts'. The root of this verb is στω, 'stand', and it seems clear in this instance that the Slavonic translator has constructed a calque.

This word is not listed in any of the Russian Academy of Sciences historical dictionaries, and the Institute of Russian Language has no record of its usage in any other context, nor were staff members of the Dictionary department able to comment on the meaning or etymology of the word, which was unknown to them.[58] In the absence of an accurate reference to Sreznevskii's quoted passage, one can only surmise that in at least one redaction of the *Life* our translator rendered διχοστασίαι as *двоверства*, meaning again 'disputes' or 'seditions'.

There are numerous other Slavic redactions of the *Life*, the earliest a twelfth-century Serbian manuscript which does not contain the sentence cited above,[59] and this was clearly a popular work. The *Great Menology* is a twelve-volume series of religious readings (one volume per month), compiled by the hugely influential prelate Makarii, Metropolitan of Moscow from 1542 to 1563. The collection was drawn from a variety of sources, from Makarii's own library and from manuscripts preserved in various monasteries and cathedrals, notably the Trinity-St Sergius, Kirillo-Belozerskii and Iosif Volokolamskii monasteries.[60] The *Life* as included in the sixteenth-century *Great Menology* would have had a relatively wide audience, as *Monthly Readings* collections were intended for both liturgical and personal use, and these texts would have been read twice a year during Church services.

Doubt, uncertainty, hesitation

The next series of meanings associated with *dvoeverie* is to be found in the *Sixteen Sermons of Gregory the Theologian with Commentary by Nicetas of Heracleia*. The word *dvover'e* first appears in a particularly difficult translation of chapter 38 of Gregory the Theologian's sermon *On Love of the Poor*. Again, there is no connection with paganism.

Аще ѿнмеши/рече/сооугъ/н/руконимлю. малословье/же/глю. н/се/нскуш-
енье. нлн/двовѣрье. н/глъ/роптаныа/что/будетъ.⁶¹

If you take away, [God] said, the bond and hand-taking,⁶² miserliness⁶³ I say, and this examination or *hesitation*, and speech of grumbling, what will be?

A recent translation of the Greek text reads '"If you do away with the fetters and with selectiveness" – with your stinginess, in other words, and with your close scrutiny [of the poor], or perhaps with your hesitancy and your grumbling words – what will happen?'⁶⁴ The Greek here is ἀμφιβολίαν, *amphibolian* (accusative of ἀμφιβολία), meaning doubt, uncertainty, hesitation. The Slavic translation of the Greek is, as with the previous text, so poor that it cannot be understood without reference to the Greek original. How clear it would have been to the medieval reader is uncertain.

The word *dvoverna* also appears in another difficult translation, the *Sermon on the Maccabees*. The harrowing death of the mother and her seven sons (Maccabees Book II, 6:18–7.42 and Book IV, 16) in defence of the Law of Moses was seen as a precursor to Christian martyrdom, and Gregory the Theologian apparently saw the mother as a forerunner of Mary, the 'mother of sorrows'.⁶⁵ This text may well relate to paganism, since these Jewish martyrs died at the hands of Hellene pagans for refusing to eat unclean food and to conform to pagan customs.

Мтн/тамо/оуношьскъі/н/добла/дѣтолюбнва/кꙋпно/н/бꙋолюбнва. н/мтрьню/
оутробу/трасуцн. чресъ/правьду/кства. не/стражюцpа/бо/мнловаше/
дѣтн. но/тружаше/а/кже/не/пострадатн. нн/ошедшн/любаше/па/
нежелн/за/оставшн/молаше/са/н/се/бѣ/кн/паче/слова/нежелн/
преставльшнхса. о/вѣ/оубо/двовѣрна/брань. овѣх/же/твердо/разорѣе/
н/овъі/оуже/бу/предлагаше. сн/же/тако/да/прнмме/бъ/печаше/са. ѡ/дша/
мꙋжьска/в/женьстѣмь/телесн/о/днвнаго/преданыа/н/велнкодшıва/н/ѡ/
аврамьскъıа/жертвъı/ѡноıа/аце/нѣчто/дерзо/н/боле.⁶⁶

A mother [was] there, vigorous and strong,⁶⁷ children-loving and also God-loving. And shaking [her] maternal womb against the law of nature, she did not have mercy on [her] suffering children, but belaboured them lest [they] not suffer. Nor did she love those who had departed more than she prayed for those who remained, and this was to her more of a word than those who had died.[68] For all therefore the struggle [was] *uncertain.* For some [there was] certain destruction, and others she had already offered to God. She was concerned that God receive [them all]. Oh a man's soul in a woman's body, oh [she] of wonderful dedication and great-souled, and oh of Abraham's sacrifice of her yet something bold and greater.[69]

The Greek word which has been translated as *dvoverna* is ἀμφίβολος, *amphibolos* – uncertain, doubtful.[70] In the RAN historical dictionary the meaning of this use is given as *somnitel'nyi* (doubtful), *s dvoiakim iskhodom* (with two outcomes).[71]

The third appearance, as *dvover'e,* is in the commentary of Nicetas to the *Sermon on the Burial of St Basil.* The absence of a Greek entry in the RAN dictionary suggests that this may be a fragment that has been lost.

Н҃ /ꙁѣло/рече/похотѣ/великꙑн/василнн. н/оусерно/мужьскꙑ/подвнꙁаса.
н/смꙑсленѣ/н/не/беꙁ/дѣлнѣ.   ннчто/же/ославнвъ/собѣ/къ/евсевъевн/
печалнн. но/абье/смнраетса/с/нн̄. н/рѣшнтъ/межю/собою/соблаꙁнꙑ. нмн/
же/надѣюще/ ꙁловѣрннн/еппн/на/насъ/въꙁвоеваша. по/нстннѣ/б̄о/не/
хоташе/великꙑн/ василнн. евсевьевн/опечалнвшемоу/кго/помоцн. тѣ/же/
налѣгахоу. но/тако/смѣрнвъса/н/раꙁдроушнвъ/малодꙑше. ополчаетса/по/
блꙃочтью. амфнлолон. н/двовѣрье/людін/прнкмлетъ. нꙁвѣсто/кже/в/
правовѣрьноу/держа[72]

Commentary: And very much he said the great Basil desired [this], and zealously [and] manfully strove [for it], both thoughtfully and not without action. Nothing having left for himself towards Eusebius [but] sorrow,[73] but immediately is reconciled with him, and resolves between themselves the temptations,[74] by them hoping the heretical bishops attacked us. In truth the great Basil did not want to help Eusebius, who had grieved him. In this way they were pressing [him]. But thus having humbled himself and destroyed faint-heartedness, [he] arms himself by grace, amfiloloi [*sic*] and the *doubt* of the people endures, firmly holding to orthodox belief.

It seems probable that the doubting people Nicetas refers to here are those tempted by fourth-century Christian heresies challenging the status of the Trinity. St Basil the Great was called to defend Orthodoxy in *c.* 364 against the Arian emperor Valens,[75] and the section of the commentary from which this excerpt is taken possibly refers to this struggle with the Arians, who maintained that the son of God was a creature who should be honoured for his righteousness but was neither divine, nor co-equal with the Father. The mysterious *amfiloloi* might be an unusual rendition of the name Amfilochius, cousin of Gregory, who was present at the Council of Iconium in 376 in which the full divinity of the Holy Spirit was defended, and was head of the Council of Side that excommunicated the Messalians.[76] This is, however, a difficult passage and it seems unlikely that амфнлолон means Amfilochius.[77] What can be said with certainty is that in this passage *dvover'e* means 'doubt', and is not related to paganism.

Nicetas of Heracleia, who lived in the eleventh to the first quarter of the twelfth century, was a deacon of the Hagia Sophia in Constantinople before becoming Metropolitan of Heracleia in 1117. His commentary to the sermons of St Gregory the Theologian appeared in the eleventh century, was translated into Georgian by a contemporary, and – according to Bulanin – first appeared in Russian translation in the twelfth century. The sermons themselves were widely known in Russia. Bulanin lists nine seventeenth-century monasteries that contained more than one edition of Gregory's sermons and accounts for their popularity by the fact that they entered into the circle of prescribed reading via the Studite and Jerusalem typikons (liturgical manuals indicating how the services are to be recited during the ecclesiastical year).[78] These typikons ideally would have been kept in every Orthodox church and monastery, and it seems safe to assume that the sermons – and therefore these meanings of the word – would have been well known in monastic circles, and probably also among parish clergy.

The *Римский Патерик* (*Rimskii Paterik*), or *Беседовник Григория Двоеслова* (*Besedovnik Grigoriia Dvoeslova*), a translation of the *Dialogues of Gregory the Great*, contains the phrase 'в двоверїи' (*v dvoverii*) as a translation of ἐν δυσπιστία (*en dyspistia*), 'in disbelief', from Book Four of the *Dialogues*. The passage containing the phrase appears in the *Uspenskii* redaction of the *Great Menology* of Metropolitan Makarii, under 11 March,[79] and also in the *Prolog* under 23 June:

Ѿ тогѡ плѡ́ти мы̀ в҆се́й заточенїа. слѣпотѣ рождьшесѧ, о҆те́чество оу҆бѡ нб҃ное слышимъ, й тогѡ жителѧ а҆́гг҃лы слышимъ, ѡ҆бѣщники же тогѡ бл҃женныхъ а҆́гг҃лъ, дꙋ҃хи праведныхъ скончавшихъсѧ. плотѧни же нѣцыи, не видимаѧ ѻна видѣти немогꙋ́ще, и ради не й҆скоꙋсьства, в страхъ низ҆падающе в҆двовѣрїи соꙋть, вмѣнѧюще быти ѻна, ꙗ҆же тѣлесныма ѻчи́ма видѣти немоѓꙋтъ.[80]

from that flesh we [are] in this exile,[81] having been born [in] blindness, for we hear [about] the heavenly homeland, and the angels of that dwelling-place we hear, [and] those companions of the blessed angels, the righteous spirits of those who have died. Some carnal [people], not being able to see those invisible [things], and because of ignorance, into fear falling downward *in doubt* they exist, thinking those [invisible things?] to be, [that] which with bodily eyes they are unable to see.[82]

This appears to correspond with the passage 'Born as we are of his flesh into the darkness of this exile, we hear, of course, that there is a heavenly country, that angels are its citizens, and that the spirits of the just live in company with them; but being carnal men without any knowledge of the invisible, we wonder about the existence of anything we cannot see with our bodily eyes'.[83] Again, the sense here is 'to wonder', 'to doubt', 'to hesitate'. The *Church Dictionary* of Petr Alekseev gives the meaning of *dvoeverie* as 'сумнѣніе, нетвердое упованіе', 'doubt, uncertain hope', citing the *Prolog* for 23 June.[84]

It is possible that the phrase 'в двовѣрїи' is a mistranslation of ἐν δυσπιστία (*en dyspistia*), which the translator misread as either ἐν δυοπιστία (*en duopistia*, literally 'in two-faith') or by iotacism as ἐν διπιστία (*en dipistia*, literally 'in bi-faith'), neither of which words exist in Greek, so that 'in incredulity' has become 'in bi-faith'.[85] Given the evidence from other texts, however, it seems more likely that the translator was competently choosing *dvoeverie* as expressing doubt or uncertain faith.

The sixth-century Pope Gregory the Great is usually believed to be the author of the *Dialogues*, although there is some disagreement about this. The stories were translated into Greek (from their original Latin) by Pope Zacharius in the eighth century, and found popularity in Byzantium. Various translations of the *Dialogues* are known – the first, which is incomplete, dating from the very earliest period of Slavic literature. Some researchers, on the basis of lexical evidence, attribute it to the circle surrounding Methodius in Moravia, others to the circle of Bulgarian pupils of Cyril and Methodius at the end of the ninth or beginning of the tenth century.[86] This text would no doubt have been relatively well dispersed. Vereshchagin identifies the most widely read books in pre-Petrine Russia as the Psalter, the Gospels, the Acts of the Apostles, the *Sluzhebnye minei* (*Service Menaion*, containing church services chronologically arranged) and, in fifth place, the *Prolog*, based on a translation (probably accomplished in Rus in the second half of the twelfth century) of the Greek *Synaxarion*, which quickly transformed itself into a Russian text with the addition of native saints. He also notes that it was much copied, extant in some three thousand manuscripts, and printed first in Moscow in 1643.[87] The *Prolog* is a collection of saints' lives, intended for contemplative or communal reading. However, the material was often replicated at least in part in the *Menaion*, books containing devotional readings for each day of the month. Since in this case the material also appears in the *Menaion* for March, the text would have been known to the attentive illiterate at least.

Another example of *dvoeverie* as 'hesitation', 'doubt' or 'uncertainty' is found in the *Commentary of Theophylact on the Gospel of St Luke*, which also appears in the sixteenth-century *Great Menology* of Metropolitan Makarii, under 4–18 October. The portion of the Gospel commentary by Theophylact, Archbishop of Ochrid and Bulgaria (*c.* 1050–1126)[88] which contains the word *dvoevernyi* accompanies the Gospel according to Luke 24:13–24 – the story of the meeting between Jesus and the disciples on the road to Emmaus.

По́ что же инѣмъ образомъ ювися и удер҄ жастася очі ею? Да весь двоевѣрный ею разумъ откръета и гной обнажита, и тако зелію пріимета, да сладокъ има ювится по мнозѣмъ, и тій да научить отъ Мѡѵсеа и пророкъ, и тогда познается, и паче вѣруета . . .[89]

Why in a different image did [Jesus] appear and hold back their eyes [prevent their eyes from recognizing him]? So that all their *doubting* thought they disclose and expose the pus, and thus the medicine receive, that sweet

He appear to them at length,[90] and that He teach [them] from Moses and the prophets, and then be recognized, and they more believe . . .

The Greek word translated as *dvoevernyi* is διστάζουσαν, *distazousan*, from the verb διστάζω, *distazō*, hesitate, doubt, be unsure.[91] The commentary uses the term to describe the disciples' spiritual state while they were unable to recognize the risen Christ. It is not until Jesus has broken bread that the disciples recognize him, and recall how their hearts burned within them while he spoke about Moses and the prophets. The implication of the Gospel passage is that the minds of the disciples prevent their bodily eyes from recognizing Christ, despite the fact that their hearts feel his presence.

According to William Ryan, Theophylact's commentaries on the Gospels were the only ones known in Russia during this period.[92] The oldest extant manuscript of Theophylact's commentaries (which is incomplete) dates to the thirteenth century and is of Russian origin.[93] As part of the *Great Menology*, this commentary would have been relatively well known.

Ambiguity and hypocrisy

The *Chronicle* of George Hamartolos, 'George the Sinner', a ninth-century Byzantine monk, was a history of the world beginning with the Creation, and was available in Russia by the eleventh century. The word 'двовѣрна' appears in a most unexpected context, a discussion of the 'abomination' of homosexuality.[94] The Slavic translation of the *Chronicle* published by Istrin gives the following:

юко оубіици естьствоу и родоу крамолници и скверненіи житию и жиꙁни досадители бъвають. юко блоуднъıа женъı любъı творать бес числа, въ сквернены˟ веселатса грѣховъ, скверненое житие и тлѣнно ѡканноую жизнь смѣсивше, двовѣрна и ненавидима или имоуца и списание родомъ незаконномъ.[95]

like murderers of nature and rebels against family and [like] defiled offenders of society and life [homosexuals] are. Like lascivious women [they] commit fornication countless times, [they] rejoice in abominable sins, uniting abominable society and corruptly accursed life, *ambiguous* and detestable or having and writing by illegitimate birth.

The crucial part of this passage is particularly opaque, but two scribal errors potentially account for the impossibility of finding a meaningful reading of this passage. Firstly the scribe has misread 'лик' ('lik') or perhaps 'лицо' ('litso', meaning 'face') as 'или' ('ili', meaning 'or'),[96] since the Greek text has the word for 'countenance' as the subject of the adjectives 'ambiguous' (ἀμφίβολα, also 'doubtful') and 'detestable' – so the first translation probably read 'having an ambiguous and detestable face' and was miscopied thereafter. A correct translation of *dvoverna* in the text given above might offer the sense of either 'ambiguous' in the sense of neither clearly male nor female, or perhaps 'hypocritical' – a meaning that is implicit in the much later text about Lutherans with 'double-believing faces' (see below). The second error is one of translation, and was clearly an earlier error. The translator has misunderstood the Greek for 'adulterated' (literally 'bastardized') as 'of illegitimate birth', since the Greek text reads 'having an ambiguous and detestable countenance and adulterated writing'.[97]

Two Slavic redactions of the *Chronicle* exist, independent but differing 'negligibly' from each other.[98] Istrin uses the so-called Russian redaction, but refers to it as the 'Slavic-Russian', and considers that it was translated in Kievan Rus in the eleventh century. This is contested by a number of scholars, who believe it was translated in Bulgaria in the tenth century and transmitted to Rus in the eleventh century – a theory that Thomson suggests is the most probable.[99] Regardless, this text was both popular and influential, and is preserved in various manuscripts up to the seventeenth century, when it was prepared for publication. It was used as a historical source by numerous chronicle compilers, including one of the compilers of the *Primary Chronicle*.[100] It would, however, have remained the preserve of the educated élite.

Further evidence of a meaning of 'ambiguous' or 'hypocritical' for *dvoeverie* is to be found in the appearance of the antonym 'недвовѣрно' in the *Ustav Studiiskii*, the *Studite Typikon*, cited in an unpublished entry from the card catalogue (XI–XIV centuries) of the Institute of Russian Language in Moscow. The meaning attributed by the catalogue is 'manifestly', 'obviously', 'unambiguously', but this reading poorly fits the context, which implies that the vow of poverty was being made insincerely and should have been a cause of shame to the monastic community.[101] It appears in a twelfth-century manuscript of East Slavic origin, the oldest extant text of the *Typikon*,[102] in the chapter ѡ отъриц҄нии ∴— 'On denial':

дивлю же с҄ како не срамл҄ютъ с҄ ѿречению имѣнии · тацѣмь образъмь д҄кмоую присаж҄ю҄е · кгд҄ не двовѣрьно ксть и свѣт҄ испълнь · д҄не свѣтьлѣк·[103]

I wonder how they are not ashamed at the renunciation of possessions, in this way being made, taking the vow [of poverty]. When it is not *insincere* (*hypocritical*) and full of light, [it is] brighter than day.

While it appears that the Greek original of the monastic *Studite Typikon* is lost, and the content of the Rule is preserved only in the Slavic translation,[104] the context here seems clear. The possession of private wealth was strictly forbidden by the Studite Rule, although this was an issue that the Kievan Caves monks struggled with,[105] as did many monastic communities.

Although the original 'blueprint' *Studite Typikon* was written by St Theodore of Studium in the ninth century, shortly before St Cyril began his mission to the Slavs, it was adopted and rewritten for a number of monasteries. Our text is a translation of a version prepared by Patriarch Alexios the Studite for his own monastery in Constantinople, which was founded in 1034. Thus this was a reasonably recent, up-to-date eleventh-century version of the *Typikon* when imported to Rus.[106] The earliest Cyrillic copies with Russian orthography date from the eleventh to twelfth centuries, and while it is not clear exactly how the earliest copies of the *Studite Typikon* reached Russia (see later), it seems fairly certain that this was during the eleventh century. As a monastic rule, this text is unlikely to have been disseminated beyond the black clergy.

From translation to creation

There seems little doubt that the term *dvoeverie* entered the Slavonic language as a calque from Greek via the translated nomocanon. While no less than six Greek constructions are translated as *dvoeverie* or a lexical derivative thereof, there are three 'families' of meaning that can be identified, united by one common thread. The most common group is that pertaining to 'doubt', 'uncertainty', 'hesitation'; the second group includes 'dispute', 'controversy', 'differ/maintain on the contrary'; and the final group includes 'ambiguous' and perhaps 'insincere' or 'hypocritical'.

One could argue that the common thread is that of being 'in two minds'; being unable to decide or agree, or being unable to perceive the true nature of something. These meanings evidenced in the translated texts were included in manuscript collections that were recopied over centuries, and read in church services and in private devotions by clergy of all stations. It is therefore safe to assume that the clerical authors of our next selection of 'native' texts would have been to some degree influenced by these early meanings in their choice of the word *dvoeverie*,[107] particularly in the light of Picchio's observations on the close reading of ecclesiastical texts.[108]

Duplicitous foreigners

While in none of the translated texts discussed above is more than one faith in evidence (except perhaps in the *Sermon on the Maccabees*), in the following examples *dvoeverie* is used in passages concerning relations between Orthodox and foreign – mostly Roman Catholic – believers.

The first three texts date from the eleventh and twelfth century, but were reproduced in much later compilations, indicating a continuous understanding of the term as used in this context. Before addressing the texts themselves, and the meaning conveyed in them by the term *dvoeverie*, we should consider their historical context and the degree to which 'Latins' were perceived as 'other' and their faith as distinct, separate. Without that perception, the interpretation of *dvoeverie* as pertaining to two faiths (Orthodox and Latin) cannot be supported, and the word as used in these texts might perhaps be better understood as meaning 'duplicitous', 'doubting' or 'hesitant', as it does in the translated texts.

The evidence for Russian Orthodox relations with the 'Latins' is contradictory, and historians are divided over the question of just how 'real' the differences and divisions between the two Churches were, particularly in the period before the Fourth Crusade of 1204, which shocked the Eastern Orthodox world and hardened attitudes towards their schismatic brethren. The texts considered shortly indicate a fairly antagonistic approach on the part of the 'black' or monastic clergy to their Western rivals, but it is often suggested that, at least among the lay Orthodox community, there was little conception that the Latins were members of a different faith.

The Byzantine polemic against the Latins began in the second half of the ninth century, under Patriarch Photius. This period is significant not merely because of the so-called 'Photian schism', when Patriarch Photius excommunicated the Pope for the heretical insertion of the *filioque* clause into the Creed (and for supporting the deposed Patriarch Ignatius), but for the struggle for ownership of Eastern European souls. The race to cultivate these spiritually unploughed territories, while no doubt politically motivated, aggravated differences of theology and ritual as rival missionaries sought to convince the pagans of their own particular versions of the Truth. There is evidence to suggest that initially this rivalry was in some respects more noticeable on the ground, among the missionary clergy rather than the Papacy, since Cyril and Methodius successfully appealed to Pope Hadrian II to legitimize use of the Slavonic liturgy when they encountered objections from Latin clergy, and Pope John VIII also defended Methodius in no uncertain terms in the face of German-Frankish opposition, securing his release from the imprisonment imposed on him by German bishops.[109] By the late ninth century however – a hundred years before the conversion of Vladimir – Pope Stephen V had banned use of the Slavonic liturgy and thus placed a further barrier between the neophyte Slavic churches and Western Christendom.[110]

The *Primary Chronicle* gives an indication of the Kievan monastic clergy's perception of this rivalry in the description of visits made to Vladimir's court in the year 986 by representatives of the major faiths. The Germans visit as emissaries of the Pope, and are swiftly dismissed by Vladimir, who is then impressed by a long discourse on the Greek faith which includes a rebuttal of all others, including the Latin:

> Then the scholar said, 'We have likewise heard how men came from Rome to convert you to their faith. It differs but little from ours, for they commune with wafers, called *oplatki*, which God did not give them, for he ordained that we should commune with bread . . . they have modified the faith'.[111]

This reasonable and relatively mild criticism of the Latin missionaries is followed shortly after by a stream of accusations against the Latins, during the exposition of the Orthodox faith made after Vladimir's baptism by the attendant priests:

> Do not accept the teachings of the Latins, whose instruction is vicious. For when they enter the church, they do not kneel before the images, but

they stand upright before kneeling, and when they have knelt, they trace a cross upon the ground and they kiss it, but they stand upon it when they arise . . . In earlier times the Romans did not so act, but took part in all the councils, gathering together from Rome and all other Sees . . . After the seventh council, Peter the Stammerer came with others to Rome and corrupted the faith, seizing the Holy See. He seceded from the Sees of Jerusalem, Alexandria, Constantinople and Antioch. His partisans disturbed all Italy, disseminating teaching in various terms. For some of these priests who conduct services are married to one wife, and others are married to seven. Avoid their doctrine; for they absolve sins against money payments, which is the worst abuse of all. God guard you from this evil, oh Prince![112]

This passage may have been written in the late eleventh century, since Pope Gregory VII issued decrees against 'the simony and incontinence of the clergy' in 1074, and the chronicler may have heard about the charges in this way.[113] However this may be, it seems clear that this view of Latins was held, at least by some monastic clergy, before 1200.

It has been suggested by many historians that Russian Orthodox relations with the West did not truly disintegrate until the disastrous Fourth Crusade and sacking of Constantinople in 1204, although the Chronicle of Novgorod contains an entry describing the Sack of Constantinople during the Fourth Crusade under the year 6712 (1204 AD) which recognizes the fact that it was the crusaders themselves who were at fault rather than the Latin Church: 'the Franks and all their voyevvodas conceived lust for the gold and silver . . . and forgot the commands of Tsar and Pope'.[114] The Greek hierarchs' early efforts to persuade the Rus that Latins were heretics seem to have borne substantial fruit only after Catholics demonstrated that they shared this belief about the Orthodox. By the thirteenth century, the Papacy viewed Rus as mission territory to be won for the Church like a pagan land, and relations deteriorated thereafter.[115]

Another date offered by historians as a turning point in Russian Orthodox relations with Western Christendom is the abortive Council of Florence of 1438–9, although the Florentine Union was not announced publicly in Moscow until 1441. In the *Story of Metropolitan Isidor* (the prelate who signed the Union on behalf of the Russian Church), which is found in the late fifteenth-century Moscow Chronicle, the author states with conviction that 'the Latins are not Christians':[116]

Латыни не суть христиане, како могуть христиане быти, нынѣ же и сице бысть, не могут слышати правды, како могут поити путем правым и како может нам быти единачество с ними и едина церковь, отмѣтающися истинны божиа . . .[117]

the Latins are not Christians, how could they be Christians, nowadays and it being so, they cannot hear the truth, how then can they walk the true path and how can we be united [literally 'a unity'] with them and one church, they who renounce the true God . . .

That the Florentine Union undoubtedly dealt a significant blow to relations between the Russian Orthodox and their fellow Christians is evidenced by regulations relating to the reception of Roman Catholic converts. In this later period (from 1441 to 1667, or from 1620 according to some scholars) Russians generally rebaptized converts from the Roman Catholic Church, indicating that they were viewed as heretics rather than schismatics during this period.[118]

We also know that the seeds of suspicion and enmity were sown long before the fifteenth, or even the thirteenth century, and it is from this early period that our texts to be discussed date. Russia inherited a suspicion of Latins, and a number of myths about Catholic practices ranging from the bizarre (they drink their own urine) to the blasphemous, along with the textual heritage of Byzantine anti-Latin polemics. The *Primary Chronicle* provides plenty of evidence of this inheritance, although Francis Thomson points out that

> In spite of the strenuous efforts of the Greek metropolitans of Kiev, especially George I (*c.* 1067–*c.* 1077), John II (*c.* 1077–1089) and Nicephorus I (1103–1121), to inculcate anti-Latin hostility it was not until the thirteenth century that complete polemical works were translated.[119]

Metropolitan Ioann and possibly his predecessor Georgii, to whom the *Commandments of the Holy Fathers* is often attributed, both wrote instructions on how to conduct oneself with regard to the Latins. These included a prohibition on concelebration with those using unleavened bread (in other words, clerics of the Latin Church) and intermarriage, and in the *Commandments*, a prohibition on taking communion or prayers from Latins, or sharing food with them.[120]

While the official date of the schism between the Eastern and Western Churches of 1054 remains disputed, this period of friction was unquestionably significant. The *Primary Chronicle* remains silent about the events of 1054, although Kievan clergy and nobles must have known of the schism immediately, since the Papal Legate Humbert returned to Rome via Kiev in August 1054. Similarly, the *Novgorodian Chronicle* makes no references to inter-Church disputes during this period. However, we have seen how the mid-eleventh century monastic author(s) of the *Primary Chronicle*'s precursor viewed the Latins – as corrupters of the faith. The 1070s and 1080s were also fraught with inter-Church tension among the great; Pope Gregory VII excommunicated the Emperor Alexius Comnenus, who closed all the Latin churches in Constantinople.[121]

There is also some curious evidence of friendly relations between Orthodox and Latin during this period. The Feast of the Translation of the Holy Relics of Saint Nicholas (9 May) was instituted in 1089, and accepted by the Russians but rejected by the Greeks – understandably, since the relics of Nicholas the Wonder-worker had been stolen by Italian merchants from Myra in 1087 and taken to Bari in Italy. In 1091 the relics were sent to Russia with a delegation from the Pope,[122] and an Office for the Feast was composed in Church Slavonic, celebrating the fact that 'Like a star the relics have gone from the east to the west'.[123] Dvornik rightly cites this along with several other texts as an example of the 'friendly religious intercourse' that existed between Kievan Russia and the Western Church, despite the Byzantine inheritance.

Western European monks operated in early Kievan Rus, apparently successfully. A community of Scottish monks built a church and a monastery in Kiev, probably at the end of the twelfth century, serving the foreign merchants and traders operating in Kiev at that time,[124] and it is worth remembering that the evidence of the canonical literature prohibiting intercommunion is a fair indication that there was a problem worth addressing. Clearly Kievan clerics needed guidance on how much contact they should properly have with their Western brethren. The account given by Abbot Daniil of his pilgrimage to the Holy Land offers further textual evidence of cordial relations between Greeks and Latins *c.* 1104–6.[125]

On balance, the evidence shows that the Latins were certainly perceived as schismatics or perhaps even as heretics by certain individuals in the higher echelons of the Kievan Church, who were closer to Byzantine culture and society, and therefore more aware of inter-Church animosity in the post-1054 period. This perception could not have been uniform, however, since the organizational contacts evidenced by the translation of relics and the establishment of a foreign monastery in Kiev would have required a degree of cooperation from the higher Rus clergy. The lower clergy and their parishioners appear to have continued to fraternize with their Latin counterparts either in ignorance or confusion about the Orthodox position, or because the official divide was an unimportant issue compared to the practicalities of maintaining good trading, diplomatic and social links.

Two of the texts to be discussed in this section are attributed to Feodosii Pecherskii, abbot of the Kievan Caves Monastery from 1062 until his death in 1074. Feodosii was a significant and influential figure in the spiritual and political spheres of Kievan Rus, and the first text under consideration, *On the Christian Faith and the Latin*, purports to be a letter from Feodosii to Prince Iziaslav. The vexed question of authorship is properly the preserve of palaeographers and specialists on the works of Feodosii, and cannot be dealt with in great detail here. Since Eremin and the *Slovar' knizhnikov i knizhnosti Drevnei Rusi* (edited by D. S. Likhachev) are satisfied that Feodosii of the Caves Monastery is the original author, I shall not quibble, but authorship remains disputed.[126]

According to the *Primary Chronicle*, Feodosii received a copy of the *Studite Typikon* (discussed earlier) from a Greek monk of the Studion Monastery in Constantinople who had accompanied Metropolitan Georgii to Rus:

> He also interested himself in searching out the monastic rules. There was in Kiev at the time a monk from the Studion Monastery named Michael, who had come from Greece with the Metropolitan George, and Theodosius inquired of him concerning the practices of the Studion monks. He obtained their rule from him, copied it out, and established it in his monastery . . .[127]

This story is confirmed in part by the *Life of St Feodosii* in the Kievan Caves Paterikon, although in one version of the story Feodosii sends one of the brothers to Constantinople to have the Rule copied and brought back to him:[128]

> After this the blessed one sent one of the brethren to Constantinople to Efrem to have the entire rule of the Stoudios Monastery copied and brought back. He at once carried out the order of the venerable father, wrote down the complete monastic rule, and sent it to him. After he had received this, our father Feodosij ordered it to be read out before the brethren, and henceforth he began to do everything in his monastery according to the rule of the holy Stoudite house, and his disciples maintain it, even to this day.[129]

This provides a lexical link of sorts with the early use of the word *недъвовѣрно*, meaning 'not hypocritically' or 'sincerely', found in the twelfth-century Slavic translation of the *Studite Typikon* and discussed earlier. It is possible that Feodosii was also familiar with the *Efremovskaia* version of the *Kormchaia kniga*, and the use there of дъвовѣрик to mean 'disagreement', 'dispute'; but as no catalogue of the Kievan Caves Monastery library exists from this period, we can only guess.

In this 1069 letter to Grand Prince Iziaslav, commonly known as *O вере крестьянской и о латиньской*, *On the Christian Faith and the Latin*, Feodosii uses the term to describe those fluctuating between the Eastern and the Western Churches. Following the Schism, this important and influential cleric seems to have perceived Christians of the Latin rite as heretics, who were particularly dangerous because they were deceptive. Masquerading as Christians, Western Catholics posed a greater threat to God's Church than the pagans did:

> They are the most pagan and evil nation, because it is impossible to protect oneself against them, but one can against pagans. The Latins have the Gospel, the Apostle, and the holy icons. They go to church, but their faith and their law are unclean. They have dishonoured the whole land with the multitude of their heresies, because there are Varangians throughout the land.[130]

We have seen that Feodosii's opinions were shared by other Rus and Byzantine clerics of the eleventh and twelfth centuries. A number of senior clerics wrote polemics explicitly condemning Latin practices,[131] but these views were certainly not shared by all and a relatively harmonious state of affairs may have been what provoked Feodosii to write his discourse. In addition to enumerating the unorthodox practices of the Latins, he gives instructions on how the Orthodox should relate to them:

> Christians should not give their daughters to them in marriage, nor receive them into their own homes, nor swear any oath of brotherhood with them, nor have them as godparents, nor exchange kisses with them, nor eat with them, nor drink from any single vessel.[132]

One could interpret Feodosii's list of prohibitions as an indication that Kievans were engaged in such relations, since he felt the need to specify that such actions were unacceptable. However, there may have been a more specific reason. Feodosii and the monks of the Caves Monastery were notably involved in the political affairs of the day, and the 1043 marriage of Prince Iziaslav – to whom this missive is apparently directed – to the Polish (Roman Catholic) princess Gertrude may have, in part, prompted this text. Inter-faith marriages were forbidden by law:

> Аще ли жидовин или бесерменин будеть с рускою или иноязычник на иноязычницех митрополиту 50 гривен а руску поняти в дом церковныи.

> If a Jew or Muslim [takes] a Rus' woman [to marriage], or [if some] other [non-Orthodox] foreigner [takes a Rus' woman], [he is to pay] the Metropolitan 50 grivnas; and take the Rus' woman into a convent.[133]

This ruling in the *Statute of Prince Iaroslav* awards the Metropolitan higher compensation for an act of inter-faith marriage than for an act of incest, bigamy or bestiality, but it is by no means certain that a marriage to a 'Latin' would have contravened this ruling at the time the *Statute* was written, since the Churches were still not formally separated. Diplomatic marriages between non-Orthodox foreigners and Russian nobles were celebrated despite these strictures, and this marriage was in fact part of Iaroslav's (Iziaslav's father) attempt to cement the Russo-Polish alliance.[134] The couple were apparently unpopular with the Kievan populace. Shortly before the letter was written, Gertrude and her husband were forced to flee Kiev during a revolt in favour of Vseslav of Polotsk, then a prisoner in Kiev, and Iziaslav only managed to re-establish his authority in 1070 with Polish military aid.

Whether Gertrude's devout Catholicism contributed to their unpopularity with the populace is hard to say,[135] but Feodosii may well have been concerned about the potential spiritual influence she could wield over her husband. However, Dvornik points out that it was Gertrude who appealed to her husband to forgive the Pecherskii monks' tonsuring of his favourite eunuch without royal permission, citing the misfortune experienced in her own land when the ruler persecuted a monastic community. Despite her alien faith, Gertrude clearly perceived the Kievan Orthodox monastic community as holy and protected by God,[136] or perhaps, since the monks she refers to were chased out of Poland before the year 1025 (when Boleslaw died allegedly as a result of his blasphemous campaign),[137] she simply did not perceive a difference between the two communities. While some scholars have interpreted this persecution as evidence of a campaign by Boleslaw against monks supporting the *Slavonic* liturgy, there is no evidence in the *Paterik* to support this theory.

It is also possible that Feodosii had better grounds to be suspicious of Iziaslav's commitment to Russian Orthodoxy than his unfortunate choice of bride. Some historians record Iziaslav as making an abortive attempt to unite Russia with Western Christendom.[138] Koncevicius remarks that according to the annals of Baronius, Iziaslav sent his son Iaropolk to Pope Gregory VII proposing that the Pope accept the allegiance of Russia and place it under the auspices of St Peter. The Pope apparently sent an ambiguous letter of reply to Iziaslav in 1075.[139] According to Fennell, however, there is no evidence in other sources to support this view – citing the *Primary Chronicle*, Lampert of Hersfeld's chronicle, and Pope Gregory's letters as devoid of references to Iziaslav's proposal.[140]

A number of historians have identified the influence of a Byzantine sermon *On the Franks and Other Latins* (*Opusculum contra Francos*) upon this work.[141] It is possible that this sermon (attributed to Patriarch Photius) and other documents such as the *Letter of Michael Cerularius Patriarch of Constantinople to Peter, Patriarch of Antioch*, existed in translation in Rus in the eleventh century – introduced by the Greek metropolitans perhaps – but we cannot be sure.[142]

In the redaction of *On the Franks and Other Latins* published by Popov (from the Novgorodian *Kormchaia kniga* of the 1280s, with variants from the Ryazan *Kormchaia* of 1284)[143] there does not appear to be a passage corresponding to the one in Feodosii's letter which mentions *dvoeverie*, nor in the Serbian *Kormchaia* available in Russia from 1262.[144] However, whether Feodosii had strong textual precedents to draw on or not, the culture of the higher Kievan clergy, particularly those close to the Greek metropolitans, must have been prone to anti-Latin feeling. The *Paterik* – as we have seen – records that Feodosii had contact with the retinue of Metropolitan Georgii over the *Studite Typikon*, and it is probable that his contact with Georgii was greater than this limited intercourse.

The key passage in which dvoeverie appears is:

> Аще ли начьнеть непрѣстанно хвалити и свою и чюжюю, то обрѣтается таковый двовѣрье держа и близъ есть ереси . . . И аще ти речеть прьць: «Сию вѣру и ону Богъ далъ есть», ты же, чадо, рци: «То ты, кривовѣрне, мниши ли Бога двовѣрна! Не слыши ли, оканьне и развращене злою вѣрою, Писанье тако глаголеть: "Единъ Богъ, едина вѣра, едино крещенье" . . . »[145]

> Should anyone start to incessantly praise both their own and a foreign [faith], then such a person is holding *double-faith* and is close to heresy . . . If someone arguing should say to you: 'this faith and that God has given', then you, child, say to him, 'So you, heretic [crooked-believer], think that God is *double-believing*? Have you not heard, accursed one, corrupted by an evil faith, what Scripture says: 'One God, one faith, one baptism' . . .

This passage is perhaps the clearest indication that the term could mean 'holding two faiths', and the final sentence might best be translated 'do you think that God has two faiths?' There can be only one faith, Feodosii asserts; therefore all others are false even if they bear a resemblance to Christianity. 'Right-believing', *православие, правоверность*, defines itself against 'wrong-believing', and during this period immediately after the Schism Feodosii seems to have viewed acknowledgement that the Roman Catholic Church might have some things right as tantamount to heresy. The epithet *кривоверне* is interesting, and appears in more than one of Feodosii's sermons. This surely comes from Isaiah 40:4, 'Every valley shall be filled and every mountain and hill laid low, the crooked ways made straight and the rough paths made smooth'. This prophecy relates to the coming of the true faith, Christianity, and is repeated in Luke (3:5), where the preaching of John the Baptist is seen as 'the voice crying in the wilderness "Prepare the way for the Lord, make straight paths for Him"'.

The sin that Feodosii objects to in this homily is that of not being sufficiently Orthodox, of not establishing and maintaining clear boundaries between Orthodox and non-Orthodox. It has been observed (in other periods and in other places) that a crisis of some sort can precipitate a rejection of confident and complex theology for a belief-system with clear definitions of the permissible, the 'right'.[146] A mere eighty years after the official acceptance of Christianity, the clerics of Rus were faced with a break in the Body of Christ, and a choice forced upon them. It was no longer acceptable to celebrate with Frankish or Varangian priests because they had become part of the 'other', and anyone who would or could not distinguish their false faith from the true, and condemn it whole-heartedly, was a potential threat.

Religious-national awareness adds another layer of nuance to this text.[147] 'Other' or 'strange' equals 'foreign' (*чюжюю, chuzhiuiu*) in Feodosii's letter, and this may well relate to Iziaslav's aforementioned flirtation with Catholic Poland and his marriage to a foreign 'heretic'.[148] A conception of Orthodoxy as a specifically Russian faith seems to be present in this text, and is reinforced by the second of Feodosii's writings to use the term *dvoeverie*. Fairy Von Lilienfield suggests that

> in the thirteenth century, there arose in Eastern Europe a new exclusiveness, a consciousness of 'Rus' nationality – whatever this means in the thirteenth century! – and of Orthodoxy. Nothing of this sort is to be found in the K[ievan] C[aves] M[onastery] in the eleventh and twelfth centuries, according to the oldest sources, not even in the P[osilaniia of] S[imon and] P[olikarp] (thirteenth century) or in the K[ievan] C[aves] P[atericon] (fifteenth century).[149]

While there may have been no exclusiveness in the sense that the monastery welcomed individuals from different lands as brothers after conversion to Orthodoxy (such as Simon the Varangian), I believe that there was a developing sense both of Rus identity and of a Russian faith during this period, the two inextricably linked. This is evidenced not only in the writings of Feodosii but also in texts such as Ilarion's sermon *On Law and Grace*. Fedotov sees 'Russia' as having being created with the conversion to Christianity:

> Life within the oecumenical organism of the Church favourably shaped young Russia's national consciousness. Russia as a nation was born out of the mixture of Slavic and non-Slavic tribes, simultaneous with her conversion. In meditating about the destiny of their people, baptised 'after all others', the authors of the eleventh century . . . created a doctrine of national calling of Russia which is more orthodox, because it is more Christian than later Muscovite messianism.[150]

The early tenth-century South Slav text *On Letters*, which argues the superiority of the Slavonic alphabet over the Greek and Latin, indicates a developing sense of religious-national identity among the neophyte Slavs, which Picchio has termed *Slavia orthodoxa*, 'a sort of religious patriotism in accordance with the medieval notions of *nationes et confessiones*'. Picchio also observes that the term *Slavia orthodoxa* 'does not imply any belief in the existence of fixed territorial boundaries, nor does it suggest any underevaluation of the role played by local traditions, ethnic or political particularism, even ecclesiastical autonomies'.[151] That there are approximately eighty extant Cyrillic manuscripts of *On Letters* gives some indication of its popularity in the early Eastern Orthodox Church.[152]

'Foreign believers' also appear in our second text attributed to Feodosii,[153] a sermon entitled *Поучение Феодосия Печерскаго о казняхъ Божіихъ*, *The Teaching of Feodosii Pecherskii on the Punishments of God*, and found in the *Paisievskii sbornik*. This collection, which has regrettably been little studied as a whole, contains a significant number of the texts discussed in this book: *On the Christian Faith and the Latin*, *The Sermon of the Christlover*, and several other anti-pagan polemics discussed in Chapter 1.[154]

This sermon, which begins стй/ѿци/ycтавш/постнаиа/дни[155] ('the holy fathers ruled [about] fast days'), concentrates almost exclusively on drunkenness and the need to follow the teaching of the Fathers of the Church (naming St John Chrysostom and Gregory the Theologian in particular) on celebrating Christmas and Easter respectively. The preacher discusses the need to celebrate spiritually, rather than bodily, not to attend secular celebrations during the fast period, and to be reconciled (to 'make peace') not only with those one loves but also with one's enemies. However, the preacher identifies certain enemies of God with whom one should not make peace, and the word *dvoeverie* is used in this context.

А/се/вии/cy/врази/жидо/єретици. держаще/кривую/вѣру, ї/совращающе/ на/іновѣрье. ї/праще/по/чюжеї/вѣре. ї/хвалаще/чюжюю/вѣру. ї/ двоёвѣрье/любаще. с/тѣми/николй/мира/дерп?[ж[156]]а.[157]

For God these are the enemies: Jews, heretics, [those] holding to a crooked faith, and led astray to a foreign faith, and disputing in accordance with a strange faith, and praising a strange faith, and loving *double-belief*, with these never make peace.

The word 'crooked' is again used to describe Jews and heretics – the Jews because they would not accept the New Testament teaching and straighten their paths; heretics because they twist and turn the truth of Orthodox Christianity into something else. The use of the word 'foreign' to identify 'false' faith is in itself significant, but given Feodosii's use of the term in the sermon discussed earlier, one is tempted to assume that *inoverets* refers again to Roman Catholics. However, the attribution of this sermon to Feodosii is even more contested than *On the Christian Faith and the Latin*. The dispute over this sermon addresses two issues – firstly which Feodosii is the true author (as with *On the Christian Faith and the Latin*), and secondly whether it is a translation from the Greek, although the redactions discussed in this context differ so significantly from the *Paisievskii* version that it is not clear that this has any bearing on our text at all.

There is one mention of paganism within this sermon, where the author discusses the Devil's joy at witnessing drunkenness among Christians:

> All because of the doings of my desires. Of drunks the very best are drinkers and drunks from [among the] Christians, than from [among the] pagans and idol worshippers . . . and this said the Devil to the demons: I say go and teach Christians drunkenness.[158]

This passage does not seem to relate directly to the part where the sermonizer discusses making peace with one's enemies (or at least the Orthodox ones), and is part of a long and virulent attack on drunkards. The point of the contrast with pagans is surely only to emphasize that drunkenness is all the more vile among Christians, who should know better. He does not compare intoxicated Christians to 'double-believers', and there is no implication that the drunken celebrations are the familiar 'devilish games' discussed earlier. It may be that the sermonizer was attempting to instil in his audience the correct way for Christians to behave at the holy festivals, in comparison with the way that pagans celebrate. While one might expect pagans to get drunk and celebrate, he seems to be saying, it is a greater sin for Christians to behave so. Lectures on drunkenness aside, this sermon appears to provide evidence of the use of the term only with regard to Orthodox Christians who fraternize with Western Catholics (foreign believers), and possibly those who mix with Jews and heretics.

According to Fedotov, chapter 24 of the unpublished first *Izmaragd* (fourteenth century) also contains the passage 'The Jews and the heretics and all who keep a wrong faith pervert themselves to heterodoxy and argue about a strange faith and praise a strange faith and love the double faith – with them it is not becoming to keep peace',[159] but he surprisingly concludes 'we are far from the relative tolerance of the Kievan clergy, even of the Greek metropolitans, toward the heterodox. In earlier days no one was excluded from the general duty of Christian charity'. Iakovlev records chapter 24 of the fourteenth-century *Izmaragd* as containing our sermon, observing that 'here is the last part of the sermon *On the Punishments of God* attributed to the Venerable Feodosii Pecherskii'.[160] He also makes reference to the authorship dispute, seeing the doubt cast on this sermon as the work of Feodosii as 'completely justifiable'.

A nineteenth-century published version of the sermon *On the Punishments of God* does not contain the word *dvoeverie* but includes a passage in the latter part of the text that resembles the *Paisievskii* manuscript. 'But God has enemies: Jews, heretics, those holding to a crooked faith, and disputing in accordance with a foreign faith'.[161] This part of the sermon also contains similar material on the sin of drunkenness and the correct way to celebrate festivals. A number of scholars have observed that the first half of the sermon appears in the *Primary Chronicle*, under the year 6576 (1068), but this chronicle entry bears little resemblance to the *Paisievskii* version of the sermon. The three versions of this sermon cited by Bel'chenko (*По Златострую, По Летописи, По Торжественнику*) do not match the unpublished version from the *Paisievskii sbornik*, and do not contain the word *dvoeverie*.[162]

These two texts attributed to Feodosii bear more than a passing resemblance to each other, but this is not by any means indisputable evidence of shared authorship, since a great many sermons contain similar phrases, borrowing from each other or from lost prototypes, being added to by later scribes and then drawn together, sometimes in fragments, in compilations such as the *Paisievskii sbornik*. To attribute these sermons conclusively to Feodosii Pecherskii is the prerogative of specialists, and the opinion of specialists mostly favours *On the Christian Faith and the Latin* as Feodosii's work, while *On the Punishments of God* has less support. The question of authorship is not greatly significant to the general aim of this work, but if the original author were Feodosii Grek, it would indicate that the use of the word in the context of ecumenical relations arose perhaps less than a hundred years later, in the early to mid-twelfth century rather than the mid-eleventh century.

Our third text to use the term in the context of inter-Church relations is the *Questions of Kirik, Savva and Ilia*, preserved in the *Novgorodskaia Kormchaia kniga* of the thirteenth century. This text, existing in two redactions, has an extremely long shelf life and appears in sixteenth- and seventeenth-century collections and *Kormchaia* manuscripts.[163]

There appears to be some confusion about the structure of this work. According to Metropolitan Makarii:

> There are three parts to the notes of Kirik. The first, the most extensive, contains his questions and the answers to them [given] mostly by Bishop Nifont of Novgorod, and in part by a certain Klim, believed to be Kliment Smoliatich, the then Metropolitan of Kiev, by hegumen Arkadii, who was the successor of Nifont to the episcopal diocese, by the hegumen of the unknown monastery of Marina, and by an episcopal monk Luka-Evdokim; all these questions and answers are presented without any order, and in

a large part of the manuscript, not divided into chapters. The second part contains the answers of the unknown Bishop Savva in 24 chapters, or rules. The third part consists of the answers of the Novgorod high cleric Ilia, successor of Arkadii, in 28 rules . . . A few answers found among the answers of Nifont are repeated in the rules of Savva and Ilia, of course, because the questions themselves were repeated by Kirik.[164]

Metropolitan Makarii's detailed observations on the text are contested by some other scholars. The published text from the thirteenth-century (*Novgorodskaia*) *Kormchaia kniga* is titled *The Questions of Kirik, Savva and Ilia, with the answers of Nifont, Bishop of Novgorod, and of other members of the hierarchy*, and the editor notes that 'The "Questions" belong to the times of the Bishopric of Nifont (1130–1156) and not to one, but to three persons (Kirik, Savva and Ilia)'.[165] The evidence for this is firstly the headings of the three parts: the first is titled 'Се есть въпрошаніе Кюриково' 'These are the questions of Kirik', the second 'Savva's chapters' 'Савины главы', and the third 'Ilia's questions' 'Ильино въпрашаніе', and secondly the identity of the questioners – Kirik is a monk, but the second questioner is a married priest. Podskalsky also observes that it is traditional to consider Kirik the author of the whole work, which also includes the questions of Savva and Ilia.[166]

We have reasonably detailed information on the identity of Nifont, who became bishop of Novgorod in 1130 or 1131, having been tonsured at the Kievan Caves Monastery.[167] He was an educated and dedicated cleric, which is evident from his answers as much as from his known history. Podskalsky credits him with initiating the first compilation of the *Novgorodskaia Sofiiskaia letopis'*, and being an energetic church and monastery builder.[168]

Nifont uses the term *dvoeverie* in replying to a question about those who take their children to a *Varangian* priest for prayers. They are 'as double-believers':

А ѿже се носили къ варажьскомоу попоу дѣти на молитвоу? – ѕ̃ недѣль ѡпитемыѣ, рече, занеже ꙗкъ двовѣрци соуть.[169]

And if they take children to a Varangian priest to be prayed over? – Then 6 weeks penance, it is said, because they are as *double-believers*.

The exact meaning of this sentence is not immediately clear, and raises a number of questions. What does '*Varangian*' mean? And are the women *almost* 'double-believers', because while not necessarily attending a non-Orthodox Church regularly they are appealing to a non-Orthodox priest in times of need? Or do they *resemble* double-believers simply because there are two separate faiths involved? Could Nifont have had pagan/Christian double-believers in mind when he made the comparison? And finally, could 'double-believers' be translated as 'hypocrites' or 'waverers'?

Varangian is often taken to mean 'Viking', or 'of Scandinavian origin', but Robin Milner-Gulland suggests that the name *Varangian* 'may derive from *vaeringjar*, "trading agent" or "wanderer"'.[170] It seems to me very unlikely that in this context the word means specifically Scandinavian, for the reasons outlined below. Should that be the case, however, we have little hope of identifying them as Christian or otherwise, since while traditionally Varangians in Rus are identified as Swedish, it is impossible to say with absolute certainty where these twelfth-century Scandinavians in Novgorod hailed from, or if they had come to Russia via another European country.

According to Richard Fletcher, attempts to convert the Danes were made in the second quarter of the ninth century, and King Harald of Denmark was apparently converted sometime around 960, over twenty years before Vladimir. Adam of Bremen reports hearing of the appointment of priests made in Denmark in the early tenth century, and three bishoprics were created in 948, although we have no evidence that their German appointees actually took up post there. Christianity reached Norway from England and Denmark in the tenth century with royal encouragement, and by the end of the eleventh century there were bishoprics in Oslo, Bergen and Trondheim. The kings of Sweden worked to convert the Swedish population from the late tenth century with the help of German clergy and possibly English missionaries. How Christian these Scandinavian countries were (or rather what percentage of the population had been baptized) by the twelfth century is uncertain.

The issue is complicated by the fact that the early Scandinavians abroad quickly accepted the Christian faith of their 'host' countries; in Ireland, Scotland, England, and Normandy for example, so Scandinavians who travelled to Rus from Western Europe would most likely have been already Christianized.[171] Clearly these immigrants had not adopted the Russian Orthodox faith, since they maintained separate priests and churches in Novgorod.

Varangian is used to mean Roman Catholic in the story of Simon the Varangian, Discourse One of the *Kievan Caves Paterik*:

> And he who had once been a Varangian became by God's grace a Christian, having been instructed by the holy Feodosij, having abandoned the folly of the Latins, and having come to believe truly in our Lord Jesus Christ.[172]

Interestingly, here the clerical author clearly understands 'Orthodox' and 'Christian' as synonymous.

The word *Varangian* also appears signifying Roman Catholic in the *Legend about the Foundation of the Varangian Church*, referring to a church requested by *nemtsy* (North European, probably Germanic) merchants trading in the region,[173] who demand 'Дайте нам мѣсто у себѣ, . . . гдѣ поставити божница по нашей вѣрѣ и обычаю'.[174] 'Give us a place at your [town] . . . where we [may] build a church according to our faith and rite'. There is no indication in the text that the merchants are pagan, and the reference to 'rite' implies the Latin rite. They offer in return that Orthodox churches be built in their lands so that Russian traders may worship according to their faith. It seems unlikely that such a dialogue would occur between a non-Christian immigrant population and the Archbishop and Mayor of Novgorod.

The first reference to a *Varangian* Church in Novgorod in the First Novgorodian Chronicle is made under the year 1152 (6660), 'eight churches were burnt down, and the ninth, the Varangian one'.[175] In 1181 the Chronicle records the burning of 'the Varangian church in the market-place . . . by thunder at 10 of the day, after evening service'.[176] The chronicler draws no anti-Latin conclusions from this act of God, and also identifies the church by location as if there were (or had been) more than one. The position of the church too is worth remarking, not hidden away or outside the city walls but in the commercial centre, the market place.

As we have seen, at least three manuscripts of the sermon *On the Christian Faith and the Latin* also used the word *Varangian* as a synonym for Latin – the letter to Prince Iziaslav is sometimes titled *The Answer of Feodosii to Prince Iziaslav about the Varangian Faith*,[177] and the redaction included in Makarii's *Great Menology* also uses *Varangian* in the text. The final piece of evidence for *Varangian* as Roman Catholic rather than Scandinavian is found in a much later version of the *Questions of Kirik*; in the sixteenth-century *Pravila* the text reads 'Аще носили къ фрязскому попу',[178] *фрязский* meaning most commonly 'Frankish', sometimes 'Italian' or simply 'Western', but certainly Catholic.

The balance of evidence, then, suggests that the word *Varangian* is here used to signify 'Roman Catholic'; and that in Nifont's opinion these Orthodox women may as well have been practising Catholicism, by the very fact of taking their children to a Catholic priest.

While Fedotov accepts *Varangian* as meaning Western, Fennell sees it as perhaps a reference to a magician or a priest of another faith. The *Questions of Kirik* cover a variety of unorthodox practices, and this text is interesting for the comparison of passages relating to apparently pagan customs with the passage that contains the word *dvoeverie*. Kirik asks about the ritual of preparing bread, cheese and mead for *rozhanitsa*, and is told simply 'горе пьющимъ рожаницѣ!'[179] 'Sorrow upon those who drink to *rozhanitsa*'. *Rozhanitsy* worship is frequently cited as evidence of *dvoeverie*, and yet the term is not used here, nor is it in other questions that cover magical rituals such as brides' bathwater being given to husbands.[180]

A further question related to magic asks about women who take sick children to *volkhvy* rather than to a priest for prayers:

а ѥже възболать, или къ вълхвамъ несоуть, а не къ попови на молитвоу? – То ѕ҃ недѣль, или г҃, ѡже боудоуть молоди.[181]

and if [children] fall ill, or to *volkhvy* take [the children], and not to a priest for prayers? – Then 6 weeks [penance], or 3, if they are young [women].

This question evidently refers to the practice of resorting to local magicians or healers in times of illness. Some scholars, such as Zguta, believe that the *volkhvy* formed a pagan priesthood, and many interpret the activities of *volkhvy* evidenced in the *Primary Chronicle* under the year 1071 as pagan rebellions contesting the authority of the Church.[182] But the penance for this practice is almost the same as that for those resorting to Latin priests – six weeks for mature women, and half that for younger sinners. This implies firstly that the sins were of equivalent gravity, in other words the prayers of a Roman Catholic priest were as damnable as those of a magician (if not more so, since younger women were not excused so lightly for the former crime), and secondly, that the word *dvoeverie* for the scribe(s) who prepared this text was specifically related to Catholicism rather than 'paganism' or unorthodox popular practices.

Dvoeverie was used and understood in the context of Orthodox–Catholic relations for some time. As we have seen, *On the Christian Faith and the Latin* may have been written around 1069, but possibly in the mid-twelfth century. Popov observes that this sermon of Feodosii's comes to us only in multi-date miscellanies, collections (*sborniki*) of material of varying ages.[183] Three of the extant manuscripts (two sixteenth-century and the fourteenth-century version from the *Paisievskii sbornik*) replace 'the Latins' with 'the Varangians'. According to Muriel Heppell, this text does not appear in the early redactions of the *Paterik*, 'and its inclusion in the *Second Cassian* redaction in 1462 may well reflect the strong anti-Latin sentiment in the Orthodox Church after the Council of Florence in 1439'.[184] As Petrukhin observes, this work was also reproduced in much later texts,[185] including the *Great Menology* of Metropolitan Makarii, indicating a continuous understanding of the word in this context.

Feodosii's *Sermon on the Punishments of God* appears in the fourteenth-century *Izmaragd*, and there is an almost identical phrase for *dvoever'e* in the *Zlataia tsep'* of the fourteenth century.[186] The *Izmaragd* was also included in the sixteenth-century *Great Menology* of Makarii. The *Questions of Kirik* reflects a similar longevity of meaning, published repeatedly in collections intended for clerical use, including the sixteenth-century *Pravila*.[187] The audience for these texts would have been as wide as literacy and church attendance permitted, since the readers of the *Izmaragd* were, according to Fedotov, the laity and married clergy,[188] and as we have seen, texts included in the *Great Menology* of Makarii would have been read at least once a year during church services. We can safely assume from the diversity of sources that the use of the term *dvoeverie* in the context of Orthodox–Catholic relations would have been unsurprising to the medieval readers of these texts.

Later readers might have also discovered *dvoeverie* in a far more unusual context – that of Orthodox–Protestant relations. Paul Bushkovitch refers to a 'general hardening of confessional lines in Europe'[189] during the seventeenth century, which is certainly reflected in the Russian legislation of the period. This 'general hardening' is evidenced not only in relations between the old adversaries of the Orthodox and Catholic Churches, but also in Orthodox–Protestant dialogue, where we find *dvoeverie* used again pejoratively, to mean 'hypocritical' or 'insincere'.[190]

Although Russia for the most part escaped the influence of the Protestant Reformation that shattered Western Christendom, by the late sixteenth century Protestant congregations existed within her borders, consisting mostly of war

prisoners deported from the Baltic States. In 1576 a Lutheran Church was operating in Moscow, headed by Timan Brakel, a Latvian minister taken hostage
(along with other notables) by Ivan IV.[191] By 1649, the number of Protestants
living in Russia was great enough to merit the inclusion of regulations concerning inter-denominational relations in the *Ulozhenie*. In keeping with the spirit
of the times, the *Ulozhenie* ordered the destruction of such Protestant churches
built within the walls of Moscow:

> И которых Немецких дворах поставлены Немецкие кирки: и те кирки
> сломати, и в впередь в Китае и в Белом и в Земляном городе на
> Немецких дворах киркам не быти; а быти им за городам за Земляным,
> от церквей Божих в дальних местях.

> Concerning the North European churches which were set up in the yards
> of Northern Europeans: demolish those churches. In the future there shall
> be no churches in Northern Europeans' yards in Kitaigorod, Belyi gorod,
> and Zemlianoi gorod. They shall be out of town, beyond Zemlianoi gorod,
> in places distant from God's [Orthodox] churches.[192]

Clearly these measures were insufficient to protect Moscow citizens (and God's
churches) from heretic foreign influence, since in 1652 the Tsar took further
steps to control contact between the denominations, commanding all foreigners
to live outside the walls of Moscow.[193]

Hebly, in his *Protestants in Russia*, also states that laws dating from 1649 for-
bade Orthodox Russians to eat with or live under the same roof as Protestants.[194]
However, the only regulation I have been able to find in the *Ulozhenie* which
uses vaguely comparable phrasing relates to the owning of Orthodox slaves
by unbaptized foreigners, which may include Muslims and Jews, since in this
Law Code the word *Nemtsy* is usually used to describe Northern Europeans.[195]
The regulation concludes 'И ныне по тому же у иноземцев некрещенных
Руским людем во дворах не быти ни которыми делы', 'And accordingly
now Russians shall not be in the houses of unbaptized foreigners for any reason
whatsoever'.[196] 'Accordingly' refers to a related section which cites the orders
of Patriarch Filaret that Orthodox Christians serving 'unbaptized foreigners of
other faiths' be removed from their houses 'so that there would be thereby no
profanation of Christian souls'.

Patriarch Filaret reacted to the influx of foreign and heretical influences with
increasingly isolationist and 'hard-line' tactics. Even Ukrainian and Byelorussian
Orthodox intellectuals fleeing to Russia from the Polish–Lithuanian State (which
by the 1596 Brest Church Union had united part of the Orthodox population
to the Roman Catholic Church while preserving traditional Eastern rite and
customs, creating the Uniate Church) were viewed with suspicion. According
to Bushkovitch, Filaret required the rebaptism both of Catholic converts (as
heretics, rather than schismatics) and of Orthodox Ukrainians and Byelorussians
– who poured water over rather than immersed their infants – following a

Church Council in 1620, where previously this had not been required.[197] The first sitting of this Council was held in Moscow in October, and condemned the Latin 'heresies', and according to Florovsky,

> this council was reconvened in December, and directed that Ukrainians and West Russians who were not baptized by triple immersion be rebaptized while those baptized by Uniate priests undergo a week's fast and formally abjure the Catholic faith. These rules were inserted in the 1639 Trebnik and were the law until 1667.[198]

Filaret's suspicions of Ukrainian and Byelorussian intellectuals extended to books published in these areas. In 1627 the purchasing of these books was forbidden by law,[199] and in 1628 a decree was passed ordering that all such books held in churches be inventoried and replaced by Muscovite editions. Privately-owned 'Lithuanian' books were confiscated, and even Orthodox works published in 'Roman' cities were considered to be tainted by heresy. Florovsky observes that 'from practical necessity, the Moscow editors used these suspect Kievan or "Lithuanian" and Venetian books',[200] and for all the rhetoric, arguments were borrowed from both the Reformation and the Counter-Reformation by Orthodox writers struggling to combat the rival churches.[201] However, it is important to distinguish between the early seventeenth century, when Ukrainian Orthodox innovations were suspect, and the later period, when they were fully accepted. Ukrainians had been brought in to run the Patriarchal printing press in Moscow, and by the last quarter of the seventeenth century they were fully incorporated into the hierarchy of the Russian Orthodox Church.[202]

The Russian church in this period felt itself under threat from all sides, and the text to which we now turn comes from a collection of polemics which reflects the suspicion ingrained in the Russian clergy of both Roman Catholic and Protestant, those 'two sides of the same coin'.[203] The *Debates about the Faith* is a seventeenth-century work compiled by Moscow theologians engaged in debate with the Court pastors of the Danish Prince Valdemar.[204] Valdemar was betrothed to Tsarevna Irina, the eldest daughter of Tsar Mikhail, but refused to be baptized as an Orthodox Christian. He resolved to return to Denmark, but the Tsar apparently liked him so much as a prospective son-in-law that he made great efforts to persuade him to stay. Valdemar's attractiveness lay in part at least in the strategic location of Denmark, with its Polish border and access to the Baltic and North seas, and it is a sign of the times that the issue of baptism prevented a royal diplomatic marriage so successfully.[205] *Debates about the Faith* is the result of the process of persuasion that Tsar Mikhail had his Orthodox advisers engage in. Valdemar arrived in January 1644, although the betrothal had been suggested some two years before, and while the debates raged, Prince Valdemar found himself unable to leave.[206] The reluctant suitor did not escape until the spring of 1645, after Aleksei's succession.

Vernadsky writes at some length about the process of negotiation between the two Courts, and emphasizes the fact that Valdemar was initially offered freedom of choice in the matter of conversion by Mikhail's ambassadors. The matter of the rebaptism was a demand made by the Patriarch and some influential boyars, for differing reasons. The Patriarch insisted that the possibility that Valdemar might one day become Tsar (Aleksei being Mikhail's only surviving son) made rebaptism a prerequisite.[207] Political agendas rather than religious sensibility may have influenced boyar support for or objections to the match, but certainly the prospect of a Protestant Tsar or high-ranking member of the royal family could not have been palatable to the general public. However, there were precedents for such a marriage without rebaptism as a prerequisite: Ivan IV had married off a cousin to another Danish Lutheran Prince for reasons of state. At least one boyar, Prince Semen Shakhovskoi, attempted to argue that in the case of Irina's betrothal to Valdemar, religious considerations were secondary to political interests. For his pains (and his unwise committal of these ideas to paper) he was tried for heresy and condemned to death. This was commuted to exile (which may reflect the Tsar's more lenient view of the matter), but his dismissal of the significance of confessional differences, along with his elevation of needs of state above the purity of the Orthodox faith, was clearly too much for the church authorities.[208]

Golubtsov describes this text as 'an extensive but incomplete and tendentious analysis' of the first half of Matthias Velhaber's account of the debates of 1644,[209] Matthias being Valdemar's Protestant pastor. Tsar Mikhail Feodorovich had ordered Ivan Nasedka to write a refutation of the Pastor's work on 10 August 1644.[210] Nasedka was clearly a significant actor in the affairs of the day: ordained a priest in 1608, from 1612 he was resident at the Trinity-St Sergius Monastery before being transferred to the Kremlin's Annunciation Cathedral.[211] He had also been sent to Copenhagen in 1621 to help negotiate another abortive engagement between Tsar Mikhail and a niece of the Danish King, and during his four-month stay made the observations of Lutheranism that were to form the basis of his later polemics. Golubtsov also observes that 'many of [the texts in the debates] consist of south-western Russian sources, and did not imagine themselves to be original . . . but this does not diminish their historical value'.[212] Nasedka, unlike Filaret, was open to Ukrainian sources, while remaining a traditionalist on matters of ritual.

The refutation ordered by the Tsar was composed by Nasedka on the foundation of his *Izlozhenie na liutory* (*Exposition against the Lutherans*), completed in 1623,[213] and cited the works of St John Chrysostom, John of Damascus, Dionysious the Pseudo-Areopagite and Josephus Flavius, the Gospels and other sources. The relevant passage of the particular text containing the word *dvoeverie* (text No 25: *Spisanie bogoroditskogo kliucharia Ivana ot' bozhestvennago pisaniia oblichitel'no na korolevicha Nemchina Matveia*) relates not to the issue of baptism, but to the Lutheran celebration of communion with unleavened bread, a source of heated dispute between the Roman Catholic Church and the Russian Orthodox since Feodosii's time:

Къ томуже еще и о причащеніе тѣла Христова да видимъ здѣ отъ божественныхъ же писаній, понеже лютори лестнѣ у себе двоевѣрнымъ лицемъ исповѣдаютъ причащеніе свое и истинно бутто и паки не истинно являютъ въ словесехъ и въ писаніихъ своихъ, занеже вси по-папежски причащаются прѣсному хлѣбу . . .[214]

> Besides, also about the communion of the body of Christ [Holy Communion]
> we see here from the Holy Scriptures, because the Lutherans duplicitously
> among themselves with *double-believing* faces[215] profess their own com-
> munion [as] true and yet they show [it to be untrue] in their own words and
> writings, since all in popish fashion celebrate communion with unleavened
> bread . . .

This is a difficult passage, but appears to say that while the Lutherans profess to
hold the true faith (*istinno*, from *istina*, is generally used to designate religious
truth, the truth of the Orthodox Church, although in a more general sense it
can also mean 'sincere'), they do not, since they celebrate with unleavened
bread like Roman Catholics.

This may be a case of an Orthodox (i.e. 'true')–Catholic 'double-belief',
with Lutherans unable to wholly identify with either denomination,[216] or the
double may be Protestant–Catholic: the Lutherans have their own theological writings and maintain that they 'исповѣдаютъ причащеніе свое',
'profess their *own* sacrament of communion', while they in fact preserve the
Roman Catholic communion.

However, the implication here is again one of *deception*: the Lutherans are
'duplicitous' or 'deceitful', with 'double-believing' faces, much like the Latins
of Feodosii's letter against whom it is 'impossible to protect oneself' since they
have the Gospel, the Apostles and the holy icons and are therefore maintaining
an appearance of Christianity.[217] In this text the most appropriate translation of
dvoevernyi is probably 'hypocritical' or 'insincere', or possibly 'ambiguous',
a meaning reflected in earlier translated sources of the *Chronicle* of George
Harmartolos and the *Studite Typikon*, since they are clearly being accused of
masquerading as 'true' Christians, while maintaining the heathen custom of
celebrating with 'dead' bread.

Although these debates were prepared specifically to record the arguments
for the Court, this type of text was widely disseminated during the seventeenth
century. The 1648 *Kniga o vere* (*Book about the Faith*), a compendium of
anti-Catholic, anti-Uniate, anti-Protestant and anti-Jewish writings compiled
by the Kievan hegumen Nafanail, was popular enough to sell 850 copies in
four months.[218]

Some of the material prepared for this debate with the Lutherans was published in 1644 in a popular volume on the Orthodox faith called *Kirillova kniga*
(*Kirill's Book*), which sold 1,032 copies in four months.[219] From these statistics
one can assume that the reading public of Moscow took a keen interest in the
inter-Church polemic of the time, perhaps as a result of the increase in contact
with foreigners. The *Kirillova kniga* addresses the truth of teachings of the
'one holy Eastern Church', the institution of the Orthodox Church in Russia,
and gives the Orthodox position on points of difference from the other untrue
churches, including the celebration of the Eucharist with unleavened bread,

focusing mainly on the polemic with the Roman Catholic Church. While I have been unable to locate the term in these published books, one may presume that the meaning attached to *dvoevernyi* by Nasedka was current at least among the higher clergy, and presumably comprehensible to the Court elite.

Uncertainty again

Our final example of native usage dates from the sixteenth-century *Житие и чудеса Антония Сийскаго*, the *Life and Miracles of Antonii Siiskii*.[220] Antonii, the founder of the Siiskii monastery in what is now the Arkhangelsk region, was born in 1478 and died in 1557.[221] The relevant passage of the saint's life is part of a chapter recounting how a priest of the monastery is led spiritually astray, until Antonii posthumously and miraculously intervenes. It begins:

Чюдо, д҃і: ѡ̃ попѣ нѣкоемъ. его́ же прп҃бный а'нтонїй наказавъ ҙамаловѣрїе егѡ̃ гавленїемъ нѣкоимъ. и паки йсцѣлѣнїе даровà емȣ, поклавшȣіа емȣ чистѣ:[222]

Miracle 14: About a certain priest, he that the venerable Antonii punished for his lack of faith by a certain phenomenon. And afterwards healing gave to him, [the priest] having vowed to honour [Antonii].

My understanding of the passage containing the word *dvoeveren* is that this foolish priest listened to the slanderous murmuring of the surrounding villagers, who were reluctant to worship at the monastery and cast aspersions on Antonii's sanctity.

жителем/же во/ѡкрестны̀ весѣх̀ не/хотѧщимъ мн҃тирю повинȣтисѧ: /l. 176/ гако/же повелѣно имъ бысть, по ц҃рковȣ наказанию. и/сегѡ ради молвȣ в/людехъ немалȣ воздвигоша, и/ропотъ великъ, на/ст҃аго с/хȣлами соспавиша . . . ѡни/же вмѣсто бл҃годаренїа хȣлȣ на/ст҃агѡ гл҃аше.[223]

Жителем же во окрестных весех не хотящим монастыреви повинутисся, яко же повелѣно бысть по царскому наказанию, и сего ради молву в людѣх немалу воздвигоша, и ропотъ великъ на святого с хулами поставиша. . . . Они ж /f.244/ вмѣсто благодарения хулу на святаго глаголаше.[224]

Inhabitants in the surrounding villages did not want to submit to the monastery, as ordered by the Tsar's decree, and because of this they stirred up a big murmuring among the people, and a great grumbling about the saint with blasphemies they raised up . . . Instead of thanksgiving they spoke abusively about the saint.

Being weak of mind ('не крѣпцыи в разумѣ') the priest became confused, and 'forgetting his place as a teacher and an enlightener', became a doubter – a 'double-believer' at heart – and similarly slandered Antonii's holy name:

сице оубѡ несмысленны[и] попъ сеи двоевѣренъ бывъ в/срцы своемъ
ко/стомȣ. единаче безпрестани повⷨ дни хȣлȣ нанъ глⷶаше.²²⁵

Сице оубо несмысленыи попъ сей двоевѣренъ бывъ в сердцы своемъ
ко святому единаче беспрестани по вся дни хуля на нь глаголаше.²²⁶

Thus therefore the senseless priest having this *double-belief* in his heart towards the saint still ceaselessly on all days spoke reproaches against him.

Turilov interprets this passage similarly, seeing in it only doubt over Antonii's
sanctity. However, Shchapov interpreted it as a 'return to the people', in the
sense that the priest had not been adequately converted, and returned to the
pagan faith of the native peoples surrounding the monastery.²²⁷ As yet, I have
found no evidence in the text to suggest that this is the case, although at points
the monks did experience conflict with the native Finnic population. This was
due not to a desire for religious autonomy, but in reaction to a ruling by the
Muscovite state that put them politically under monastic rule – essentially
changing them from free peasants to monastery dependents.²²⁸ The Tsar also
awarded considerable areas of the surrounding lands to the monastery.²²⁹ The
word 'pagan' does not appear anywhere in this section of the text, as one
might reasonably expect it to in an anecdote about reverting to paganism,
and the priest is accused quite specifically of doubting Antonii's sanctity, not
abandoning Christianity.

The *Life* is preserved in two sixteenth-century redactions, one written by a
Siiskii monk Iona (1577–1578), and the second by the Tsarevich Ioann, elder
son of Ivan the Terrible, in 1579. The *Slovar' knizhnikov i knizhnosti* notes that
on the basis of the two earlier redactions, a third redaction of the *Life* with
supplements of stories about the miracles of the saint was composed in the
1660s.²³⁰ The version held in the archives of the Russian State Library is that
written by the monk Iona, and includes the supplementary miracle stories, so
it is probably the third redaction.

Bushkovitch notes that establishment of local celebrations in honour of
Antonii is unreliably dated by Golubinskii to 1579, a mere 22 years after his
death, while his feast day is recorded for the first time in the 1610 *Ustavy*
– indicating that a national festival may have been established at this time.²³¹
The *Life* appears in the *Prolog*, and was therefore widely read.

Ivan Timofeev – the missing link?

It is difficult to say with absolute certainty at what point historians of Russia
first used the term *dvoeverie* as a cultural concept, but the nearest we have to
a link between the medieval clerical uses of the term investigated earlier and
its revival in modern historiography is to be found in the seventeenth-century
Vremennik (*Annals*, or *Chronicle*) of Ivan Timofeev. Timofeev, one of the earliest historians of Russia – chroniclers aside – uses *двоеверны* when describing
the Oprichnina of Ivan IV.

Eve Levin has identified this use of the term as an example of the eclectic use of the word in early Russian sources,[232] but it differs from other pre-Petrine texts considered within the scope of this chapter, in that Timofeev uses the term in a historiographical context. The author, audience and context of Timofeev's *Vremennik* are not exclusively or even primarily spiritual, but secular, although as Daniel Rowland has pointed out, 'While modern historians often find social causes for social and political events, Timofeyev consistently searched for (and found) the causes of events . . . on the personal, spiritual level'.[233] God intervenes in history, and Timofeev repeatedly takes Biblical events to demonstrate the 'eternal patterns'. Dividing the secular from the sacred is always difficult in pre-modern historical mentalities, but it is probably safe to say that despite the religious foundations of his argument, this is still a piece of historical analysis rather than a Church polemic. It is a record of events and an attempt to explain them, not a sermon.

Timofeev's readers were presumably approaching the text for intellectual rather than spiritual enlightenment, since Ivan Timofeev had no authority to offer spiritual guidance. Rowland summarizes the biographical information available on Timofeev succinctly: he came from a petty service family of the Moscow region and became a *дьяк* (secretary) in the Artillery Chancellery in 1598. Timofeev appears to have progressed in service under Boris Godunov, but was demoted by Vasilii Shuyskii and sent to Novgorod in 1607. His enforced stay in Novgorod until 1617 was the period during which he wrote most of his material.[234] The author (despite the fact that he is listed as a 'дьяк' of the Metropolitan of Novgorod by Filaret)[235] is writing as a lay historian, a member of the administration, rather than as a member of the Church hierarchy. However, as Tamara Kondratieva and Claudio-Sergio Ingerflom point out,[236] he says he does so on the instruction of Metropolitan Isidor:

Он [Isidor] тихим голосом принудил меня начать писать о наказании божием, о прошедших в русской земле событиях, и о всем, совершившемся с нами за последнее время.[237]

He [Isidor], in a quiet voice, implored me to begin to write about the punishment by God, about past events in the Russian land, and about all that has happened to us in the last years.

Kondratieva and Ingerflom observe that Timofeev begins his text by making a connection between the anger of God and the installation of the Oprichnina by Ivan IV, 'which he considered a violation of the land'.[238] Timofeev explains Ivan's merciless behaviour towards the populace in terms of Divine punishment – 'for our sins' – and describes Ivan's actions thus:

От умышления же зельныя ярости на своя рабы подвигся толик, яко возненавиде грады земля своея вся и во гневе своем разделением раздвоения едины люди раздели и яко двоеверны сотвори, овы усвояя, овы же отметашася, яко чюжи отрину, не смеющим отнюдь именем его мнозем градом нарицатися запрещаемом им, и всю землю державы своея, яко секирою, наполы некако разсече.[239]

By the contemplation of excessive rage against his servants, he was so roused that he conceived a hatred for the towns of all his land, and in his wrath he divided united people by a division of cutting into two, and made [them] as if *of two faiths*, taking some as his own, others were cast out, he rejected them if [they were] foreigners, and many towns by no means daring to be called by his name, which was forbidden by him, and all the land of his state, as if with an axe, he cut into two halves.

In Vernadsky's *Source Book for Russian History* the crucial sentence has been translated as 'divided a single people into two halves and subjected them to a kind of double allegiance',[240] implying that the 'faith' element of *двоеверны* is 'loyalty'. However, in the introductory passage to the *Vremennik*, Timofeev identifies Ivan's victims as 'присноверны'[241] (which Derzhavina translates as 'единовертци'),[242] accusing him of being more severe to these 'co-religionists' than to his enemies – meaning presumably foreign, non-Orthodox enemies. The blasphemous nature of Ivan Groznii's Oprichnina, which divided Orthodox Christian from Orthodox Christian, and in which Orthodox Christian murdered Orthodox Christian, is accentuated by Timofeev's choice of simile: 'two faiths' are made from the nation which prided itself as being the one true Christian land following the fall of Constantinople in 1453. Ivan took a unified Christian kingdom, and created a schism:

сам тогда на ню руку не благословля наложи, даже оно и доныне неутверженым от грех колеблемо, и несть ю до единаго ныне от человек утвердити могущаго, по Христову гласу, яко «всяко царство, раздельшееся на ся, не может стояти», и прочее.[243]

he himself then, not in blessing, laid his hands on [the realm], it even hitherto is being shaken by sins, not made firm, and there is not one of the people now to make it firm, as Christ said, so "every kingdom, divided against itself, cannot stand"[244] and so on.[245]

The nation has been plunged into a state of insecurity and doubt through division, and this uncertainty within the nation caused by the 'unblessed' split gives us a lexical link to the earliest uses of the term *dvoeverie* as translated from the Greek, where the word means 'uncertainty', 'doubt', 'hesitation', 'dispute', although Timofeev's use is far stronger, implying a sort of blasphemy.

Conclusion

In the 'native' texts discussed in this chapter we have three uses of the term pertaining to Orthodox Christians who fraternize or sympathize with Roman

Catholic believers, one use that refers to Lutherans holding to Roman Catholic practices, one use which indicates a state of spiritual doubt in an Orthodox believer, and one which implies a blasphemous split within Orthodoxy. All of these texts address on some level the inability to remain firmly and unwaveringly Orthodox. Believers who accept the validity of other denominations, or parts of their doctrine, and believers who doubt aspects of the one true Orthodox faith, are guilty of this *dvoeverie*.

What the authors of these texts intended by the word and its lexical derivatives is by no means certain. Both Feodosii Pecherskii and Bishop Nifont of Novgorod were senior clerics who would probably have had access to a copy of the nomocanon, possibly the *Efremovskaia*. We know that Feodosii had access to the *Studite Typikon*, and as Nifont was tonsured at the Kievan Caves Monastery we can assume that he too was familiar with the *Studite Typikon*, which was in use there at least until the thirteenth, or perhaps the fourteenth century. As we have seen, *dvoeverie* and its lexical derivatives as used in these texts meant 'ambiguous', 'insincere', 'dispute' or 'controversy' and 'differ'. Nifont may possibly have had access to the sermons of Gregory the Theologian, with the additional meaning of 'doubt', 'hesitation'. Their concept of the word may well have been more closely related to these meanings than to our modern understanding of the term, and the passages explored earlier still retain meaning if we read them differently:

> Should anyone start to incessantly praise both their own and a foreign [faith], then such a person is unclear [in faith] and is close to heresy . . . If someone arguing should say to you: 'this faith and that God has given', then you, child, say to him, 'So you, heretic [crooked-believer], think that God is controversial (or disputed)? Have you not heard, accursed one, corrupted by an evil faith, what Scripture says: 'One God, one faith, one baptism'.

> For God these are the enemies: Jews, heretics, [those] holding to a crooked faith, and led astray to a foreign faith, and disputing in accordance with a strange faith, and praising a strange faith, and loving controversy, with these never make peace.

> And if they take to a Varangian priest children to be prayed over? – Then six weeks' penance, it is said, because they are as those who are in [spiritual] ambiguity [or perhaps 'like those who are in dispute (with the Church)'].

These readings remain unsatisfactory however, and the inability to prove that the sermonizers had access to the sermons of Gregory the Theologian, the commentary of Theophylact or the *Dialogues* of Gregory the Great is frustrating, since replacing 'double-belief' in these texts with 'doubt' provides a perhaps more convincing interpretation.

The later texts, whose clerical authors were very probably familiar with these later uses of the word, and that of the *Chronicle* of George Hamartolos are more easily reinterpreted:

Besides, also about the communion of the body of Christ [Holy Communion] we see here from the Holy Scriptures, because the Lutherans duplicitously among themselves with insincere/hypocritical/ambiguous faces profess their own communion [as] true and yet they show [it to be untrue] in their own words and writings, since all in popish fashion celebrate communion with unleavened bread . . .

Thus therefore the senseless priest this doubt having in his heart towards the saint still ceaselessly on all days spoke reproaches against him.

Although establishing the precise meaning of the term *dvoeverie* and its lexical derivatives is difficult to achieve in these texts, we can say with certainty that in these native Russian 'creative' uses of the term, paganism was not the second faith. Indeed, as discussed in Chapter 1, paganism may not have been accorded the status of a faith at all. In the eleventh, as in the seventeenth century, it was heretical Christians and those weak Orthodox believers who fraternized with heretics rather than wavering neophytes who were primarily the target of this pejorative epithet.

3   A history of historians

Thanks to the pertinacity of pagan beliefs among the masses of the people, there arose the phenomenon of *dvoeverie* (ditheism), whose existence is confirmed by historians of all schools; this belief is still alive in some places today. Kievan and Muscovite history is rich in examples of the perpetual struggle waged by the Church to put down pagan survivals.[1]

N. Andreyev, 1962

This chapter traces the development of *dvoeverie* as an academic concept, identifying significant scholars who have made use of the term 'double-belief' in their interpretations of Russian history, and the key elements of the concept outlined in their work. This is not intended to be an exhaustive study of historical works from the late nineteenth to the late twentieth centuries, but rather an overview of the way in which the term has developed in the historiography of Russian spirituality and culture.

One of the most intriguing aspects of the term *dvoeverie* in the historiography of Russia is that it develops from a mid-nineteenth century 'specialist' term, apparently absent in eighteenth- and early nineteenth-century historical works, becoming such common currency by the late twentieth century that many general works refer to it as an established and basic fact of Russian culture. This chapter takes us from the embryonic *dvoeverie* to the point at which the concept of double-belief is firmly enough established to be referred to in encyclopaedias, anthologies of Russian culture and general histories, but has provoked questions about meaning and legitimacy among historians of Russian popular culture and belief.

The discovery of the 'folk' – the origins of *dvoeverie*

It seems that an academic concept of double-belief, meaning the preservation of pagan elements within the religious faith of the Russian *narod* or 'folk', preceded the appearance of the term itself in the scholarship of Russian history. This concept coincided with an increase in curiosity about the 'folk' in the late eighteenth and early nineteenth century, and the romantic, nationalist elevation of folk culture and religion that developed as a result of the work of Herder, the Grimm brothers and other European intellectuals. This phenomenon, which Burke has labelled 'the discovery of the people',[2] resulted in the general acceptance of myths that still resonate in contemporary scholarship in various ways.

In terms of *dvoeverie*, the myth that the 'folk', unspoiled by modern, enlightened ideas, preserved pure and unchanging cultural and religious traditions rooted in the primitive, pre-Christian past, has had the greatest impact. This perception of the peasantry (generally equated with the 'folk') as bearers of an essentially static national culture led to the belief that pre-Christian religion could be reconstructed by the study of peasant belief and culture, and an obsession with identifying 'pagan survivals' within peasant religiosity.

The initial research into the phenomenon of 'pagan survivals' and popular belief was conducted by early nineteenth-century ethnographers, whose main focus was to record and analyze material about the life of the Russian population in that era.[3] I. M. Snegirev's 1837 exploration of the *Festivals and Superstitious Rituals of the Russian Common People*, for example, begins with an interesting survey of the sources for the ancient beliefs of the people, since 'a large part of the folk festivals arose in ancient paganism',[4] but he does not appear to use the term *dvoeverie*. Similarly, A. V. Tereshchenko's 1848 work on the daily life of the nineteenth-century *narod* addresses calendrical rituals, rituals surrounding the dead and other areas typically considered fertile ground for double-belief, also without, apparently, using the term.[5]

While folk songs, tales and *byliny* (epic poems) began to be collected and published in Russia in the eighteenth century,[6] early Russian historians were primarily concerned with mapping out the 'origins of the State', and identifying and collating the manuscript source material that would be relied on by their nineteenth-century successors. The immensely popular and influential *History of the Russian State* by Nikolai Mikhailovich Karamzin (1766–1826) for example, as its name implies, is primarily concerned with politics, and little attention was paid to popular culture by eighteenth-century historians, with the exception of Mikhail Vasil'evich Lomonosov (1711–1765). His *Old Russian History*, first published in 1766, compares the popular beliefs, games and songs of his contemporaries with old Russian pagan beliefs, but without using the term *dvoeverie*.[7]

The model of the resistant masses struggling for a long period to preserve their own beliefs in the face of an alien Christianity rooted in élite culture was introduced to a broad readership by Sergei Mikhailovich Solov'ev (1820–1879). Solov'ev interpreted the 'superstitious' practices of the peasantry (as Soviet historians were to later) as evidence of the initial resistance of pagan Rus to the imposition of Christianity:

> for a long time the demands of Christianity had force only in the highest layers of society and with difficulty penetrated beneath, to the masses, where paganism lived on still in the workings of their rituals. We have

seen that because of the clan [nature of] everyday life of the Eastern Slavs [paganism] could not develop public worship, could not form a priestly class; had nothing to oppose Christianity with, paganism had easily to give up its place in society to [Christianity]; but being a religion of the clan, the family, the home, it remained here for a long time . . . The struggle, the hostility of ancient pagan society to the influence of the new religion and her servants manifested itself in superstitious signs, now without meaning, but having had meaning in the first century of Christianity in Rus.[8]

Although Solov'ev discusses the period of Christianization in some detail in his *History of Russia from the Earliest Times*, and addresses issues often raised as essential components of Russian double-belief, he does not use the term *dvoeverie*. The key themes of the concept are laid in place, however – the superficiality of the initial Christianization, the hostility of pagan society, the continuation of rituals which, although after a time desemanticized, are stubbornly maintained by the populace.

   In terms of historiography of the Church, Metropolitan Makarii Bulgakov (1816–1882) is the most significant figure of this period, described as 'the first major historian of the Russian Church who laid the foundation for subsequent studies'.[9] Makarii appears to use the term *dvoeverie* just twice in his huge work *A History of the Russian Church*, when paraphrasing two of the primary sources (discussed in Chapter 2) that actually use the word.[10] While Makarii acknowledges the possibility that some of those baptized in Vladimir's reign 'perhaps were Christian in name only, and in spirit remained pagans, performed the external rites of the holy Church, but preserved at the same time the superstition and rituals of their fathers',[11] he discusses the struggle against paganism without recourse to the term. This bears out what the negative evidence in Orthodox theological dictionaries and encyclopaedias demonstrates – *dvoeverie* is not a term propagated by the Church from the seventeenth century onwards.[12] The eighteenth-century dictionary produced by the Institute of Russian Language does not include the term (unlike historical dictionaries covering earlier periods), confirming that it fell into disuse during this century.

The nineteenth-century rise of *dvoeverie*

Without having read every nineteenth-century publication on Russian history, ethnography and religion, it is perhaps rash to make firm declarations about the earliest use of the term *dvoeverie* in a modern work, but an anonymous article published in 1861 is the earliest work found during the preparation of this book. The author was probably a teacher at the Kazan Ecclesiastical Academy, which published the journal in which it appeared. The article, titled 'The mix of Christianity with paganism and heresy in old Russian folk tales about the world', discusses various apocryphal works and the evidence in them of pagan and heretical thought. The anonymous contributor does not offer any definition of *dvoeverie*, or analyze this double-belief in any detail, and uses the term about both pagan- and heretically-influenced texts. Discussing the apocryphal *Dialogue of Three Holy Men*, the author observes that:

> God is proclaimed by Christendom in the Trinity, yet occurs in the dia-
> logue as natural light and fire, which indicates the superstition of those
> double-believingly living Christians, who still in the twelfth or thirteenth
> century, in the words of the Christlover, 'prayed to the fire, calling it fire
> Svarozhich' [i.e. 'Son of Svarog'].[13]

In this early scholarly usage we have an immediate link with the now famous *Sermon of the Christlover*, the most frequently cited medieval text in the study of *dvoeverie*, explored in Chapter 1.

Prompted by the increasing number of philological publications, including the 1862 publication of an influential collection entitled *Sermons and teaching directed against pagan beliefs and rituals* which included the *Sermon of the Christlover*,[14] a number of researchers turned to early medieval sources in an effort to understand apparent 'pagan survivals' in popular culture. One of the first was M. Azbukin, who in his 'Essay on the literary struggle of Christianity's representatives with survivals of paganism in the Russian people' covered a great number of medieval texts in five articles.[15] Azbukin declared that 'Double-belief is a basic fact of Russian religious life',[16] and firmly endorsed the belief that *dvoeverie* was a medieval concept used by sermonizers attacking pagan survivals:

> Hence other ancient sermonizers characterized the religious life of this time
> completely differently from Metropolitan Ilarion. . . . That condition of the
> religious life of the ancient Russian people is quite aptly characterized by
> the representatives of Christianity with the word 'double-belief'.[17]

Azbukin made use mainly of sermons published by Tikhonravov, but he also introduced a number of texts which subsequently became accepted into the canon of works providing evidence of double-belief: the *Sermon on the Fast*, the *Sermon on Things Made by Man*, the *Sermon of St Nifont on the Rusalii*, and the writings of Metropolitan Ioann II and Kirill II among others, many of which were subsequently published by Gal'kovskii (to be discussed later).

In Azbukin's articles we find the first systematic exposition of *dvoeverie*, outlining the various stages in its development, the first of which is a purely 'mechanical' mixing of Christianity and paganism. The new Christian was a Christian in name only, and

> from fear of punishment fulfilled the exterior rites of the new religion . . . and
> after the almost compulsory prayers in a Christian church, set off for the
> lake, the river, the forest or under the grain store, and there carried out
> prayer to his own former gods.[18]

After the mechanical stage, where the newly baptized pretends to be Christian while continuing to worship in pagan fashion, comes the second stage, when Christianity has made more headway. The Russian Christians are now worshipping sincerely, 'since the former worldview was clothed in the garb of Christian externals'. This might be characterized as the 'thin veneer' stage. Lurking behind the images of Christian saints were the pagan gods; behind the façade of the Christian holy day was the pagan festive gathering.

The final stage of *dvoeverie* is when worshippers have forgotten the very 'basic, essential characteristics' of paganism, and their former world-view, and all that remains to them are fragments of beliefs and rites which have been completely 'mixed with the substance of Christianity', when Christianity has partly accommodated paganism, and partly been adapted by it. Not touching the 'essence of religion' in any way, the resulting mass of beliefs, rituals and symbols 'is commonly called folk superstition'.[19] This structure of the various stages of double-belief sets in place the model of *dvoeverie* followed and revised by many subsequent historians including Golubinskii, Smirnov, Vernadsky and Kartashev.[20]

The concept of *dvoeverie* was introduced to Anglophone academia in 1872 by W. R. S. Ralston, in his monumental survey of Russian folk song 'as illustrative of Slavonic mythology and Russian social life':

> in Russia, as in other countries, even the 'faithful' proselytes of the new religion could not at once forget the teaching of the old, so they retained a mass of familiar traditions, chiefly of a mythical nature, but they substituted in them for the names of their elementary gods and demigods, others which they took from the calendar of the Church. The consequence was a confusion of ideas which justified the epithet 'two-faithed' which an old ecclesiastical writer bestowed upon the Russian people.[21]

Ralston proceeds to list denunciations of witchcraft, sorcery and magic, declaring that 'witches and wizards held their own, just as the people, in spite of the remonstrances of their pastors, continued the 'satanic games', attended by dance and song, which had come down to them from their heathen ancestors'.[22] Predating modern debates about the boundaries between magic, superstition and religion, Ralston wrestled with two possible theories for the apparent persistence and ubiquity of witchcraft and superstition: that witchcraft is a natural part of 'savage' or 'primitive' culture; or (a theory he finds more comfortable) that it represents the survivals of an ancient mythological culture.

A medieval term

A crucial theme in the scholarship of Russian medieval and popular belief is that double-belief was a sin that much exercised the minds of clerics. Anichkov clearly identifies *dvoeverie* as a term that originated in the medieval period:

In their struggle against paganism the authors of such works invented a special word, 'double-faith'. They say that the new Christians . . . secretly confess their old belief. They insist on the duty of the Christian not to cleave to the old pagan rituals, but to give them up entirely and to cease offering sacrifices. We must note – and this is particularly important – that they persuade the people to always address themselves not to creatures but to their Creator, which means that the people should not implore 'nature', nor try to force her by means of magic to serve their interests, but should simply believe in the power of the Creator who is sole master on earth.[23]

This idea is to be found in numerous works, including modern publications by Gerhard Podskalsky, Linda Ivanits and Nicholas Riasanovsky.[24] Podskalsky suggests that 'the problem of double faith' is 'far closer to everyday concerns than . . . the speculative discussions about Christology and the Holy Trinity' in his 1987 article 'Principal Aspects and Problems of Theology in Kievan Rus'. He describes *dvoeverie* thus:

> the extremely long-lived evil of *dvoeverie* was among the most frequently attacked sins of the newly converted Christians. . . . In original Kievan Literature, *dvoeverie* can have two meanings: the concept usually refers to the simultaneous practice or merging of Christian and pagan cultic forms; but in several passages it also means an indecisive vacillation between the Latin and the Greek-Byzantine rite.[25]

Podskalsky also offers material culture as evidence of this long-lived double-belief, citing the controversial *zmeeviki* amulets which portray a Medusa-like head with snakes on one side and a Christian symbol on the other, often with Greek inscriptions.[26] He concludes, 'unquestionably, *dvoeverie* was more a matter of everyday domestic practices than of religious offices'. Implied, but not explicit in his article, is the argument that double-belief was long-lived because the church dealt leniently with offenders, handing out light penances and preferring to attack them with words rather than with persecution. Lacking 'rational argument' and 'positive ideas as to how to "Christianize" pagan customs', their struggle was unsuccessful. His article concludes, however, that the church addressed the problem of *dvoeverie* 'bravely and thoughtfully'.[27]

A similar conviction that medieval clerics were persistently struggling with *dvoeverie* is demonstrated by John Fennell in his posthumous publication *A History of the Russian Church*:

> as far as the history of the spread of Christianity in Russia is concerned, perhaps the most insidious aspect of the old beliefs and ways of life is the curious association of paganism with Christianity. The so-called 'double-faith' (*dvoeverie*) – the simultaneous adherence to both Christianity and heathen relics – is evidenced by many of the Church's writings, not only in the period under consideration, but also deep into the seventeenth, and even as late as the nineteenth century.[28]

He proceeds to cite 'a work attributed to the Abbot Feodosy of the Caves Monastery' and Bishop Nifont on women who take their children to Varangian priests. Fennell interprets 'Varangian' as either a 'magician' or a priest of another faith, although we should remember that this work was published posthumously, and the question mark around these suggestions indicates that he would probably have revised this passage.[29]

It is clear that as late as 1992 (the year Fennell died, leaving his *History of the Russian Church* unpublished), the notion of pagan survivals as *dvoeverie* was so firmly embedded in the minds of Church historians that the evident contradiction – already highlighted by several researchers – that these two texts pose to the subject matter of Fennell's section on double-belief went unnoticed. Fennell also discusses the dangerous connections between Christian and pagan festivals, and the infamous 'revels' or games. He is careful to separate witchcraft and sorcery from the section on double-belief, though presenting them as pagan practices. That Fennell does not differentiate between eras or stages of double-belief, or explore questions of awareness and intent, may also be due to his untimely death.

Also published in 1992, Linda Ivanits's *Russian Folk Belief* addresses mainly the popular beliefs of the nineteenth and early twentieth centuries, and does not question the concept of *dvoeverie* except to observe that while the 'Russian case is extreme', Western Europe also experienced a similar phenomenon. Ivanits also implicitly accepts the idea that while double-belief is evidenced in the period under study, it was a medieval concept:

> The term most often used for the interweaving of pre-Christian and Christian elements in the belief and practice of the Russian peasant is *dvoeverie*, or 'double faith'. The 'double faith' of Christians addicted to pagan rites and superstitions is the brunt of the invective of many sermons of the first centuries of Russian Christianity, and it is the condition to which materials collected in the nineteenth and early twentieth centuries attest.[30]

Her understanding of *dvoeverie* leads her to conclude that assessing the balance of paganism and Christianity within folk belief will solve the 'problem' of whether the Russian peasant was in fact Christian at all. Falling into the trap that *dvoeverie* has led many a good scholar to – a futile and anachronistic attempt to separate out and catalogue the pagan aspects of the spiritual life of Orthodox Christians – Ivanits observes that

> the argument, of course, remains unresolved. At its basis lies not only the religious disposition of the commentator, but the crucial issue of the balance of Christian and pagan elements in the peasant's 'double faith'.[31]

Resistance and conflict

The first stage in many models of *dvoeverie* is that of resistance to the new faith – neophytes hide their pagan practices while pretending to fulfil the obligations of Christian worship, or maintain both traditions as a form of 'hedging one's bets'. *Volkhvy* (sorcerers, often interpreted as representatives of paganism – even as pagan priests) are active, and can encourage the wavering Christians to revolt.[32] George Vernadsky, writing in 1947, identifies this first stage of *dvoeverie* as the preservation of paganism beneath the outward signs of Christian allegiance, and predominantly an agrarian phenomenon:

> At first only the city people took Christianity seriously; in remote rural districts paganism held its ground for a long time under a thin veneer of Christian rites. The result was the so-called 'double-faith', *dvoeverie*. People may have worn crosses and attended Church services but they did not abandon the celebration of pagan festivals, too.[33]

According to Vernadsky, who displays a personal value judgement and Hegelian cultural assumptions as unhelpful to scholarship as the Marxist atheist line adopted by Soviet historians, Christianity was bound to triumph in this struggle since not only was it the 'higher religion' but 'it represented a higher civilisation in general'.

S. I. Smirnov – writing in the first decades of the twentieth century – like Azbukin articulates three stages in the development of double-belief. The initial stage is a crude 'mechanical' form of double-belief, when paganism still exists in organized form, and results from the population mix. 'Baptised pagans' worship both in church and under the barn, and use Christian priests and *volkhvy* indiscriminately. He also added an interesting and influential perspective to the resistance model of double-belief in his monograph *Impious Women* (published in 1909), which identified women as the main preservers and protectors of pagan beliefs and ritual after the establishment of Christianity in Rus. In this he pre-empted feminist historians, perceiving the conflict between pagan and Christian as fought on gender rather than class lines. The 'impious women' of the title were significant protagonists in this battle, who knew the old prayers and rituals, and 'double-believing women, even nobles, called them to themselves and prayed with them secretly'.[34]

As Eve Levin points out, feminist scholars adhere to the 'conflict model' dear to the Marxists, except that the conflict here is between the sexes rather than the classes, and double-belief is initiated by this conflict even before the Christianization of Rus.[35] Foremost among the works of Western feminist historians is the thought-provoking but ultimately unconvincing *Mother Russia* by Joanna Hubbs, who suggests that

> The practice of *dvoeverie* (two faiths), which would characterise later Russian culture, resulted most certainly from the aggressive expansion of the Slavic tribes and reflected the conflict of hierarchically oriented warrior elites with the still-matrifocal clans they were to protect.[36]

Hubbs's exploration of the 'feminine myth in Russian culture' is an imaginative attempt to link the evidence from palaeographic archaeological discoveries, nineteenth-century ethnographical research, very limited medieval texts and a great deal of folklore to reveal 'the Mother' in Russian culture, and her methodology reflects the type of *dvoeverie* scholarship that reconstructs paganism from much later ethnographical material, and then identifies in peasant culture traces of that latent paganism.

This approach is also in evidence in Julia Vytkovskaya's analysis of Slav mythology in the *Feminist Companion to Mythology*. Vytkovskaya conventionally interprets the concept as 'quixotic and complex combinations' of Christian and pagan belief, focusing on those aspects of popular Christianity such as the cult of St Paraskeva which she views as particularly important to women.[37] Her identification of St Paraskeva as 'a direct continuation of the Old Russian goddess Mokosh' is one made by numerous researchers, and has been convincingly refuted by Levin as circular reasoning.[38] Interestingly, Vytkovskaya translates *dvoeverie* as 'belief ambivalence' – expressing a meaning much closer to the earliest uses of the word as explored in Chapter 2 than the usual 'double-belief'.

As might be expected, Soviet scholarship enthusiastically embraced the academic concept of double-belief. Soviet historians tended to focus on pagan survivals as evidence of active resistance by the people to the institution of the Church and the ruling classes who helped impose Christianity on the populace. Perhaps the most influential and representative of Soviet scholars working in the field of early Russian society and popular belief is the archaeologist B. A. Rybakov, whose immense and imaginative canon of works about Slavic paganism and early Russian culture is predictably coloured by the Marxist-atheist axe he was obliged to grind as a scholar of the 1950s–1980s. A third of his monograph *Paganism in Ancient Rus* (first published in 1981) is devoted to *dvoeverie* in the tenth to thirteenth centuries, and double-belief is an essential component of Rybakov's historical theories:

> The paganism of old Rus from the ninth to the thirteenth century is an important part of Russian medieval culture, without which it is impossible to understand either the folk culture of the villages and merchant suburbs, or the complicated and multifaceted culture of the feudal aristocracy.[39]

Double-belief became a symptom of the class struggle. With the Church supporting the governing classes and preaching against resistance to the laws of both God and the state,[40] *dvoeverie* represented a covert, sometimes overt, rebellion against the oppressor Church: the people submitted to Christianity in name only, while stubbornly maintaining their pre-Christian practices. It is this element of resistance and rebellion that Rybakov focuses on, identifying a pagan revival in the thirteenth century that was a result of anti-clerical feeling incited by drought and famine, the 'hostile supervision' of the Church and the greed of 'ecclesiastical boyars'. Understood thus, *dvoeverie* was highly convenient to Soviet missionary-atheist scholarship.

Rybakov also starts from the premise that Christianity and paganism are fundamentally the same, the difference being one of externals (names, actions) only. Double-belief might then be seen as an understandable confusion about what actually constitutes an Orthodox Christian ritual or belief:

> Christianity cannot be counterposed to paganism, since they are but two forms, two variations of the one and the same primitive ideology, differing only in their outward manifestation . . . Being an eclectic and spontaneous combination of a number of ancient agricultural and cattle-breeding cults, in its essence Christianity was very close to the pagan beliefs of the Slavs . . . No wonder that, after Christianity was adopted, the local folk beliefs merged so closely with the Christian doctrine.[41]

Double-belief is not, however, in Rybakov's schema, a phenomenon exclusive to the peasantry. He also identifies a period of friction in the thirteenth century between Church and boyar class, basing much of his argument on material culture such as the motifs decorating the white stone churches of Vladimir and Suzdal, and archaeological finds of *zmeeviki* amulets, jewellery and headdresses. Rybakov finds in the decoration of these objects a wealth of pagan (mostly agricultural) motifs, which he sees as reflecting the tastes and aspirations of the higher ranks of society.[42] This leads him to conclude that

> Double-belief was not simply a mechanical combining of the old habits and beliefs with the new, Greek ones; in a number of cases it was a well thought-out system, in which old ideas were completely consciously preserved.[43]

The republication of Rapov's *The Russian Church from the ninth to the first third of the twelfth century: The Acceptance of Christianity*, first published in 1988, amply demonstrates the legacy of Soviet scholarship. With a foreword by Rybakov, the history concludes with the following observation:

> And B. A. Rybakov was right to note that after the baptism of Rus, Christianity of the Byzantine form merged with Russian paganism. For Russian Christians not only in the eleventh to the thirteenth centuries, but even in the nineteenth century, double-belief was characteristic.[44]

Rapov further confirms that the existence of pagan survivals was a result of the class struggle, but interestingly places the emphasis not on the active resistance of the people, but on the cynical toleration or accommodation of pagan practices by the Church. The Church did not object 'in principle' to the continued observation of *Maslenitsa* (Shrovetide or Carnival, often interpreted as a pre-Christian survival of sun worship)[45] or the 'secret worship' of Volos, Perun and Mokosh in the guises of St Blaise, Elijah and St Paraskeva-Piatnitsa, because these practices were not detrimental to the development of feudalism.

However, the Church did oppose the offering of human sacrifices, and the killing of women and slaves after the death of their lords and masters, because

> The Church viewed these phenomena as a vain waste of human resources, essential for the means of production and the receipt of profit by the feudal class.[46]

A more subtle and significant contribution to the *dvoeverie* debate was made by Lotman and Uspenskii, famous for their work on 'binary oppositions'. Much of their work on the binary oppositions of 'old versus new', which includes 'paganism versus Christianity', has been highly influential in the study of the phenomenon of double-belief, particularly with regard to the resistance/conflict model. While they refer conventionally to double-belief as the 'coexistence of Christianity and paganism',[47] or 'the coexistence of two faiths',[48] they add a great deal to the subject without specifically using the term in their article 'The role of dual models in the dynamics of Russian culture (up to the end of the eighteenth century)'. While not fundamentally challenging the phenomenon or the concept of double-belief, their discussion of the 'syncretic image of "alien faith"' is pertinent to some of the texts considered in Chapter 2,[49] and the conclusions drawn about *dvoeverie* in the following chapter, and are therefore discussed further there.

Accommodation and syncretism

In contrast to the resistance or conflict model of two distinct but clashing or competing faiths, *dvoeverie* is often portrayed as the fruit of a period of creative syncretism. This double-belief is one in which pagan and Christian elements have merged and influenced each other. Some scholars perceive this process as being a result of missionary strategies employed by the Church during the Christianization period (the replacing of pagan idols with Christian churches, for example), others as a natural human response to perceived inadequacies of the new religion. The stock examples of this synthesis – the identification of the prophet Elijah with Perun, the 'transformation' of Volos/Veles into St Vlas (St Blaise) and Mokosh into St Paraskeva, and the merging of agricultural or calendrical festivals with Christian feasts – are cited by many writers.[50]

This process of creative syncretism appears in the work of some historians as a 'second stage' of double-belief, which follows an initial period of resistance. For S. I. Smirnov, this is the most interesting phase, when Christianity and paganism operate on an equal footing, and Christianity, 'arousing religious thought among the people, itself serves as material for mythological creation'. As an example of this creative form of double-belief, Smirnov gives confession to the earth, which first appears among the heretic *Strigolniki* ('Shearers') in Pskov and Novgorod in the fourteenth century.[51]

Creative reworkings of Christian symbol and rite – confession to the earth, or any number of rituals connected with the Blessed Virgin in Western Europe (many of which have been analyzed by Marina Warner in her exploration of Marian cults)[52] – become heretical and 'false' only if condemned by the Church. If accepted or tolerated by the institutional Church they *become* the faith, in the way that popular devotion to certain healing springs creates a pilgrimage site, and turns local bones into saintly relics.[53] Smirnov appears to distinguish between these creative reworkings and surviving 'pagan rituals' that the people maintain simply for amusement's sake. The essential difference would appear to lie in the assumption that the practitioner believes in the former and attaches no special religious significance to the latter, but this is surely 'the study of souls', and unmeasurable. Smirnov admits an imaginative reworking of Christian belief and practice, starting from the premise that [true] Christianity has accumulated various [false] pagan beliefs (without defining these terms) during its propagation in the pagan Greco-Roman world. This mixed belief system then passed to Russian believers, who reworked this faith in a society that, while not officially recognizing paganism, had not yet escaped it. It is not clear whether his final stage, in which pagan rituals have lost their religious significance, represents for him belief in a 'true' Christianity.

E. V. Anichkov's understanding of the term *dvoeverie* is similar, although his chronology differs. The preservation of the old beliefs together with the new, resulting in new religious forms, is explored in a chapter on 'the double-belief of Rus and folk paganism' in his *Paganism and Old Rus* (first published in 1914). Anichkov perceives *dvoeverie* as having arisen initially in the religious environment of the towns, and argues that double-belief based on agricultural cults is a phenomenon not of the early period, but of the much later Christianization of the countryside. He suggests that this latter conversion period spanned the fifteenth to the seventeenth century, since Christianity was first disseminated among the wealthy, urban élite:

> Then will arise also those double-beliefs, based on agrarian cults, rites and beliefs, the lack of which in our sources has been indicated. Contemporary folklore investigates them. The evidence of survivals of folk belief is in the later sources, because the Christianization of the countryside was not carried out in the eleventh and twelfth centuries, but in the fifteenth and sixteenth, even the seventeenth century . . . That is why the research of popular double-belief, built on the foundations of ancient agricultural belief, and therefore also of the foundations themselves, leads us beyond the limits of this work. To do this one would need to turn to other material and other centuries – and this time not only to the fifteenth, sixteenth and seventeenth centuries, but also further to the eighteenth and nineteenth centuries.[54]

Urban religious needs (being primarily related to private enterprise and wealth) differed from the needs of agricultural communities, and the early urban population had already become distant from the pagan agricultural belief-system, therefore conversion resulted in little friction between the old and the new.

He points out that the early sermons he studies (discussed in Chapter 1) are addressed to the 'new people', to Christians, and that the Russian audience of these sermons proudly considered themselves to be Christians.

While Anichkov is primarily concerned with paganism rather than *dvoeverie*, and he goes on to dismiss most of the content of the sermons he studies as useless for the reconstruction of Slavic paganism, he makes the dubious observation that we should value the sermons as evidence of pagan ritual more highly because:

> Our authors had before them only manifestations of the former faith, which they did not know or understand, but on the other hand they were still closer to everyday life, and still had the possibility of evaluating the meaning of rituals and other displays of faith immeasurably more correctly than us, and we need not forget this. Often they heard from the performers of ritual acts themselves why they did this and what benefit, what use they expected from their acts and actions.[55]

Anichkov starts from the premise that double-believers want to be Christian, and only slide into their bad habits when firstly they are required to give up all their former pastimes and amusements (the condemnation of which he sees as the only real evidence of pagan survivals), and secondly when their spiritual needs are not fulfilled by the new religion. These unfulfilled needs result in the creation of religious rites in which the old beliefs are fused with the new faith, creating new forms. His exploration of textual evidence relating to feasts in honour of *rod* and *rozhanitsy* provides perhaps the clearest example of his understanding of these new forms:

> we see that these feasts became complicated. At them they began to read the troparion of the Mother of God. And here then it is not a simple turning back [to paganism], but something completely different, some sort of agreement of the old with the new, some sort of carrying of the old beliefs into the new forms, that is to say, a kind of religious creativity. Our sermons have given us the possibility of imagining sufficiently clearly the process of the origin of double-belief, or to put it differently, the process of welding together the old beliefs with the new.[56]

The concept of double-belief here refers not to active, deliberate resistance by the pagan populace to the new religion imposed from above, but to a Christian reworking of the old faith in order to satisfy needs unfulfilled by the new religion. Anichkov brings an interesting new twist to the debate in his division of faith into urban and agricultural realms, identifying the latter as the main source of later *dvoeverie*.[57]

Soviet scholars also utilized the model of 'syncretic' *dvoeverie*. Apparent parallels between paganism and Christianity provided evidence of their shared irrationality and the ease with which they might mix, and N. M. Nikol'skii sets the tone for the Soviet cultivation of the concept of double-belief in his 1930 *History of the Russian Church*. He begins his section on 'the baptism of Rus and double-belief' by congratulating Golubinskii for his courage in dismissing the written evidence of the baptism of Rus as 'not preserving within itself one single grain of truth', except for the detail that Vladimir and his entourage brought Byzantine Christianity to Rus around 988. On this cynical note, Nikol'skii proceeds to explain that early Christianity had assimilated numerous pagan survivals in its development both in the east and in the west, and the faith that arrived in Rus was already contaminated:

> already on Byzantine soil arose that same double-belief which official Russian historians of the church considered for some reason an original Russian phenomenon.[58]

Nikol'skii firmly establishes a perception of Orthodoxy as little or no different from paganism. He identifies relic and icon veneration as 'fetishism', describes Orthodox sacraments and rituals as 'magic', argues that the popular perception of priests was as *volkhvy* and that the Christian teachings about the immortal soul were easily combined with the pagan cult of the dead. He also sees the Church itself as primarily responsible for the continued existence of double-belief, since the conversion methods employed (turning pagan gods into demons, superimposing Christian festivals on pagan feast days, building churches over sites sacred to the pagans) created the conditions for further syncretism – arguments rather similar to those of Keith Thomas in his seminal 1971 work *Religion and the Decline of Magic*, in which he declares that the 'notorious readiness of the early Christian leaders to assimilate elements of old paganism into their own religious practice' resulted in the subsequent popular perception of the medieval Catholic Church as a magical agency.[59]

Peasant ignorance, unconscious *dvoeverie* and folk belief

Another theme prevalent in the historiography of *dvoeverie* is that the condition of double-believing arises as a result of the poor education of clergy and/or neophytes. In the post-Christianization period, this model of uneducated or unconscious *dvoeverie* is prevalent among the ignorant peasantry, who fail to understand that what they do is pagan. As discussed above, the notion that folk belief is naturally conservative and preserves tradition regardless of provenance was part of the eighteenth- and nineteenth-century 'discovery of the folk', and this legacy has had a significant impact on the historiography of peasant culture in Imperial Russia.

The unwitting preservation of pagan survivals in folk belief and culture is often described as the final stage of *dvoeverie*. Smirnov, for example, describes a final stage of 'desemanticised pagan survivals', when Christianity has been established as the dominant ideology for centuries, but 'the people have been unable to free themselves from a number of pagan rituals' which have long ago lost their mythological or religious significance.[60]

A challenge to the theory of double-belief as a mixing of pagan and Christian forms was formulated by E. E. Golubinskii, a priest's son who wrote the first part of his *History of the Russian Church* in 1880 as his doctoral dissertation. In volume one, published in 1904, Golubinskii starts from the premise that the mass of the population could not have received anything like a proper education in Christianity during the period of Christianization, and so accepted it with an entirely pagan outlook, maintaining two families of gods, and two separate and distinct forms of worship. Golubinskii sees a fusion between Christianity and paganism as impossible, there being no similarities between them:

> Christianity could not be merged with paganism, but had to take up position beside it, as a faith distinct from it. Thus, accepting Christianity and not denying paganism, the mass of Russian people had to become double-believing in the precise and literal sense of the word: the Christian God with the assembly of the saints introduced by the government and the former pagan gods – two gods or two assemblies, two families of gods, the new Christian divine service and the old paganism – two particular and separate [forms of] worship.[61]

Golubinskii does, however, identify a further period of double-belief, surviving into the late nineteenth century (the time of his writing), that of hidden, unconscious double-belief. Once the people had come to recognize that 'Christianity is the one, true faith, and that paganism is lies and the temptation of the devil', the pagan gods vanished to be replaced by 'incarnations of the devil'.[62] This later double-belief survived mainly in the folk beliefs, superstitions, festivities, customs and amusements, which were no longer regarded by the populace as pagan, but rather as a traditional folk inheritance.

Golubinskii argues that while the existence of pagan survivals in folk belief and daily life may appear 'distressing', the phenomenon of *dvoeverie* is pan-European, common 'even among the Greeks', and an inevitable and necessary part of religious development. In this reference to the Greeks, one senses a desire to legitimize the faith of the Russian *narod* which may be found over a century later in the writing of historians in the field of popular belief. Golubinskii's motivation is perhaps that of a believer concerned to prove the unadulterated success of Christianity in Russia, but the result is remarkably similar to conclusions drawn by modern cultural historians, motivated by the desire to focus attention on the popular rather than the élite and the institutionalized.

N. Gal'kovskii first published his seminal work on paganism and double-belief in medieval Russia, *The Struggle of Christianity with Pagan Survivals in Old Rus*, in 1915.[63] The second volume of this work, a collection of sermons against pagan survivals and one of the most cited sources in the field of medieval popular belief, was published first, in 1913. Despite the contribution his work has made to the *dvoeverie* debate, Gal'kovskii does not analyze the term in detail. Instead, he discusses a number of sermons traditionally cited in discussions of double-belief, arguing that by the time the sermons were written, the pagan idols and the few rituals mentioned in them had lost their meaning and were honoured simply from habit. This he deduces from the relative silence of the authors about the 'cult':

> But the meaning of ancient paganism was already forgotten: the sacrifices and above all the pagan rites were performed simply from habit, without understanding their meaning; at least the Christlover, recounting the names of the gods, says almost nothing essentially about the pagan cult, upon which without doubt he would have not failed to enlarge in his zeal to condemn.[64]

Gal'kovskii's general understanding of the term *dvoeverie* is the piecemeal preservation of the names of pagan idols and some rituals by both educated and uneducated. For Gal'kovskii, who certainly was at pains to stress his belief in the generally high moral nature of ordinary folk, there was no antagonistic intention to resist Christianity: 'Old Rus genuinely wanted to be Orthodox Christian, but did not always succeed in this', because of the low level of education, including of her clerical class, and a misguided desire to preserve tradition – 'in this respect, Rus cannot be exceptional'.[65] In the early period, represented in the *Sermon of the Christlover*, which Gal'kovskii surmises is pre-Mongol, the double-believers had already forgotten the pagan meaning of their actions, because they mixed Christian prayers with pagan ritual. The further away in time the sources are from their subjects, the more confused the sermonizers are about the nature and names of the pagan idols – referring back to other literary sources in an effort to understand them, they mix them up with Greek gods and Biblical figures.

The idea that the peasantry was the sole source of *dvoeverie* is also contested by Smirnov, who argues that double-belief is not a popular phenomenon confined to the illiterate peasantry, but also to be found in the higher stratum of society. In his analysis, *dvoeverie* arose among the upper classes partly via Byzantium, and in this he pre-empts modern arguments over the validity of *zmeeviki* and similar artefacts as evidence of the prolonged existence of Russian paganism:

> Old Russian double-belief is a very complicated, difficult to study, but extremely interesting phenomenon. Being the heritage of predominantly illiterate simple people, living by native tradition, double-belief was not alien also to the higher classes, the literate, those who came under the influence of Byzantium, and arose among them to some extent under the influence of the folk belief of the Christian East – of Greek double-belief, which itself was formed from different, rather variegated elements.[66]

The increasing tendency to equate double-belief with 'popular faith' was also challenged by Pierre Pascal in his *The Religion of the Russian People*, written in the 1970s. Pascal argues that the faith of the Russian peasant is *not* one of double-belief, that 'mixture of Christianity and pagan survivals'.[67] While suggesting that traditional Russian culture is full of rituals that contain traces of pagan festivals (the festival of *Iarilo*, the tree rituals of Whitsun, the drowning of effigies and wreathing of garlands), he regards the participants as unaware of the pagan element. They continue to celebrate in this fashion because it is fun, and 'the young peasant girls . . . who, on the night of 31 December read their fortune for the coming year in the grotesque patterns made by wax in contact with boiling water' show no more double-belief than 'the Frenchwoman who goes to have her fortune read in the cards'.[68] Pascal concludes that the only aspect of folk belief which contained pre-Christian elements for any length of time was 'the belief in the power and sanctity of the earth',[69] and his arguments on this aspect of popular belief owe much to Smirnov and Fedotov's work.

An interesting, late development and defence of the concept of double-belief is made by Evgenii Ivakhnenko in his 1997 article entitled 'The Middle Ages: the spiritual aspect of Russian double-belief'.[70] A key feature of his model of double-belief is his identification of a 'ground floor' of Russian *dvoeverie* – a sort of uncontrolled subconscious which bursts out at critical moments, when the believer feels that magic ritual may be more effective than the Church sacraments. It may also manifest itself unexpectedly, in someone who views themselves as wholly Christian: 'The deep layers of pagan consciousness continued to exist and manifest themselves in the most unexpected ways, even for those who did not suspect themselves to be pagan'.[71]

This bottom layer of consciousness is identified with demonism, and manifests itself in a variety of beliefs and actions that would not generally be included in a modern definition of paganism, without elaboration:

> Inner paganism of such a type can be defined as of demonic spiritual formation. It later constituted the 'bottom' of Russian double-belief. This layer of consciousness burst out as relapses into shamanism and idol-worship, universal sorcery and belief in fortune-telling, as fear before the transformative powers of country sorcerers and the active use of [love-] potions.[72]

A 'magical' view of the world hardly constitutes a 'pagan' view,[73] unless one were to accept that the vast majority of Europeans were pagan at least until the seventeenth century – which, as we discuss in Chapter 4, has indeed been suggested. Possibly Ivakhnenko, like Le Bras and Delumeau, would agree:

> the existence of entire historical periods in which occurred a reanimation of paganism – the Renaissance, the French Revolution, the Soviet period – gives evidence that pagan consciousness, talented at mimicry, continued to 'work' at the deepest levels of world culture.[74]

This 'demonic consciousness' manifests itself particularly in times of 'instability, sedition and unbelief', and Ivakhnenko cites the rediscovery or recreation of the Marii pagan tradition in post-Soviet Russia (as he might have the neo-paganism of extreme nationalists in Moscow)[75] as an example of instability and loss of 'firm soil' bringing forth the desire to return to an earlier spirituality.

After a brief survey of the position of scholars on 'Russian religious syncretism', Ivakhnenko draws a number of conclusions, among which is that the majority of researchers have accepted the special significance of 'Orthodox–pagan syncretism in the development and formation of folk self-consciousness over a period of more than 500 years' of Russian history, but the 'dynamic growth' and development of this mixed religious consciousness has been underestimated.

Ivakhnenko appears to want to broaden the understanding of double-belief beyond a phenomenon restricted to the actions and objects of the material world, to a fundamental part of Russian spirituality. Double-belief is the 'demonic consciousness' lurking ever present beneath a veneer of civilized Christianity, ready to surprise the believer in moments of stress or revolution. Alternatively it exists in the public face of Orthodoxy, since he also concludes that the pagan heritage within the body of Orthodoxy is revealed by elements of 'animism, fetishism and totemism'. One assumes that by 'fetishism' he means what N. M. Nikol'skii did – the adoration of relics – an indication of the sorts of value judgements that mar this article.

Double or triple faith?

Francis Conte's *Pagan Heritage of Russia*, published in 1997, demonstrates that the concept of double-belief reached continental academic circles as well as Anglophone ones. Referring to the continued domestic and communal village rituals and consulting of sorcerers by the peasant, he says:

> This situation is well summed up by an expression very often used at the end of the nineteenth century – that of 'double-belief' (*dvoeverie*) – which indicates the mixed beliefs of the rural world.[76]

Like Fedotov, Conte sees the Orthodox Church as having failed to achieve in Russia the degree of success that the Catholic Church achieved in the West in eradicating paganism, and attributes this to a lesser degree of organization and a greater degree of toleration. In his view, the Church compromised out of necessity. The clergy were living alongside the peasant, farming the land and possessing only a modest level of spiritual education, sharing a

> common feeling for the divine thoroughly impregnated by the natural world, penetrated by the familiar intercessors – the saints, the spirits of the locality and of venerated ancestors who lived in the hereafter but actively protected their family remaining on earth.[77]

In his chapter on double-belief, Conte focuses on the late nineteenth century, firmly declaring that in this period the peasant held two sets of beliefs and associated behaviours which were both distinct and complementary. The peasant could turn to either set of beliefs at will, passing 'without pangs of conscience from the observation of Orthodox rituals to the selective practice of magic'.[78] It is this conscious and deliberate choice that distinguishes double-belief from syncretism in Conte's schema, and he likens double-belief to spiritual bilingualism. The two languages of belief are interchangeable, giving the practitioner, as it were, two signifiers for each signified. The choice of spiritual language is made according to its appropriateness to the situation.

Conte is bravely unfashionable in his conception of double-belief, with his diagnosis of late nineteenth-century peasant spirituality as a consciously dual world where magic (as a distinct and identifiable belief-system) and Orthodox Christianity are alternately practised as necessary. In his conclusion, however, he refers to a further phenomenon, that of 'triple-faith', a phenomenon identified by the ethnographer N. I. Tolstoi, which does not involve a choice between one or the other languages of belief, but a 'véritable «coexistence pacifique» entre paganisme et christianisme', a true 'peaceful coexistence' of paganism and Christianity.[79]

To illustrate this 'peaceful coexistence', Conte gives the curious story of a peasant who lights two candles for the feast of St George before an icon of George slaying the dragon. When asked why two, the peasant replies that one is for the dragon, and one for the saint. Why he chooses this particular example is poorly explained, since it could perhaps better serve as an illustration of a simple human reaction of pity for the loser of this particular battle, and wherein lies the paganism is not clear.[80] Interestingly, Haney cites a similar tale involving an old woman lighting candles before an icon of St Michael and an icon depicting the defeated Satan, seeing in her self-confessed desire to have friends in both heaven and hell as evidence of 'practitioners . . . unable or unwilling to distinguish Orthodoxy from the old popular beliefs'.[81] Since Satan is a perfectly orthodox figure, she might be more appropriately accused of devil-worship, which allegedly makes use of inverted Christian ritual.

Tolstoi challenges the notion that there were two conflicting systems (paganism and Christianity) influencing the character of Russian spiritual culture, identifying a third source which came to the Slavs simultaneously with Christianity – a folk, urban culture which developed in Byzantium and partly in the West as non-Christian rather than anti-Christian – and tentatively attributes holy foolishness (*iurodstvo*), the activities of minstrels (*skomoroshestvo*) and carnival festivities to this third cultural stream.[82] A much earlier challenge to the essentially binary concept of Russian belief systems was formulated as early as 1904 by the son of a provincial priest, V. O. Kliuchevsky, in his *Course in Russian History*. This work contains little in-depth study of the religious beliefs of the Russian people, and when Kliuchevsky ventures into the realms of belief, it is with an apology:

> I am not a theologian . . . But religious as well as all other rites and texts that affect practical everyday life have a general psychological import in addition to their specific meanings, and in that respect may be the subject of historical investigation.[83]

Kliuchevsky raises the issue of *dvoeverie* in the context of Russian–Finnish relations, suggesting that the 'nondescript religious system' created by the mingling of Christian Russian settlers with pagan native Chuds during the colonization of northern Russia was a synthesis of 'popular religious ideas'.[84] Finnish inhabitants and Russian immigrants came to see in each other's beliefs an identifiable element of their own. Thus the Finnish gods of the earth became the demons of Russian Orthodoxy, and the spirits of forest and water honoured by the Finns inhabiting the Volga region 'passed wholesale into the mythology of the Great Russians'.[85]

> Already the confusion bound to arise out of a development of pagan mythology into Christian demonology had made itself felt in Rus during the eleventh century, and might very well be called, according to the apt expression applied by Abbot Theodosius of Petcherski to persons who practised both their own and an alien religion, '*dvoeviera*' or 'double-faith', while there can be little doubt that, if only the prelate could have foreseen the manner in which Finnish paganism was destined later to join hands with Russian, he would have called such a nondescript religious system '*troeviera*' or 'triple-faith'.[86]

This muddying of spiritual waters is demonstrated by another example of cultural interchange: while the eleventh-century Archimandrite Abraham was busy harvesting souls in Rostov, the inhabitants of the so-called 'Chud quarter' were worshipping the Slavonic cattle god Volos alongside Russian pagans, Kliuchevsky surmises. Whether or not the local Russian population were also actively opposing the Archimandrite's efforts is not the most important question in this instance – more pertinent to Kliuchevsky's identification of 'triple faith' is why the Finnish inhabitants should have adopted a Slavonic idol. A baptized population of 'Great Russians' or Chuds preserving a mixture of their own 'native' heathen beliefs and an 'alien' belief system are triple believers in Kliuchevsky's scheme. This implies that, unlike the Chronicler, of whom Kliuchevsky says 'To him paganism, whether Russian or Finnish, was all one, and he took no account of racial origin or ethnographical differences when writing of heathen beliefs', Kliuchevsky sees not just an amorphous mass of pagan customs and beliefs in a 'spiritualized' natural environment. He perceives distinct faiths, initially identifiable by their ethnic characteristics. This is a typically nineteenth-century approach, assuming as it does that religious beliefs can safely be identified as Slavonic or Finnish, or Germanic or Celtic for that matter, and that each ethnic paganism constituted a distinct 'faith'. However, in the realm of popular belief clear boundaries are rare, and influences are continual and multidirectional. When postulated, such ethnic boundaries should be viewed with a degree of suspicion.

The 'Russification' of Christianity

Although significant scholars have argued that double-belief is a pan-European, or Byzantine, or universal phenomenon, it has also been perceived as a specifically

Russian problem. Some have suggested that there was a particularly Russian failure to combat superstition and paganism, or that *dvoeverie* reflects a 'Russification' of Christianity, a unique blend of Russian paganism and Byzantine Christianity. This theory has been applied to other times and places – most fully perhaps in Russell's *The Germanization of Early Medieval Christianity*, which argues that the 'universal salvation religion' of Christianity was fundamentally altered by contact with Germanic warrior society during the Christianization period: 'an unintended result of implementing a missionary policy which accommodated Germanic concerns'.[87]

The Soviet scholar B. Grekov sees in *dvoeverie* one syncretic religion, a 'Russianized' faith, emerging from the slow process of Christianization:

> Christianity spread slowly from the cities to the manors and villages merging with the habitual ways of thought and sentiment. Old and new scholars insisted that the two faiths existed side by side, but there was no such thing in actual fact. It was a syncretic religion which resulted from the introduction of the Christian faith among the Russian people, in other words, its Russification.[88]

In some respects this reflects Fedotov's 'tincture of native heathendom' theory (discussed later), but as with Kliuchevsky's desire to separate out the ethnic strands of paganism, this is dangerous territory. Grekov does not dwell on the continual process of syncretism that began in the early Church and is in evidence in the Christianity of the Roman and Byzantine Empires (and in any period of Christianization, anywhere), nor does he perceive the irony of offering as his first example of this 'Russification' the celebration of Christmas:

> The Russian holidays illustrate this fact unequivocally . . . The celebration of the New Year, of spring, bore the Roman name of Calendae – *Koliada* – and coincided with Christmas. The ritual side of the celebrations remained purely pagan: on Christmas Eve the Bulgarians, Serbs, Byelorussians and the people in many parts of Russia proper until quite recently held a ritual repast symbolising an invocation for abundance and welfare in the coming year.[89]

It would of course be difficult to find a part of Christian Europe where this Christmas feasting did not occur, and if it did originate in sympathetic magic – eating rich foods in order to bring abundance – it is certainly not a specifically Russian phenomenon.

George P. Fedotov, a Russian 'exile', as he describes himself in his introduction to *The Russian Religious Mind*, made a fine attempt to write a history of 'Russian religious consciousness'. Though executed with sensitivity and imagination, the work, which was first published in 1946, unfortunately brings little new to the definition of *dvoeverie*:

Indeed, Church historians are right in describing the Russian medieval religion as 'dual faith' . . . Some historians date the true conversion of the lower classes of the Russian people as late as the fifteenth century. But exact dating has no meaning because even in the nineteenth century pagan survivals were deeply rooted. Long ago these pagan elements blended with Christian Orthodox ritualism and became hardly distinguishable from it. The Russian Church, which formerly waged a merciless war against the dual faith and had redoubled its efforts in the eighteenth century, the age of enlightenment, gave up the struggle in the nineteenth century.[90]

Fedotov also takes his evidence for the existence of double-belief from Church literature, and continues the tradition of ascribing the concept to the medieval clerics themselves: 'What these sermons and canons fight against is, in their own words, the "double faith"; they accuse the Christians of being addicted to pagan practices and superstitions'.[91] In the second volume of *The Russian Religious Mind*, covering the period of the thirteenth to the fifteenth century, he also finds evidence of double-belief in folk literature, considering for example a folk song which tells of three sins against kinship being confessed to the Earth, and concluding that the folk list of sins indicates 'the survivals of the *gens* (or *rod*) religion that has a very close tie with the cult of the Mother Earth. As such, they indicate a very deep, or very low, cultural stratum, that of "double-faith" (*dvoeverie*)'.[92]

The key attributes of Fedotov's *dvoeverie* remain the existence of pagan survivals (even to the present day), resulting in a syncretic blend of Christian and indigenous pagan beliefs. He accepts the universal nature of pagan survivals among Christian nations, while acknowledging that in Russia the heathen residue is particularly marked, as a result primarily of the lack of a Reformation and Counter-Reformation 'with their cleansing, spiritualizing and sweeping out of medieval superstitions'.[93] Fedotov suggests that what accounts for the 'characteristic national features' of Christianity is this 'tincture of native heathendom', and much of his first volume is dedicated to sifting through these apparent remnants of paganism to isolate the elements that colour Russian religious consciousness.

Challenges to *dvoeverie*

As Simon Dixon has pointed out, the challenge to *dvoeverie* which escalated in the 1990s has resulted in a sea change in Russian historiography, particularly in the study of peasant belief of the late Imperial period.[94] Several Anglophone academics have been particularly influential in challenging the concept of 'double belief' – most notably Eve Levin and Chris Chulos – but *dvoeverie* was also not accepted unquestioningly by Soviet academics, and a number of Russian historians have contributed substantially to the debate in the *glasnost'* and post-Soviet period.

D. S. Likhachev, an academician and Christian believer who managed to publish during the Soviet period without compromising his scholarship, wrestled with the term in an article about folk poetic works from the twelfth to the thirteenth century, pre-empting the modern debate about its validity:

> 'Double-belief' is a very complicated phenomenon and by no means defined by the matter which is usually extracted from the name itself: two faiths, double faith, a combination of Christianity with paganism, fulfilment of the requirements of two religions and so on. The simple combining of two religions would hardly be possible generally, the more so of two *hostile* religions.[95]

In a challenge to the concept of *dvoeverie* as a form of deliberate resistance to Christianity, Likhachev sees the merging of pagan elements with Christian as possible only when paganism has in effect ceased to be a religion. The 'sharpness of contrast' between paganism and Christianity first has to be blunted, and the pagan rituals have to become 'desemanticised', over time. Once this has happened, Likhachev sees it as 'no surprise that pagan rituals, which had ceased to be recognised as pagan by the people, joined in combination with the rituals of Christianity – at first in straight succession: one after the other, and then "fully mixed"'.

Likhachev gives the peasant wedding as evidence of this alternation of rites, and also addresses the ever popular example of the *rozhanitsy* worshippers:

> None of those who were practicing pagan rituals in the XII–XIII centuries, nor those believing in 'rozhanitsy', set themselves up in opposition to Christianity, as something possessing equal rights with it, and in this was one of the main conditions for the endurance of that which is called 'double-belief'.[96]

This mixture of desemanticized pagan rites and Christian ritual appears as a poetic stimulus in Likhachev's essay: 'in the depths of that which is called "double-belief" [ritual poetry] was gradually freed from faith and became for the most part a phenomenon of artistic creation'. He discusses in this context the fate of the folk 'lament' (*плач, plach*), a famous example of which appears in the *Igor Tale*.

In short, Likhachev implies that the term *dvoeverie* is misleading, while acknowledging the existence of the phenomenon, albeit interpreted again slightly differently. He dismisses the notion of a first, conscious stage of 'literal' double-belief as impossible, but apparently accepts the idea of 'unconscious' *dvoeverie*, when in the later period desemanticized pagan elements enter Christianity and are preserved there. It is significant, however, that in his article on Russian Orthodoxy for the 1998 *Cambridge Companion to Modern Russian Culture*, which gives a historical overview of the Church, he makes no reference to the concept or the phenomenon.[97]

In the post-Soviet period, although the standard interpretations of *dvoeverie* have continued to appear in encyclopedias and broad-themed historical and cultural works,[98] the term has been debated by a small group of Russian academics for over a decade. More recently, Western publications on Russian religion have expressed doubts about the usefulness of the term, and several articles have sharply critiqued the concept. The Russian scholars most active in the debate are A. V. Chernetsov, his colleague and sometime co-author A. A. Turilov,[99] A. E. Musin, V. P. Darkevich, Evgenii Ivakhnenko, V. M. Zhivov[100] and V. Ia. Petrukhin.[101] It is to this debate that we now turn.

As early as 1988, A. M. Panchenko published an article on the 'Aesthetic aspects of the Christianization of Rus' that served as a warning to all those who cite medieval authors as originators of the concept of double-belief. His article is not concerned primarily with double-belief, but in the wider context of relations with other denominations, he discusses the letter of Fedosii Pecherskii to Prince Iziaslav, with its condemnation of those who praise foreign faiths. He observes that although in contemporary 'historical-philological terminology', *dvoeverie* means the synthesis of paganism and Christianity:

> Meanwhile Feodosii Pecherskii (and that means also, the intelligentsia of Kievan Rus in general) understood by 'double-belief' something completely different, namely confessional tolerance.[102]

This observation (expanded upon by Petrukhin, who concludes that the term meant wavering between Catholicism and Orthodoxy for the entire medieval period) rightly posed a challenge to the concept of 'medieval double-belief'. The ensuing debate raised emotionally loaded questions for Russian scholars – the collapse of the Soviet Union, and the surge of interest in and admiration for the Russian Orthodox Church which began with *glasnost'* and the Millennium celebrations of 1988, have significantly altered the face of Russian historiography. Russian historians have had to contend with a legacy of atheist Soviet scholarship which has placed ideological value on research findings in this field in particular, and falsely divided historians into 'pro' and 'anti' Church camps.

A. E. Musin, an academic and a deacon of the Russian Orthodox Church, raised the 'problem of double-belief' in an article published in 1991.[103] Musin divides *dvoeverie* scholars into two camps: those who – like Anichkov and Solov'ev – see Orthodox Christianity as having adapted to entrenched paganism, a view which developed into the Soviet idea of 'undefeated paganism'; and those who see Orthodoxy as having assimilated paganism and eventually arrived at a syncretic blend acceptable to the Church. In this latter group he includes Gal'kovskii, Grekov and Likhachev, noting that researchers of this camp often object to the term itself as inaccurate – it is not two faiths but rather one syncretic belief-system.

From the two usages cited by Musin, in the *Sermon of the Christlover* and *Questions of Kirik* (the former referring to idol-worshippers,[104] the latter to those who bring their children to Varangian priests), Musin deduces that the term *dvoeverie* had no fixed meaning, but that the concept arrived ready-made from Byzantium, in translated sermons by the Church Fathers which denounced paganism, and in rituals and materials similarly imported.

Musin's article contains a number of important and interesting ideas which deserve individual consideration, the most significant of which is that Christianity evolved from paganism and Judaism, giving Christian content to old symbols in that process. He goes on to discuss the Christian tradition of using 'desemanticized' pagan symbols for proselytism in the Russian context, finding some examples (*siriny* – half bird, half woman – with halos representing Divine Wisdom for example) which are puzzling, others (such as crosses decorated with lily-like ends) clearly supporting his thesis. While Musin is not wholly convincing in his dismissal of pagan influence (particularly his argument that priests attending the feasts of the *rozhanitsy* were there solely for proselytizing, see Chapter 1, earlier), his challenge to those who would divide the pagan from the 'truly Christian' is an important one.

The problems now surrounding post-*glasnost'* scholars of early popular belief have been most clearly articulated by the archaeologist Aleksei Chernetsov, who sprang to the defence of *dvoeverie* in a 1994 article for *Zhivaia starina* (*Living Antiquity*), a journal dedicated to articles about Russian folklore and traditional culture.[105] Chernetsov describes those who oppose use of the term *dvoeverie* as 'naïve idealists' whose real objections are to the very idea of pre-Christian elements being identified in later beliefs. The Soviet approach, as we have seen, often identified pagan survivals as evidence of resistance to patriarchal and oppressive Christianity, and/or evidence of the tenuous hold Christianity had in 'Holy Russia'. Chernetsov's article implies that this has provoked a simplistic response from certain 'pro-Church' academics, and misdirected the energies of researchers. As acceptance of the existence of *dvoeverie* is seen as discrediting the Church in some way, it must therefore be denied.

> The position of today's battlers against 'double-belief' is unfortunately less Olympian [than that of medieval clerics]. In them I see mainly a naïve idealisation of the country with elements of 'folk-worship'. The idealization of old Russian times as untroubled Orthodoxy is naïve, because it does not bear the tests of the most elementary questions.[106]

Chernetsov acknowledges that the world-view of the medieval Russian was an 'organic' whole, thereby accepting *dvoeverie* as a syncretic blend of Christianity and paganism rather than a mode of conscious, deliberate resistance adopted by nominal Christians. Though there may have been a unified belief-system, he argues, it was not wholly Christian. If folk Orthodoxy had been pure and irreproachable, medieval clerics would not have expended so much energy condemning elements of it as pagan, nor would it have capitulated so easily beneath the 'catastrophe' (*katastrofa*) of the Bolshevik revolution, which he rather cryptically associates with the forces of darkness.

Chernetsov defends his right to research the past using terms in vogue during the period:[107]

> At the same time, the word 'double-belief' was widely used by Old Russian clergy; in it were invested notions about entirely concrete phenomena of spiritual culture. An attempt to arrive at an understanding of the past using those categories which were in vogue in the epoch being studied is one of the possible and completely legitimate scholarly approaches.[108]

Unfortunately he does not explore this wide usage of the word *dvoeverie* further within the boundaries of this article. Chernetsov is also concerned to encourage further research in the field of historical popular belief:

> the academic argument should address not justification of the use of the word 'double-belief', but such concrete questions as the dynamic of the interaction of the varied elements of this syncretic phenomenon, and the mechanism of their mutual interaction.[109]

He supports this suggestion with numerous examples of double-belief (according to his understanding of the term) from archaeological and textual sources, some of which have been challenged, such as *zmeeviki*, snake-amulets. Chernetsov is also careful to stress that these material evidences of *dvoeverie* are crucial to an understanding of the 'traditional national culture' of Russia, in contrast to some scholars who prefer to emphasize the pan-European nature of such belief patterns.

V. P. Darkevich's 1995 article 'On the question of "double-belief" in Old Rus' attempts to distinguish between the use of the term *dvoeverie* by medieval observers of the process of Christianization and its use by modern scholars:

> The so-called 'double-belief' is two sides of one unified, linked mechanism, of its synchronous structure. In the estimation of contemporaries (the term is found in Feodosii Pecherskii of the eleventh century), both layers are perceived as hostile. But in the understanding of scholars of our times, this antagonism should be removed. There is present an interaction of different, as it were mutually exclusive, categories of consciousness.[110]

Darkevich's reference to Feodosii Pecherskii is confusing, since Feodosii was concerned primarily with 'Latins' rather than with any pagan 'layer' in the sermons in which he used the term, and while some modern scholarship insists on the removal of the note of 'antagonism' between the old and the new layers of religious culture, there remain those who subscribe to what Eve Levin calls the 'conflict model'. He refutes the use of the term *dvoeverie* by modern scholars to describe later peasant spirituality, preferring the phrase 'folk Christianity' (*narodnoe khristianstvo*), but accepts it as legitimate when discussing the early period:

One can talk about 'double-belief' in the early period of Christianization, which, judging by the written and archaeological sources, lasted for at least one and a half centuries . . . But when 'pagan' sanctuaries were destroyed, when former gods were overthrown and humiliated, to talk then about 'double-belief', not from the viewpoint of a medieval cleric, but as a representative of contemporary academia, is hardly legitimate.[111]

Darkevich offers no discussion of the dating of this post-*dvoeverie* period, so we must assume he means around 1130. The archaeological half of his brief summary of the 'written and archaeological' sources assesses the evolution of burial rituals, the evidence from which is complicated and varies according to region. Franklin and Shepard observe that

By the end of the [twelfth] century almost all urban graves were Christian, while rural burial-grounds even in the previously retarded land of the Viatichi had begun to include some Christian pit-graves as well as traditional barrow-graves containing crosses and other Christian symbols. Some 200 years after Vladimir Sviatoslavich the process of Conversion was close to becoming plausibly, rather than just eulogistically, complete.[112]

It is worth noting that Musin also raises the question of burial rituals as evidence of Christianization, seeing the tradition of 'kurgan' or barrow-burial as not out of keeping with Christian belief (despite complaints about it by high-ranking sixteenth-century clerics), as it appeared in Novgorod after the official conversion (in the late eleventh century) and was found in the vicinity of Orthodox churches.[113]

Darkevich concludes by citing E. V. Anichkov's argument that *dvoeverie* was not a mechanical combination of former beliefs with the new, but rather 'a transfer of old beliefs into new forms'. That double-belief is accommodation rather than resistance appears to be the crux of his argument.

In perhaps the most important Western contribution to the *dvoeverie* debate, '*Dvoeverie* and Popular Religion', Eve Levin justly makes the point that we cannot judge medieval Christianity 'by the standard of a contemporary intellectualised and rationalised philosophical system'.[114] She makes an eloquent plea for a reconsideration of the term, a return to 'its original meaning, cleansed of its pejorative connotation: the conscious and deliberate practice of Christianity and paganism by the same person'.[115] Levin may have misjudged the original meaning if by that she intends the original medieval meaning, which as we have seen was multiple, certainly intended to be pejorative in some contexts and, with one exception, does not appear to refer to the practice of paganism and Christianity. However, this article convincingly dispels several myths about the topic, and clearly summarizes many of the problems faced by the scholar using the term 'double-belief'.

Levin has suggested in her article that the original meaning of *dvoeverie* was the 'conscious and deliberate practice of Christianity and paganism by the same person', which is a perfectly logical definition if we consider the initial uses of the term in late nineteenth- and early twentieth-century scholarship.[116] No historian has used the term in relation to faiths other than the Orthodox and the pagan, although 'anti-Orthodox' behaviour has been seen as part of this duality and reference has been made to the texts in which it relates to 'Latins'. A great many have used it to describe the practice of 'pagan' rituals or aspects of belief and worship that are neither deliberately nor consciously pagan. As we have seen, the general consensus among modern historians is that double-belief refers either to Christians who have preserved elements of pagan belief in their worship or daily lives either by a process of accommodation (Church-approved or reluctantly accepted), resulting in a syncretic blend of 'pure' Orthodoxy and ancient paganism, or to pagan elements preserved as a form of resistance to patriarchal, autocratic, aristocratic culture imposed on the masses.

Levin is primarily objecting to the use of the term *dvoeverie* as shorthand for 'popular belief', and its abuse either by scholars who have a political axe to grind (Soviet or feminist), or by those who cannot see beyond the confrontational model of popular/pagan versus official/Orthodox. Summarizing the various definitions and their adherents, she neatly dispenses with the 'syncretic' group by a reconsideration of some of their favourite examples – among them the cult of St Paraskeva. Her arguments are similar to Musin's; she notes that 'the immediate inspiration for the popular cult of St Paraskeva came from three distinct ecclesiastical traditions, not pagan ones'.[117] Levin is careful to indicate the circular reasoning by which pagan beliefs are sometimes reconstructed from peasant cults and little else, and then subsequent scholars identify pagan elements in those very cults, predictably enough since the cults furnished the material for the reconstruction of those beliefs. She also points out that similar cults are to be found in Bulgaria, Serbia, Greece and Romania.[118]

Although both Musin and Chernetsov are aware of the Byzantine influence, neither of them compares the Russian experience with that of other Orthodox or Western European countries, a notable omission particularly for Chernetsov, who maintains that 'these phenomena [*zmeeviki* amulets, Novgorodian crosses with genitalia, etc.] were widely distributed; they are very important for the characteristics of traditional national culture, of its nationally specific nature'.[119]

While Levin's treatment of the various meanings of double-belief in modern scholarship is illuminating, she leaves one major point unexplored. The original meaning of *dvoeverie* is surely to be found in the medieval texts where it first appeared, but she, like Musin, passes swiftly over some of the better-known citations in order to dissect complex cases of double-belief. This is a valuable exercise, but perhaps premature. *Dvoeverie* as a term needs to be re-defined before decisions can be made about whether a particular belief, artefact or practice is a 'true' example of double-belief, and as Levin herself suggests, to do that one must return to, and re-examine, the original meaning.

Other commentators have gone further. Chris Chulos declares that '[o]ne of the most trite misnomers about pre-revolutionary peasant religion has been that it can best be described as a dual faith or *dvoeverie*', and this label tells us more about the ignorance of the observer than the faith of the peasants.[120] Chulos has also pointed out that early twentieth-century clerical observers condemned not only superstitions but antireligious activity, atheism, 'drunkenness, swearing and disorder' as pagan behaviours.[121] J. Eugene Clay suggests that the term *dvoeverie* be dispensed with altogether, since

> terms, such as dual-faith [*dvoeverie*] which implies that the Russian peasant was basically pagan with a thin veneer of Russian Orthodoxy, were coined not so much to describe peasant religion as to denigrate, modify and monitor it.[122]

Clay sees such nineteenth-century terminology (and with *dvoeverie* he considers 'sectarian' and 'schismatic') as carrying with it the 'theological baggage' of the missionary, restricting the historians' freedom and channelling him into unnecessary and fruitless activity, such as trying to determine whether a practice is Orthodox or not. He makes the valid points that the term 'double-belief' implies that the Orthodoxy of the urban seminary is the norm, that Orthodoxy is a 'rationalised, immutable system', and that 'the sophisticated urban practice of reading pagan philosophers' is Orthodox, while the peasant customs such as the carnival revels of *Maslenitsa* are not.

Clay suggests that the historian should allow 'historical actors to define themselves in their own terms', and dismisses *dvoeverie* for denying the Orthodox peasant this self-definition. While I have every sympathy with his argument, it has to be remarked that the further back in time we look, the more difficult it is to ascertain the self-image of the peasant, as it is to establish his or her religious rituals. This is why we must accept the definition of 'Orthodox' as accepted by the hierarchy of the period in question – which indeed is not a static, immutable system, and does vary according to status, location and education of the cleric in question, but as the written records of the literate clerical class are the chief window we have onto the medieval religious mind, we have little choice.

Conclusion

'The devil is in the detail' is an apt aphorism for the *dvoeverie* debate. To summarize the plethora of themes and interpretations of the concept outlined in this chapter: a significant point of difference between interpretations of double-belief is the question of whether double-belief is a syncretic phenomenon, or whether two faiths remain identifiably distinct and separate. This conundrum is sometimes overcome by the division of double-belief into stages. *Dvoeverie* has been seen both as a static condition, and as a progressive phenomenon with identifiable stages, where the Christian (or 'baptized pagan') moves from simultaneous, conscious and deliberate practising of pagan and Christian rituals to a final stage of unconscious preservation of desemanticized, fragmented pagan rites and belief.

This preservation of pagan rituals has been viewed alternately as a form of resistance on the part of the peasantry – but sometimes also by the upper strata of society – to the Church and State-enforced ideology, or as an unconscious desire to preserve the religious pattern of the ancestors, or as a creative response to needs unfulfilled by the new religion. Double-believers are seen as either Christians unfulfilled or under stress, misguided, uneducated or otherwise unaware Christians, or baptized pagans, in rebellion or under duress.

The existence of double-belief in Russia is supported by evidence drawn from medieval texts, archaeological evidence, ethnographical and folkloric research, but many of the most significant contributors to the debate have depended heavily on citations from and references to medieval sermons, which are then re-quoted by other academics, often out of context. Thus developed the highly misleading notion that medieval Russia – and sometimes the later period – was awash with complaints by clerics about 'double-believers' stubbornly resisting the process of Christianization.

A notable feature of *dvoeverie* scholarship is the degree to which the debate has been coloured by the ideological or confessional background of the contributors. The republication in 1998 of Rapov's Soviet-style historiography is extraordinary, but in some respects he is no more guilty than Nikolay Andreyev, for example, who proclaimed double-belief still alive in some places in the twentieth century – relating his own observation of peasant women offering butter and eggs to the statue of St Nicholas in the 1930s.[123] Rapov, Andreyev and other scholars of the Church have simply viewed popular beliefs through their own socio-political (or religious) prism, and judged them accordingly, and in doing so reveal as much about their own beliefs as they do about their subjects. This is, of course, an issue for all historians of religion, not just Russianists.

Contemporary scholars are still disagreeing, not only about whether *dvoeverie* is a syncretic, unified world-view or a conscious preservation of pagan traditions; but also about what constitutes 'paganism'. This is an important element of the study of *dvoeverie*, and deserves close scrutiny. Chernetsov avoids the issue entirely, because he is less concerned with the naming of things than proving their existence – if there is a demonstrably unchristian element to beliefs to be found in texts and material objects, what does it matter by what name this phenomenon is known?

> In the end, one term is not worth the argument, if those arguing understand the phenomenon under discussion the same way, and only name it differently.[124]

While I sympathize with his frustration as a researcher who just wants to get on and write about his findings without being drawn into a debate about academic semantics, the phenomenon *is* hotly contested, and an understanding of what this term meant to medieval clerics is crucial both to the debate about the validity of the term, and to a deeper understanding of Russian medieval spirituality.

Both Chernetsov and Levin touch on the validity of approaches to medieval faith that either use medieval terminology, or attempt to dispense with a modern, rational, value-laden attitude to medieval Christianity. To understand the spirituality of medieval people we must seek to understand the terms they used to define their religious world as they understood them. It is with language that we express our understanding of the world, define, and to a certain extent create, our societies. *Dvoeverie* is a particularly significant term in Russian cultural history, partly perhaps because it has been so much used by historians, but mostly because it has been cited as an important medieval concept which reflects the spiritual life of early Russian society. If that reflection of medieval spirituality is tarnished by a modern misinterpretation of the word, this has serious implications for our study of the period.

The *dvoeverie* debate has revealed many areas worthy of further research, despite not having resolved the fundamental issue of definition. The nature of the so-called 'pagan' or 'demonic' games, the role of priests in unorthodox popular practices, the medieval attitude to and understanding of 'other' or 'foreign' faith, and the Church's role in sanctioning or prohibiting aspects of popular faith are just a few of the most tempting topics raised by the debate. However, until a thorough understanding of the medieval use of the term *dvoeverie* has been reached, and academics agree either to dispense with the term entirely, or agree upon a working definition, the study of popular belief will remain muddied by vague terminology and arguments about that terminology.

4 How Russian is 'double-belief'?

> Although I understood what that metaphorical word [*nepantla*] means, that is to say, 'in the middle', I insisted he tell me which 'in the middle' he referred to. The native told me that, since the people were not yet well rooted in the Faith, I should not marvel at the fact that they were neither fish nor fowl: they were governed by neither one religion nor the other. Or, better said, they believed in God and also followed their ancient heathen rites and customs.[1]
>
> Fray Diego Durán, *c.* 1589

In Chapter 2 of this book, we explored medieval uses of the term *dvoeverie* and concluded that they do not provide evidence of a medieval concept of double-belief, where Christians preserve their pagan practices and beliefs either unconsciously or consciously, in stubborn resistance to the new faith or by a process of creative accommodation. Our modern day double-belief, then, is a historiographical construct that developed in the nineteenth century out of a preoccupation with the 'folk' and a belief that by sifting through the sediment of traditional culture, one can find preserved pure elements of pre-Christian paganism.

While the meaning and value of double-belief as an academic construct has been questioned in post-Soviet scholarship, the impact of this historiographical trope has been huge. As we have seen, *dvoeverie* has been considered a specifically Russian phenomenon by many scholars, despite the arguments contesting this thesis that were made quite clearly at the very beginning of *dvoeverie* scholarship.[2] This chapter will explore some of the most important implications of this, specifically the view that Russian society was particularly resistant to the introduction of Christianity (in comparison to other societies), that Russian Orthodoxy is or was particularly prone to pagan survivals, and that the alleged persistence of *dvoeverie* is evidence of innate dualism in Russian culture, as epitomized by the 'binary oppositions' of Lotman and Uspenskii. *Dvoeverie* may not be what it seems, but are there nevertheless grounds for arguing that Russian Orthodox culture is, or was, somehow more 'pagan' than the Catholic or Protestant cultures of Western Europe?

As explored in Chapter 3, many historians have perceived the development of *dvoeverie* as a series of progressive stages, which can be broadly divided

into three chronological periods reflecting the perceived processes of Christianization. The first stage is the conversion period of conscious *dvoeverie*, in
which the neophyte community consists of baptized pagans who either overtly
or covertly resist Christianity, or attempt out of ignorance, habit or fear to fulfil
both pagan and Christian rites simultaneously. The old forms of paganism are
preserved under a thin veneer of Christianity, as converts accept St Paraskeva as
Mokosh, Elijah as Perun, and have their pagan shrines replaced with churches.
This is followed by a stage which might be described as creative syncretism or
unconscious *dvoeverie*, when the community consists of sincere Christians who
are nevertheless maintaining their 'former world-view clothed in the garb of
Christian externals',[3] and new forms of worship develop out of a mixture of the
old and the new. The final stage is where the fragmented and desemanticized
flotsam of paganism exists as a collection of 'bad habits', folk superstition
(including demonized versions of pagan entities) and amusements to which
the people attach no religious significance. While there have been variations
upon these stages, and historians have disagreed about the time frames within
which these stages supposedly developed, they offer a useful structure for this
chapter, roughly corresponding to the questions we need to address.

Was Rus more resistant to Christianity than other European cultures? The conversion period

To explore the notion that the inhabitants of Rus were particularly resistant
to Christianity, we must return to the period of conversion, which is centred
upon the 'official' baptism *c.* 988 of the Kievan Prince Vladimir ('Volodimir' in
the sources) but spreads over two centuries at least. As we have seen, various
academics have argued that Russia has never been successfully Christianized,
or at least that it was still undergoing the process of conversion in the fifteenth,
sixteenth or seventeenth centuries, but for the purposes of comparing the reception of Christianity in Russia with that of other European nations, we will focus
on the tenth and eleventh centuries. Mindful of the multiple perils a historian
faces when relying on conversion narratives compiled by Christian bookmen,[4]
we shall turn first to the textual evidence.

One of the earliest references to Christianity in Rus was made by Patriarch
Photius of Constantinople, who wrote in 867 that the Rhos 'have exchanged
the Hellenic and godless faith they previously held for the pure and blemish-
free religion of the Christians', that they had accepted a 'bishop and pastor'
and were fulfilling Christian rites.[5] This 'first baptism' warrants a mention in
other Byzantine sources: the tenth-century *Life* of Emperor Basil I (867–886)
records that Basil 'conciliated the indomitable and utterly godless nation of the
Rhos with the lure of generous gifts . . . [and] persuaded them to partake of the
salutary baptism'.[6] Basil apparently sent an archbishop back to Rus with them,
who by miraculous means induced the 'barbarians' to accept Christianity. This
initial Byzantine mission proved unsuccessful, which might explain in part why
subsequent baptisms of the Rus rulers Olga and Vladimir are such non-events

in Byzantine sources. Instead of concluding a lasting peace and providing the military support the Byzantine empire expected from peoples it had welcomed into the family of Eastern Christendom, the Rus warriors continued to act in a godless manner, raiding and slaughtering along the Black Sea coast as they did even after the successful conversion of Vladimir a century later.

While we know very little about these ninth-century converts and how (or whether) they propagated their religion to the next generation, there is other evidence that Christianity existed on the territory of Rus prior to the official institution of Christianity. A treaty concluded around the year 945 between the Rus and Byzantines makes reference to the different vows made by baptized and unbaptized Rus, and to a church of St Elijah/Elias in Kiev:

> In the morning, Igor' summoned the [Byzantine] envoys, and went to a hill on which there was a statue of Perun. The Russes laid down their weapons, their shields, and their gold ornaments, and Igor' and his people took oath (at least, such as were pagans), while the Christian Russes took oath in the church of St Elias, which is above the creek, in the vicinity of the Pasÿncha square and the quarter of the Khazars. This was, in fact, a parish church, since many of the Varangians were Christians.[7]

Other early chronicle references to Christians include the 'Varangian [who] had immigrated from Greece', who tries to save his son from being sacrificed to Vladimir's pantheon in the year 983 and is murdered with him by an angry crowd.[8]

According to the sources, the tenth-century conversion of Rus was a top-down affair. While it was the personal decision of the ruler that instigated the mass conversion of the people, there was, nevertheless, some prevaricating in the royal house, and at least one further failed attempt to institute Christianity before it finally took root. The *Primary Chronicle* records that the Kievan Princess Olga was received into the Christian faith in Constantinople some time between 948 and 955 and baptized by the Emperor Constantine VII himself, in a tale designed to elevate her status as a Christian ruler and to emphasize her wisdom and cunning.[9] Byzantine sources also record Olga's visit to the court: John Skylitzes' *Synopsis Historiarum* confirms that she visited Constantinople and was baptized during the reign of Constantine VII, and Constantine himself describes her reception at court in 957 or 958 in the *Book of Ceremonies*, but makes no mention of her baptism. He does, however, record that a chaplain accompanied her on this visit, indicating that she had at least been receiving instruction in Christianity, and may have already been baptized. Both sources refer to her as Helga, however, her pagan name rather than the name she took at baptism (Helena), and Obolensky has convincingly argued for a later baptism conducted during a further visit to Constantinople in 960.[10]

When and wherever she was baptized, Olga had little apparent success in spreading her new faith, failing even to convert her son Sviatoslav. She appealed to Otto I in 959 for a bishop and priests and was eventually sent Adalbert of Trier (subsequently Archbishop of Magdeburg) in 961, who returned home in 962 complaining that he had been unable to succeed in any of his missionary endeavours.[11] This may have been because by the time Adalbert arrived, Olga had been baptized by the Byzantines and had secured priests from them,[12] although Thietmar of Merseburg (975–1018) records that Adalbert 'had previously been ordained bishop for Russia but [was] expelled by the heathen',[13] which implies a rejection by pagans rather than by rival missionaries; possibly this reflects the hostility of Sviatoslav and his retainers to Adalbert's mission.

Fletcher has observed that seventh-century English kings, like the tenth-century rulers of Kievan Rus, 'did not "govern" in any sense that we should recognize today. Their primary business was predatory warfare and the exaction of tribute from those they defeated'.[14] Kings who failed to deliver the goods to their retainers would lose armed support and find themselves ousted by more powerful rivals. Sacrifices were made to ensure victory in battle, and gods who did not support the needs and goals of these martial 'courts' would not win converts.

Some hint of this may be found in Sviatoslav's reluctance to be baptized:

> Now Olga dwelt with her son Svyatoslav, and she urged him to be baptized, but he would not listen to her suggestion, though when any man wished to be baptized he was not hindered, but only mocked . . . Olga remarked oftentimes, 'My son, I have learned to know God, and am glad for it. If you know him, you too will rejoice'. But he did not heed her exhortation, answering, 'How shall I alone accept another faith? My followers will laugh at that'.[15]

Concerned that his retainers would mock a conversion to Christianity, Sviatoslav ignores his mother and pursues a resolutely pagan career. Vladimir – Olga's grandson – is equally swayed by the attitude of his retainers, and in seeking their advice and approval, he demonstrated a wisdom that the eleventh-century King Inge of Sweden lacked. Inge accepted Christianity in what appears to have been a genuine personal conversion, and refused to sacrifice to pagan gods at the bloody Uppsala shrine. His retainers promptly deposed him and elevated his pagan brother-in-law, Sven, to the throne.[16] Although Inge eventually triumphed, and established Christianity by force, it was a painful process. King Edwin of Northumbria, on the other hand, was personally convinced of the verity of Christianity (by a mix of traditional levers such as a Christian wife, a miraculous victory in battle and the persuasive preaching of a missionary priest) but insisted on consulting with his 'advisors and friends' before baptism. They agreed with his inclination, and as a result, 'King Edwin, with all the nobility and a large number of the humbler folk, accepted the Faith and were washed with the cleansing waters of Baptism' in 627.[17] Ensuring the support of one's armed retainers was a necessity for early royal converts.

In failing to convert her son, Olga is not unusual. We know of several neophyte rulers who died and left an unbaptized heir to unravel all their good work – Ethelbert of Kent, for example, who died in the early seventh century:

> The death of Ethelbert and the accession of his son Eadbald proved to be a severe setback to the recently established church, for not only did he reject the Faith of Christ, but he was also guilty of such fornication as the Apostle Paul mentions as being unheard of even among the heathen; in that he took his father's (second) wife as his own. His immorality was an incentive to those who, either out of fear or favour to the king his father, had submitted to the discipline of faith and chastity, to revert to their former uncleanness.[18]

For some time it appeared that Vladimir was as impervious to the seeds his grandmother had sown as his father. He murdered his brother, fought, raped and fornicated with legendary enthusiasm, and attempted to establish some sort of public polytheism. The chroniclers record that he set up a pantheon of wooden idols (Perun, Khors, Dazh'bog, Stribog, Simar'gl and Mokosh) in Kiev, and in Novgorod, an idol of Perun on the banks of the river Volkhov,[19] before eventually deciding to embrace Byzantine Christianity for himself and his subjects.

The Chronicle narrative has Vladimir courted by representatives of Islam, Western or Latin Christianity, Judaism and Byzantine or Greek Christianity, before seeking the advice of his nobles and elders. They counsel him to send out emissaries to the Bulgarians, North Europeans (*nemtsy*, probably Germanic), and the Greeks, to ascertain for themselves which religion would suit the Rus best. The Jews are omitted in this second round of testing faiths. The envoys naturally prefer the Christianity that Constantinople offers, together with the rich gifts and status it conveys, and Vladimir's boyars remind him that Byzantine Christianity was good enough for Princess Olga, who was no fool. Still, Vladimir waits a year, and attacks the Greek port of Chersonesos, demanding the hand in marriage of Anna, sister of the Emperors Basil II (976–1025) and Constantine VIII (976–1028), as payment to prevent further attacks on Byzantine territory. As with Olga's baptism, there are a number of theories about when and where Vladimir's baptism took place, as some sources place this in Kiev before the attack on Chersonesos.[20] One theory suggests that Vladimir was enrolled in the catechumenate in Kiev in 988, and then was baptized a year or so later, after the capture of Chersonesos, raising interesting questions about the rite of catechumenate creating a 'non-baptized Christian'.[21]

A Christian wife, concubine or mother is a common feature in conversion narratives, but Anna is not the first Christian woman in Vladimir's life. She is preceded by his brother's widow, a Greek Christian whom Vladimir raped after murdering her husband, and possibly others. She subsequently gave birth to the unfortunate Sviatopolk, whose 'father did not love him; for he had two fathers',[22] Iaropolk and Vladimir. This Greek woman is not named in the chronicle, but we learn earlier, as the chronicler recounts the internecine struggle of 976–977, that Iaropolk had a Greek wife who had been a nun, brought home by his father Sviatoslav and married to Iaropolk 'on account of the beauty of her countenance'.[23] This Sviatoslav, it may be remembered, was the obdurately pagan son of Olga, who in 971 marched against the Greeks, advancing almost to Constantinople 'fighting as he went' until, deflected by payment of tribute, he concluded a peace treaty sworn in the names of Perun and Volos, 'the god of flocks'.[24] We may assume that it was during this campaign that the Greek woman was captured. Nothing more is said about her, so we cannot tell what her status was in Vladimir's household, which was full of women of equal or higher status – his 'lawful wife' Rogneda (after she refused to marry Vladimir, calling him 'a slave's son', he murdered her family and forcibly 'married' her), two Czech women and a Bulgarian, all of whom bore sons to whom Vladimir subsequently allocated towns to govern. Whether she had any influence over Vladimir's search for a unifying faith (like the Christian women Bertha, d. *c.* 612, who was instrumental in the conversion of her husband Ethelbert of Kent, and Clotild, d. 548, wife of the Merovingian king Clovis)[25] cannot be known, but Vladimir's marriage to Princess Anna certainly precipitated his baptism. Anna refused to marry a pagan, and after some negotiation, it was agreed that she should bring priests from Constantinople to administer the sacrament of baptism before the wedding at Chersonesos.

Vladimir's conversion narrative also includes a miraculous cure of the eye disease which strikes him in Chersonesos, which is witnessed by his retainers and prompts many of them to accept baptism after him. Such public demonstrations of the superior supernatural power of the Christian faith, sometimes in competition with pagan magicians (such as the Permian shaman with whom St Stefan battles in the fourteenth century, or the druid who features in the late seventh-century *Life of St Patrick*),[26] are another common feature of European conversion narratives. Miracles were perceived as an important means of evoking Christian awe in pagan communities, and miracle cures in particular feature heavily in early Christian literature of both Western Christianity and Byzantium, perhaps reflecting the increase in infectious disease in late Antiquity and the early Middle Ages.[27]

The tale of Vladimir's investigation and rejection of Judaism, Islam and Western Christianity is probably substantially apocryphal, although some have argued for its basic plausibility.[28] His personal conversion is, however, of less importance for our discussion of the concept of *dvoeverie* than the methods he used to convert his subjects. Vladimir first has the idol of Perun publicly beaten and dragged into the river Dnieper (to punish the demon that had hoodwinked the people of Rus in the guise of Perun), and then orders a mass baptism:

> Thereafter Vladimir sent heralds throughout the whole city [Kiev] to proclaim that if any inhabitant, rich or poor, did not betake himself to the river, he would risk the Prince's displeasure. . . . he ordained that wooden churches should be built and established where pagan idols previously

stood. He thus founded the Church of St Basil on the hill where the idol
of Perun and other images had been set, and where the Prince and people
had offered their sacrifices. He began to found churches and to assign
priests throughout the cities, and to invite the people to accept baptism
in all the cities and towns. He took the children of the best families, and
sent them for instruction in book-learning. The mothers of these children
wept bitterly over them, for they were not yet strong in faith, but mourned
as for the dead.[29]

Within this historiographical narrative compiled by monks with victorious
hindsight, probably in the late eleventh or early twelfth century,[30] we may
discern a number of elements that appear in the conversion narratives of other
societies. An order to present for baptism is issued by the ruler, with threats
of punishment if not fulfilled, and there is an immediate, tangible impact on
urban society. Not only is there a mass baptism of the populace, but the children
of the nobility are removed from their families in order to be educated, to the
distress of their mothers. Although where they are removed *to* is not clear,
the reaction of their mothers suggests geographic distance or perhaps monastic isolation. We know that Tsar Boris of Bulgaria (*c.* 852–889) had subjects,
including his own son, sent to Constantinople for religious instruction, and that
he also opened monastic schools in Bulgaria,[31] and it is possible that Vladimir
did the same with the encouragement of Byzantine missionaries. Child oblation developed in tandem with monasticism, and authorities such as St John
Chrysostom enthusiastically supported the raising of children in monasteries.[32]
We also know that this practice was used by Catholic missionaries in sixteenth-
century South America as a means of rapid Christianization.[33]

    This maternal lamentation among the Rus has often been interpreted as
evidence of resistance to the new faith, the implication being that the children
are lost to the pagan faith and this is what provokes their mothers' tears. One
might equally read fear (since Vladimir had previously removed children for
sacrifice to his pantheon) or sorrow at physical separation into this passage,
since the children are taken from their families and 'given away', presumably
to monks, for intensive education. If these children were intended to become
monastic clergy rather than becoming the family protectors and progenitors
that might have been expected, this grief is all the more understandable. In
such neophyte communities, a priest in the family could not yet have been
perceived as a positive asset. We have another portrait of a mother's distress
at losing her child to the monastic life in Nestor's *Life of St Feodosii*, probably written in the mid 1080s. Feodosii's mother weeps for him and beats her
breast 'as if lamenting for a dead person' when he absconds to a monastery
seventy-odd years after Vladimir's official conversion drive. When she dis-
covers his whereabouts she begs him to return home at least until he can bury
her body, for she cannot bear to live without him. Feodosii, somewhat brutally,
persuades her that the only way she can see him is by being tonsured herself,
and entering a nearby convent.[34]

The first churchmen in Russia focused on princes, as missionaries to Germanic and other European societies did, since princes had the economic capacity to build churches, sustain clergy, and endow 'family' monasteries as an extension of their estates.[35] Rulers could institute new law codes, and ensure that new codes of behaviour were adhered to by a mixture of education, example and coercion. Tsar Boris of Bulgaria, so taken with his Christian faith that he eventually abdicated in favour of his son and retreated to a monastery, was converted and guided by the joint efforts of Pope Nicholas I and Patriarch Photius in the ninth century. The correspondence addressed to him by his mentors has revealed the sorts of issues that he was concerned with in his efforts to Christianize Bulgaria. Boris may have been involved in the process to a more than usual degree, but it seems likely that at least some of the same quandaries troubled Vladimir and his successors. We know they shared a concern over the Christian way of punishing criminals, and Boris's concern over the sacramental and ritualistic aspects of Christian life – when and how to fast, what animals one might safely eat, when one might be prohibited from taking communion, regulations surrounding marriage, copulation and childbirth for example – is reflected in later, native Russian texts such as the eleventh-century *Answers of Metropolitan Ioann II* and the twelfth-century *Questions of Kirik*, discussed in Chapter 1.

The nobility, or rather the warrior élite, commissioned manuscripts and icons, promoted the causes of individual saints (particularly saints from within their own dynasty, such as the 'martyred' princes Boris and Gleb), and through their example or on their instruction, retainers and servants were converted. They also had the armed capacity to destroy pagan shrines and suppress insurgencies, often working in tandem with the clergy. There are a number of instances recorded in the *Primary Chronicle* where princes or their retainers suppress the activities of 'magicians' (*volkhvy*), who are leading the people astray: in 1071, two itinerant *volkhvy* from Iaroslavl' are captured and killed at the instigation of the prince's tax collector in the Beloozero area, after they have 'caused the death of many women along the Volga and the Sheksna'. These *volkhvy* are not adherents of any recognizable Slavic pre-Christian paganism, however; they believe in God, but explain that Satan made man, and that they worship Antichrist who dwells 'in the abyss'.[36] Under the same year, the chronicler records that a 'magician' appeared in Novgorod and, blaspheming against the Christian faith, incited the people against their bishop: 'So the people were divided into two factions, for Gleb and his retainers took their stand beside the bishop, while the common people all followed the magician'. This working relationship between bishop and prince is in evidence from the earliest period – Vladimir entrusts Archbishop Akim of Chersonesos (*Korsun*, where Vladimir received baptism) with the task of destroying the idol of Perun in Novgorod. Akim sees to it that Perun is dragged and beaten before being flung in the waters of the river Volkhov.[37] A much later source (Adam Olearius, a German diplomat writing in the seventeenth century) records that:

At the place where the idol [Perun] once stood they built a monastery, which preserves the god's name, for it is called Perun Monastery. The idol was in the form of a man holding in his hands a flint that looked like a thunderbolt or an arrow. In honor of this god they burned oak wood day and night; if the attendant negligently allowed the flame to go out, he paid with his life. When the Novgorodians were baptized as Christians, they flung the idol into the Volkhov. It is said that the idol floated against the current; when it came to the bridge a voice said, 'Novgorodians, here is something to remember me by', and immediately a cudgel was thrown up onto the bridge. The voice of Perun was heard afterward on certain days of the year, and then the inhabitants fled in panic and beat each other with sticks so cruelly that the voevoda was hard put to pacify them. According to a reliable [sixteenth-century] witness, Baron von Herberstein, similar things occurred in his time too. Nothing of the sort is heard of any more.[38]

Vladimir's decision to establish Christian sites of worship where idols had previously stood has multiple comparable precedents. This approach might mean a violent replacement of the old with the new – like Vladimir, the fourth-century Bishop Martin of Tours destroyed pagan shrines and replaced them with churches – or it might be a matter of relocating activity, where pagan rituals were transferred to Christian sites or Christian rituals conducted at pagan sites.[39] The strategy of accommodation, allowing some elements or structures of paganism to remain within Christian communities in order to make the new faith more palatable or accessible to the converts, is most famously encapsulated in Pope Gregory the Great's letter to Abbot Mellitus on how to progress the conversion of the English, in AD 601:

When by God's help you reach our most reverend brother, Bishop Augustine, we wish you to inform him that we have been giving careful thought to the affairs of the English, and have come to the conclusion that the temples of the idols in that country should on no account be destroyed. He is to destroy the idols, but the temples themselves are to be aspersed with holy water, altars set up, and relics enclosed in them. For if these temples are well-built, they are to be purified from devil-worship, and dedicated to the service of the true God. In this way, we hope that the people, seeing that its temples are not destroyed, may abandon idolatry and resort to these places as before, and may come to know and adore the true God. And since they have the custom of sacrificing many oxen to devils, let some other solemnity be substituted in its place, such as a day of Dedication or the Festivals of the holy martyrs whose relics are enshrined there. On such occasions they might well construct shelters of boughs for themselves around the churches that were once temples, and celebrate the solemnity with devout feasting. They are no longer to sacrifice beasts to the Devil, but they may kill them for food to the praise of God, and give thanks to the Giver of all gifts for His bounty.[40]

Here Gregory offers God's guidance of the Israelites from idolatry to monotheism as a precedent, and likens the process of converting 'obstinate minds' to climbing a mountain, step by step. Gregory's letters reveal that this was not a standard policy for missionaries, but rather one that he had mused over and decided was most appropriate in this instance.[41] In the *Primary Chronicle*, Vladimir is depicted as having made a similar decision. Although there is no mention of temples in the Chronicle account of the conversion,[42] the sacred sites on which the idols stood are customized for Christianity, while the idols themselves are destroyed:

> When the Prince arrived at his capital, he directed that the idols should be overthrown, and that some should be cut to pieces and others burned with fire. He thus ordered that Perun should be bound to a horse's tail and dragged down Borichev [path] to the stream. He appointed twelve men to beat the idol with sticks, not because he thought the wood was sensitive, but to affront the demon who had deceived man in this guise, that he might receive chastisement at the hands of men . . . While the idol was being dragged along the stream to the Dnieper, the unbelievers wept over it, for they had not yet received holy baptism.[43]

> [Vladimir] ordained that wooden churches should be built and established where pagan idols had previously stood. He thus founded the Church of St. Basil on the hill where the idol of Perun and the other images had been set, and where the Prince and the people had offered their sacrifices.[44]

The chronicle makes it clear that for Vladimir and his community, Perun continues to exists as a spiritual entity, but is now perceived as deserving dishonour rather than as worthy of veneration, as befits a *daimon*, a pagan god. Although this treatment of the idol has been interpreted as reflecting Vladimir's pagan mindset,[45] the belief that pagan worship was the prompting of demons has many Christian precedents, most obviously Biblical (Deuteronomy 32:16–17; Psalm 106:36–38; I Corinthians 10:19–21).[46] Nor was it an uncommon missionary strategy: the sixth-century Bishop of Braga in Spain, Martin, began his *De Correctione Rusticorum* with an explanation of how demons live in natural elements such as rivers and woods, and deceive men into worshipping them. A Saxon baptismal creed extant in an early ninth-century manuscript declares 'I forsake all the works and words of the devils, Thunaer and Woden and Saxnote and all the fiends that are their companions'.[47] Some historians have perceived in this strategy a key reason for the longevity of pagan ideas; turning gods into demons was '[t]he most common way in which pagan ideas survived the coming of Christianity to Saxony'.[48] Lotman and Uspenskii have also argued that pagan gods continued to exist in Russian culture in one of two ways – either 'united with saints who replaced them functionally' or as 'identified with demons'.[49] In the twelfth-century Russian apocryphal text *The Descent of the Virgin into Hell*, the first sinners visited by Mary are those who made gods out of the devils Troyan, Khors, Veles, and Perun, and they worshiped [*sic*] these evil devils. And even now they are possessed by evil darkness, and therefore they suffer such torments.[50]

There is no hint of backsliding in the chronicler's account of Vladimir's conversion: he demonstrates none of the tendency to 'hedge his bets' displayed by Redwald of East Anglia, for example, of whom Bede writes:

> like the ancient Samaritans, he tried to serve both Christ and the ancient gods, and he had in the same temple an altar for the holy sacrifice of Christ side by side with an altar on which victims were offered to devils.[51]

Here Bede, like the Christlover, uses an Old Testament example of inconstancy (the Samaritans who both fear the Lord and worship idols, II Kings 17:33, 41) to show up the failings of the East Anglian ruler. Thietmar of Merseburg also tells of a Hungarian noble Deuvix,

> who was very cruel and killed many people because of his quick temper. When he became a Christian, however, he turned his rage against his reluctant subjects, in order to strengthen this faith. Thus, glowing with zeal for God, he washed away his old crimes. He sacrificed both to the omnipotent God and to various false gods. When reproached by his priest for doing so, however, he maintained that the practice had brought him both wealth and great power.[52]

Redwald and Deuvix seem to be guilty of precisely that 'mechanical mixing' of faiths identified by Azbukin as the first stage of *dvoeverie*, in which the neophyte fulfils his Christian duties while continuing to worship his pagan idols, either overtly or covertly, whereas Vladimir, on the contrary, is promoted by his chroniclers as a superb example of a converted king. So Christian is he, that less than a decade after his baptism the bishops have cause to complain to him about the proliferation of crime in his realm. Fearing that to punish criminals would entail sinning, Vladimir has inadvertently allowed them to prosper. The text implies that the types of punishment he was failing to mete out were corporal and capital, and that he had instituted a system of fines in place of these less merciful options. Vladimir's response to being told that he is 'appointed by God for the chastisement of malefaction and for the practice of mercy towards the righteous' is to abolish the *wergild* and 'set out to punish the brigands'. He is persuaded subsequently that the *wergild* is a useful source of revenue, and reinstates it. The text is confusing here, as the (pre-Conversion) 911 treaty with the Byzantines makes clear that murder was punishable by death, but robbery and assault were subject to financial compensation 'according to Rus' law'.[53] The later *Russkaia pravda*, ostensibly composed in the eleventh century, allows male family members to avenge the murder of their male relatives by killing the murderer (if the victim is one of the Prince's men, a Rus or Slav of free status), and confirms a complicated table of financial compensation and fines for the murder of those who have no-one to avenge them, or who are too lowly to merit revenge – slaves, women, peasants.[54] The expanded redaction indicates the desire of early Rus rulers to 'abolish vengeance justice' and institute a payment system instead.[55]

Vladimir's neophyte leniency is an endearing and unusual feature of conversion narratives, but he was not alone in feeling that Christian justice entailed something different from the pagan justice he was used to administering. Again, the correspondence of Tsar Boris of Bulgaria reveals that weighing up Christian mercy against authoritative punishment was a particularly troubling area for the neophyte ruler.[56]

A different picture of Vladimir is suggested by the German chronicler Thietmar of Merseburg, who records that

> Vladimir accepted the holy Christian faith which, however, he did not adorn with Christian deeds. He was an unrestrained fornicator and cruelly assailed the feckless Greeks with acts of violence.[57]

Worse, Vladimir apparently ill-treats his son Sviatopolk, his daughter-in-law (daughter of the Polish ruler Boleslaw) and her confessor Bishop Reinbern of Kolberg, who accompanies her and dies in the solitary confinement imposed by Vladimir, 'that unjust man', around 1015. Thietmar tells us that this bishop worked hard to proselytize in his new community:

> He destroyed the shrines of idols by burning them and purified a lake inhabited by demons, by throwing into it four rocks anointed with holy oil and sprinkling it with consecrated water.[58]

A more gradual process of diffusion continued missionary work in Rus, once the ruling household had been persuaded to support Christianity officially. A Russian clerical hierarchy was established, although it was heavily reliant on the importation of Greek metropolitans for several centuries, and a programme of church building spread across the urban centres of Rus. Vladimir's son Iaroslav – after a murderous struggle with his siblings – took over where his father left off, founding several churches, the Monastery of St George and the Convent of St Irene in Kiev.

> During his reign, the Christian faith was fruitful and multiplied, while the number of monks increased, and new monasteries came into being. Yaroslav loved religious establishments and was devoted to priests, especially to monks.[59]

Monasticism played a crucial role in the Christianization of Rus as it did in the dissemination of Christianity in other northern European cultures, notably those of the Irish and the Franks. Rus, like Ireland, was not 'Romanized', and received the civilization of Byzantium with Christianity as Ireland received the culture of Latin Christendom. It has been pointed out that the Christianization of Ireland as a pastoral, non-urban society was conducted by monasteries rather than by bishops, who functioned in Ireland as they did elsewhere but who had less spiritual weight than the abbots of the flourishing monasteries that colonized the geographic wilds. Monasteries were founded by clan groups, who would populate the hierarchy of the monastery, sustain it with gifts and in return, receive prayers and Christian burial within the grounds.[60] The situation was similar in Rus – princely families founded and sustained monasteries, where their relatives might become superiors and where they were buried and prayed for by the inhabitants.[61]

While statistics, particularly ones from the dim and distant past, should be regarded with suspicion, recent calculations suggest that nineteen monasteries and convents were founded in the eleventh century, and a further forty in the twelfth century. The majority of the eleventh-century foundations were in Kiev, although Tmutarakan, Chernigov, Pereiaslavl', Murom, Suzdal', Vladimir-Volynsk and Rostov have also been proposed as early seedbeds of monasticism. In the twelfth century, fourteen foundations in Novgorod are recorded, and Polotsk, Galich, Vladimir, Turov, Smolensk and Vyshgorod join the list of provincial towns with their own monasteries and convents.[62] It is even harder to ascertain how large these religious houses might have been. We know most about the Kievan Caves Monastery – which apparently speedily gained a hundred monks after its creation in the mid-eleventh century – but precious little about less famous establishments.[63]

Monasteries were not simply refuges within which new Christians might save their souls – they were dispensers of the sacraments, educators, and most importantly, generators of books. Though substantial doubt has been cast on the chronicler's assurance that Iaroslav had many books translated from Greek into Slavic, there seems less reason to doubt that he initiated or promoted the copying of manuscripts and their distribution to churches. The chronicler describes Iaroslav's activities in this sphere under an entry for the year 1037, and the *Ostromir Gospel*, the oldest surviving manuscript that can be accurately dated, was completed in 1057. Two further collections of edificatory prose survive from the 1070s, and Simon Franklin has observed a significant growth in written culture from the 1050s,[64] no doubt prompted and succoured by the spread of Christianity within the towns.

Finally, it should be remembered in dating the conversion period that the spread of Christianity followed the spread of the Christian Russian state. As new geographic areas and peoples were assimilated, conquered or colonized into Russian territory, a process which continued into the nineteenth century, new souls were won for the Russian Orthodox Church. The Russian conquest of Kazan in 1552 brought the pagan Mari, Chuvash and Urdmurts of the Volga-Kama region (as well as significant numbers of Muslim Tatars and Bashkirs) within reach of Ivan IV's government and Russian Orthodox mission. Khordakovsky has pointed out that before the sixteenth century, mission was limited and sporadic, the fruit of the personal inspiration and labour of individuals (generally monks) like St Stefan of Perm, but from then on it became systematized, 'one of the most important tools of Russia's imperial policies', and 'conducted more in a manner of Charlemagne than that of the contemporary New World'.[65] Introduced to Christianity by missionaries ignorant of local culture and language, who adopted the stick and carrot approach in tandem with the State, it is small wonder that backsliding among these non-Russian converts was a continual problem.

> На самом же деле один из крещеных снова возвращались в свою прежнюю веру – ламайскую или шаманскую; а другие делали из всех этих вер самое странное и нелепое смешение: . . . Двоеверие держалось не у одних кочевников, а почти и повсеместно в моей пастве . . .[66]

> In fact some of the baptized went back to their former belief – in lamaism or shamanism; while others made out of all these beliefs the most strange and absurd mixture: . . . Double-belief was maintained not only among the nomads, but almost everywhere among my flock . . .

This Orthodox missionary, apparently based on Archbishop Nil of Irkutsk (1799–1874), is bemoaning the laxity of nineteenth-century Siberian converts in a tale by Nikolai Leskov.[67] While he no doubt echoes the sentiments of earlier pastors to their newly converted flocks, the complaints of priests, bureaucrats and observers of missions to new subject peoples before the nineteenth century did not use the terminology of double-belief. Non-Russians who continued to practice animism were regarded as Orthodox by virtue of their baptism, and as Khordakovsky observes, there is little discussion of the 'newly-enlightened' Christians' perception of their adopted faith, or of any new unorthodox forms of worship and belief which they may have developed, before the nineteenth century. This was not a matter of concern – the need to create a single political and religious national identity was the primary goal, and the degree of individual conversions of far less interest.[68] We may assume that for the rulers of Rus, similar concerns prevailed, and in this they surely differed little from their Western European counterparts.

How successful was the Christianization of Russia in comparison with Western Europe? Clerical protests in the Middle Ages

For all the praise lavished on Vladimir, 'the new Constantine of mighty Rome, who baptized himself and his subjects',[69] the centuries following Christianity's establishment as a 'national' faith were barbaric and rapacious. If this violence is evidence of the imperviousness of society to Christian values, it is certainly not exclusive to Russia (nor, indeed, to the medieval period). Post-conversion, the Frankish king Clovis I continued to split the heads of his relatives with an axe in the same way that the Rus princes descended into internecine strife, and brought upon themselves (in the words of the chroniclers) the punishments of God in the form of pagan invasions.[70] In a reflection that might equally well apply to the warring princes of Rus, Cusack observes that:

> Gregory of Tours presented a lurid vision of Frankish society, where adultery, murder and other violences were daily occurrences . . . The Frankish aristocracy was a Germanic warrior aristocracy which had converted to Christianity, but had not changed its mode of living at all.[71]

It is, as we discussed in the introduction to this book, pointless to speculate on how Christian a medieval society was from a modern, post-Vatican II perspective. If we want to ascertain whether or not a society was successfully Christianized, we are again predominantly reliant on textual evidence written by clerics at the time. While archaeological evidence is sometimes used by historians to demonstrate how far Christian practice had spread, or how well entrenched it was, material evidence is harder to interpret than written sources. The proliferation of stone churches in urban areas was such that by the end of the twelfth century, 'the lands of the Rus bristled with little Kievs',[72] a fair indication that Christianity was woven into the normal fabric of life even in smaller towns. The continuation of mound burials up to the fifteenth and even sixteenth centuries in some areas of Russia, plus the absence of rural churches, has been considered evidence of prolonged paganism among the peasantry.[73] Other historians have declared that while burials from the eleventh and twelfth centuries show a period of transition from paganism to Christianity, from the mid-twelfth century only Christian burials are found, marking that Rus is a 'fully christianized land'.[74] However, material objects do not necessarily reflect the beliefs of the owner: grave goods bearing Christian emblems may have simply been fashionable; tumuli may have simply indicated status.[75] Conclusions drawn from grave goods and burial practices should be treated with caution – what religious significance was attached to the inclusion of victuals and beloved or useful objects we cannot know, and the human desire to incorporate items of 'comfort' to the dead in burial and bereavement rituals is not a clear indicator of pagan faith. If it were, then the bereaved of the twenty-first century should be supposed as pagan as their eleventh- and twelfth-century predecessors.[76]

Penitentials, regulatory or canonical literature (like the *Stoglav* and the *Answers of Metropolitan Ioann II*), sermons and epistles all record to some extent the concerns of those responsible for spreading, monitoring and maintaining Christian standards among the laity. What issues bothered the hierarchy and the clergy 'on the ground'? Did they perceive themselves to be wrestling with apostasy or latent paganism? If so, how did they describe this struggle?

We have already recognized that while the clerical élite was well placed to decide what constituted correct Christianity, and to define Orthodoxy at any given time or place, we cannot necessarily rely on their definitions of 'pagan', since in some instances their use of the term may have no connection with pre-Christian belief systems, but rather be a damning term of abuse levelled at non-Christian, anti-Christian or heterodox behaviours. Various scholars have highlighted the fluctuating definitions of and hazy boundaries between 'paganism', 'superstition' and 'magic' in both medieval texts and historiography.[77] We have difficult qualitative judgements to make for each text, since context is all. The paganism identified by a missionary bishop working within local communities a generation or two after the acceptance of Christianity by the ruling élite will be different from the paganism castigated in a sermon preached two hundred years after the Christianization of a people or region. That said, the chronological and geographical transmission of such texts means that often material composed in a conversion period may be completely or partially reproduced in very different circumstances. This particular minefield is well stocked: deciding whether material is simply a result of the haphazard reproduction of earlier texts, reproduced deliberately as reflecting a common concern, or an original addition based on local circumstances, is a delicate process. Bernadette Filotas has produced an excellent survey of Western European pastoral literature from *c.* 500 to *c.* 1000 (including penitentials, sermons and letters, and legislative texts such as *capitula*) which attempts to do just that, and this chapter has greatly benefited from her labours.[78]

Even the most cursory of comparisons reveals that the complaints of Russian clerics were very similar to their Western counterparts, although why this might be the case is a less straightforward question to answer. Clerics, as Peter Burke has observed, have been condemning popular culture in much the same terms for centuries.[79] To a great degree this is the result of a shared textual heritage: Biblical condemnations of idolatry, drunkenness, debauchery and other unseemly human behaviours offer a ready and unchallengeable precedent; the canons of the ecumenical Church Councils and the sermons of the early Church Fathers also offer honourable and trustworthy models for the missionary or reformer at home or abroad. Lebbe has pointed out that a survey of medieval Western attitudes from different times and places will offer a 'highly coherent' picture. The clergy received the same sort of training, used the same patristic, liturgical and theological texts, and gloried in borrowed themes and phrases: 'Medieval man thought in clichés and that's all there is to it'.[80]

The scope of this book does not permit a close comparison of the canon of available texts in Rus and Muscovy with that of the medieval West, but it should first be pointed out that the Latin Fathers (including the hugely influential Augustine of Hippo)[81] were generally unknown in medieval Russia.[82] Furthermore, there is no evidence that writings which proved so influential in the Western literature of Christianization (the sermons of Caesarius of Arles, for example, or Sulpicius Severus' *Life of St Martin of Tours*), ever reached medieval Russia. Nevertheless, there are clearly shared themes and motifs to be highlighted, and where possible, an attempt has been made to suggest possible reasons for this commonality.

The earliest condemnations of popular festivals and amusements by Augustine, Tertullian and other Church Fathers were well known to the later sermonizers in the West. Copying sermons of predecessors and applying them to different regions in different times was seen as a perfectly adequate way of dealing with problems; pagan gods might have different names and faces, but the same force was behind them all – Satan and his demons. There was, therefore, nothing anachronistic about applying the same remedies across the ages, wherever a new battle with paganism was to be fought, as Peter Brown has pointed out. As Gregory of Nazianzus' writings on Greek paganism were reworked for the neophyte Slavs, Caesarius of Arles copied from St Augustine, and was copied himself three centuries later by those working in the neophyte regions of central Germany. It mattered little whether Provençal and Germanic paganism differed in form or content; missionaries perceived the same evil root to the problem.[83] As Daniel Reff has explored, the narratives of these 'old' conversions were also reused by missionaries of the new world, for similar reasons.[84]

Caesarius, Bishop of Arles from 502 until his death in 542, was a reformer and prolific sermonizer who wanted his congregations to follow Christianity with dedication and enthusiasm.[85] He also, according to the *Life of Caesarius*, sent sermons out to clerics in 'Frankish lands, Gaul, Italy, Spain and other provinces'.[86] Christianity reached Arles around the middle of the third century, but the cathedral and Christian cemeteries were probably not built before the fourth century and it is not until the middle of the fifth century that the majority of citizens participated in Christian festivals. The countryside around the city was Christianized even more slowly.[87] Caesarius seems to have had little confidence in some of his flock, and bemoaned the now familiar problem of Christians who decided to 'hedge their bets' for some reason:

> But, although we rejoice at this, dearly beloved, to see you hasten faithfully to church, we are sad and grieve because we know that some of you rather frequently go over to the ancient worship of idols like the pagans who have no God or grace of baptism. We have heard that some of you make vows to trees, pray to fountains, and practice diabolical augury . . . What is worse, there are some unfortunate and miserable people who not only are unwilling to destroy the shrines of the pagans but even are not afraid or ashamed to build up those which have been destroyed . . . Why then did these miserable people come to church? Why did they receive the sacrament of baptism – if afterwards they intended to return to the profanation of idols?[88]

Caesarius' sermons raise other themes that remind us of the *Christlover* and later proscriptive Russian texts. He condemned the toasting of angels and saints at drunken parties (sermon 47.5) and the celebration of holy festivals with feasting, drinking, dancing and singing (sermons 188.5, 201.1; 13.4; 55.2) as behaviour one might expect of pagans rather than Christians. As Klingshirn has pointed out, however, this is evidence of 'alternative' piety rather than paganism.[89] He also chastized parishioners who ate at sacrificial feasts out of gluttony, reminding them of the Biblical injunction 'You cannot drink the cup of the Lord and the cup of devils'.[90] Caesarius also singled out the Kalends celebrations at New Year – widespread across Europe – for rebuke, since they involved obscene dancing and singing, cross-dressing and heavy drinking, citing again I Corinthians 10:21 to convince those who sympathized with the revellers and did not seek to correct them.[91]

A generation later than Caesarius, what Gregory, Bishop of Tours (573–594) was confronting in Gaul

> was not tenacious paganism, surviving unchanged in a peasant world which was untouched by the Catholicism of the cities. What he found, rather, was a world characterized, in city and country alike, by fertile religious experimentation. Christian rituals and Christian holy figures were adapted by local religious experts to serve the needs of persons who would have considered themselves to be good Christians.[92]

It would appear that, in Brown's estimation, we have reached a stage in which (to use Azbukin's phrasing) sincere Christians are nevertheless maintaining a pagan world-view 'clothed in the garb of Christian externals', and new forms of worship are developing out of this mixture of the old and the new.[93]

It is not only the uneducated lay people, but monks and clerics who are accused of these faults. Caesarius complained about priests and monks who distributed healing or apotropaic charms,[94] and as we have seen, Russian clergy too were often implicated in magical and unorthodox behaviours (such as the placing of soap, salt and cauls on the altar) in medieval texts. Even bishops in sixth-century Spain were reprimanded for chanting the Alleluia at the January festival of Kalends, thereby blessing the 'pagan' fun.[95]

Calendrical celebrations such as Lupercalia and the Kalends, which interrupted Christian time, plus ostensibly secular pastimes such as the races, games and theatre formerly associated with pagan Roman culture, were particularly difficult to deal with. Clerical responses to them varied over time and place, but the Kalends festival was a particular bugbear for clerics in both the Western and Eastern Churches,[96] and highlights one of the problematic issues faced by the Church – how far traditions which predated Christianity but which were perceived as 'civil', or had lost any religious component, could be permitted. A bishops' council at Tours in 567 declared that anyone celebrating the Kalends 'cannot be said to be a genuine Christian in so much as he clings to bits of paganism'.[97] While Caesarius stressed the pagan nature of this feast, most of his complaints were about immorality (cross-dressing, lewd dancing and singing, drunkenness), lack of charity (not sharing a New Year fire), and the sympathetic magic expected by the peasantry who loaded their tables with food on New Year's eve, in the hope that this would ensure plenty throughout the year (sermon 192.3).[98] In twelfth-century Byzantium, Balsamon notes that the Kalends was celebrated 'even until the present day', while discussing canon 62 of the seventh-century Council of Trullo which castigated the celebration of the Kalends (among other festivals discussed later).

Riotous behaviour on the eve of Christian festivals was apparently widespread. As we explored in Chapter 1, unorthodox celebrations on the eves of Christmas, Epiphany and St John's feast are often mentioned in Russian texts, and further references to inappropriate behaviour on Trinity Sunday, Radunitsa (a festival to commemorate the dead celebrated on Tuesday of Saint Thomas's Week, the second week after Easter), Maundy Thursday and the first Monday of Peter's Fast are to be found in the sixteenth-century *Stoglav*. Less specific complaints that on feast days, even during Easter season, people prefer to celebrate with dancing and drinking rather than by going to church are found in the earliest chronicles and in the thirteenth-century *Pravilo* of Metropolitan Kirill II, and similar complaints are easily identified in Western sources.

In a manner reminiscent of the *Stoglav*, *The Precept of King Childebert I* (France, *c.* 533–58) declares;

> Complaint is made to Us that many sacrileges are performed among the people. From this God is injured and the people through sin go down to death, passing nights in drunkenness and scurrilous songs, even on the holy days of Easter, of the Lord's Nativity, and the other [Church] feasts, or dancing on the Lord's day through towns.[99]

This could be interpreted as general 'carnival behaviour', especially on the eve of extended fast periods, but the midsummer and midwinter festivities may have included magical and divinatory practices that made them doubly irritating for reforming clerics. One early sixteenth-century Russian clerical source complains about the hunt for magical herbs on and before the feast of St John the Baptist, and instructions for the gathering of certain herbs on this feast were even issued in the name of Tsar Aleksei Mikhailovich (1629–1676).[100] Midsummer fires seem to have been widespread across medieval Europe,[101] and Hutton cites a monk of Winchcombe Abbey, Gloucestershire, who preached in the fifteenth century against the 'vain, stupid, profane' midsummer games which involved drinking and the lighting of fires, including wheels of fire which were rolled down hills.[102] The monk speculates that 'the wheel which they roll, which, with the rubbish [including bones] they burn, they have from the pagans'.[103] A thirteenth-century French bishop, William of Auvergne, suggests that although some think this is 'done in memory of the burning of blessed John the Baptist', only 'youths and silly people' participate, and veneration is not their intention. Rather, this behaviour is 'the remnants of idolatry'.[104] The Russian *Stoglav* does not mention fires but does identify bathing in rivers at dawn,[105] activities recorded by earlier Western sources such as Caesarius of Arles, who – as did Augustine – condemned bathing in springs and rivers on the eve or feast of John the Baptist. There is clearly potential Christian symbolism in bathing in rivers on the day one celebrates the man who baptized Jesus in a river, but we can only guess at the intentions of these bathers:

> We desire to celebrate joyfully the nativity of St. John the Baptist, just as we do the other feasts that come around. Since that illustrious feast is

coming soon, let us all observe perfect chastity and honesty the several days preceeding, in order that we may be able to celebrate that feast with joy and may merit to approach the Lord with a clear and upright conscience. I beseech and adjure you by the dreadful day of judgement to admonish your neighbours, your household, and all who are related to you, and to reprove them severely out of zeal for God. Let no one on the Feast of St. John dare to bathe in the fountains or marshes or rivers either at night or early in the morning; that wretched custom still remains from pagan observances. Although not only souls, but so much the worse, bodies very frequently die as a result of that impious bathing . . . We likewise admonish you, brethren, not to allow your household to sing shameful, dissolute songs, which are opposed to chastity and upright living. Indeed, it is not right for a mouth into which the Eucharistic Christ enters, to sing dissolute love songs.[106]

Since Caesarius is anxious to point out that this is a custom that 'remains from pagan practice', one can only assume that the practitioners needed to be told this – in other words, that they did not perceive these customs as pagan. Another curious sermon by the tenth-century Italian bishop Atto of Vercelli includes references to magical and divinatory practices, and to a baptism of plants which may reflect the mysterious 'splashing' (if such it is) of the Russian texts:

Certain little trollops [*meritriculae*] abandon the churches and the divine offices; they pass the whole night any which where, in the streets and crossroads, by springs and in the countryside; they form round dances, compose songs, draw lots and pretend that people's prospects are to be predicted from things of this sort. Their superstition has given rise to madness to such a point, that they presume to baptize grass and leafy boughs, and hence they dare to call [the turf and trees?] godparents [co-parents? – *compatres vel commatres*]. And for a long while after-wards, they strive to keep them hung up in their houses, as though for the sake of piety.[107]

This 'baptizing' of trees and grass is clearly unorthodox behaviour rather than any pagan practice, and it seems that Christians in twelfth-century Byzantium similarly 'baptized' their houses. Balsamon recorded rites on the eve of the feast of St John the Baptist – prohibited by Patriarch Michael III (1170–1176) – that involved water, fire and divination. Men and women would feast, dance and shout frenziedly, and conduct divinatory rites by pouring seawater into a brass vessel and fishing various objects out. During the night the revellers would burn haystacks and leap over them, and in the morning they would collect seawater and pour it on their houses.[108]

In addition to sermons focusing on unorthodox behaviours, penitentials are another source addressing practices that clerics were keen to stamp out. However, although they offer an interesting insight into the sort of questions clerics were supposed to ask their penitents, these texts are perhaps even more heavily interdependent than sermons. Russian penitential manuscripts dating from the fourteenth, fifteenth and sixteenth century display a great deal of interest in sexual behaviour, and questions about adultery, sodomy, rape, masturbation and oral sex, fornication within prohibited degrees of consanguinity or at prohibited times, or with animals, slaves or monastics, predominate in texts aimed at lay penitents. Other sins of violence, anger, oath-breaking, robbery, slander, blasphemy, drunkenness, and inappropriate behaviour in church, on feast days or during fasts do feature, but less prominently. Eve Levin has observed that while such manuscripts show a great deal of editing to suit local conditions, the predominance of sexual sins was ubiquitous and indicates that sexual behaviour was perceived above all as the indicator of Christian righteousness, rather than 'faith, good intentions, or ethical conduct'.[109]

One has to read the Russian penitentials fairly closely for sins that might be interpreted as evidence of paganism, although various questions reveal facets of unorthodox belief and practice. One frequent question, addressed to clerics as well as to laity, is whether penitents go to *volkhvy* or have *volkhvy* or witches (*vedmy*) visit them.[110] Other questions include whether they believe in dreams and meetings, or lie on the ground as if 'playing on a woman',[111] play games or sing *skomorokhi* songs.[112] In texts composed specifically for female penitents, clerics are advised to ask whether they have practiced sorcery with 'impious women' (*baby bogomerskye*), if they have prayed to 'idols' or 'to *vily*', sometimes even '[have you] prayed to *vily*, *rod*, *rozhanitsy*, and Perun and Khors and to Mokosh [have you] drunk and eaten?' or 'have you prayed to demons, or drunk a cup to them?' In one seventeenth-century penitential men are also asked if they have prayed, eaten or drunk to idols.[113] Women are also asked if they have worked sorcery by means of rubbing themselves with oil, milk and/or honey and feeding it to someone;[114] or drunk fertility potions;[115] whether they have bowed down to the sun, moon, stars or the dawn, or have heated porridge for the birth of Christ;[116] or drunk, danced and sung 'devilish songs'.[117] Curious as this mix of magic ritual and revelry may be, it offers little hard evidence of active or latent paganism. Numerous historians have speculated on whether magic was (or was sometimes) a form of pagan survival,[118] but in this instance it is clear that only the questions about idol worship, bowing to celestial bodies and lying on the earth indicate religious or quasi-religious rituals of a possibly pre-Christian nature, and the latter two may just as easily be interpreted as parts of magical spells. Again, the question of provenance arises, especially where the idols are listed as *vily*, *rod*, *rozhanitsy*, Perun, Khors and Mokosh, as they are only in penitentials dating from the sixteenth to the seventeenth century. As Korogodina points out, the *Sermon of St Gregory*, which declares that Perun, Khors, Mokosh, *vily*, *rod* and *rozhanitsy* are prayed to 'even today on the outskirts', was widely circulated in the sixteenth century,[119] and the similarity indicates the literary nature of this paganism. It is clear also that some copyists could not make sense of these names – changing '*vila*' to '*delo*' and 'Khors' to '*krona*'.[120]

Similar protests against magic and carousing are found in penitentials such as the unusual *Corrector* of Burchard of Worms (d. 1025), which displays an originality lacking in many such texts. Burchard, like Serapion of Vladimir, objects as much to *belief* in magical ritual and 'vulgar folly' as to the related practices. Burchard also asks about women who smear themselves in honey for maleficent magical purposes, explaining that they roll in grain and then bake loaves from the wheat collected on their bodies and feed them to their unfortunate husbands.[121] Sorcery, divination, believing in auguries or omens based on birds and dreams are also the subject of questioning from the seventh-century English *Penitential of Theodore* to the eleventh-century German *Corrector* of Burchard, but again, other sins dominated.

Canons of the 'First Synod of St Patrick', which probably dates from the first half of the sixth century, indicate a world in which paganism and Christianity are coexisting, a century or so after the small Christian community of Irish were sent their first bishop, Palladius, precursor of the more famous 'apostle of the Irish', St Patrick. Canon 8 makes reference to a cleric standing surety for a pagan (*gentili*),[122] canon 13 stresses that alms offered to the Church by a pagan are not permissible, and canon 14 punishes Christians who have sworn before a soothsayer 'in the manner of pagans'. Metropolitan Ioann II was addressing similar concerns a century after the official baptism of Rus. Although the pagans are mostly seen as outside of the community (he answers a question about the cleanliness of a priest's wife returned after capture by a foreign tribe, for example), Ioann also addresses questions about those who voluntarily trade with pagans (response 28) or who inadvertently eat with them (response 19).[123] He also describes those who sacrifice to 'devils and bogs and wells [or shafts]' as 'foreign to our faith' (response 15), along with those who do not communicate once a year or who abandon their wives.

The majority of Metropolitan Ioann's responses, however, address less exotic issues. The morality of the laity clearly preoccupies the Metropolitan and his interlocutors, with bigamy, remarriage, adultery and fornication predominating: in addition to response 15, response 30 castigates those taking a wife with dancing and singing rather than a church service, and response 12 reiterates the permissibility of remarriage for those whose spouses have taken monastic vows. Liturgical and hierarchical issues also feature: response 14, for example, addresses whether a priest may officiate while wearing leather, and response 1 permits the baptism of a baby too weak to feed. Ritual impurity is also of concern (response 2 grants that a ritually unclean mother can nurse her baby if a wet-nurse is not available, and response 3 discusses the eating of carrion) as, understandably, is correct Christian behaviour for laity and clerics in particular: response 22, for example, forbids the selling of Christian slaves, while responses 16 and 28 discuss the deportment of clerics and monastics invited to secular feasts.

It would be easy to overstate the case for a prolonged battle with paganism – or indeed unorthodox beliefs and rituals – across the whole of Europe, since we are focusing on those texts which do mention it, rather than the sum of

Christian literature as a whole. Filotas has set this problem in context, suggesting that:

> Of the over five hundred and fifty canons enacted by Gallican Councils
> between 511 and 695, barely over thirty, about six percent, concern what
> might be called paganism and superstition. Less than ten percent of the
> three hundred and thirteen clauses of the influential *Penitential* of Theodore
> deal with this topic. The overwhelming majority of medieval sermons
> never touched it at all.[124]

Hen has pointed out that of Caesarius' prolific body of sermons, 'only seven are
dedicated to the subjects of paganism and superstitions' (sermons 50, 51, 52, 54,
192, 193, 53.1) while six more (1, 13, 14, 19, 33, 184) address these issues 'in
passing'.[125] He further argues that Caesarius' sermons, far from demonstrating
the unchristian nature of Gallic society, offer scant support for the thesis that
paganism coexisted with Christianity in Merovingian Gaul.[126] In both Russia and
Western Europe, medieval clerics were more concerned with pastoral matters
and ecclesiastical discipline than with fighting obdurate paganism.

The question remains as to why such complaints as there are about popular
unorthodoxy are so similar, despite chronological and geographical distances.
While some commentators suggest that ecclesiastical texts such as Caesarius'
sermons were simply transcribed and circulated regardless of the current social
and cultural conditions, and are therefore worthless as indicators of the religious milieu, others interpret these repetitions as evidence that certain unorthodox practices were particularly widely established and persistent. Gurevich,
for example, suggests that while the medieval cleric's preference for textual
antecedents should make historians wary of ecclesiastical texts as sources for
popular culture, 'one must be prepared to see the expression of the actual
needs which dictated appealing to ancient authorities . . . Repetitions in them
should rather be regarded as evidence of the stability of the vital phenomena
which they interpret'.[127]

The matter is slightly more complex, however, as the example of 'devilish'
or 'pagan games' illustrates. The earliest condemnations of pagan games in
canonical and polemical texts refer to the Roman circuses and performances
which had gradually changed from a civic function attended by both Christians
and pagans in late Antiquity and tolerated by the younger and more moderate
Augustine, to a profane temptation and a source of confusion for Christian and
pagan alike, with the increasing asceticism that Caesarius represents. When
repeated in Russia in the sixteenth century, the condemnations of 'games' may
be equally (and simultaneously) replications of fourth-century canonical texts
castigating phenomena for which there were no parallels in sixteenth-century
Muscovy, and an indication of clerical disapproval of the traditional recreations
of Russian popular culture, perceived through the prism of Byzantine Christian
heritage. What is certain is that such condemnations were neither original nor
unique, for Russia inherited a textual tradition of condemnation of the profane,
the frivolous, the 'immoral'.

It is increasingly suggested that the conversion or Christianization of Europe was a long process. The second edition of Hillgarth's *The Conversion of Western Europe, 350–750*, published fifteen years after the original, was retitled *Christianity and Paganism, 350–750: The Conversion of Western Europe*, to acknowledge the fact that 'Western Europe, Britain and Ireland were very imperfectly Christian in 750'.[128] The editor of *The Pagan Middle Ages* goes one step further, declaring that 'Paganism's lengthy resistance – in all manner of ways – to the Christian takeover justifies the title of this book'.[129] Some historians have suggested that the guardians of Eastern Christianity were *less* troubled by paganism than Western Christendom. Discussing the fifth and sixth century, Brown declares that:

> Eastern Christians were undisturbed by the existence in their midst of considerable pockets of paganism. The fact that they lived in a successful and stridently Christian empire was enough to persuade them that theirs was a basically Christian world.[130]

As evidence of this, Brown offers Greek sources such as Theodoret of Cyrrhus' fifth-century *Cure for Hellenic [Pagan] Maladies*, which triumphantly declares a 'bright new age' where the new faith has replaced the old in a manner reminiscent of Ilarion's *Sermon on Law and Grace*.[131]

While Brown is not suggesting that the process of Christianization was any faster or more effective in the East, he identifies a different, less confident attitude in the West:

> paganism was now [after the collapse of the Western Roman Empire] seen to lie close to the heart of all baptised Christians. It was always ready to re-emerge in the form of 'pagan survivals'... evidence of the force of evil habits at work within the Church itself. As a result of this somber view of the Church, the master narrative of Christianization, as it came to be propounded from henceforth in the Latin West, was not one of definitive triumph. It was, rather, one in which an untranscended pagan past perpetually shadowed the advancing footsteps of the Christian present.[132]

Brown is writing about the sixth-century Western Europe of Caesarius of Arles and Gregory of Tours, but as Markus has pointed out, Severus, Patriarch of Antioch in the early sixth century, was horrified by the 'idolatrous' celebration of Antioch's 'Fortuna', with spectacles and races. Like Caesarius, Severus also found a variety of reasons to protest against these celebrations – they were demonic, but they also stirred up passions, caused conflict, wasted money which might be spent on the poor and were cruel to horses.[133]

The canons of the seventh-century Council of Trullo, replicated in Russian texts from the eleventh century, also offer a different picture of Byzantine Christendom. Canon 61 castigates all sorts of diviners, amulets and charms. Canon 62 protests the continued worship of Dionysus, the celebration of Brumalia (associated with Dionysus), Bota (a festival of Pan), the Kalends and the first of March. The Brumalia, however, was celebrated at the Imperial Court in the eighth century, which suggests that it had been secularized and made respectable despite clerical objections.[134] This canon also forbade dancing in honour of pagan gods, wearing masks and cross-dressing.

This council addressed problems faced by Eastern Christian communities following the Arab and Bulgar invasions, which some have speculated caused a demoralization which led to the proliferation of pagan practices.[135] The Council's concern to weed out any behaviours which might be identified as pagan may be evidence of a type of Christian thinking that follows a crisis situation (about which more will be said later), but the question of how long the flotsam of a pre-Christian past was perceived to be a feature of both Western and Eastern European Christianity is particularly pertinent to the *dvoeverie* debate, and it is to this question that we now turn.

Was Russian Orthodoxy particularly prone to 'pagan survivals'?

We have seen in Chapter 3 that a key argument in the historiography of *dvoeverie* is the suggestion that Russian Orthodoxy was more than usually riddled with 'pagan survivals' because of the lack of an 'illuminating' Renaissance or a 'cleansing' Reformation and Counter-Reformation.[136] This suggests firstly that Western Christianity was similarly riddled with pagan survivals (or rather unorthodox popular practices opposed by the Church) before – but not after – the Reformation, and secondly, that Russian Christianity never underwent an equivalent process of reform.

A short survey of the recent historiography of Western Christianity would seem to support this first supposition at least in part. While the specific term 'double-belief' is limited to Russian and Soviet studies,[137] scholars of other fields have talked about 'semi-Christians', 'half-Christians' or 'pagan-Christians', and the language of cultural historians of the West reflects similar concerns. In questioning the fundamentally Christian nature of medieval and early modern belief in Western Europe, some scholars have stressed the longevity of 'pagan survivals' in a manner reminiscent of Soviet double-belief scholarship:

> Granted that paganism and pagan practices will have lost much of their social relevance, some forms of them still survive even after a thousand years (and often more) of punishment and marginalisation. With a few exceptions (such as the horoscope, expressly and strictly forbidden in 1310) superstition disappeared only recently, as a result not of the growing impact of the church but of the increasing rationalisation of our society, if it really disappeared at all.[138]

In the mid-twentieth century, historians of Western Europe rediscovered latent paganism within Christian communities, and contested whether Europe was ever really Christianized. This has been in part a reaction against the previously received wisdom that during the Middle Ages – the 'golden age of religious orthodoxy' – Europe was a monolithic Christendom,[139] and in part prompted by a reaction against the secularization theory, which suggests that religious belief declined from the seventeenth century onwards, as Europe gradually became 'rational'.[140]

It is no coincidence that this debate – which centres upon the familiar 'binary oppositions' of pagan/Christian, magic/religion, rural/urban and popular/élite – was to a great extent driven by scholars of the Reformation. The debate began in the 1960s,[141] although the first contribution is generally recognized as having been made by the sociologist Gabriel Le Bras in 1955.[142] Le Bras challenged the thesis that Europe was 'properly Christian' in the medieval period, and had been 'dechristianized' since, working from a contentious thesis:

> the fulfilment of periodic duties in no way attests to true Christianity. Whoever believes in the divinity of Christ and in eternal life, whoever follows the commandments even from habit, is better Christianized than the faithful mass-goer who practices the law from habit and doesn't practice the virtues.[143]

Church attendance and participation in the sacraments is not, he argues, sufficient evidence of Christian faith – one must be visibly a *good* Christian, and 'good' in a manner which would be recognized as such by modern, Western European academics, or perhaps Le Bras personally, since participation in the sacraments certainly indicates Christian faith to this Western European academic. Le Bras concludes that the concept of a Christian medieval France is a nostalgic, post-Revolution myth – Roman Catholicism was the official Church and the religion of royalty before 1789, but not by any means accepted by all classes and professions, and forced upon much of the population rather than freely and genuinely embraced.

Le Bras is not concerned directly with the survival of pre-Christian belief, but rather with the idea that medieval Europe constituted a successfully Christianized world. The classic tenet of double-belief, that paganism survived in the religiosity of the rural population under a cloak of superficial Christianity, was raised within the discipline of Western European history by another French scholar, Jean Delumeau, in his 1971 study of early modern Catholicism.[144] Delumeau argues, however, that while the Reformation and Counter-Reformation 'did much to eliminate a deep-seated and persistent paganism frequently camouflaged with the most superficial veneer' of Christianity, this process of Christianization was far from complete when the French Revolution struck: 'How could it have been, when half the inhabitants could neither read nor write?'[145] Christianity is here associated with literacy, and it is implied that true faith without the ability to read the Bible is impossible.

A closer reading of Delumeau's work reveals that although he frequently observes a 'persistent pagan mentality with the occasional vestiges of pre-Christian ceremonial',[146] this 'pagan mentality' has less to do with pre-Christian belief than a 'magical' approach to religion. Witchcraft is 'residual paganism',[147] and pagan mentality is 'animist mentality'. As evidence of this he cites popular practices such as throwing the dust from a church into the air to ensure a favourable wind for sailors, divination, and healing rituals involving offerings of eggs for the intercession of the saints and, representing the illness, the rather more surprising element of horse manure.

Delumeau recognizes that the behaviours he identifies as evidence of a pagan mentality are not straightforward pagan survivals, but rather a folklorization of Christianity akin to the 'creative syncretism' of unconscious *dvoeverie*. As an example of this folklorization, Delumeau offers the folk traditions associated with the nativity of St John the Baptist, particularly the collecting of magical herbs, lighting of bonfires, and bathing at night: 'Christian festivals tended to be "folkorized" because they were addressed to a populace that was in general uneducated, and concretized in a civilization impregnated until a relatively late period by an animist mentality'.[148]

'Paganism' is therefore identified by the *quality* of the religion, rather than by the object of worship or the origins of belief and ritual, and is synonymous with irrational, illiterate, uneducated Christianity. However, the Christianity of the Ancien Régime's élite fares little better in Delumeau's estimation – like Le Bras, he rejects 'constraint, conformism and official worship' as much as 'magic, Manichaeism and fear . . . Have we not for too long called "Christianity" what was in fact a mixture of practices and doctrines with frequently but little connexion with the gospel message?'[149]

Keith Thomas's contemporaneous study of magic and early modern religion in England makes similar judgements about medieval English Catholicism. The problem with medieval Christianity, Thomas argues, stems from the well documented policy of 'accommodation' or assimilation that the Church pursued, which turned pagan sites into Christian shrines, and pagan festivals into holy days. This left clerics with a problem, since the people expected the functions of paganism to be fulfilled by the Church:

> An eclectic range of ritual activities was conducted under the auspices of the Church: 'leading the plough about the fire' on Plough Monday, 'for good beginning of the year, that they should fare the better all the year following'; the annual fires kindled on the hillsides on May Day, St John the Baptist Eve and other occasions; the flowers draped by the villagers around holy wells; the offerings of oats, cheese and other commodities at the shrines of saints. Some were customary calendar rituals whose pagan origins had long been forgotten, whereas others retained a frankly magical purpose.[150]

Despite his recognition of the fact that '[a]s Catholic theologians never ceased to emphasize, it was the presence or absence of the Church's authority which determined the propriety of any action',[151] Thomas seems unaware of the confessional bias of his approach, which implies that some Roman Catholic and

Eastern Orthodox communities – and indeed, the rural Anglican communities which have preserved or revived the tradition of well-dressing – are conducting acts of magic or (by implicit equation) paganism. Swanson and Duffy in their recent reappraisals of late medieval Catholicism betray an impatience with this sort of historiography, which fails to acknowledge that practices which may appear to have little to do with contemporary British, Protestant Christianity, were nevertheless an integral part of parish life and the Church calendar, and thereby part of Christianity.[152] However, Duffy too offers the plough fertility rites conducted on the first working day after Christmas as an example of a 'patently pagan' ritual legitimized by the Church, with a plough-light that might burn before the Sacrament on that day.[153]

Subsequent historiography of medieval and early modern belief has continued to focus on these apparently impure popular beliefs, but the binary opposition of folk religiosity/Christianity evident in the work of Delumeau, Schmitt,[154] Thomas and others has been challenged in ways reminiscent of the recent *dvoeverie* debate. Medieval Christianity should not be perceived as two distinct world-views, one belonging to illiterate peasants and/or the laity, and the other to the ruling classes and/or clergy, but rather as a spectrum of beliefs or a highly regionalized culture,[155] in which 'there was an interaction between church ideology and pre-Christian (or more accurately non-Christian) popular culture'.[156] Philip Gorski suggested in 2000 that the historiography of the Middle Ages has now 'come full circle', in that medieval culture is once again regarded as Christian, but as a now unified culture of magic and ritual rather than an 'Age of Faith'.[157] The debate, however, has continued unabated since.[158]

Despite this flurry of recent publications challenging an apparently widely held concept of the 'Age of Faith', there are much earlier precedents for the debate about how Christian 'Christendom' really was. In 1903, the approach of the British scholar E. K. Chambers revealed a familiar attitude to 'pagan survivals':

> if the comparative study of religions proves anything it is, that the traditional beliefs and customs of the medieval or modern peasant are in nine cases out of ten but the *detritus* of heathen mythology and heathen worship, enduring but with little external change in the shadow of a hostile creed.[159]

Chambers acknowledged himself a follower of James Frazer in the study of 'primitive religion', and his observations that the heathen heritage survived in Christendom in two ways – underground (revealing itself in witch trials and 'the shameful secrets of the confessional')[160] and by assimilation or accommodation (the building of churches on the sites of heathen temples, and the absorption of heathen gods by Christian saints) – bear a close resemblance to *dvoeverie* historiography of the same period.

The problem with the approach epitomized by Le Bras but embracing a wide range of academics from Chambers to Thomas, is that it (implicitly or explicitly) compares popular belief and practices with an imaginary (or at least highly subjective) Christian norm. This 'good' Christianity is either measured by knowledge and understanding of Scripture (particularly the New Testament), which largely excludes the illiterate and uneducated from the Christian community, or by morality, which excludes perhaps the vast majority of baptized sinners, or by rationality – indicated by a selective rejection of the magical, miraculous or supernatural. It is, for example, acceptable to believe that a woman was healed by touching the cloak of Jesus, but not acceptable to believe that one may be healed by touching the shroud of a saint or an icon of the Saviour.[161] Furthermore, this approach rejects the sacramental markers laid down by the Catholic and Orthodox Churches as indicators of Christian allegiance or identity – baptism, Church attendance, Easter duties. This is a particularly Protestant perspective, reflecting the same sorts of sentiments evident in the writings of Reformation clergy, who also perceived in pre-Reformation Christianity (and post-Reformation Catholicism) a pernicious mass of pagan survivals and inadequate evidence of true Christian faith.

For Protestant observers, the pagan antecedents they identified within the rituals of the Roman Catholic Church were important because they revealed the damnable origins of 'papism', and how distant it was from 'true' Christianity. Conyers Middleton (1683–1750), a Protestant clergyman and fellow of Trinity College, wrote in his *Letter from Rome* that:

> For nothing, I found, concurred so much with my original intention of conversing solely or chiefly with the Antients [*sic*], or so much help'd my Imagination to fancy myself wandering about in *Old Heathen Rome*, as to observe and attend to their *Religious Worship*; all whose Ceremonies appeared plainly to have been copied from the *Rituals of Primitive Paganism*, as if handed down by an uninterrupted Succession from the *Priests of Old* to the *Priests of New Rome* . . . So that as oft as I was present at any Religion Exercise *in their Churches*, it was more natural to fancy myself looking on at *some solemn Act of Idolatry in Old Rome*, than assisting at a Worship, instituted on the Principles, and formed upon the Plan of Christianity.[162]

Pre-empting the modern tendency to seek out the structures and beliefs of paganism by observing the exotic activities of living people, Middleton objects to elements firmly embedded in prescribed Catholic tradition: incense; the use of holy water (from the blessing of the congregation in the church to the January blessing of horses at the church doors); candles and lamps; votive gifts of clay and metal limbs (citing Polydore Vergil's complaints about this);[163] statues such as the Black Madonna at Loretto, who is compared to 'the *old Idols of Paganism*, which in *sacred* as well as *profane Writers* are described to be *black with the perpetual Smoak* [*sic*] *of Lamps and Incense*';[164] and the continued presentation of infants at the Temple of Romulus, now a church dedicated to St Theodorus.[165] Not only has the Church rededicated pagan temples as churches (e.g. the Pantheon or Rotunda reconsecrated by Pope Boniface the Fourth), but saints have, of course, replaced demigods. Middleton also castigates popular piety, stressing that 'the whole Face of the Country has the visible *Characters of Paganism* upon it',[166] listing the roadside shrines, flower-bedecked crosses (compared to the sacred oak of Ovid!), religious processions, the penitential acts of the flagellants, and miraculous images as all having pagan precedents and therefore being effectively pagan in nature.

As Peter Burke has pointed out, however, educated reformers of sixteenth- and seventeenth-century Western European Christianity, both Catholic and Protestant, identified in popular culture the 'traces of ancient paganism',[167] so is this as much evidence of 'élite' or 'educated' thinking as 'Protestant' thinking? Erasmus, to cite a prominent example, declared that the sort of popular customs associated with the cult of saints that 'the learned and devout' would wish to dispense with 'survive from the ancient pagans', referring to the rowdy processions of saints' statues and relics. These, he suggests, were tolerated because 'it was more difficult to change the religious belief of those who became Christians than their civic customs', and the Fathers of the Church considered it 'great progress' if sailors called on the Virgin Mary rather than Venus, and the harvest was purified with hymns and a procession with a cross rather than 'foolish rituals' to appease Ceres.[168]

In an intriguing study of classical models in sixteenth-century Spanish America, David A. Lupher explores the Dominican friar Bartolomé de Las Casas's study of the 'pagan survivals' in European culture, his *Apologética historia sumaria* written in the 1550s. This work circulated in manuscript, although it was not published until recent times, and favourably compares the religion of the Indians with that of Europe, in which he identifies the insidious roots of Roman paganism. Lupher speculates that Las Casas's interest relates to the problems preoccupying Catholic clerics in the New World, where the neophyte Indians were suspected of maintaining their pagan idolatry, although rather than tackling these accusations, Las Casas stressed that Indian pagan beliefs in some ways anticipated the Catholic rituals the missionaries subsequently brought.[169] More direct evidence of this missionary concern with continued idolatry can be found in the writings of another sixteenth-century Dominican, Fray Diego Durán, who records a conversation with an 'idolatrous' Indian Christian, cited at the beginning of this chapter. The Indian explains his continued attachment to native deities (already associated with Satan and his demons in the mind of the converts, and therefore part of a Christian world-view) as *nepantla*, the state of 'being in the middle'.[170] He both believed in a Christian God and continued to practice traditional rites – apparently classic stage one double-belief.

Some of the classic themes of double-belief also appear in Las Casas's work. In Catholic remembrances of the dead such as All Saints Day, Las Casas identifies a continuation of the Roman feast of Parentalia, when families gathered at ancestral tombs to pray for their dead. Candlemas he interprets as a feast designed to accommodate the tradition of exchanging candles in the last days of Saturnalia,[171] and the St Nicholas Day tradition of *obisoillos* (little bishops) when choirboys dressed as bishops and mimicked their actions, resembled the mock kings and magistrates of Saturnalia.[172]

Lupher identifies Polydore Vergil (1470–c. 1555) as one of the more unusual Catholic precedents. An Italian humanist, priest and friend of Erasmus, Vergil expanded his popular tome *De inventoribus rerum* in 1521 to explore the origins of rituals and customs of Roman Catholicism, within which he identified many survivals of (pagan) Roman religion. Vergil differentiates between the less worrying adaptations of pagan practices he detected in official Catholic ritual, and the more damnable popular customs attached to the fringes of feast days and sacraments,[173] such as the New Year gift-giving, singing and dancing at May Day and the decorating of churches and houses with foliage at weddings and feast days, explored in Book Five. Vergil's work was abridged and translated for the English, who naturally had use for sentiments such as the following:

> the rite of hanging up Images of Wax, and Tapers before Saints, or as often as any member is diseased, to offer the same in wax, as legges, arms, feet, Paps, Oxen, Horse, or sheep, which were hanged up in the Church, before that Saint, by whom (as they believed) they had obtained health, of the said member or beast: for this came of an old Heathenish fashion of sacrifices, that the Pagans offered to Saturnus and Pluto, in the Isle of Italy, named Cotillia, whereof I spake before.[174]

Las Casas, Vergil and their reforming colleagues were hardly unique, although it was more often Protestants who strove to point out the pagan nature of Catholic tradition.[175] Post-Reformation Anglican Christianity did not escape similar condemnation, however. Sixteenth-century Protestant Phillip Stubbes's observations of Elizabethan England included the suggestion that the May-pole decorated as part of popular festivities was 'a stinking idol', danced around 'as the heathen people did at the dedication of the Idols'. At these festivities 'a great Lord is present among them, as superintendent and Lord over their pastimes and sports, namely Satan, prince of Hell'.[176] Parish feast days and wakes originated in the celebrations and banquets of 'Pagans and heathen people', as did the wanton and wicked practice of dancing, expressly (Stubbes reminds us) banned by the Council of Laodicea.[177] Clearly, the degree to which any Christianity is perceived as 'pagan' is a subjective matter: for Stubbes, reformed Elizabethan Protestantism was still 'idolatrous'. Like Bishop Tikhon Zadonskii responding to the decadence and idolatry he perceived in the popular celebrations of eighteenth-century Voronezh, Stubbes does not accuse the participants of conscious idol worship, but of unwittingly preserving pagan behaviours. Similar attitudes are revealed in the eighteenth-century records of the Holy Synod, where popular practices (such as dunking those who miss Easter liturgical services in the village pond) are likened to idolatry from Kievan times – in this instance, offering a sacrificial victim to the 'disgusting idol' Kupalo.[178]

While Russian Christianity, like Greek Orthodoxy,[179] escaped the Protestant and Catholic reformations that swept Western Europe, there was both a process of 'tidying' and 'standardizing' of Russian Orthodoxy led from the top (epitomized in the rulings of the *Stoglav* and Metropolitan Makarii's efforts to compile a definitive compendium of the spiritual heritage of Russia in his *Great Menology*) in the sixteenth century. The seventeenth century saw both a limited grassroots reform movement – the 'Zealots of Piety' – and wider efforts by Tsar Aleksei Mikhailovich and the clerical hierarchy to improve the Christian behaviour of the laity and to raise standards among the clergy, including literacy levels and basic religious education.[180] This was coupled with Patriarch Nikon's attempts to bring the Russian Church into line with Greek Orthodoxy, an exercise which resulted in a fracture of the Church into traditional conservative 'Old Believers', who stood by the rulings of the *Stoglav* council, and the reformers led by Patriarch Nikon and Tsar Aleksei Mikhailovich. The priest Avvakum, an early Zealot and later leader of the 'Old Believers', was a stern crusader against what he perceived as improper behaviour, and frequently beaten for his reforming zeal:

> There came to my village dancing bears with drums and lutes, and I, though a miserable sinner, was zealous in Christ's service, and I drove them out and I broke the buffoons' masks and drums, on a common outside the village, one against many, and two great bears I took away – one I clubbed senseless, but he revived, and the other I let go in the open country. And after that Basil Petrovich Sheremetev, who was sailing up the Volga to Kazan to take over the Governorship, took me on board, and sternly reprimanded me and ordered me to bless his son who had a shaven face. And when I saw that image of shame I would not bless him, but condemned him from the Scriptures. And so my lord waxed terribly wrath and ordered that I should be flung into the Volga . . .[181]

The evidence suggests that Avvakum and his fellow zealots inspired violent reactions from diverse communities and social strata, and that they had very little support apart from a few disciples, drawn mostly from the merchant and noble classes. The Archpriest Daniil was beaten by the inhabitants of Kostroma in 1652, complaining to investigators that on one night in May he had tried to stop peasants on the banks of the Volga singing. Daniil had also forbidden *skomorokhi* (itinerant minstrels) from performing and had attempted to curtail drunkenness.[182] Another prominent Zealot, Ivan Neronov – a parish priest in Nizhnii Novgorod in the 1630s – complained that the Pecherskii monastery was being mocked by a popular festival involving 'salesmen of alcohol . . . strolling players, bear trainers, and minstrels with their devilish instruments', plus masks and 'shameful sexual paraphernalia'.[183] Neronov, together with a group of Nizhnii Novgorod priests, petitioned Patriarch Iosaf in 1636 to address a long catalogue of low standards among the clergy and 'demonic' popular revels. The priests were particularly bothered by inappropriate behaviour on holy days, and gave a detailed description of the sorts of activities involved in the 'hellenic and devilish games' conducted on these days: masquerading in shaggy masks and tails 'in the appearance of demons', making goat-like noises, 'singing devilish songs and shouting Koleda' on the eve of Christmas and the Epiphany; at Easter, the shameful festival near to Pecherskii monastery; on the seventh Thursday of Easter 'women and girls gather under trees, under birches, and bring, like sacrifices, pies and porridge and eggs, and bow before the birches', indulge in kissing rituals which create 'godparents', sing 'satanic songs' and dance. At Christmas, and from the eve of the Nativity of St John the Baptist to St Peter's Day, they light fires in the fields and 'play all night to the very dawn', with women and girls jumping through the fire.[184] Again, the proximity of these activities to holy places and holy feasts, and the inappropriateness of Orthodox believers behaving in such a fashion, is what alarms the reformers: the sacred and the profane are too close for comfort.

Neronov's *Life* also records that when he challenged revellers (from the Bishop's house, no less) in the town of Vologda who were indulging in 'demonic spectacles' involving masks and the imitation of 'demons and ghosts', he was beaten until 'barely alive'.[185] Efforts were also made by some clergy to regulate the use of icons and limit the cult of the saints, in a manner reminiscent of the Council of Trent (1545–63),[186] which proved very unpopular with the laity. Michels concludes that the Russian clerics' attempts to evangelize the masses in the seventeenth century, unlike the efforts of their Western peers, failed. Freeze comes to a similar conclusion, although he locates the Church's attempt at a fundamental reformation in the eighteenth century:

> Despite vigorous attempts at reform from above, the Church gradually lost its grip on the emerging society and culture. It made but little headway against the abiding problems of superstition and pagan custom . . . [a]nd, in elite culture, the Church lost the battle almost by default. It produced few intellectual figures of note and lost its former cultural primacy to a Westernized intelligentsia.[187]

The period of ecclesiastical reform from the mid-eighteenth century to the mid-nineteenth has been called 'the rechristianization of Russia', but Freeze is quick to point out that the piety of the populace was not in question – what needed reform, as far as the clerical élite were concerned, was 'the laity's capacity to understand and articulate what exactly they professed to believe'.[188] He concludes that these reforms had little impact on popular religion beyond urban communities. Freeze's assessment of the eighteenth century as a crucial period of spiritual reformation, and of the clerical élite's failure to combat popular unorthodoxy, is supported by other scholars.[189] Efforts by the clerical élite were supplemented and even directed by the monarchy – Tsar Aleksei Mikhailovich was instrumental in the reforms of the seventeenth century, banning *skomorokhi*, rowdy popular practices and festivals in 1648 in missives titled 'On the Righting of Morals and the Abolition of Superstition' and 'Concerning *Koliada*, *Usen'* and Other Popular Games'.[190] The former letter complains that:

in Belgorod and other towns and in the regions (*uezda*) lay people of all ranks and their wives and children on Sunday and on the Lord's days and great feast days at the time of holy services do not go to the churches of God, and all manner of drunkenness has increased in the people, and all manner of rebellious, devilish activity, mockery, and minstreling (*skomoroshestvo*) with all manner of devilish games. And much brutality is committed by these satanic disciples among Orthodox Christians, and many people, forgetting God, and the Orthodox Christian faith, are led by such deceivers and minstrels to go in the evening to their disorderly attractions, and to all night shameful events on the streets and in the fields, and they listen to sacrilegious and filthy songs and all manner of devilish games, men and women, and to the youngest child, and have fights between themselves in fisticuffs, and sway around on swings, and on ropes; and there are other tempters of male and female sex in the towns and in the regions with much magic (*charodeistvie*) and sorcery (*volkhovanie*), and many people are attracted by their witchcraft; and other people of such enchanters (*charodeev*) and magicians (*volkhvy*) and impious women . . . and from the right faith of Orthodox Christians they differ. Yes, in the towns and regions a devilish throng is made from deceivers and simple-minded people: many people, male and female, go enchanting by dawn and by night, from sun rise of the first day of the moon they watch, and at times of loud thunder in rivers and in lakes they bathe, charming themselves from such health, and washing themselves with [water from] silver, and they lead bears, and dance with dogs, with dice, and cards, and chess, and knuckle-bones (*lodygi*) they play, and unruly skipping and dancing, and they sing devilish songs; and in Holy Week women and girls swing on boards; and around Christmas and Epiphany many people, male and female gather in devilish throngs for demonic temptations, many devilish activities they play in all manner of devilish games; and on the eves of Christmas and St Basil's Day and the Epiphany they cry devilish cries – to Koleda, and Tausen, and Plug, and many stupid people believe in dreams and meetings . . .'[191]

Peter I's *Ecclesiastical Regulation* of 1721 attempted to quash 'whatever may be called by the term "superstition" [*sueverie*] . . . that which is superfluous, not essential to salvation, devised by hypocrites only for their own interest, beguiling the simple people, and like snowdrifts, hindering passage along the right path of truth'.[192] The *Regulation* specifically mentions 'falsely fabricated tales' in the *Lives of the Saints*, 'fabrications' such as the veneration of dubious icons and relics, and 'shameful idolatry' (*stydnoe idolosluzhenie*) such as praying in front of oaks (with the participation of the local priest).[193] That Russian attempts at reform of popular belief had less impact than those in Western Europe seems clear: most obviously, there was no equivalent to the devastating iconoclasm of the Protestant Reformation, and efforts to restrict the way people used icons and relics were largely rejected by the mass of believers. Burke has argued that what ensured the success of the sixteenth- and seventeenth-century reformers where previous attempts had failed was the increased possibility for communication in early modern Europe: printing, literacy and improved travel meant that reformers were less isolated and could disseminate their zealotry more quickly than in medieval Europe. One might argue that the lack of success the Russian reformers experienced was correspondingly linked to bad communications – huge geographic distances, inclement weather, poor conditions for travel, slow development of mass printing and widespread illiteracy all combined to restrict the reforming impulse.

This does not mean, however, that the Russian Orthodoxy of the modern period was, or is, somehow or other more 'pagan' than Western Christianity. It may have remained closer to its medieval precursor than Methodism or Lutheranism, but, given our working definition of a Christian as a baptized individual who identifies him or herself as a Christian, modern (pre-Soviet) Russia was perhaps *more* Christian than her Western European neighbours. We know that by the late fourteenth century peasants called themselves Christians, confirming a self-conscious Christian identity among the 'common people',[194] and that in early modern Russia, the Church calendar regulated time, and the majority of the population marked the transitions of birth, marriage and death with Orthodox sacrament and ritual.[195] The vast mass of the pre-revolutionary Orthodox populace (substantial Jewish, Muslim and 'other believer' communities excepted) continued to fulfil their annual obligation to confess and receive communion at Easter in the nineteenth and early twentieth century,[196] and a consensus is emerging that views Imperial Russia as a thoroughly Christian society, where 'Orthodox lay people, especially peasant laity, were passionate about the matters they considered holy and sought assertively to manage them as they saw fit'.[197] It is not perceived as a monolithic Christendom, however, but as a rich and variegated fabric of regional Christianities – 'Russian heterodoxy', as one historian would have it[198] – a conclusion shared by recent historiography of Western Christianity.

Boundaries, binary oppositions and the neutral sphere

While avoiding the suggestion that the reform movement which swept Europe in the sixteenth and seventeenth centuries was monolithic, Burke manages to convey the remarkably similar concerns of the early modern reformers across England, Belgium, Italy, Portugal, Bavaria and the Russia of the *Stoglav*, Tsar Aleksei Mikhailovich's 1648 edict and Avvakum's Zealots. Popular culture was perceived as preserving pagan remnants, as muddying the sacred with the profane, and serving flesh and the Devil with drunkenness, lewdness and violence. Burke's exploration of clerical attacks on the popular culture of Western Europe also led him to conclude that

> the crucial point in all these examples [from sixteenth-century England, Antwerp, Bavaria, Italy and Portugal] seems to be the insistence of the reformers on the separation between the sacred and the profane. This

separation now became very much sharper than it had been in the Middle Ages.[199]

This apparent Europe-wide sharpening of the division between the sacred and the profane interestingly corresponds with Boris Uspenskii and Iurii Lotman's theory of 'binary oppositions' in Russian culture, which is based on the argument that 'the Russian medieval system was constructed on a marked dualism'.[200] Starting from the premise that pre-eighteenth century Russian culture exhibits a 'fundamental polarity', whereby 'basic cultural values . . . are arranged in a bipolar value field divided by a sharp line and without any neutral axiological zone',[201] Lotman and Uspenskii identify a number of key oppositions, such as 'old' versus 'new', 'Christianity' versus 'paganism', and 'Orthodox' versus 'non-Orthodox'. In the latter binary opposition Russian Orthodoxy comes to represent the truth, and all others are seen as false faiths, as inversions of the truth. Paganism, Catholicism and Judaism are all demonic/untrue/alien and 'identical for polemical purposes' – a conclusion convincingly supported by Petrukhin.[202] Correct belief and behaviour needs an opposite against which it can define itself, and medieval clerics used the unorthodox to define Orthodox. As one of their most influential theories, the concept of 'binary oppositions' has had repercussions outside of the historiography of Russian Orthodoxy, and impacted upon Russian studies as a whole.

Although they are increasingly challenged,[203] Lotman and Uspenskii's key oppositions (like those of Lévi-Strauss) have proved a source of inspiration for many students and scholars. Moshe Lewin, for example, writing about popular religion in twentieth-century Russia in *The Making of the Soviet System*, comes to the conclusion that 'the term "dual faith" (*dvoeverie*), may, after all, be misleading'. He suggests, however, that researchers of popular belief (here we must note that he is concerned with a far later period – twentieth-century interwar Russia – and appears to be conflating *dvoeverie* with 'rural Christianity') opt for discussing instead:

> a *system* of antipodes, not just 'pagan versus Christian' but also 'Church versus the *izba*', 'miracle versus (or complemented by) magic', 'Orthodox versus Christian anti-Orthodox', and more.[204]

The gradual move towards a more nuanced view of 'lived Orthodoxy' has discredited these sorts of binary oppositions in the recent historiography of pre-Soviet Russia, but it is worth exploring this notion of a dichotomy of sacred and profane as somehow differentiating Russian religious culture from that of Western Europe. Scholars of Western Europe and the Mediterranean world, particularly in late Antiquity and the early Middle Ages, have also identified this particular 'binary opposition' as pivotal in the development of European Christian culture.[205]

In exploring pre-eighteenth-century Russian culture, Lotman and Uspenskii conclude that Russia's lack of a spiritually neutral zone, a secular sphere, fundamentally differentiates it from the Christian culture of the medieval West. Western Christianity developed the concept of purgatory and accepted the existence of neutral behaviour which was neither sinful enough to merit damnation nor pure enough to merit direct access to heaven: in contrast, Russian behaviours were always either holy or damnable.[206]

The thesis that the fundamental difference between medieval Russian and Western European cultures is a binary/tertiary divide is supportable only in part, in certain periods but not in others. In Le Goff's seminal study of the development of purgatory, he observes that the outlook of the Christian intelligentsia underwent a broad change in the eleventh century, when the Christian élite moved from a binary pattern of thought to a pluralistic model, with particular emphasis on tertiary models:

> In the early Middle Ages thought naturally organised itself in binary patterns. The powers that ruled the universe were two: God and Satan (though it is important to note that Christianity subordinated the devil to God in rejecting Manichaean dogma). Society naturally divided itself into pairs of opposites: the powerful and the poor, the clergy and the laity. Moral and spiritual life were conceived in terms of the opposition between the virtues and the vices.[207]

The powerful and the poor began to be linked by a third section of society, the bourgeois; the division between clerics and laity was blurred by the Third Orders; the sharp division between virtues and vices was compromised by a new complex category of venial sin; and the boundary between heaven and hell expanded into a spatial reality of its own – purgatory. For Le Goff, the primary engine of these changes was socio-economic; the middle classes did not create purgatory, but purgatory emerged with the transformation of the dualistic model of feudal Christendom.[208] Other historians have identified a 'neutral zone' in Western medieval culture unrelated to Christianity: Bernard Hamilton has suggested that a 'three-layered view of the supernatural' persisted throughout the medieval period into the modern, 'consisting of the good and evil forces of Christian orthodoxy, together with a third, neutral force, which did not fit into Christian categories'. This third force, despite its 'pagan roots', is neither the conscious preservation of paganism nor consciously anti-Christian, but encompassed those areas of the supernatural 'which drew their power from the pagan imaginative tradition' that the Church failed to accommodate – the fairies and wizards of the Arthurian legends, for example.[209]

Burke's reformers were, however, both Catholic and Protestant, and the doctrine of purgatory remains to this day an essential element of Roman Catholicism – and therefore an essential element of the Catholic cultures of seventeenth-century Spain, Portugal and France, for example. Burke's suggestion is that the early modern shift in religious mentality was an impulse to 'destroy the traditional familiarity with the sacred, because they believed that familiarity breeds irreverence'.[210] His argument suggests that the sacred and profane in medieval Europe were not so much separated by a neutral zone as blurred by a familiarity which refused to distinguish clearly between these elements of life. The reformers focused their attack on popular culture because it was among the laity and lower clergy, in rural or uneducated urban communities, that this 'muddying' was most pronounced.

While chronological boundaries are as problematic as geographical boundaries in studies of religion and culture, historians who have focused on the transition from 'late Antique Christianity' to the 'Christian (or Pagan) Middle Ages', have identified the attitudes of clerics and reformers to concepts of 'sacred', 'civic' and 'profane' as a crucial indicator of cultural change. Peter Brown, for example, argues that in AD 1000 the sacred and profane were inextricably mixed, but that by end of the twelfth century, purely secular values of chivalry and courtly love have emerged. The period in between shows a gradual disentangling of the sacred from the secular – he gives as an example the judicial ordeal, used in secular law suits and blessed by the Church until the Lateran Council (1215) forbade clerics to do so. This chronology fits well with Le Goff's suggestion that the move to a tertiary model of thinking began in the eleventh century in Western Europe.

It has been pointed out that Eastern and Western Christianity differed over their responses to the secular world or 'neutral zone' in this early, apparently 'binary' period. Taking the Lupercalia as an example, Robert Markus suggests that while in the tenth century the Lupercalia were celebrated in Constantinople as a 'spring festival in which civic, political and religious elements were combined without the least tension', the Papacy launched an attack on the very notion of the secular in the fifth century in its attempt to curb Christian participation in the Lupercalia celebrations. Pope Gelasius I (492–6), or perhaps Felix III (483–92), 'was determined to force a choice on its participants – whom he called "neither Christian nor pagans" – a choice where none had been expected before'.[211] The sudden identification of the celebrations – which had previously been viewed by Christians as harmless fun, stripped of any religious significance – with paganism, happened 'in the wake of crisis':

> The trichotomy which had prevailed before the crisis – of Christian (or sacred), secular (neutral, civic), pagan (profane) – vanished, to be replaced by a simpler dichotomy: sacred and profane, or simply 'Christian' and 'pagan'.[212]

This suggests a Western Christian cycle of trichotomy of sacred, civic/neutral, profane in the fourth century, followed by a dichotomy of sacred–profane from the fifth to the eleventh century, a trichotomy again from the eleventh to the sixteenth century, superseded by a dichotomy in the reformed seventeenth century. Eastern Christianity apparently follows a different pattern, with a longer 'confident' period in which the trichotomy prevails. This is simply too neat. 'Radical dualism'[213] is innate in the fundamental texts of

Christianity – the choice is between God and Satan, between the 'cup of the Lord and the cup of devils'.[214] Clerical concern to see the boundaries of faith firmly established, and their fear of anything that might blur those boundaries, is evidenced in moments of crisis and periods of conversion: fifth-century Rome, eleventh-century Rus, sixteenth-century South America, seventeenth-century Muscovy. As we have seen in Chapter 2, Russian medieval clerics and their Byzantine predecessors saw spiritual indecisiveness and indeterminate faith as particularly pernicious, and this fear of the indeterminate – and the corresponding hardening of boundaries – is a common feature of religious communities who feel themselves under threat, or in crisis. Studies of modern fundamentalism have confirmed that this is a human trait which has survived the massive changes of the last two centuries.[215]

A further flaw in the neat and attractive 'binary oppositions' theory of Lotman and Uspenskii is that it neglects the importance of the liminal in Russian popular culture. The dangerous threshold area of neither one thing nor the other (twilight – between day and night, riverbanks – between water and land, for example), and liminal or transitory states such as childbirth, marriage and death, are neither sacred nor entirely profane. Rituals, as well as places and states, may not fall into neat categories. As Zhivov has pointed out, the ethnographical research of N. I. Tolstoi established the existence of a transitional zone between paganism and Christianity 'in which the separate elements on principle cannot be attributed to one or the other pole – to the Christian or the pagan (antichristian)'.[216] Corresponding with Hamilton's theory of a neutral, neither Christian nor pagan zone in Western popular culture, Zhivov suggests that the folk ritual of summoning rain once belonged to the system of 'unclean' behaviour, which as a 'desemanticized' activity has lost its 'synchronal link' with the system of pagan behaviour. It has not become an organic part of Christian behaviour either, and therefore remains in the transitional zone, ever preserving the possibility of reverting to its unclean state.

As Zhivov points out, the archetypal denunciation of double-belief, the *Sermon about how firstly the pagans were idol worshippers*, essentially contradicts the supposition that Russian medieval consciousness was dualistic. The 'dualism' is in the mind of the reforming cleric, rather than his audience. As with the worshippers in the *Sermon of the Christlover*, the Christians being corrected were unaware of any profanity in their behaviour:

> Evidently, what is being denounced here is namely a social norm, toleration of the mixing of Christian piety with profane rituals. Their profane, pagan content was not clear to society as a whole, in other words, they were desemanticized, and therefore it was essential to 'teach' this society – precisely because its normal members were not conscious of themselves as double-believers. On the basis of similar sources it is entirely illegitimate to talk about a dualistic clash of piety and antibehaviour as a paradigm of Russian religious consciousness of the Middle Ages.[217]

Zhivov also challenges the notion that double-belief is a specifically Russian phenomenon, since a 'systematic criticism of the sources for Russian spiritual culture of the Middle Ages' leads to the conclusion that there are no significant differences between Russian and Western European medieval spirituality, comparing the Italian and French Carnival with Russian *Maslenitsa* in passing. That which he does identify as different (the lack of a tradition of intellectual play and parody, the religious rigourism preserved in the sphere of literary culture) goes beyond the boundaries of this chapter.

Conclusion

The historiography of religious belief, driven in particular by a revised approach to popular culture and – in Russian studies – post-Soviet academic freedom, has developed in curious counterpoint. The drive in Russian studies is to demonstrate that pre-Soviet Russia was overwhelmingly Christian, although perhaps heterodox rather than Orthodox or at least richly, regionally, variegated. Academic studies of Western Europe have been engaged in the reverse process, contesting the notion that medieval and early modern Europe was swiftly, or thoroughly, Christianized. We are perhaps seeing an emerging consensus that acknowledges the difficulty, perhaps impossibility, of developing a 'one size fits all' terminology or schema to support analysis of the basic structures of medieval Christian thought while accurately reflecting the infinite variety of belief. Every term we use – double-belief, pagan survivals, syncretism, superstition, even folklorized Christianity – is tainted with ideological baggage and prone to conceptual flaws. Every model that attempts to identify and pin down basic underlying structures – binary oppositions, trichotomies, stages of *dvoeverie* – can be easily challenged with a sideways look at another time, or another place.

So are we able to draw any overall conclusions about European medieval popular belief with certainty? We can say that allegations of paganism were made widely across medieval and early modern Europe, and were no more prevalent in Russia than in, say, France. How accurate these allegations were matters less than the undeniable fact that popular practices have been conceived of as 'pagan' (or 'demonic', 'idolatrous', 'Hellenic' or 'Satanic') by reforming clerics in diverse communities, across several centuries – indeed, across the entire span of the Christian millennium, if one includes current fundamentalist Christian objections to Hallowe'en and the like. Periods of uncertainty and conflict may escalate such accusations, but the literary heritage of Christianity ensures that clerics and zealots always have access to a fount of texts with which to contest the popular unorthodoxy that is the inevitable fruit of human creativity and difference.

Conclusion

The validity of the term *dvoeverie*, as it has been commonly employed since the mid-nineteenth century, has been rightly challenged by some scholars in the past two decades. Scholarly use of the word has often been justified by reference to its medieval origins and this work has set out to survey these medieval usages in order to ascertain whether double-belief (as it is understood in modern historiography) was in fact a medieval concept.

This textual evidence of medieval usage, as we have seen, does not reflect modern understanding of the term. Of the eighteen uses of the word or lexical derivatives discussed, eleven are indisputably about uncertainty, doubt, hesitation, dissension, ambiguity or insincerity. There is no question of there being two faiths in which the practitioner believes simultaneously or even alternately, and sometimes no question of religious faith at all. The term as used in these eleven examples has the common thread of a *lack* of firmness of opinion – and religious belief in the medieval period required certainty. Those who questioned the verity of the true faith, or doubted the rightness of right-worship were heretics, not Orthodox believers.

As we observed in Chapter 2, early Russian had a fluidity that permitted multiple meanings and idiosyncratic use of vocabulary. A. M. Panchenko has observed that medieval clerics understood *dvoeverie* to mean 'confessional tolerance', and some of the textual evidence presented in Chapter 2 supports such an interpretation. We can say with certainty that in almost all untranslated uses of the term in which Orthodoxy appears as the 'first' faith, paganism was not the 'second' faith. In the eleventh, as in the seventeenth century, it was 'heretical' Christians rather than the semi-converted who were the primary target of this pejorative epithet. However, while *dvoeverie* in this context can be read as confessional tolerance, the possibility that the word also meant 'doubt', 'uncertainty' or perhaps 'hypocrisy' in these texts cannot be ruled out.

The evidence for *dvoeverie* in the medieval period as meaning Christians practising paganism appears to rest on one text. To my knowledge, no historian has directly quoted a passage containing the term other than from the *Questions of Kirik* and the sermons attributed to Feodosii Pecherskii discussed in Chapter 2, and the famous sentence from the *Sermon of the Christlover*.[1] Negative evidence can never be conclusive, but its notable absence in other anti-pagan polemics and texts directed at correcting unorthodox belief and practices such as the *Stoglav*, plus the seventeen examples using the word in different contexts, lead me to conclude that the term was not primarily understood as a pejorative epithet directed against Christians 'addicted to pagan practices'.[2] Even in the *Sermon of the Christlover* it may simply have implied 'weak in faith', 'doubting' or 'hypocritical'.

An understanding of what *dvoeverie* meant to medieval clerics is crucial to the current debate about the validity of the term, and perhaps more importantly, to dispelling some of the myths that influence our perception of Russian medieval spirituality. The concept of *dvoeverie* has coloured this perception for over a century, leading to a preoccupation among historians and scholars in fields such as ethnography, art history, archaeology and cultural studies with identifying latent paganism in many areas of Russian material and spiritual culture. Furthermore, it has led to an unsubstantiated belief that pre-Petrine Rus was particularly resistant to Christianity, and that Russian culture was (or even is) particularly laden with 'pagan survivals', on the grounds that Russian medieval clerics invented a special word to describe this phenomenon.

Recent scholarship has accepted the validity of approaching history through the concepts of the period under study, and attributing modern concepts to medieval minds limits our ability to make a proper assessment of the textual evidence that remains to us. As far as possible, we should seek to understand cultures 'in their own terms' and, as Bossy suggests, we cannot assume that a concept existed in the past where there was no word for it: 'Words matter', and 'without a sense of their history they become manipulable in the cause of obfuscation'.[3] The term *dvoeverie* was considerably more nuanced than our modern interpretation of it allows, and unless historians uncover substantial evidence to the contrary, we have to conclude that there was no medieval concept of double-belief at all.

So is it valid for scholars to continue to use the term *dvoeverie* or its modern English translation 'double-belief', if we acknowledge that medieval clerics would not have recognized the interpretation we place upon it? Scholars do, of course, use terms in ways that would have been alien to the subject populations under scrutiny, and provided that they are clear about this, and do not attribute modern concepts to medieval minds, this is a legitimate and sometimes unavoidable practice – especially where the historian is studying a population who speak the same language.[4] Even within the short span of our own lifetimes we can see the meanings of words change radically, or mean entirely different things to different communities within one language group.

In the case of *dvoeverie*, the scholarly concept has been clouded by its use in discussion of very diverse phenomena – the initial Christianization process (in any historical period, from the 'baptism of Rus' to nineteenth-century missionary efforts in Siberia), when the neophyte is unsure of what may and what may not be preserved from their former non-Christian lives;[5] the calendrical and life-cycle 'folk rituals' of Slavic agricultural communities in any century from the eleventh to the twentieth; the use of magic (charms, curses, amulets, divination) to manipulate nature or fate, at any time, in any area. It has been used as a synonym for 'syncretism' – itself a term that has been the subject of much debate – and to encompass 'accommodation', 'resistance' and 'pagan survivals'. A more interesting interpretation of the term has been that of 'spiritual bilingualism'.[6] It may be that there is use for a term which encompasses the notion that practitioners have access to two distinct belief systems simultaneously, and may choose to use the vocabulary of either (perhaps preferring one or the other in different contexts or registers) in the way that bilinguals do.[7] But this is a discussion for another book, and perhaps one better tackled by anthropologists. Suffice to say that in the Russian medieval context, the use of *dvoeverie* and lexical derivatives did not reflect these modern interpretations of the term, and until there is consensus among the academic community about what we modern scholars mean by double-belief, its use can only confuse.

Notes

Preface

1 The dictionaries and encyclopedias consulted are listed separately in the bibliography.
2 Contemporary Russian sources referred to the Mongols as 'Tatars', along with other steppe peoples. See Donald Ostrowski on the identities of Tatar and Mongol in relation to the invasions and subsequent overlordship in *Muscovy and the Mongols: Cross-cultural influences on the steppe frontier, 1304–1589* (Cambridge: CUP, 1998), especially pp. xiii, 32–4, 144–9.

Introduction

1 J. Ellis, 'Religion and Orthodoxy', in C. Kelly and D. Shepherd (eds), *Russian Cultural Studies: an introduction* (Oxford: OUP, 1998), p. 295.
2 Throughout, I will use the modern Russian spelling of *dvoeverie* in transliteration, as this is the form most commonly used by historians, or double-belief, hyphenated to emphasize the compound nature of the word (except where I am citing a text in which the word is spelt differently).
3 D. Harmening has taken a similar approach in his *Superstitio: überlieferungs- und theoriegeschichtliche Untersuchungen zur kirchlich-theologischen Aberglaubensliteratur des Mittelalters* (Berlin: E. Schmidt, 1979). See also Peter Biller's 'Words and the Medieval Notion of "Religion"', *Journal of Ecclesiastical History* 36, no. 3 (1985), 351–69, which alerts us to the fact that the absence of the word does not always indicate the absence of the concept.
4 Jacques Le Goff, *The Birth of Purgatory*, translated by Arthur Goldhammer (London: Scholar Press, 1984), p. 3.
5 See for example Aleksander Pluskowski and Philippa Patrick '"How do you pray to God?" Fragmentation and Variety in Early Medieval Christianity', in Martin Carver (ed.), *The Cross Goes North: processes of conversion in northern Europe, AD 300–1300* (Woodbridge, Suffolk: York Medieval Press, 2003).
6 M. Mazo, ' "We Don't Summon Spring in the Summer": traditional music and beliefs of the contemporary Russian village', in W. C. Brumfield and M. M. Velimirovic (eds), *Christianity and the Arts in Russia* (Cambridge: CUP, 1991), p. 77.
7 Peter Burke, *Popular Culture in Early Modern Europe* (London: Temple Smith, 1978; revised reprint Aldershot: Ashgate, 1996). I also appreciate Andrew D. Brown's observation that 'popular piety' can mean simply the piety of the people (gentry included), which may include practices that did not conform to standards set by the Church hierarchy. See his *Popular Piety in Late Medieval England. The Diocese of Salisbury, 1250–1550* (Oxford: Clarendon Press, 1995), pp. 2–3.
8 See for example Miri Rubin, 'The Middle Ages, or Getting Less Medieval with the Past', in Peter Burke (ed.), *History and Historians in the Twentieth Century*

(Oxford: OUP, 2002), pp. 11–36, for a perspective particularly pertinent to Western (Catholic) Europe.

9 Natalie Zemon Davis, 'From "Popular Religion" to Religious Cultures', in Steven Ozment (ed.), *Reformation Europe: a guide to research* (St. Louis: Center for Information Research, 1982), pp. 321–42. See also Ellen Badone (ed.), *Religious Orthodoxy and Popular Faith in European Society* (Princeton, NJ: Princeton University Press, 1990), pp. 3–9.

10 The history of clerical celibacy in the Catholic world is long and complicated, but rules against clerical marriage (rather than concubinage) began to be successfully enforced after the Fourth Lateran Council of 1215. See for example Henry C. Lea, *The History of Sacerdotal Celibacy in the Christian Church* (New York: Russell & Russell, 1957).

11 See Badone, *Religious Orthodoxy and Popular Faith*, pp. 10–11.

12 Mary R. O'Neil, '*Sacerdote ovvero strione:* ecclesiastical and superstitious remedies in 16th century Italy', in Steve L. Kaplan (ed.), *Understanding Popular Culture: Europe from the Middle Ages to the nineteenth century* (New Babylon Studies in the Social Sciences 40: Berlin and New York: Mouton Publishers, 1984), pp. 67–8, 76.

13 Russell Zguta suggests, however, that the *volkhvy* were pagan priests. See for example his article 'The Pagan Priests of Early Russia: Some New Insights', *Slavic Review* 33, no. 2 (1974). While they may have preserved an unorthodox belief system, I do not believe that there is enough evidence collated yet to prove that they officiated over a widespread pagan cult.

14 Ioann, Metropolitan of Saint Petersburg and Ladoga (ed.), *Pravoslavnaia tserkov': Sovremennye eresi i sekty v Rossii* (St Petersburg: Izd. Pravoslavnaia Rus', 1995), p. 4.

15 G. P. Fedotov, *The Russian Religious Mind. Vol. 1: Kievan Christianity, the tenth to the thirteenth centuries* (New York, Evanston and London: Harper & Row, 1960), Chapter VII.

16 I accept that I may be influenced by my own cultural assumptions here, although even among the less institutionalized denominations, a system of elders and a body of accepted knowledge usually exists to guide the neophyte. However, since this work is primarily concerned with the denominations of Orthodoxy and Catholicism, I shall refer to the structures recognized by these. See also Stanley Brandes, 'Conclusion: Reflections on the Study of Religious Orthodoxy and Popular Faith in Europe', in Badone, *Religious Orthodoxy and Popular Faith*, pp. 185–200.

17 Richard Fletcher, *The Conversion of Europe: from paganism to Christianity 371–1386 AD* (London: HarperCollins, 1997), p. 9.

18 Letter of Alcuin to Charles the Great, 796, in H. R. Loyn and J. Percival (eds), *The Reign of Charlemagne: documents on Carolingian government and administration* (London: Edward Arnold, 1975), p. 122.

19 R. A. Markus, *The End of Ancient Christianity* (Cambridge: CUP, 1990), p. 53. See also Richard Lim, 'Converting the Un-Christianizable: the baptism of stage performers in late antiquity', in Kenneth Mills and Anthony Grafton (eds), *Conversion in Late Antiquity and the Early Middle Ages: seeing and believing* (Rochester, NY: University of Rochester Press, 2003), pp. 84–126, esp. pp. 98–102, and Robin Lane Fox, *Pagans and Christians in the Mediterranean world from the second century AD to the conversion of Constantine* (London: Penguin, 1988), pp. 338–9, for a discussion of prebaptismal preparation and delayed baptism in late Antiquity.

20 John Van Engen, 'The Christian Middle Ages as an Historiographical Problem', *American Historical Review* 91, no. 3 (1986), 519–52, especially pp. 540–1.

21 *The Laws of Rus – tenth to fifteenth centuries*, tr. and ed. Daniel H. Kaiser (Salt Lake City, UT: Charles Schlacks Jr, 1992), p. 49.

22 *The Muscovite Law Code (Ulozhenie) of 1649. Part 1: text and translation*, tr. and ed. R. Hellie (Irvine, CA: Charles Schlacks Jr, 1988), p. 194.

23 *Ulozhenie*, p. 189.
24 See for example E. Levin, *Sex and Society in the World of the Orthodox Slavs, 900–1700* (Ithaca, NY and London: Cornell University Press, 1989), pp. 85, 123.
25 Kaiser, *The Laws*, p. 44.
26 P. Walters, 'The Russian Orthodox Church and Foreign Christianity: The Legacy of the Past', in J. Witte Jr and M. Bourdeaux (eds), *Proselytism and Orthodoxy in Russia: the new war for souls* (Maryknoll, NY: Orbis, 1999), pp. 31–50, especially p. 32.
27 Paul W. Werth, 'Orthodoxy as ascription (and beyond): religious identity on the edges of the Orthodox community, 1740–1917', in Valerie A. Kivelson and Robert H. Greene (eds), *Orthodox Russia: belief and practice under the tsars* (University Park, PA: Pennsylvania University Press, 2003), pp. 239–51, especially p. 242.
28 Daniel H. Kaiser, 'Quotidian Orthodoxy: domestic life in early modern Russia', in Kivelson and Greene (eds), *Orthodox Russia*, pp. 179–92, especially p. 180.
29 Kivelson and Greene, *Orthodox Russia*, p. 8. See Debra Coulter, 'Church Reform and the "White Clergy" in Seventeenth Century Russia', in *Modernizing Muscovy: reform and social change in seventeenth-century Russia*, eds Jarmo Kotilaine and Marshall Poe (London and New York: Routledge, 2004), especially pp. 311–13, on records kept by seventeenth-century parish clergy.
30 On the problem of characterizing societies as 'Christian' (with different conclusions), see chapter two of James C. Russell, *The Germanization of Early Medieval Christianity: a sociohistorical approach to religious transformation* (New York and Oxford: OUP, 1994).
31 Eve Levin, 'Lay Religious Identity in Medieval Russia: the evidence of Novgorod birchbark documents', *General Linguistics* 35, nos. 1–4 (1997), 131–55.
32 Eve Levin, 'Supplicatory Prayers as a Source for Popular Religious Culture in Muscovite Russia', in Samuel H. Baron and Nancy Shields Kollmann (eds), *Religion and Culture in Early Modern Russia and Ukraine* (DeKalb, IL: Northern Illinois University Press, 1997), pp. 96–114.
33 Jennifer Lee Anderson, 'Gender Role Construction, Morality and Social Norms in Early Modern Russia', unpublished PhD thesis (Ohio State University, 2001), p. 201.
34 I. Ia. Froianov, A. Iu. Dvornichenko and Iu. V. Krivosheev, 'The Introduction of Christianity in Russia and the Pagan Traditions', in M. M. Balzer (ed.), *Russian Traditional Culture: religion, gender and customary law* (Armonk, NY and London: M. E. Sharpe, 1992), p. 3.
35 'Slovo o zakone i blagodati mitropolita Kievskogo Ilariona', in *BLDR t. 1 (XI–XII veka)* (St Petersburg: Nauka, 1997), pp. 25–61; see p. 38.
36 Simon Franklin (trans.), *Sermons and Rhetoric of Kievan Rus'* (HLEUL 5; Cambridge, MA: Harvard University Press, 1991), p. 14.
37 See for example P. P. Tolochko, *Drevniaia Rus': Ocherki sotsial'no-politicheskoi istorii* (Kiev: Nauka Dumka, 1987); P. P. Tolochko, 'Religious Sites in Kiev During the Reign of Volodimer Sviatoslavich', *HUS* 11, nos. 3/4 (1987), 317–22, and in the same volume, Volodymyr I. Mezentsev, 'The Masonry Churches of Medieval Chernihiv', 365–83.
38 'Slovo o zakone i blagodati', *BLDR* 1, p. 50.
39 Franklin (trans.), *Sermons and Rhetoric*, p. 25.
40 *Adam von Bremen Hamburgische Kirchengeschichte* (Hannover and Leipzig: Hahnsche Buchhandlung, 1917; reprinted 1993) p. 80.
41 Adam von Bremen, *A History of the Archbishops of Hamburg-Bremen*, translated with an introduction and notes by Francis J. Tschan, with new introduction and bibliography by Timothy Reuter (Records of Western Civilization; New York: Columbia University Press, 2002), p. 67.
42 *The Russian Primary Chronicle: Laurentian text*, trs and eds S. H. Cross and O. P. Sherbowitz-Wetzor (Cambridge, MA: Mediaeval Academy of America, 1953), pp. 116–17.

43 Recent calculations suggest that nineteen monasteries and convents were founded in the eleventh century, and a further forty in the twelfth century. See Metropolitan Makarii (Bulgakov), *Istoriia Russkoi Tserkvy, kn. 2: Istoriia russkoi tserkvy v period sovershennoi zavisimosti ee ot konstantinopol'skogo patriarkha (988–1240)*, pp. 668–71.

44 *Ottonian Germany: the chronicon of Thietmar of Merseburg*, translated and annotated by David A. Warner (Manchester and New York: Manchester University Press, 2001), p. 384 (book 8, chapter 32); *Thietmari Merseburgensis Episcopi Chronicon*, ed. Fridericus Kurze (Hannover: 1889), p. 258.

45 S. Franklin and J. Shepard, *The Emergence of Rus 750–1200* (London and New York: Longman, 1996), p. 352.

46 The eleventh century Homilies of Gregorii the Philosopher, for example, were found both in service books and in private reading books, indicating that they were intended both for private edification of the lettered, and public preaching. See *The Edificatory Prose of Kievan Rus'*, introd. and tr. W. R. Veder (HLEUL 6; Cambridge, MA: Harvard University Press, 1994).

47 Vera Shevzov, 'Letting the people into Church: reflections on Orthodoxy and community in late Imperial Russia', in Valerie A. Kivelson and Robert H. Greene (eds), *Orthodox Russia: belief and practice under the tsars* (University Park, PA: Pennsylvania State University Press, 2003), p. 62.

48 See for example Anderson, *Gender Role Construction*.

49 See for example V. P. Darkevich, 'K voprosu o "dvoeverie" v Drevnei Rusi', in *Vostochnaia Evropa v drevnosti i srednevekov'e: iazychestvo, khristianstvo, tserkov'* (Moscow: RAN, 1995), p. 13.

50 See for example T. A. Bernshtam, 'Russian Folk Culture and Folk Religion', in Balzer, *Russian Traditional Culture*, p. 35.

51 See for example *Converging Worlds: religion and community in peasant Russia, 1861–1917* by Chris J. Chulos (DeKalb, IL: Northern Illinois University Press, 2003), and his overview of research on local religion in Russia: 'The End of Cultural Survivals (*perezhitki*): Remembering and Forgetting Russian Peasant Religious Traditions', *Studia Slavica Finlandensia* 17 (2000), 190–207.

52 See for example Brown, *Popular Piety in Late Medieval England*. As Peter Burke has pointed out, the notion of 'microhistory' has earlier precedents: *History and Historians*, p. 8.

53 See for example Harmening, *Superstitio*; Michele R. Salzman, ' "Superstitio" in the Codex Theodosianus and the persecution of pagans', *Vigiliae Christianae* 41 (1987), 172–88; P. A. Florenskii, 'O Sueverii', *Simvol* 20 (1988), 241–67.

54 E. B. Smilianskaia, 'O kontsepte "sueverie" v Rossii veka Prosveshcheniia', in Zh. V. Kormina, A. A. Panchenko and S. A. Shtyrkov (eds), *Sny Bogoroditsy. Issledovaniia po antropologii religii* (St Petersburg: Evropeiskii universitete v S-Peterburg, 2006), pp. 19–31.

55 This fear of contamination by unbelievers is by no means specific to Russian Orthodoxy, but common to many, if not all religious faiths.

56 'Kanonicheskie otvety mitropolita Ioanna II', in *Russkaia istoricheskaia biblioteka VI: Pamiatniki drevne-russkogo kanonicheskogo prava, chast' 1 (Pamiatniki XI–XV v.)* (St Petersburg: Tip. Imp. Akademii Nauk, 1880), col. 9.

57 R. Kieckhefer, *Magic in the Middle Ages* (Cambridge: CUP, 1995), p. 37.

58 W. F. Ryan, *The Bathhouse at Midnight: an historical survey of magic and divination in Russia* (Thrupp, Stroud: Sutton Publishing, 1999), pp. 2–4. See also Simon Franklin on definitions of 'magic' and 'pagan', in *Writing, Society and Culture in Early Rus, c. 950–1300* (Cambridge: CUP, 2002), pp. 255–60 and Dieter Harmening's 'The history of Western magic: some considerations', *Folklore* 17 (2001), 85–95.

59 Carole M. Cusack, *The Rise of Christianity in Northern Europe, 300–1000* (London and New York: Cassell Religious Studies, 1999), p. 177.

60 Alexander Murray for example has pointed out that 'In its missionary phase the purpose of Christian language was to win hearts from both paganism *and* magic, so it lumped them together, charging us, much later, with the task of their separation'. See his 'Missionaries and Magic in Dark-Age Europe', in Lester K. Little and Barbara H. Rosenwein (eds), *Debating the Middle Ages: issues and readings* (Oxford and Malden, MA: Blackwell Publishers, 1998), p. 101. See also R. A. Markus, 'Gregory the Great's Pagans', in Richard Gameson and Henrietta Leyser (eds), *Belief and Culture in the Middle Ages: studies presented to Henry Mayr-Harting* (Oxford and New York: OUP, 2001), pp. 23–34.

61 See for example David Porter's *Hallowe'en: trick or treat?* (Tunbridge Wells: Monarch 1993).

62 Ronald Hutton, *The Stations of the Sun: a history of the ritual year in Britain* (Oxford: OUP, 1996; reissued 2001), p. 384.

63 Peter Brown, *The Rise of Western Christendom: triumph and diversity, AD 200–1000* (Malden, MA and Oxford: Blackwell, 2003), pp. 146–7.

64 *OED*, vol. 11 (Second edition; Oxford: Clarendon Press, 1989), p. 59.

65 Eve Levin, '*Dvoeverie* and Popular Religion' in S. K. Batalden (ed.), *Seeking God: the recovery of religious identity in Orthodox Russia, Ukraine, and Georgia* (DeKalb, IL: Northern Illinois University Press, 1993), p. 37.

66 Syncretism is, of course, another loaded term with a voluminous literature. A useful recent reappraisal of the term can be found in David Frankfurter, 'Syncretism and the Holy Man in Late Antique Egypt', *Journal of Early Christian Studies* 11, no. 3 (2003), 339–85. See also Charles Stewart's 'genealogical consideration' of the term in 'Syncretism and its synonyms. Reflections on cultural mixture', *Diacritics* 29, no. 3 (1999), 40–62 and Appendix 1 'Syncretism – the term and the phenomenon', in Irina Levinskaya's *The Book of Acts in Its Diaspora Setting* (Book of Acts in Its First Century Setting, 5; Grand Rapids, MI: Wm. B. Eerdmans, 1996), pp. 197–203.

67 R. R. Milner-Gulland, *The Russians* (Oxford and Malden, MA: Blackwell, 1997), pp. 85–7. For a more conventional analysis of East Slavic paganism, see M. Gimbutas, *The Slavs* (London: Thames & Hudson, 1971), pp. 156–9, 162–9.

68 The authenticity of the Igor Tale is debated. See for example J. L. I. Fennell's 'The Recent Controversy in the Soviet Union over the Authenticity of the *Slovo*', in Lyman H. Legters (ed.), *Russia: essays in history and literature* (Leiden: E. J. Brill, 1972), pp. 1–17; Edward L. Keenan's *Josef Dobrovsky and the Origins of the Igor' Tale* (Cambridge, MA and London: Harvard University Press, 2004) and A. A. Zimin's work: *Slovo o polku Igoreve* (St Petersburg: Dmitrii Bulanin, 2006).

69 'Slovo o polku Igoreve, Igoria, syna Sviatslavlia, vnuka Ol'gova', in L. A. Dmitriev and D. S. Likhachev (eds), *Literatura Drevnei Rusi: khrestomatiia* (Moscow: Vysshaia shkola, 1990), p. 151.

70 'Zadonshchina', in *BLDR* t. 6 (*XIV – seredina XV veka*) (St Petersburg: Nauka, 1999), pp. 104, 108. See also R. Jakobson and D. S. Worth (eds), *Sofonija's Tale of the Russian–Tatar Battle on the Kulikovo Field* (The Hague: Mouton, 1963).

71 See Fletcher, *The Conversion of Europe*, pp. 504–7, and S. C. Rowell's *Lithuania Ascending: a pagan empire within east-central Europe, 1295–1345* (Cambridge: CUP, 1994).

72 I. I. Sreznevskii, *Materialy dlia slovaria drevne-russkago iazyka po pis'mennym pamiatnikam*, t. 1 (St Petersburg: Tip. Imp. Akademii Nauk, 1893), col. 1012, from the Pskov Chronicle year 1265 (6773) and the Novgorod Chronicle year 1406 (6914) respectively.

73 Sreznevskii, *Materialy*, t. 1, col. 1012.

74 M. V. Korogodina, *Ispoved' v Rossii v XIV–XIX vekakh: Issledovanie i teksty* (St Petersburg: Dmitrii Bulanin, 2006), p. 244.

L

166 *Notes*

75 *OED*, vol. 7 (Second edition; Oxford: Clarendon Press, 1989), p. 927.
76 'The return of Patriarch Filaret to Moscow', in L. Wiener (ed.), *Anthology of Russian Literature*, vol. 1 (New York and London: Putnam's Sons, 1902), p. 134.
77 D. P. Costello and I. P. Foote (eds), *Russian Folk Literature: Skazki, liricheskie pesni, byliny. Istoricheskie pesni. Dukhovnye stikhi.* (Oxford: Clarendon Press, 1967), p. 161.
78 Although it does sometimes seem to have also held the meaning of 'vampire', 'dead sorcerer' or 'witch'; see L. J. Ivanits, *Russian Folk Belief* (New York and London: M. E. Sharpe, 1992), p. 122.

1 Christian idol-worshippers and 'pagan survivals'

1 *Modern Encyclopedia of Russian and Soviet History*, vol. 10, ed. J. L. Wieczynski (Gulf Breeze, FL: Academic International Press, 1979), pp. 73–5.
2 See for example G. P. Fedotov, *The Russian Religious Mind. Vol. 1: Kievan Christianity, the tenth to the thirteenth centuries* (New York, Evanston and London: Harper & Row, 1960), p. 346.
3 Francis Thomson has pointed out that 'христолюбьць' is more properly 'Christian' than 'Christlover', but conventionally the sermon is referred to as the *Sermon of the Christlover*. 'On the Problems Involved in Translating Slavonic Texts into a Modern Language', *Byzantinoslavica* 55, no. 2 (1994), 360–75.
4 Professor S. P. Shevyrev describes his discovery of the *Sbornik* in the Kirillo-Belozerskii Monastery library in his *Poezdka v Kirillo-Belozerskii monastyr': vakatsionnye dni professora S. Shevyreva v 1847 godu*, chast II (Moscow: Universitetskaia tipografiia, 1850), pp. 32–9.
5 A consensus of academic opinion dates this collection as late fourteenth to early fifteenth century. The manuscript bears the inscription 'Prince Stefan Vasil' evich Komrin, year 6320 [1412]'. See N. Gal'kovskii, *Bor'ba khristianstva s ostatkami iazychestva v drevnei Rusi. T. 2: Drevne-russkiia slova i poucheniia, napravlennyia protiv ostatkov iazychestva v narode* (Moscow: A. I. Snegirev, 1913), p. 37.
6 It was first published in F. I. Buslaev (ed.), *Istoricheskaia khristomatiia: tserkovno-slavianskago i drevne-russkago iazykov* (Moscow: Universitetskoi tip., 1861) with a helpful footnote explaining that 'those of the Russians who, accepting the Christian faith did not give up the pagan faith, are here called *dvoeverno zhivushchim*', see col. 535.
7 Anichkov concludes firmly that the sermon was written in Kiev, in the mid-eleventh century. See E. V. Anichkov, *Iazychestvo i Drevniaia Rus'* (St Petersburg: Tip. M. M. Stasiulevicha, 1914; reprinted Munich: Verlag Otto Sagner, 1995), pp. 132–7. Mansikka is reluctant to date the *Christlover* at all; see V. J. Mansikka, *Die Religion der Ostslaven* (Helsinki: Suomalainen Tiedeaktemia, 1922), p. 160.
8 See for example Filaret (Gumilievskii), Archbishop of Chernigov, *Obzor' Russkoi dukhovnoi literatury: kniga pervaia i vtoraia, 862–1863* (St Petersburg: Izd. I. L. Tuzova, 1884; third edition reprinted Oxford: Meeuws, 1984), p. 13.
9 Anichkov, *Iazychestvo*, pp. 135–6.
10 This phrase is difficult as *dvoeverno* is an adverb and, in combination with *vo* ('in'), doesn't make sense. One can either ignore the *vo* or assume that it originally read *vo dvoeverii* 'in double-belief', as Sreznevskii does: See I. I. Sreznevskii, *Materialy dlia slovaria drevne-russkago iazyka po pis'mennym pamiatnikam*, t. 1 (St Petersburg: Tip. Imp. Akademii Nauk, 1893), col. 640.
11 M. Mazo, ' "We Don't Summon Spring in the Summer": traditional music and beliefs of the contemporary Russian village', in W. C. Brumfield and M. M. Velimirovic (eds), *Christianity and the Arts in Russia* (Cambridge: CUP, 1991), p. 76.
12 'Slovo nekoego khristoliubtsa', in F. I. Buslaev (ed.), *Istoricheskaia khristomatiia: tserkovno-slavianskago i drevne-russkago iazykov* (Moscow: Universitetskoi tip., 1861), cols 519–20 [*Paisievskii* redaction].

13 Mansikka suggests that this should be read as 3 × 9 rather than 39, as suggested by T. V. Chertoritskii for example, in *Krasnorechie Drevnei Rusi: XI–XVII vv.* (Moscow: Sov. Rossiia, 1987), p. 123. Generally, 39 would be written as л҃ѳ.

14 A number of scholars have identified Il'ia as the prophet Elijah; see for example Gerhard Podskalsky 'Principal Aspects and Problems of Theology in Kievan Rus'', *HUS* 11, nos. 3/4 (1987), p. 276.

15 I Kings 19:10 (KJV).

16 III Kings 18:21 in the Slavonic Bible, where there are four Books of Kings. Some early sources have a different reading – see for example *Paremeinik* no. 4, Trinity-St Sergius Monastery (Moscow State Library Archive, Fond 304), l.133ob, available online at www.stsl.ru/manuscripts/medium.php?col=1&manuscript=004& pagefile=004-0138 (accessed 7 December 2006). M. A. Johnson dates this to the fourteenth century (rather than to the thirteenth century as indicated on the website) in 'Observations on the Hymnography of Certain Medieval Slavic Parimejniks', *Srpski jezik* 2, nos. 1/2 (1997), 363–76. The Septaguint reads 'ἕως πότε ὑμεῖς χωλανεῖτε ἐπ' ἀμφοτέραις ταῖς ἰγνύαις;' – 'how long will ye limp on both knees?' A literal translation of the Hebrew is 'hopping on the two boughs': see I Kings 18:21, *Tanakh: The Holy Scriptures: the new JPS translation according to the traditional Hebrew text* (Philadelphia: Jewish Publication Society, 1985).

17 Interestingly, Golubinskii makes the point that the Israelites often fell into the 'sickness' of double-belief. See E. E. Golubinskii, *Istoriia russkoi tserkvi, t. 1, vtoraia polovina toma* (Moscow: Univ. tip., 1904; reprinted The Hague and Paris: Mouton, 1969), p. 851.

18 R. Picchio, 'The impact of ecclesiastical culture on old Russian literary techniques' in H. Birnbaum and M. S. Flier (eds), *Medieval Russian Culture*, vol. 1 (Berkeley, CA: University of California Press, 1984), pp. 277–8.

19 *The Russian Primary Chronicle: Laurentian text*, trs and eds S. H. Cross and O. P. Sherbowitz-Wetzor (Cambridge, MA: Mediaeval Academy of America, 1953), p. 93.

20 Although Cross suggests that the Simar'gl of the *Primary Chronicle* is a 'copyist's combination of the two deities, Sim, a household spirit, and Rogl, a spirit of the harvest', without suggesting sources for these latter two. See Cross, *Primary Chronicle*, p. 227. Others have suggested Simargl as a winged creature and/or fertility god of Iranian provenance.

21 *PSRL 2: Ipat'evskaia letopis'* (St Petersburg: Tip. M. A. Aleksandrova, 1908; reprinted Moscow: Izd. Vostochnoi literatury, 1962), cols. 278–9.

22 Malalas was probably translated in Bulgaria in the tenth century. See F. J. Thomson, 'The Distorted Mediaeval Russian Perception of Classical Antiquity: The Causes and the Consequences', in F. J. Thomson, *The Reception of Byzantine Culture in Mediaeval Russia* (Aldershot: Ashgate Variorum, 1999), p. 320; Simon Franklin, 'Malalas in Slavonic', in E. Jeffreys et al. (eds), *Studies in John Malalas* (Sydney: Australian Association for Byzantine Studies, 1990), 276–90.

23 See in particular the appendices in Anichkov, *Iazychestvo*.

24 I Corinthians 10:20–22 (KJV).

25 'Slovo nekoego khristoliubtsa', *Istoricheskaia khristomatiia*, col. 524.

26 Anichkov, *Iazychestvo*, p. 37.

27 'Slovo nekoego khristoliubtsa', *Istoricheskaia khristomatiia*, col. 522.

28 V. Ia. Petrukhin, 'Drevnerusskoe dvoeverie: poniatie i fenomen', *Slavianovedenie* (1996), no. 1, p. 45.

29 'Slovo nekoego khristoliubtsa', *Istoricheskaia khristomatiia*, col. 520.

30 This should probably read 'such are worse', or as a rhetorical question perhaps: 'are such not worse than . . . ?'

31 *Die Chronik des Georgios Hamartolos: in altslavischer Übersetzung, Band 1* (Munich: Wilhelm Fink Verlag, 1972), p. 63. See also Mansikka, *Die Religion*, p. 153; Gal'kovskii, *Bor'ba khristianstva t. 2*, p. 39.

32 The late fourteenth-century *Paisievskii sbornik* version, a version included in the late fifteenth-century collection of the *Novgorodskii Sofiiskii Sobor* and a third version from the late fourteenth-century *Zlataia tsep'* of the Trinity-St Sergius Monastery.

33 Anichkov, *Iazychestvo*, pp. 32–3.

34 Anichkov, *Iazychestvo*, p. 29.

35 Mansikka, *Die Religion der Ostslaven*, p. 159.

36 'Slovo nekoego khristoliubtsa', in N. Tikhonravov, 'Slova i poucheniia, napravlennyia protiv iazycheskikh verovanii i obriadov', in *Letopisi Russkoi literatury i drevnosti*, t. 4 (Moscow: Tip. Gracheva, 1862), p. 92.

37 Or 'having fashioned a phallus' – my thanks to both Daniel Collins and Maria Korogodina for help with this sentence.

38 Or 'sniff [it] and lick [it] and kiss [it]'.

39 Literally, 'they are no worse than Jews, and heretics, and Bulgars'.

40 'Slovo nekoego khristoliubtsa', *Istoricheskaia khristomatiia*, col. 523.

41 Wheat and honey, according to Sophia Senyk, *A History of the Church in Ukraine. Vol. 1: To the end of the thirteenth century* (Rome: Pontificio Istituto Orientale, 1993), p. 189.

42 Or 'an unlawful table'.

43 Tikhonravov, 'Slova i poucheniia', pp. 94–5.

44 See for example M. Warner, *Alone of All Her Sex: the myth and the cult of the Virgin Mary* (London: Picador, 1985), pp. 281–2. See also Vasiliki Limberis, *Divine Heiress: the Virgin Mary and the creation of Christian Constantinople* (London and New York: Routledge, 1994), pp. 118–20.

45 See Chapter 2.

46 Warner, *Alone of All Her Sex*, p. 275. See also Stephen Benko, *The Virgin Goddess: studies in the pagan and Christian roots of Mariology* (Leiden and New York: E. J. Brill, 1993), especially pp. 170–95.

47 Mansikka, *Die Religion*, p. 156. See also p. 157 for his discussion of '*baby kashi*'.

48 In the *Kormchaia kniga* this appears as 'мѹкѹ', 'flour': V. N. Beneshevich (ed.), *Drevne-slavianskaia kormchaia XIV titulov bez tolkovanii*, t. 1, vyp. 1–3 (St Petersburg: Imperatorskoi Akademii Nauk, 1906–7), p. 191.

49 Henry R. Percival, *The Seven Ecumenical Councils of the Undivided Church: their canons and dogmatic decrees together with the canons of all the local synods which have received ecumenical acceptance* (Nicene and Post-Nicene Fathers of the Christian Church, Second Series, vol. 14; Oxford: James Parker and Company, 1900), p. 399.

50 Tikhonravov, 'Slova i poucheniia', p. 86. See also the first fourteenth-century fragment pp. 85–6 which is another possible source for the *rozhanitsy*/Mother of God feasts.

51 See for example the 'Questions to women and girls' from a sixteenth-century manuscript, in A. Almazov, *Tainaia ispoved' v Pravoslavnoi vostochnoi tserkvi, t. III: Prilozheniia* (Odessa: Tipo-litografiia Shtaba Odesskago voennago okruga, 1894; reprinted Moscow: Palomnik, 1995), p. 167.

52 *Russkaia istoricheskaia biblioteka, t. VI: Pamiatniki drevne-russkogo kanonicheskogo prava, chast' 1 (Pamiatniki XI–XV v.)* (St Petersburg: Tip. Imp. Akademii Nauk, 1880), col. 31.

53 Unfortunately the scope of this book does not permit further exploration of this fascinating area. For a detailed analysis of the textual evidence, possible origins and meanings of *rozhanitsy*, see I. Sreznevskii's 'Rozhenitsy u slavian i drugikh iazycheskikh narodov', in N. Kalachov (ed.), *Arkhiv istoriko-iuridicheskikh svedenii otnosiashchikhsia do Rossii, kn. 2, polovina pervaia* (Moscow: Tip. A. Semen, 1855). See also Mansikka's discussion of *rod* and *rozhanitsy* in *Die Religion*, pp. 142–7; Petrukhin's section on *rod* and *rozhanitsy* in 'Drevniaia Rus': Narod.

Kniaz'ia. Religiia', in V. Ia. Petrukhin (ed.), *Iz istorii russkoi kul'tury t.1: Drevniaia Rus'* (Moscow: Iazyki Russkoi Kul'tury, 2000), pp. 236–43; N. I. Zubov, 'O periodizatsii slavianskogo iazychestva v drevnerusskikh spiskakh "Slovo sv. Grigoriia"', *Zhivaia starina* (1998), no. 1, 8–10. A good summary of *rod* scholarship from 1850 to 1990 is L. C. Klein's 'Pamiati iazycheskogo boga roda', in I. V. Dubov (ed.), *Iazychestvo vostochnykh slavian: Sbornik nauchnykh trudov* (Leningrad: Ministerstvo Kul'tury SSSR, 1990), pp. 13–26. Klein also strongly argues against the existence of a Slavic deity 'Rod'.

54 Mansikka, *Die Religion*, pp. 142–3. See also Rybakov's comparison of the *Sermon of Isaiah the Prophet* with the Biblical text of Isaiah 65:8–15 in *Iazychestvo drevnikh slavian* (Moscow: Russkoe slovo, 1997), pp. 602–5. See also *Paremeinik* no. 4, Trinity-St Sergius Monastery (Moscow State Library Archive, Fond 304), l.71, available online at www.stsl.ru/manuscripts/medium.php?col=1&manuscript=004&pagefile=004-0075 (accessed 7 December 2006).

55 A. E. Musin, 'K kharakteristike russkogo srednevekovogo mirovozzreniia (Problema "dvoeveriia": metodologicheskii aspekt)', in V. A. Khrshanovskii et al. (eds), *Rekonstruktsiia drevnikh verovanii: istochniki, metod, tsel'* (St Petersburg: GMIR, 1991), p. 210.

56 Ronald Hutton, *The Stations of the Sun: a history of the ritual year in Britain* (Oxford and New York: OUP, 1996), pp. 1–3. See also Anton Wessels, *Europe: was it ever really Christian? The interaction between Gospel and Culture* (London: SMC Press Ltd., 1994), pp. 41–5.

57 N. M. Gal'kovskii, *Bor'ba khristianstva s ostatkami iazychestva v drevnei Rusi*, t. 1 (Kharkov: Eparkhial'naia tip., 1916), p. 125.

58 Gal'kovskii, *Bor'ba khristianstva* 1, p. 126.

59 Gal'kovskii, *Bor'ba khristianstva* 1, p. 1.

60 'Slovo nekoego khristoliubtsa', *Istoricheskaia khristomatiia*, col. 523.

61 Tikhonravov, 'Slova i poucheniia', pp. 83–112.

62 See for example G. Podskal'ski, *Khristianstvo i bogoslovskaia literatura v Kievskoi Rusi (988–1237 gg.): izdanie vtoroe, ispravlennoe i dopolnennoe dlia russkogo perevoda*, trans. A. V. Nazarenko (St Petersburg: Bizantinorossika, 1996), pp. 408–9; B. A. Rybakov, *Iazychestvo drevnei Rusi* (Moscow: Nauka, 1988), p. 514; Golubinskii, *Istoriia* 1.2, p. 859; M. Azbukin, 'Ocherk literaturnoi bor'by predstavitelei khristianstva s ostatkami iazychestva v russkom narode (XI–XIV veka)', *RFV* 35, no. 2 (1896), 246–9.

63 Rybakov, *Iazychestvo drevnei Rusi*, p. 514.

64 This sermon exists in manuscript in the fourteenth-century *Paisievskii sbornik*, the fifteenth-century *Novgorodskaia Sofiiskaia biblioteka* No. 1295, the *Kirillo-Belozerskii Monasterii* No. 43/1120 and the sixteenth-century manuscript of the *Chudovskii Monasterii* No. 270 l.221.

65 Anichkov, *Iazychestvo*, pp. 146–7.

66 Anichkov, *Iazychestvo*, p. 66.

67 Tikhonravov, 'Slova i poucheniia', p. 105.

68 Gregory Nazianzus, 'Oration on the Holy Lights', *A Select Library of Nicene and Post-Nicene Fathers of the Christian Church*, Series II, Vol. VII, Philip Schaff and Henry Wace (eds), translated by Charles Gordon Browne and James Edward Swallow (Grand Rapids, MI: Wm. B. Eerdmans Publishing Company, 1894), p. 353. A recent translation of the sermon is also available in Brian E. Daley, S. J., *Gregory of Nazianzus* (London and New York: Routledge, 2006), pp. 128–38.

69 See for example Francis Thomson, 'The Nature of the Reception of Christian Byzantine Culture in Russia in the Tenth to Thirteenth Centuries and Its Implications for Russian Culture', *Slavica Gandensia* 5 (1978), 107–39; Simon Franklin, *Byzantium – Rus – Russia: studies in the translation of Christian Culture* (Aldershot: Ashgate Variorum, 2002), especially p. 184.

70 This could mean the 'honouring of Rod', but given the Greek, 'reading of birth/fate' seems more probable.
71 'Slovo sv. Grigoriia', in Gal'kovskii, *Bor'ba khristianstva* 2, pp. 24–5.
72 See for example Mansikka, *Die Religion*, p. 178 and Rybakov, *Iazychestvo drevnei Rusi*, p. 463.
73 Mansikka describes the reference to *vily* as 'an echo of the South Slav literary tradition' (*Die Religion*, p. 153) and sees it as a Turkish/Tartar loan word, firmly related to the spirits of the dead (p. 160). See also A. N. Afanas'ev, *Poeticheskiia vozzreniia slavian na prirodu*, t. 3 (Moscow: Izd. K. Soldatenkova, 1869; reprinted Moscow: Izd. Indrik, 1994), p. 153, who points out that in the chronicle of George Harmartolos *vily* are equated with sirens; and Marija Gimbutas, *The Slavs* (London: Thames and Hudson, 1971), p. 164, who describes the *vila* worshipped by Slovaks, Croats, Serbs and Bulgarians as 'battle-maidens' for whom offerings were left under trees, at springs, caves and stones. In some penitentials, *vily* are clarified simply as 'idols'; see M. V. Korogodina, *Ispoved' v Rossii v XIV–XIX vekakh: Issledovanie i teksty* (St Petersburg: Dmitrii Bulanin, 2006), p. 226.
74 See also Anichkov, *Iazychestvo*, p. 385.
75 II Kings 17:9–10, 16–17.
76 'Slovo sv. Grigoriia', in Gal'kovskii, *Bor'ba khristianstva* 2, p. 23; Tikhonravov, 'Slova i poucheniia', p. 103.
77 'Slovo sv. Grigoriia', in Gal'kovskii, *Bor'ba khristianstva* 2, pp. 34–5.
78 'Slovo sv. ottsa nashego Ioanna Zlatoustago', in Gal'kovskii, *Bor'ba khristianstva* 2, p. 60; Tikhonravov, 'Slova i poucheniia', p. 108.
79 Rybakov argues that these are not the spirits of ancestors but of 'other' dead, and connects them with the *upiry*. See *Iazychestvo drevnei Rusi*, pp. 462–3.
80 'O poste k nevezham', in Gal'kovskii, *Bor'ba khristianstva* 2, p. 15.
81 This may be 'for delight', rather than 'for footprints', but given the context I prefer the latter.
82 See for example Afanas'ev, *Poeticheskiia vozzreniia*, p. 236.
83 Rybakov, *Iazychestvo drevnei Rusi*, p. 514. Later penitentials also mention heating the bathhouse for the dead on the eve of Trinity Sunday, see Korogodina, *Ispoved' v Rossii*, p. 230.
84 S. A. Zenkovsky (tr. and ed.), *Medieval Russia's Epics, Chronicles, and Tales* (New York: Dutton, 1963), p. 123.
85 On later Russian Orthodox missionary attitudes to Siberian paganism as 'manifestations of infantile "ignorance" . . . under the influence of dark forces', see Andrei A. Znamenski, *Shamanism and Christianity: native encounters with Russian Orthodox missions in Siberia and Alaska, 1820–1917* (Westport, CT and London: Greenwood Press, 1999), pp. 75–8.
86 Fedotov, *Russian Religious Mind* 1, p. 347.
87 *The Laws of Rus – tenth to fifteenth centuries*, tr. and ed. Daniel H. Kaiser (Salt Lake City, UT: Charles Schlacks Jr, 1992), p. 43.
88 Bernadette Filotas, *Pagan Survivals, Superstitions and Popular Cultures in Early Medieval Pastoral Literature* (Toronto: Pontifical Institute of Mediaeval Studies, 2005), p. 169.
89 See Filotas, *Pagan Survivals*, pp. 169–70. My thanks to Bernadette Filotas for this suggestion, originally by e-mail on the medieval-religion mailing list, 16 August 2003.
90 G. P. Fedotov, *The Russian Religious Mind. Vol. 2: The Middle Ages: the thirteenth to the fifteenth centuries* (Cambridge, MA: Harvard University Press, 1966), p. 133.
91 'Slovo sv. ottsa nashego Ioanna Zlatoustago', in Tikhonravov, 'Slova i poucheniia', p. 107.
92 Possibly from Romans 16:18: 'For they that are such [them which cause divisions and offences contrary to the doctrine which ye have learned (v. 17)] serve not

our Lord Jesus Christ, but their own belly; and by good words and fair speeches
deceive the hearts of the simple'.
93 Fedotov's translation (*Russian Religious Mind* 2, p. 133). This Biblical citation is
Philippians 3:19: 'whose God is their belly, and whose glory is in their shame'.
94 Fedotov, *Russian Religious Mind* 2, p. 134.
95 Fedotov, *Russian Religious Mind* 2, p. 133.
96 Will Ryan has suggested these sisters may be related to the *triasavitsy* or 'shaking
fever' demons (sometimes identified as twelve, seven, forty or seventy-seven evil
women, and/or 'daughters of Herod'), who appear in later Russian beliefs, derived
from the Greek demon Gylou. See W. F. Ryan, *The Bathhouse at Midnight: An
Historical Survey of Magic and Divination in Russia* (Thrupp, Stroud: Sutton
Publishing, 1999), especially pp. 244–52.
97 Tikhonravov, 'Slova i poucheniia', p. 87.
98 All five are published by E. V. Petukhov in *Serapion Vladimirskii, russkii propovednik XIII veka* (St Petersburg: Tip. Imp. Akademii Nauk, 1888).
99 Podskalsky, 'Principal Aspects', p. 270.
100 Petukhov, *Serapion Vladimirskii*, p. 11 (sermon 4).
101 Petukhov, *Serapion Vladimirskii*, p. 14 (sermon 5).
102 Petukhov, *Serapion Vladimirskii*, p. 14 (sermon 5).
103 The Tatar-Mongols effectively ruled over Russia from 1240 to 1480 after a series
of devastating campaigns from 1237 to 1240, when Kiev was razed. See Charles J.
Halperin's *Russia and the Golden Horde: the Mongol impact on medieval Russian
history* (Bloomington, IN: Indiana University Press, 1987).
104 The Golden Horde converted to Islam only in the early fourteenth century. Halperin,
Russia and the Golden Horde, p. 123.
105 J. Fennell, *A History of the Russian Church to 1448* (London and New York:
Longman, 1995), p. 88.
106 See Anichkov, *Iazychestvo*, chapter 4, although he also emphasizes the need to be
aware of the possible Greek origin of some of this material. The *Kormchaia kniga*
does in fact contain similar prohibitions; see Buslaev, *Istoricheskaia khristomatiia*,
cols 377–8, 382–4.
107 Fedotov, for example, declares it an 'exaggeration'; *Russian Religious Mind* 1,
p. 352.
108 For background on these minstrels or buffoons, see Z. I. Vlasova, *Skomorokhi i
fol'klor* (St Petersburg: Aleteiia, 2001) and Russell Zguta, *Russian Minstrels: a history of the skomorokhi* (Philadelphia: University of Pennsylvania Press, 1978).
109 'Opredeleniia vladimirskago sobora, izlozhennyia v gramote mitropolita Kirilla II',
*Russkaia istoricheskaia biblioteka VI: Pamiatniki drevne-russkogo kanonicheskogo
prava, chast' 1 (Pamiatniki XI–XV v.)* (St Petersburg: Tip. Imp. Akademii Nauk,
1880), cols 83–102. Citation from col. 95.
110 'Opredeleniia vladimirskago sobora', *RIB VI: Pamiatniki drevne-russkago kanonicheskago prava, chast' 1 (Pamiatniki XI–XV v.)* (St Petersburg: Tip. Imp. Akademii
Nauk, 1880), col. 100.
111 See later for 'rusalii', not necessarily 'pagan games'.
112 Cross, *Primary Chronicle*, pp. 147–8.
113 Discussed further in the following chapter.
114 See however Azbukin's discussion on the 'pagan character' of drunkenness
in 'Ocherk literaturnoi bor'by', *RFV* 39, nos. 1–2 (1898), 248–50, in which he
proposes a link with pagan feasts.
115 Kaiser, *The Laws*, p. 50. Again, this may well have a canonical precedent referring
to early Roman games.
116 Golubinskii, *Istoriia* 1.2, p. 850.
117 E. Levin, *Sex and Society in the World of the Orthodox Slavs, 900–1700* (Ithaca,
NY and London: Cornell University Press, 1989), p. 280.

118 'Kanonicheskie otvety mitropolita Ioanna II', *RIB* VI, cols 8–9.
119 *Codex Canonum Ecclesiæ Universæ: the canons of the first four general councils of the Church, and those of the early local Greek synods* (London: R. D. Dickinson, 1870), p. 171.
120 Beneshevich, *Drevne-slavianskaia kormchaia* 1, p. 277.
121 Percival, *Seven Ecumenical Councils*, p. 157.
122 Percival, *Seven Ecumenical Councils*, p. 376
123 Korogodina, *Ispoved' v Rossii*, pp. 292–3, 501, 492–3. See also Almazov, *Tainaia ispoved'*, t. III, pp. 177, 183–4.
124 Ryan, *Bathhouse at Midnight*, pp. 320–3.
125 'Kanonicheskie otvety', *RIB* VI, col. 8.
126 *Stoglav: issledovanie i tekst*, E. V. Emchenko (ed.), (Moscow: Izd. Indrik, 2000), ch. 1, pp. 238–9.
127 J. E. Kollman, 'The *Stoglav* Council and the Parish Priests', *Russian History* 7, nos. 1–2 (1980), p. 65.
128 J. E. Kollmann, 'The Moscow *Stoglav* (hundred chapters) Church Council of 1551', unpublished PhD thesis (University of Michigan, 1978), p. 565.
129 See ch. 41, questions 2 and 3, Emchenko, *Stoglav*, pp. 304–5; Kollmann, 'The Moscow *Stoglav*', pp. 269–70.
130 See ch. 41, question 26, Emchenko, *Stoglav*, pp. 314–5.
131 See ch. 41, questions 17 and 22, Emchenko, *Stoglav*, pp. 310, 312–3.
132 See ch. 41, questions 16, 19 and 23, Emchenko, *Stoglav*, pp. 309–10, 311, 313.
133 See ch. 41, question 23, Emchenko, *Stoglav*, p. 313.
134 See ch. 41, questions 25 and 26, Emchenko, *Stoglav*, p. 314.
135 See ch. 41, question 27, Emchenko, *Stoglav*, p. 315.
136 Almazov, *Tainaia ispoved'*, t. III, p. 170. My thanks to Eve Levin for this reference. See also Korogodina, *Ispoved' v Rossii*, pp. 229–30.
137 Emchenko, *Stoglav*, ch. 41, pp. 313–4.
138 Sreznevskii, *Materialy dlia slovaria drevne-russkago iazyka po pis'mennym pamiatnikam*, t. 2 (St Petersburg: Tip. Imp. Akademii Nauk, 1902), col. 965 suggests *igry*, 'games', with a question mark for this word. Given the modern Russian *pleskat'*, 'to splash', and what we know about the rituals of St John's Eve (see Chapter 4), it is very tempting to translate this as 'splashing'.
139 See Korogodina, *Ispoved' v Rossii*, p. 236 for penitentials where 'clapping' is related to women's dances. Again, 'splashing' is a tempting translation here.
140 Possibly 'create spectacles' or 'nonsense', or 'ridicule'.
141 Emchenko, *Stoglav*, pp. 399–400 (my translation).
142 Rybakov, *Iazychestvo drevnei Rusi*, p. 659.
143 Emchenko, *Stoglav*, p. 402.
144 See the introductory note to the canons of the Council in Trullo in Percival, *Seven Ecumenical Councils*.
145 Percival, *Seven Ecumenical Councils*, p. 393.
146 Percival, *Seven Ecumenical Councils*, p. 393.
147 Kollman, 'The Moscow *Stoglav*', p. 541.
148 All of these canons were enshrined in the *Kormchaia kniga*. See Beneshevich, *Drevne-slavianskaia kormchaia* 1.
149 *The Domostroi: rules for Russian households in the time of Ivan the Terrible*, ed. and tr. Carolyn Johnston Pouncy (Ithaca and London: Cornell University Press, 1994), p. 117.
150 Ryan, *Bathhouse at Midnight*, p. 409.
151 See Emchenko, *Stoglav*, p. 403 for the Dionysus reference.
152 *Tvoreniia izhe vo sviatykh ottsa nashego Tikhona Zadonskago*, t. 1 (Moscow: Sinodal'naia Tipografiia, 1898), pp. 90–1.
153 See Charles E. Gribble, 'Earliest Slavic Attestations of the Custom of Rusalii', *Paleobulgarica* 13, no. 2 (1989), 41–6, for references and a discussion of early

manuscript evidence of medieval Rusalii, allegedly a pagan forerunner of the later *Rusal'naia nedeliia* and related to the Roman Rosalia, but sometimes simply indicating 'Pentecost'. See also F. K. Litsas, 'Rousalia: the ritual worship of the dead', in Agehananda Bharati (ed.), *The Realm of the Extra-Human: agents and audiences* (The Hague and Paris: Mouton, 1975), pp. 447–66.
154 See for example Elizabeth Warner, *Russian Myths* (London: British Museum Press, 2002), pp. 43–4.
155 See Ivanits, *Russian Folk Belief*, p. 11; Rybakov, *Iazychestvo drevnei Rusi*, p. 682; M. Zabylin, *Russkii Narod: ego obychai, obriady, predaniia, sueveriia i poeziia* (Moscow: Kniga Printshop, 1990; reprint of 1880 edition), pp. 80–3.
156 *Tvoreniia izhe vo sviatykh ottsa nashego Tikhona Zadonskago*, p. 92.
157 *Tvoreniia izhe vo sviatykh ottsa nashego Tikhona Zadonskago*, p. 92.
158 *Tvoreniia izhe vo sviatykh ottsa nashego Tikhona Zadonskago*, p. 92.
159 I am indebted to Irina Levinskaia for pointing this out to me.
160 See for example Anichkov, 'Old Russian Pagan Cults', in *Transactions of the Third International Congress for the History of Religions*, vol. 2 (Oxford: Clarendon Press, 1908), p. 258.
161 As suggested by Eve Levin, in her '*Dvoeverie* and Popular Religion', in S. K. Batalden (ed.), *Seeking God: the recovery of religious identity in Orthodox Russia, Ukraine, and Georgia* (DeKalb, IL: Northern Illinois University Press, 1993), pp. 31–52.

2 Heretics, doubters and 'wrong-believing'

1 G. P. Fedotov, *The Russian Religious Mind. Vol. 1: Kievan Christianity, the tenth to the thirteenth centuries* (New York, Evanston and London: Harper & Row, 1960), p. 346.
2 E. Fält, *Compounds in Contact: a study in compound words with special reference to the Old Slavonic translation of Flavius Josephus' Peri tou Ioudaikou polemou* (Uppsala: Uppsala University, 1990), p. 65. Fält is citing the work of Zett, 1970.
3 A. M. Schenker, *The Dawn of Slavic: an introduction to Slavic philology* (New Haven, CT and London: Yale University Press, 1995), p. 194.
4 See F. J. Thomson, 'The Nature of the Reception of Christian Byzantine Culture in Russia in the Tenth to Thirteenth Centuries and its Implications for Russian Culture', *Slavica Gandensia* 5 (1978), especially pp. 115–17. Dmitrii Bulanin also made this observation with regard to the *Sermon on the Maccabees* discussed later (personal communication, 24 October 1998).
5 In comparing the Greek originals to their Slavonic translations, I have been greatly helped by Persephone Liulio, Vassiliki Roupa and Gavin Ashenden. Simon Franklin, Dmitrii Bulanin, Ia. Shchapov, Anatolii Turilov, Francis Thomson and William Ryan also made contributions that helped shape this chapter. However, my time at the Hilandar Research Library, Ohio State University proved invaluable in tackling these texts, and in particular, I am grateful for the tuition, support and advice of Professor Daniel Collins.
6 F. J. Thomson, 'The Corpus of Slavonic Translations Available in Muscovy: The Cause of Old Russia's Intellectual Silence and a Contributory Factor to Muscovite Cultural Autarky', in B. Gasparov and O. Raevsky-Hughes (eds), *Christianity and the Eastern Slavs. Vol. 1: Slavic cultures in the Middle Ages* (California Slavic Studies 16; Berkeley, CA: University of California Press, 1993), pp. 179–214.
7 Francis Thomson has laboured to establish such a corpus, surveying works in Slavonic translation available in Russia from the tenth to the fourteenth century, in 'The Nature of the Reception'; and from the fourteenth to the seventeenth century, in 'The Corpus of Slavonic Translations'.
8 Thomson, 'The Nature of the Reception', p. 115.

9 A lecture given at the Medieval Slavic Summer Institute, Hilandar Research Library, July 1999.
10 Thomson, 'The Nature of the Reception', p. 115.
11 From the eleventh century *Macedonian Folio*, as cited in Schenker, *The Dawn of Slavic*, p. 195.
12 Saint John of Damascus, *Des Hl. Johannes von Damaskus 'Ekthesis akribēs tēs Orthodoxou pisteōs' in der Übersetzung des Exarchen Johannes*, ed. L. Sadnik (Wiesbaden: Otto Harrassowitz, 1967), pp. 4–6.
13 *Des Hl. Johannes von Damaskus*, pp. 22–4.
14 G. P. Fedotov, *The Russian Religious Mind. Vol. 2: The Middle Ages: the thirteenth to the fifteenth centuries* (Cambridge, MA: Harvard University Press, 1966), p. 44.
15 R. Picchio, 'The impact of ecclesiastical culture on old Russian literary techniques', in H. Birnbaum and M. S. Flier (eds), *Medieval Russian Culture*, vol. 1 (Berkeley, CA: University of California Press, 1984), p. 259.
16 'O chtenii knig', *Istoricheskaia khristomatiia: tserkovno-slavianskago i drevne-russkago iazykov*, ed. F. I. Buslaev (Moscow: Universitetskoi tip., 1861), col. 289.
17 Picchio, 'The impact of ecclesiastical culture', p. 258.
18 Picchio, 'The impact of ecclesiastical culture', p. 260.
19 *The Vita of Constantine and the Vita of Methodius*, translated with commentaries by Marvin Kantor and Richard S. White (Michigan Slavic Materials 13; Michigan: University of Michigan, 1976), p. 45.
20 Kantor and White, *Vita of Methodius*, p. 89.
21 S. Franklin and J. Shepard, *The Emergence of Rus 750–1200* (London and New York: Longman, 1996), p. 234; *Sbornik otdeleniia russkago iazyka i slovesnosti*, t. 65 (St Petersburg: Tip. Imperatorskoi Akademii Nauk, 1899), p. 16.
22 *Svodnyi katalog slaviano-russkikh rukopisnykh knig, khraniashchikhsia v SSSR, XI–XIII vv.*, ed. S. O. Shmidt et al. (Moscow: Nauka, 1984), p. 116.
23 V. N. Beneshevich (ed.), *Drevne-slavianskaia kormchaia XIV titulov bez tolkovanii*, t. 1, vyp. 1–3 (St Petersburg: Imperatorskoi Akademii Nauk, 1906), pp. 780–1.
24 Sreznevskii also records the phrase 'Дъвовѣриѥ имѣти' from the *Efremovskaia Kormchaia*, giving the reference Efr. Krm. LXXXVII 57. He proposes a translation of ἀμφισβήτησιν, *controversiam* for this, and it is likely that Sreznevskii duplicated his material in this instance, since the above text is found under Chapter 57, shares the same meaning, and no other alternatives present themselves: I. I. Sreznevskii, *Materialy dlia slovaria drevne-russkago iazyka po pis'mennym pamiatnikam*, t. 1 (St Petersburg: Tip. Imp. Akademii Nauk, 1893), col. 639.
25 It seems to me possible that it was calqued from ἀμφίγνοια, *amphignoia*, meaning 'doubt'.
26 Ia. N. Shchapov, *Vizantiiskoe i iuzhnoslavianskoe pravovoe nasledie na Rusi v XI–XIII vv.* (Moscow: Nauka, 1978), p. 219. My thanks to Professor Kaiser for this reference.
27 For an explanation of the significance of *Calendae*, *Nonae* and *Eidus* – names of marker-days in the Roman Calendar from which all days are counted backwards – see B. Blackburn and L. Holford-Strevens, *The Oxford Companion to the Year: An exploration of calendar customs and time-reckoning* (Oxford and New York: OUP, 1999), pp. 672–3.
28 V. N. Beneshevich (ed.), *Drevneslavianskaia kormchaia XIV titulov bez tolkovanii*, t. 2 (Sophia: Izd-vo Bolgarskoi Akademii Nauk, 1987), p. 18.
29 In e-mail correspondence January 2000. See also W. F. Ryan, *The Bathhouse at Midnight: an historical survey of magic and divination in Russia* (Thrupp, Stroud: Sutton Publishing, 1999), p. 384.
30 *Staroslavianskii slovar' (po rukopisiam X–XI vekov)*, eds R. M. Tseitlin, R. Vecherka and E. Blagov (Moscow: Russkii Iazyk, 1994), p. 165.

31 F. Dvornik, *The Slavs: their early history and civilization* (Boston: American Academy of Arts and Sciences, 1956), p. 48. See also C. D. Buck, *A Dictionary of Selected Synonyms in the Principal Indo-European Languages: a contribution to the history of ideas* (Chicago and London: University of Chicago Press, 1949) for a list of synonyms for 'believe', including 'choose', 'be persuaded' and 'have confidence in'.

32 Beneshevich, *Drevne-slavianskaia kormchaia* 1, p. 684. Sreznevskii's *Materialy* similarly lists it as this, see col. 85.

33 Frederick Chase observes that the first eighty heresies of St John of Damascus' *On Heresies* 'are taken verbatim' from Epiphanius' *Panarion*, and that the text includes 'two important fragments of the *Arbiter* of John Philoponus in Heresy 83. These fragments of the *Arbiter* are all that exists of the original Greek text'. This may explain Beneshevich's slightly misleading title. *Saint John of Damascus: Writings*, tr. F. H. Chase, Jr. (Fathers of the Church vol. 37; New York: Fathers of the Church, Inc., 1958), pp. xxix, xxxi.

34 My thanks to Professor Daniel Collins for identifying this source for me. Francis Thomson notes that two separate translations of *De haeresibus compendium unde ortae sint et quomodo prodierunt*, Book Two of *The Fount of Knowledge*, are to be found in the two versions of the *Nomocanon xiv titulorum*, the Efremovskaia and the Ryazan (Serbian) redaction, which reached Russia in 1262. See Thomson, 'The Nature of the Reception', 111.

35 Beneshevich, *Drevne-slavianskaia kormchaia* 1, p. 684.

36 Professor Collins notes that here the Slavonic translator has misunderstood: literally 'which things they of the walking friend call indivisibles'. The Greek adverb *philon* (accusative in form), translated here as 'like to', has been taken as 'beloved one, friend'.

37 Personal communication, 27 July 1999.

38 I am also grateful to Ia. Shchapov for initially advising me that this translation from the Greek is incorrect (interview at the Institute of Russian History, Moscow, July 1998), and to Simon Franklin for help with this passage.

39 *The Laws of Rus – tenth to fifteenth centuries*, tr. and ed. Daniel H. Kaiser (Salt Lake City, UT: C. Schlacks Jr, 1992), p. 42.

40 Kaiser, *The Laws*, p. xx.

41 I. Žužek, *Kormčaja Kniga: studies on the chief code of Russian canon law* (Orientalia Christiana Analecta, no. 168; Rome: Pont. Institutum Orientalium Studiorum, 1964), p. 122.

42 Simon Franklin, *Writing, Society and Culture in Early Rus, c. 950–1300* (Cambridge: CUP, 2002), p. 137.

43 Žužek, *Kormčaja Kniga*, p. 125.

44 Franklin, *Writing, Society and Culture*, p. 137.

45 This latter theory is, according to Žužek, the opinion of A. S. Pavlov. See also F. J. Thomson, *The Reception of Byzantine Culture in Mediaeval Russia* (Aldershot: Ashgate Variorum, 1999), ch. 1, pp. 131–3 and D. H. Kaiser, *The Growth of the Law in Medieval Russia* (Princeton: Princeton University Press, 1980), p. 20.

46 *Sbornik otdeleniia russkago iazyka i slovesnosti*, t. 65 (St Petersburg: Tip. Imperatorskoi Akademii Nauk, 1899), p. 16; Žužek, *Kormčaja Kniga*, pp. 23–4.

47 Žužek, *Kormčaja Kniga*, pp. 23–4.

48 See Franklin, *Writing, Society and Culture*, pp. 147–9.

49 Sreznevskii, *Materialy*, t. 1, col. 639.

50 Published in *Velikiia Minei Chetii sobrannyia vserossiiskim Mitropolitom Makariem: sentiabr' dni 25–30* (St Petersburg: Izd. Arkheograficheskoi Kommissii, 1883), col. 1616.

51 *Sofiiskaia Biblioteka No. 1317*, *Velikaia Mineia Chet'ia na m. sentiabr'*, Ll.396a–415d (Archive of the State Public Library, St Petersburg).

52 *Sofiiskaia Biblioteka No. 1321, Velikaia Mineia Chet'ia na m. mai*, Ll.250a–270d (Archive of the State Public Library, St Petersburg).

53 *Sofiiskaia Biblioteka No. 1321*, l.259.

54 *Sofiiskaia Biblioteka No. 1317*, l.404.

55 I was unable to consult this manuscript as it was in Germany being prepared for publication, along with the *Uspenskii* manuscript, while the research for this book was being conducted.

56 A Russian recension of the *Life of St John the Theologian and Interpretation of the Apocalypses* dating from the third quarter of the sixteenth century also reads "воудж двонстанства, и распра многы" *Fekula 16*, l.51v. [*Fekula #15* in the Matejic Catalogue] (Hilandar Research Library, Ohio State University).

57 *Acta Joannis unter Benutzung von C. v. Tischendorf's Nachlass*, ed. T. Zahn (Erlangen: Verlag von Andreas Deichert, 1880), p. 71.

58 Interview at the RAN Institute of Russian Language Dictionary department, March 1999.

59 I. I. Sreznevskii publishes this and others in *Svedeniia i zametki o maloizvestnykh i neizvestnykh pamiatnikakh XLI–LXXX* (St Petersburg: Tip. Imperatorskii Academii Nauk, 1875).

60 M. V. Shchepkina and T. N. Protas'eva, *Sokrovishcha drevnei pis'mennosti i staroi pechati; obzor rukopisei russkikh, slavianskikh, grecheskikh, a takzhe knig staroi pechati Gosudarstvennogo istoricheskogo muzeia*, ed. M. N. Tikhomirov (Pamiatniki kul'tury, vyp. 30; Moscow: Sovetskaia Rossiia, 1958), p. 13.

61 *GIM Sin No. 945*, l.107.

62 Professor Collins suggests the 'stretching forth of hands', observing that this is a citation from Isaiah 58:9, not 58:6 as given in *Patrologia Graeca*: 'If thou take away from the midst of thee the yoke, the putting forth of the finger, and speaking vanity'.

63 This has been identified as a translation of the Greek *mikrologia* by Professor Collins – another calque. How comprehensible it would have been to a reader unfamiliar with the Greek is unclear – they might perhaps have read 'petty speaking' or 'speaking little' (*brachologia* – 'brevity in speech' – is also calqued as *maloslovesiie*) rather than 'miserliness'.

64 Brian E. Daley S. J., *Gregory of Nazianzus* (London and New York: Routledge, 2006), p. 97. The Greek is found in J.-P. Migne (ed.), *Tou en hagiois patros hemon Gregorou tou theologou Archiepiskopou Konstantinoupoleos, Ta heuriskomena panta = Sancti Patris Nostri Gregorii Theologi, vulgo Nazianzeni, Archiepiscopi Constantinopolitani, Opera quae exstant omnia*, vol. 1 (Patrologiae cursus completus. Series Graeca, t. 35; Paris: Migne, 1857; reprinted Turnhout: Brepols, 1960), col. 909. I am grateful also to Dmitrii Bulanin for help with this passage.

65 B. M. Metzger and M. D. Coogan (eds), *Oxford Companion to the Bible* (New York and Oxford: OUP, 1993), p. 482.

66 *GIM Sin No. 945*, l.133; my word divisions.

67 Daniel Collins suggests that 'tamo' is perhaps a mistake for 'tako': 'so', 'thus'. He suggests the reading 'The mother [acting] so firmly and [was] valorous'. Personal communication, April 2000.

68 Professor Collins has pointed out that this is a 'literalistic and yet muddled rendition of the Greek: "and of these was to her greater the word than the dead", with "word" probably indicating "reckoning, account, matter."'

69 Professor Collins suggests the much more palatable reading 'And o her [sacrifice] if perhaps [it is not too] bold [to say this] – even greater than Abraham's sacrifice'.

70 Migne, *Patrologia Graeca* t. 35, col. 915.

71 *Slovar' drevnerusskogo iazyka (XI–XIV vv)*, t. 3, p. 112.

72 *GIM Sin No. 945*, l.157, with my word divisions.

73 Professor Collins suggests 'Not permitting himself to hold any feelings of enmity towards Eusebius'.
74 Professor Collins suggests 'sins' for *soblazny*.
75 *Oxford Dictionary of the Christian Church*, ed. F. L. Cross (London: OUP, 1957), p. 138.
76 *Oxford Dictionary of the Christian Church*, pp. 44–5.
77 Professor Collins suggests that *amfiloloi* is probably 'a scribal corruption – a ditto-graphy for *amfilo(g)i*, borrowed from Greek *amphilogía*. The rendition of Greek [gi] as [j] would then parallel *naloj* "lecterne" from *analogia*'. The sentence might then read 'he endures the equivocations [or disputes] and doubt of the people'.
78 D. M. Bulanin, *Antichnye traditsii v drevnerusskoi literature XI–XVI vv.* (Munich: Verlag Otto Sagner, 1991), p. 139.
79 *Die grossen Lesemenaen des Metropoliten Makarij: Uspenskij Spisok. Band 1: 1–11 Marz*, eds E. Weiher, S. O. Smidt and A. I. Skurko (Freiburg: Weiher Verlag, 1997), p. 331.
80 *Prolog*, GIM Sin (*iz sobranii Mnshch.*) F. No. 1668–1.
81 The *Uspenskij Spisok, 1–11 Marz* gives 'otpushchenie'.
82 My thanks again to Professor Collins for helping me unravel this convoluted passage. His suggested reading is 'Some carnal [people], not being able to see those invisible [things], and falling into fear because of ignorance, are in doubt, considering [sc. 'when they consider'] [that] there exist those [things] which they cannot see with bodily eyes'. (Personal correspondence, 25 April 2000).
83 *Saint Gregory the Great: Dialogues*, tr. O. J. Zimmerman (Fathers of the Church vol. 39; New York: Fathers of the Church, Inc., 1959), p. 189. The original Latin text (with parallel Greek) is to be found in J.-P. Migne (ed.), *Sancti Gregorii papae I, cognomento Magni, Opera omnia*, vol. 3 (Patrologiae cursus completus. Series Latina, 77; Paris: Garnier, 1896), cols 317–20.
84 *Tserkovnyi slovar', ili istolkovanie rechenii slavenskikh drevnikh, takozh inoiazych-nykh bez perevoda polozhennykh v sviashchennom pisanii i drugikh tserkovnykh knigakh*, chast' 1, compiled by Petr Alekseev, Archpriest of the Moscow Archangel Cathedral and member of the Moscow Spiritual Consistory (St Petersburg: Ivan Glazunov, 1817), p. 237.
85 My thanks to Francis Thomson for this suggestion (personal correspondence, 18 January 2000).
86 See *Slovar' knizhnikov i knizhnosti Drevnei Rusi. Vyp 1: XI-pervaia polovina XIV v.*, ed. D. S. Likhachev (Leningrad: Nauka, 1987), pp. 314–15. For a more detailed discussion of translations and manuscript redactions see K. Diddi, *Paterik Rimskii. Dialogi Grigoriia Velikogo v drevneslavianskom perevode* (Moscow: Indrik, 2001), which also publishes the relevant passage on p. 361, with parallel Greek.
87 E. M. Vereshchagin, *Khristianskaia knizhnost' Drevnei Rusi* (Moscow: Nauka, 1996), p. 84.
88 Filaret, *Obzor' Russkoi dukhovnoi literatury*, p. 150.
89 *Velikiia Minei Chetii sobrannyia vserossiiskim Mitropolitom Makariem: oktiabr' dni 4–18* (St Petersburg: Izd. Arkheograficheskoi Kommissii, 1874), col. 1499.
90 For this difficult construction Professor Collins suggests either (a) 'in order that He appear sweet to them at length' or (b) 'in order that He appear very sweet to them'. The implication seems to be that the delay in recognition will make His revelation all the more sweet.
91 J.-P. Migne (ed.), *Theophylaktou archiepiskopou Boulgarias, Ta heuriskomena panta = Theophylacti, Bulgariae archiepiscopus, Opera quae reperiri potuerunt omnia*, vol. 1 (Patrologiae cursus completus. Series Graeca, t. 123; Paris: Migne, 1864), col. 1113.
92 Early Slavic Studies Mailing List (ESS-L), 7 January 1999.
93 *Slovar' knizhnikov i knizhnosti* 1, p. 76.

94 I am grateful to Oleg Panchenko of *Pushkinskii dom* for directing me to this passage, which is not cited in the historical dictionaries.
95 V. M. Istrin, *Knigy vremen'nyia i obraznyia Georgiia mnikha: khronika Georgiia Amartola v drevnem slavianorusskom perevode. T. 1: Tekst* (Petrograd: Izd. Otdeleniia Russkago iazyka i slovesnosti Rossiiskoi Akademii Nauk, 1920), p. 425.
96 All the redactions that Istrin has used in his edition appear to have contained this mistake.
97 *Georgii Monachi Chronicon*, ed. Carol de Boor, vol. II (Leipzig: Teubner, 1904), p. 651 (lines 12–13). I am most grateful to Professor Daniel Collins for suggesting these scribal errors, and for help unscrambling this passage in comparison with the Greek.
98 *Slovar' knizhnikov i knizhnosti* 1, p. 468.
99 See *Slovar' knizhnikov i knizhnosti* 1, p. 468; F. J. Thomson, '"Made in Russia": a survey of translations allegedly made in Kievan Russia', in *The Reception of Byzantine Culture*, p. 339.
100 *Slovar' knizhnikov i knizhnosti* 1, pp. 468–9.
101 Again, my thanks to Daniel Collins for helping me find a more convincing reading of *nedvoverno* here.
102 Schenker, *The Dawn of Slavic*, p. 223. See also D. M. Petras, *The Typicon of the Patriarch Alexis the Studite: Novgorod-St Sophia 1136* (Cleveland, OH: Pontificium Institutum Orientale, 1991), who lists this manuscript as twelfth or thirteenth century.
103 'Ustav monastyrskii', *GIM Sin No. 330* (Archive of the State Historical Museum, Moscow) l.236ob., as published in A. M. Pentkovskii, *Tipikon Patriarkha Aleksiia Studita v Vizantii i na Rusi* (Moscow: Izdatel'stvo Moskovskoi Patriarkhii, 2001), pp. 391–2.
104 M. Heppell, (introd. and tr.), *The 'Paterik' of the Kievan Caves Monastery* (HLEUL 1; Cambridge, MA: Harvard University Press, 1989), footnote, p. 44.
105 See Heppell, *The 'Paterik'*, p. 139.
106 My thanks to Simon Franklin for pointing this out.
107 I somewhat tentatively identify these as 'native' uses of the word *dvoeverie*, because it is difficult to say with absolute certainty that no part of the following texts, which span seven centuries, is translated from another language. However, all the texts are ascribed to native Russian clerics, and appear to be, in part or in entirety, original works, composed in response to issues that were being addressed by the Russian Orthodox Church at the time of writing.
108 Picchio, 'The impact of ecclesiastical culture', p. 260.
109 Wil van den Bercken, *Holy Russia and Christian Europe: East and West in the religious ideology of Russia*, trans. John Bowden (London: SCM Press, 1999), p. 35.
110 For an excellent summary of the attitude of the Papacy to the use of Slavonic in the liturgy see Schenker, *The Dawn of Slavic*, pp. 36–40.
111 *The Russian Primary Chronicle: Laurentian text*, trs and eds S. H. Cross and O. P. Sherbowitz-Wetzor (Cambridge, MA: Mediaeval Academy of America, 1953), p. 98.
112 Cross, *Primary Chronicle*, pp. 115–16.
113 *Oxford Dictionary of the Christian Church*, p. 584. Also see Bercken, *Holy Russia and Christian Europe*, p. 25.
114 *The Chronicle of Novgorod: 1016–1471*, trs R. Michell and N. Forbes (Camden Third Series, vol. XXV; London: Offices of the Society, 1914), p. 44.
115 See for example Bercken, *Holy Russia and Christian Europe*, p. 124; and Sophia Senyk, *A History of the Church in Ukraine. Vol. I: To the end of the thirteenth century* (Rome: Pontificio Istituto Orientale, 1993), pp. 298–326, 442–3.

116 Fedotov, *Russian Religious Mind* 2, p. 180.
117 *Moskovskii letopisnyi svod kontsa XV veka* (*PSRL* t. 25; Moscow: Akademii Nauk SSSR, 1949), p. 255.
118 T. Ware, *The Orthodox Church* (2nd edn; London: Penguin, 1993), p. 98; P. Bushkovitch, *Religion and Society in Russia: the sixteenth and seventeenth centuries* (New York and Oxford: OUP, 1992), pp. 52–3.
119 Thomson, *The Reception of Byzantine Culture*, Chapter I, pp. 111–12.
120 J. Fennell, *A History of the Russian Church to 1448* (London and New York: Longman, 1995), p. 97.
121 Fennell, *A History*, p. 96.
122 Rev. J. B. Koncevičius, *Russia's Attitude towards Union with Rome (9th–16th centuries)* (2nd edn; Washington, DC: Catholic University of America Press, 1927), p. 40.
123 Dvornik, *The Slavs*, p. 241.
124 F. Dvornik, 'The Kiev State and its Relations with Western Europe', in *Transactions of the Royal Historical Society* (Fourth Series Vol. XXIX; London: Offices of the Royal Historical Society, 1947), p. 40; also see his *The Slavs*, p. 242.
125 *The Pilgrimage of the Russian Abbot Daniel in the Holy Land 1106–1107 A.D.*, annotated by Colonel Sir C. W. Wilson (London: Palestine Pilgrims' Text Society, 1895); Russian text available in *BLDR* t. 4.
126 I. P. Eremin, 'Literaturnoe nasledie Feodosiia Pecherskogo', *TODRL* 5 (1947), p. 159; *Slovar' knizhnikov i knizhnosti* 1, pp. 457–9 (entry by O. V. Tvorogov). For an opposing view, see for example Podskalsky, 'Principal Aspects and Problems of Theology in Kievan Rus'', *HUS* 11, nos. 3/4 (1987), 270–86, who attributes it to the later Feodosii Grek (d.1156), and Heppell's summary of opinions on p. 211 of *The 'Paterik'*.
127 Cross, *Primary Chronicle*, p. 142.
128 The *Paterik* contains two stories of the introduction of the *Studite Typikon* – one in Discourse 7 (see Heppell, *The 'Paterik'*, p. 23) which closely resembles the *Primary Chronicle* entry, and one in Discourse 8 (see Heppell, *The 'Paterik'*, p. 45).
129 Heppell, *The 'Paterik'*, pp. 44–5.
130 Heppell, *The 'Paterik'*, p. 213.
131 See for example A. S. Pavlov, *Kriticheskie opyty po istorii drevneishei greko-russkoi polemiki protiv latinian* (St Petersburg: Tip. Imp. Akademii Nauk, 1878); Ia. N. Shchapov (ed.), *Drevnerusskie pis'mennye istochniki X–XIII vv.* (Moscow: Krug, 1991), p. 25.
132 Heppell, *The 'Paterik'*, p. 212.
133 Kaiser, *The Laws*, p. 47.
134 A. P. Vlasto, *The Entry of the Slavs into Christendom: an introduction to the medieval history of the Slavs* (Cambridge: CUP, 1970), p. 287.
135 Heppell, *The 'Paterik'*, p. 211.
136 Dvornik, *The Slavs*, p. 243; Heppell, *The 'Paterik'*, p. 38.
137 Heppell, *The 'Paterik'*, p. 168.
138 G. Vernadsky, *A History of Russia. Vol. 2: Kievan Russia* (New Haven and London: Yale University Press, 1948; paperback edition 1976), p. 86; Dvornik, *The Slavs*, p. 214.
139 Koncevičius, *Russia's Attitude towards Union*, p. 46.
140 Fennell, *A History*, pp. 99–100.
141 See for example M. Colucci, 'The Image of Western Christianity in the Culture of Kievan Rus', *HUS* 12/13 (1988/9), 576–86.
142 F. J. Thomson argues that the Serbian *Kormchaia* introduced Nicetas Stethatus' *Libellus contra Latinos* and the pseudo-Photian *Opusculum contra Francos* to the Russians in full for the first time in the thirteenth century. See 'The Nature of the Reception', pp. 111–12.

143   A. Popov, *Istoriko-literaturnyi obzor drevne-russkikh polemicheskikh sochinenii protiv latinian (XI–XV v.)* (Moscow: Tip. T. Ris, 1875; reprinted London: Variorum Reprints, 1972), pp. 58–69.

144   *Zakonopravilo, ili, Nomokanon svetoga Save: ilovicki prepis 1262 godina: fototipija/ priredio i priloge napisao Miodrag M. Petrovic* (Gornji Milanovac: Decje novine, 1991); Chapter 51: 'On the Franks and against the Latins' appears on f.262v–4v.

145   'Poslanie k kniaziu o vere latinskoi togo zhe Feodosiia k tomu zhe iziaslavu', *BLDR* 1, p. 450 (from the *Sofiiskii* manuscript of the fifteenth century).

146   R. Markus, *The End of Ancient Christianity* (Cambridge: CUP, 1990), p. 134.

147   Reams of paper could be (and have been) filled discussing the origins of nationalism and the appropriateness of applying the term 'nationalism' to the medieval period, before the establishment of the nation-state 'proper'. I mean here an awareness of communal identity as created by political allegiance (to an Orthodox prince) and religious affiliation.

148   Haney (following V. V. Ivanov and V. N. Toporov) identifies *svoi/chuzhoi* (*our own/other*) as the 'basic dichotomy' of Russian peasant life, ancient and modern. This, like all binary oppositions, is an oversimplification, but is neverthless an interesting approach. See J. V. Haney, *Introduction to the Russian Folktale* (Armonk, NY and London: M. E. Sharpe, 1999), p. 48.

149   F. von Lilienfeld, 'The Spirituality of the Early Kievan Caves Monastery', in B. Gasparov and O. Raevsky-Hughes (eds), *Christianity and the Eastern Slavs. Vol. 1: Slavic cultures in the Middle Ages* (California Slavic Studies 16; Berkley CA: University of California Press, 1993), p. 73.

150   Fedotov, *Russian Religious Mind* 1, p. 405.

151   Picchio, 'The impact of ecclesiastical culture', p. 250.

152   Schenker, *The Dawn of Slavic*, p. 227.

153   The *Slovar' drevnerusskogo iazyka (XI–XIV vv)*, t. 3, p. 64, lists this sermon as Feodosii Pecherskii's.

154   I. I. Sreznevskii has written about this collection in *Svedeniia i zametki o maloiz-vestnykh i neizvestnykh pamiatnikakh XLI–LXXX* (St Petersburg: Tip. Imperatorskoi akademii nauk, 1875), p. 297, and – according to E. V. Anichkov – in an 1851 article I have been unable to access; see *Iazychestvo i Drevniaia Rus'* (St Petersburg: Tip. M. M. Stasiulevicha, 1914; reprinted Munich: Verlag Otto Sagner, 1995), p. 26.

155   'Pouchenie Feodosiia Pecherskago o kazniakh Bozhiikh "sviatyi ottsy ustavsha postnye dny"', *Paisievskii sbornik*, Kirillo-Belozerskii No. 4/1081 No. 230, l.95 (Archive of the State Public Library, St Petersburg); my word divisions.

156   The text here is unclear – the *Slovar' drevnerusskogo iazyka (XI–XIV vv)*, t. 3, p. 112, suggests we read 'zh' for the corrupted 'p'.

157   *Paisievskii sbornik*, l.97.

158   *Paisievskii sbornik*, l.98.

159   Fedotov, *Russian Religious Mind* 2, p. 55.

160   V. A. Iakovlev, *K literaturnoi istorii drevne-russkikh sbornikov: opyt izsliedovaniia 'Izmaragda'* (Odessa: Tip. Sht. Voisk Odesskago voen. Okruga, 1893; reprinted Leipzig: Zentralantiquariat der DDR, 1974), p. 15.

161   *Russkaia istoricheskaia khrestomatiia (862–1850) s teoreticheskim ukazatelem*, ed. K. Petrov (St Petersburg: Tip. Morskago ministerastva, 1866), p. 44.

162   G. P. Bel'chenko, *Pouchenie blazhennago Feodosiia, igumena Pecherskago, o kazniakh Bozhiikh* (Odessa, 1899). See also I. I. Sreznevskii, *Svedeniia i zametki o maloizvestnykh i neizvestnykh pamiatnikakh I–XL* (St Petersburg: Tip. Imperatorskoi Akademii Nauk, 1867), pp. 34–43 for the twelfth-century *Zlatostrui* redaction with variations from the fourteenth century.

163   S. I. Smirnov, *Drevne-russkii dukhovnik: izsledovanie po istorii tserkovnago byta* (Moscow: Sinodal'naia tipografiia, 1914; reprinted Westmead: Gregg International Publishers, 1970), p. 17.

164 Makarii (Bulgakov), Metropolitan of Moscow and Kolomenskoe, *Istoriia russkoi tserkvi, kn. 2: Istoriia russki tserkvi v period sovershennoi zavisimosti ee ot konstantinopol'skogo patriarkha (988–1240)* (Moscow: Izd. Spaso-Preobrazhenskogo Valaamskogo monastyria, 1995), p. 388.
165 'Voprosy Kirika, Savvu i Ilii', *RIB VI: Pamiatniki drevne-russkago kanonicheskago prava, chast' 1 (Pamiatniki XI–XV v.)* (St Petersburg: Tip. Imp. Akademii Nauk, 1880), cols 21–2.
166 G. Podskal'ski, *Khristianstvo i bogoslovskaia literatura v Kievskoi Rusi (988–1237 gg.): izdanie vtoroe, ispravlennoe i dopolnennoe dlia russkogo perevoda*, translated from the German by A. V. Nazarenko (St Petersburg: Bizantinorossika, 1996), p. 307.
167 Filaret, *Obzor' Russkoi dukhovnoi literatury*, p. 33.
168 Podskal'ski, *Khristianstvo i bogoslovskaia literatura*, p. 307.
169 'Voprosy Kirika', *RIB* VI, col. 60.
170 R. R. Milner-Gulland, *The Russians* (Oxford and Malden, MA: Blackwell, 1997), p. 52.
171 See R. Fletcher, *The Conversion of Europe: from paganism to Christianity 371–1386 AD* (London: HarperCollins, 1997), chapter 11.
172 Translation by Muriel Heppell, *The 'Paterik'*.
173 I am indebted to Eve Levin for pointing this out and providing me with the text.
174 N. Kostomarov (ed.), *Pamiatniki starinnoi russkoi literatury, izdavaemye grafom Grigoriem Kushelevym-Bezborodko; skazaniia, legendy, povesti, skazki i pritchi*, vyp. 1 (St Petersburg: Tip. P. A. Kulisha, 1860), p. 251.
175 Michell and Forbes, *Chronicle of Novgorod*, p. 21.
176 Michell and Forbes, *Chronicle of Novgorod*, p. 31.
177 Filaret, *Obzor' Russkoi dukhovnoi literatury*, p. 14.
178 *Slovar' russkogo iazyka XI–XVII vv*, vyp. 4, ed. S. G. Barkhudarov (Moscow: Nauka, 1977), p. 184.
179 *RIB* VI, col. 31, question 33. Rybakov notes that this is a quote from the *Slovo Isaii proroka*.
180 *RIB* VI, col. 60.
181 *RIB* VI, col. 60.
182 See for example N. Gal'kovskii, *Bor'ba khristianstva s ostatkami iazychestva v drevnei Rusi*, t. 1 (Kharkov: Eparkhial'naia tip., 1916), pp.131–2; L. J. Ivanits, *Russian Folk Belief* (New York and London: M. E. Sharpe, 1992), pp. 85–7.
183 Popov, *Istoriko-literaturnyi obzor drevne-russkikh*, p. 69.
184 Heppell, *The 'Paterik'*, p. xx.
185 V. Ia. Petrukhin, 'Drevnerusskoe dvoeverie: poniatie i fenomen', *Slavianovedenie* (1996), no. 1, p. 45.
186 *Slovar' drevnerusskogo iazyka (XI–XIV vv)*, t. 3, p. 112.
187 *Slovar' russkogo iazyka XI–XVII vv*, p. 184.
188 Fedotov, *Russian Religious Mind 2*, p. 36.
189 Bushkovitch, *Religion and Society in Russia*, p. 53.
190 This use of *dvoeverie* is mentioned in the card catalogue of the dictionary department of the Institute of Russian Language in Moscow, but not included in the published dictionaries. I am grateful to Simon Franklin for suggesting this line of enquiry.
191 J. A. Hebly, *Protestants in Russia*, tr. J. Pott (Belfast: Christian Journals, 1976), p. 17.
192 *The Muscovite Law Code (Ulozhenie) of 1649. Part 1: text and translation*, tr. and ed. R. Hellie (Irvine, CA: Charles Schlacks Jr, 1988), p. 161.
193 Hebly, *Protestants in Russia*, p. 18.
194 Hebly, *Protestants in Russia*, p. 18.

195 This term could refer to Northern European Protestants or Catholics. Eve Levin has pointed out that 'often Russian propagandists referred to Protestants as "Arians" – a serious misconception of Protestant theology, but a neat way of extending the earlier condemnation by an ecumenical church council to new heretics'. (Personal correspondence, August 2002).
196 *Ulozhenie*, p. 182.
197 Bushkovitch, *Religion and Society*, pp. 52–3. See also Ware, *The Orthodox Church*, p. 98 for a different view.
198 G. Florovsky, *Ways of Russian Theology*, tr. R. L. Nichols (Belmont, MA: Nordland Publishing Company, 1979), p. 310.
199 G. Vernadsky, *A History of Russia. Vol. 5: The Tsardom of Moscow, Part I* (New Haven: Yale University Press, 1969), p. 320.
200 Florovsky, *Ways of Russian Theology*, p. 89.
201 See for example Ware, *The Orthodox Church*, p. 123; Kliuchevsky, *The Seventeenth Century*, pp. 294–5.
202 Eve Levin, personal correspondence, June 2002.
203 Ware, *The Orthodox Church*, p. 2.
204 Published in *Chteniia v imperatorskom obshchestve istorii i drevnostei rossiiskikh pri Moskovskom Universitet 1892g. Kn. 2, cht. 2: Materialy istoriko-literaturnye pamiatniki prenii o vere, voznikshikh po delu korolevicha Val'demara i tsarevny Iriny Mikhailovny*, ed. A. Golubtsov (Moscow: 1892).
205 P. Longworth, *Alexis, Tsar of All the Russias* (London: Secker, 1984), p. 17.
206 Vernadsky notes that it was considered as early as 1640; *A History of Russia* 5.1, p. 379.
207 Vernadsky, *A History of Russia* 5.1, p. 381.
208 Bushkovitch, *Religion and Society*, p. 135.
209 Golubtsov gives 1664, but this must be a typographical error.
210 Golubtsov, *Materialy istoriko-literaturnye pamiatniki prenii o vere*, p. xxiv.
211 Bushkovitch, *Religion and Society*, p. 134.
212 Golubtsov, *Materialy istoriko-literaturnye pamiatniki prenii o vere*, p. iv.
213 Vernadsky, *A History of Russia* 5.1, p. 378.
214 Golubtsov, *Materialy istoriko-literaturnye pamiatniki prenii o vere*, p. 335.
215 Literally 'with double-believing face', singular.
216 As suggested by Anatoli Turilov (personal communication, July 1999).
217 Heppell, *The 'Paterik'*, p. 213.
218 Vernadsky, *A History of Russia* 5.1, p. 424. The Slavic Reference Service at the University of Ilinois records this book as published in 1644, rather than 1648, the same year as *Kirill's Book*.
219 Vernadsky, *A History of Russia* 5.1, p. 382.
220 Since the research for this book was completed, the *Life* has been published by St Petersburg University with a brief foreword. *Zhitie Antoniia Siiskogo: Tekst i slovoukazatel'*, ed. A. C. Gerd (St Petersburg: St Petersburg University Press, 2003).
221 A. I. Ponomarev provides a brief outline of the saint's life in *Pamiatniki drevnerusskoi tserkovno-uchitel'noi literatury: Vyp. 2, Slaviano-russkii prolog. Ch.1: Sentiabr'-dekabr'*, ed. A. I. Ponomarev (St Petersburg: Tip. Dobrodeeva, 1896), pp. 65–7, as does I. U. Budovnits, *Monastyri na Rusi i bor'ba s nimi krest'ian v XIV–XVI vekakh: po "zhitiiam sviatykh"* (Moscow: Nauka, 1966), pp. 270–6. See also Makarii, Episkop Arkhangel'skii i Kholmogorskii (ed.), *Istoricheskiia svedeniia ob Antonievom Siiskom Monastyre* (Moscow: Universitetskoi Tip., 1878) and E. A. Ryzhova's *Antonievo-Siiskii monastyr': Zhitie Antoniia Siiskogo* (Syktyvkar: Izd-vo SyktGU, 2000).
222 'Zhitie i chudesa Antoniia Siiskago', *Soch. ieromonakha Iony*, 1578g, GBL f.310 (Und.) No. 284, XVIIv (Archive of the Lenin Library, Moscow). 1.175a.
223 *Soch. ieromonakha Iony*, 1.175b–1.176a.

224 'Zhitie i chudesa Antoniia Siiskago', RGADA, F.187, *Kollektsia rukopisnykh knig*, TsGALI, op. 1, No. 12, f.243v–244 (transcript provided by Eve Levin).

225 *Soch. ieromonakha Iony*, l.177a.

226 *Kollektsia rukopisnykh knig*, f.244v.

227 At a meeting arranged by the Department of the History of Religion, in the Institute of Russian History, Moscow, July 1998.

228 I am grateful to Eve Levin for pointing this out.

229 Budovnits, *Monastyri na Rusi*, p. 275.

230 *Slovar' knizhnikov i knizhnosti Drevnei Rusi. Vyp. 2: vtoraia polovina XIV–XVI v., chast' 1, A–K*, ed. D. S. Likhachev (Leningrad: Nauka, 1988), p. 248.

231 Bushkovitch, *Religion and Society*, p. 87.

232 Eve Levin, '*Dvoeverie* and Popular Religion', in S. K. Batalden (ed.), *Seeking God: the recovery of religious identity in Orthodox Russia, Ukraine, and Georgia* (DeKalb, IL: Northern Illinois University Press, 1993), pp. 32, 47 (footnote).

233 D. Rowland, 'Towards an Understanding of the Political Ideas in Ivan Timofeyev's *Vremennik*', *Slavonic and East European Review* 62, no. 3 (1984), p. 383.

234 Rowland, 'Towards an Understanding', especially pp. 375–7.

235 Filaret (Gumilievskii), Archbishop of Chernigov, *Obzor' Russkoi dukhovnoi literatury: kniga pervaia i vtoraia, 862–1863* (St Petersburg: Izd. I. L. Tuzova, 1884; 3rd edition reprinted Oxford: Meeuws, 1984), p. 222.

236 T. Kondratieva and C.-S. Ingerflom, '"Bez carja zemlja vdova": Syncrétisme dans le *Vremmenik* d'Ivan Timofeev', *Cahiers du monde russe et soviétique* 34, nos. 1–2 (1993), p. 258.

237 I. Timofeev, *Vremennik Ivana Timofeeva*, ed. V. P. Adrianova-Peretts; tr. and commentary O. A. Derzhavina (Moscow and Leningrad: Akademii Nauk SSSR, 1951), p. 327 (from the modern Russian translation of O. A. Derzhavina).

238 Kondratieva and Ingerflom, '"Bez carja zemlja vdova"', p. 259.

239 Timofeev, *Vremennik*, pp. 11–12.

240 G. Vernadsky et al. (eds), *A Source Book for Russian History from Early Times to 1917. Vol. 1: Early times to the late seventeenth century* (New Haven and London: Yale University Press, 1972), p. 145.

241 Timofeev, *Vremennik*, p. 11.

242 Timofeev, *Vremennik* (translation), p. 173.

243 Timofeev, *Vremennik*, p. 12.

244 Matthew 12:25 'And Jesus knew their thoughts, and said unto them, "Every kingdom divided against itself is brought to desolation; and every city or house divided against itself shall not stand"'.

245 My thanks to Daniel Collins for helping me find a comprehensible reading of this passage, assuming that до is a mistake for ни.

3 A history of historians

1 N. Andreyev, 'Pagan and Christian Elements in Old Russia', *Slavic Review* 21, no. 1 (1962), pp. 17–18.

2 See Peter Burke's *Popular Culture in Early Modern Europe* (London: Temple Smith, 1978; revised reprint Aldershot: Ashgate, 1996) for a useful summary of the European 'Discovery of the People', pp. 3–22.

3 E. Ivakhnenko, 'Srednevekovoe dvoeverie i russkaia literaturno-filosofskaia mysl' novogo vremeni: Srednevekov'e: dukhovnyi aspekt russkogo dvoeveriia', *Rubezhi* no. 2 (1997), p. 51.

4 I. M. Snegirev, *Russkie prostonarodnye prazdniki i suevernye obriady*, vyp.1 (Moscow: Univ. tip., 1837), p. 2.

5 See for example A. Tereshchenko, *Byt russkago naroda* (St Petersburg: Tip. Ministerstva vnutrennikh diel, 1848), chast 4: pp. 6–7, chast 3: pp. 28, 53. He prefers the word *sueverie*, 'superstition'.

6 Visiting foreigners such as the Englishmen Richard James and Dr Samuel Collins also recorded Russian folk songs and folk tales in the mid-seventeenth century.

7 M. V. Lomonosov, *Polnoe sobranie sochinenii. T. 6: Trudy po russkoi istorii, obshchestvenno-ekonomicheskim voprosam i geografii 1747–1765 gg.* (Moscow and Leningrad: Akademii Nauk SSSR, 1952), pp. 251–2.

8 S. M. Solov'ev, *Istoriia Rossii s drevneishikh vremen* t. 1 (Moscow: Izd-vo sotsial'no-ekonomicheskoi literatury, 1962), p. 262.

9 G. Vernadsky, *Russian Historiography: a history* (Belmont, MA: Norland Publishing Company, 1978), p. 374.

10 Metropolitan Makarii (Bulgakov), *Istoriia russkoi tserkvi, kn. 2: Istoriia russkoi tserkvi v period sovershennoi zavisimosti ee ot Konstantinopol'skogo patriarkha (988–1240)* (Moscow: Izd. Spaso-Preobrazhenskogo Valaamskogo monastyria, 1995), pp. 192, 394.

11 Makarii (Bulgakov), *Istoriia russkoi tserkvi 2*, p. 26.

12 The term appears only in the 1817 edition of Petr Alekseev's *Tserkovnyi slovar'* (orginally compiled in the eighteenth century), meaning 'doubtful', 'uncertain hope', with reference to the *Prolog*. See Chapter 2, earlier.

13 'Smes' khristianstva s iazychestvom i eresiami v drevne-russkikh narodnykh skazaniiakh o mire', in *Pravoslavnyi sobesednik*, ch. 1 (Kazan: Kazanskaia Dukhovnaia Akademiia, 1861), p. 255.

14 N. Tikhonravov, 'Slova i poucheniia, napravlennyia protiv iazycheskikh verovanii i obriadov', in *Letopisi russkoi literatury i drevnosti*, t. 4 (Moscow: Tip. Gracheva, 1862), pp. 81–112.

15 M. Azbukin, 'Ocherk literaturnoi bor'by predstavitelei khristianstva s ostatkami iazychestva v russkom narode (XI–XIV veka)'. The first part is published in *Russkii Filologicheskii Vestnik* 28, no. 3 (1892), 133–53; the second part in *RFV* 35, no. 2 (1896), 222–72; the third in *RFV* 37, nos. 1–2 (1897), 229–73; the fourth in *RFV* 38, nos. 3–4 (1897), 322–37; and the final part in *RFV* 39, nos. 1–2 (1898), 246–78.

16 Azbukin, 'Ocherk literaturnoi bor'by', *RFV* 35, no. 2 (1896), p. 265.

17 Azbukin, 'Ocherk literaturnoi bor'by', *RFV* 28, no. 3 (1892), p. 140.

18 Azbukin, 'Ocherk literaturnoi bor'by', *RFV* 35, no. 2 (1896), p. 265.

19 Azbukin, 'Ocherk literaturnoi bor'by', *RFV* 35, no. 2 (1896), p. 265.

20 A. V. Kartashev, *Ocherki po istorii russkoi tserkvi* t. 1 (Paris: YMCA, 1959), p. 240

21 W. R. S. Ralston, *The Songs of the Russian People, as illustrative of Slavonic mythology and Russian social life* (London: Ellis & Green, 1872), pp. 419–20.

22 Ralston, *Songs*, p. 420.

23 E. V. Anichkov, 'Old Russian Pagan Cults', in *Transactions of the Third International Congress for the History of Religions*, vol. 2 (Oxford: Clarendon Press, 1908), p. 258.

24 N. V. Riasanovsky, *A History of Russia* (5th edn; New York and Oxford: OUP, 1993; reprinted 2006), p. 52.

25 G. Podskalsky, 'Principal Aspects and Problems of Theology in Kievan Rus'', *HUS* 11, nos. 3/4 (1987), p. 274.

26 A detailed explanation of *zmeeviki* can be found in W. F. Ryan, *The Bathhouse at Midnight: an historical survey of magic and divination in Russia* (Thrupp, Stroud: Sutton Publishing, 1999), pp. 241–4. See also J. Blankoff, 'Survivances du Paganisme en vielle Russie', *Problèmes d'histoire du christianisme* 8 (1979), 29–44, and E. de Savitsch, 'Religious Amulets of Early Russian Christendom', *Gazette des Beaux-Arts* 23 (1943), 112–16.

27 Podskalsky, 'Principal Aspects', p. 286.

28 J. Fennell, *A History of the Russian Church to 1448* (London and New York: Longman, 1995), p. 87.

29 Fennell, *A History*, p. 76.

30 L. J. Ivanits, *Russian Folk Belief* (New York and London: M. E. Sharpe, 1992), p. 4.
31 Ivanits, *Russian Folk Belief*, p. 37.
32 See for example Joanna Hubbs, *Mother Russia: the feminine myth in Russian culture* (Bloomington, IN: Indiana University Press, 1993), pp. 21–2; A. P. Vlasto, *The Entry of the Slavs into Christendom: an introduction to the medieval history of the Slavs* (Cambridge: CUP, 1970), p. 264.
33 G. Vernadsky, *A History of Russia. Vol. 2: Kievan Russia* (New Haven and London: Yale University Press, 1948; paperback edition, 1976), p. 263.
34 S. I. Smirnov, 'Baby bogomerzkiia', in Ia. L. Barskov (ed.), *Sbornik statei, posviashchennykh Vasiliiu Osipovichu Kliuchevskomu ego uchenikami, druz'iami i pochitateliami ko dniu tridtsatilietiia ego professorskoi dieiatel'nosti v Moskovskom Universitetie, 5 dekabria 1879–5 dekabria 1909 goda* (Moscow: Pechatnia S. P. Iakovleva, 1909).
35 E. Levin, '*Dvoeverie* and Popular Religion', in S. K. Batalden (ed.), *Seeking God: the recovery of religious identity in Orthodox Russia, Ukraine, and Georgia* (DeKalb, IL: Northern Illinois University Press, 1993), pp. 31–52, esp. p. 35.
36 Hubbs, *Mother Russia*, p. 13.
37 J. Vytkovskaya, 'Slav Mythology', in C. Larrington (ed.), *The Feminist Companion to Mythology* (London: Pandora, 1992), pp. 102–17.
38 See 'Khristianskie istochniki kul'ta Paraskevy', in E. Levin, *Dvoeverie i narodnaia religiia v istorii Rossii*, trs A. L. Toporkova and Z. N. Isidorovoi (Moscow: Indrik, 2004); Levin, '*Dvoeverie* and Popular Religion', p. 43.
39 B. A. Rybakov, *Iazychestvo drevnei Rusi* (Moscow: Nauka, 1988), p. 6.
40 Rybakov, *Iazychestvo drevnei Rusi*, p. 457.
41 B. A. Rybakov, *Early Centuries of Russian History*, tr. J. Weir (Moscow: Progress Publishers, 1965), pp. 51–2.
42 B. A. Rybakov, 'Paganism in Medieval Rus', *Social Science* 6, no. 1 (1975), 130–54; Rybakov, *Iazychestvo drevnei Rusi*, chapter 12.
43 Rybakov, *Iazychestvo drevnei Rusi*, p. 652.
44 O. M. Rapov, *Russkaia tserkov' v IX-pervoi treti XII v.: Priniatie khristianstva* (2nd edn; Moscow: Russkaia Panorama, 1998), p. 371.
45 See for example Mary Matossian, 'The Peasant Way of Life', in *Russian Peasant Women*, eds Beatrice Farnsworth and Lynne Viola (New York and Oxford: OUP, 1992), pp. 11–40, especially p. 34; Hubbs, *Mother Russia*, pp. 68–9.
46 Rapov, *Russkaia tserkov'*, p. 372.
47 B. A. Uspenskij, 'On the Origin of Russian Obscenities', in Ju. M. Lotman and B. A. Uspenskij, *The Semiotics of Russian Culture*, ed. A. Shukman (Michigan Slavic Contributions, no. 11; Ann Arbor, MI: Ann Arbor, 1984), p. 296.
48 Ju. M. Lotman, *Universe of the Mind: a semiotic theory of culture*, tr. A. Shukman (London: I. B. Tauris, 1990), p. 256.
49 Ju. M. Lotman and B. A. Uspenskij, 'The Role of Dual Models in the Dynamics of Russian Culture (up to the end of the eighteenth century)', in Lotman and Uspenskij, *Semiotics of Russian Culture*, pp. 10–11.
50 See for example Ivanits, *Russian Folk Belief*, pp. 5–18; Michael S. Flier, 'Sunday in Medieval Russian Culture: *Nedelja* versus *Voskresenie*', in H. Birnbaum and M. S. Flier (eds), *Medieval Russian Culture*, vol. 1 (Berkeley, CA: University of California Press, 1984), pp. 105–49, especially pp. 122, 138.
51 S. I. Smirnov, *Drevne-russkii dukhovnik: izsledovanie po istorii tserkovnago byta* (Moscow: Sinodal'naia Tipografiia, 1914), pp. 254–7.
52 M. Warner, *Alone of All Her Sex: the myth and the cult of the Virgin Mary* (London: Picador, 1985).
53 See for example Eve Levin, 'From corpse to cult in early modern Russia', in Valerie A. Kivelson and Robert H. Greene (eds), *Orthodox Russia: belief and*

practice under the tsars (University Park, PA: Pennsylvania State University Press, 2003).

54   E. V. Anichkov, *Iazychestvo i Drevniaia Rus'* (St Petersburg: Tip. M. M. Stasiulevicha, 1914; reprinted Munich: Verlag Otto Sagner, 1995), pp. 306–7.

55   Anichkov, *Iazychestvo*, pp. 286–7.

56   Anichkov, *Iazychestvo*, p. 302.

57   Anichkov, *Iazychestvo*, p. 303.

58   N. M. Nikol'skii, *Istoriia russkoi tserkvi* (3rd edn; Moscow: Izd-vo polit. lit-ry, 1983), p. 25.

59   Keith Thomas, *Religion and the Decline of Magic: studies in popular beliefs in sixteenth- and seventeenth-century England* (London: Penguin, 1971; reprinted 1991), p. 54. See also Chapter 4, later.

60   Smirnov, *Drevne-russkii dukhovnik*, pp. 254–7.

61   E. E. Golubinskii, *Istoriia russkoi tserkvi, t. 1, vtoraia polovina toma* (Moscow: Univ. tip., 1904; reprinted The Hague and Paris: Mouton, 1969), p. 838.

62   Golubinskii, *Istoriia* 1.2, p. 838.

63   N. Gal'kovskii, *Bor'ba khristianstva s ostatkami iazychestva v drevnei Rusi, t. 1* (Kharkov: Eparkhial'naia tip., 1916), p. IV.

64   Gal'kovskii, *Bor'ba khristianstva* 1, pp. 124–5.

65   Gal'kovskii, *Bor'ba khristianstva* 1, pp. 371–3.

66   Smirnov, *Drevne-russkii dukhovnik*, p. 255.

67   P. Pascal, *The Religion of the Russian People*, tr. R. Williams (London and Oxford: Mowbrays, 1976), p. 8.

68   Pascal, *Religion of the Russian People*, p. 10.

69   Pascal, *Religion of the Russian People*, p. 10.

70   E. Ivakhnenko, 'Srednevekovoe dvoeverie i russkaia literaturno-filosofskaia mysl' novogo vremeni: Srednevekov'e: dukhovnyi aspekt russkogo dvoeveriia', *Rubezhi*, no. 2 (1997), 47–57.

71   Ivakhnenko, 'Srednevekovoe dvoeverie', p. 49.

72   Ivakhnenko, 'Srednevekovoe dvoeverie', p. 48.

73   Religion versus magic is a very problematic distinction. See for example Thomas, *Religion and the Decline of Magic*, pp. 51–7, 301–5, 331; Hildred Geertz's critique of Thomas's work, 'An Anthropology of Religion and Magic, I', *Journal of Interdisciplinary History* 6, no. 1 (Summer, 1975), 71–89 (and Thomas's response in the same volume); and Chapter 4 of this book.

74   Ivakhnenko, 'Srednevekovoe dvoeverie', p. 49.

75   See for example Victor A. Shnirelman, *Russian Neo-pagan Myths and Antisemitism* (Analysis of Current Trends in Antisemitism no. 13; Jerusalem: SICSA, 1998).

76   F. Conte, *L'héritage païen de la Russie: le paysan et son univers symbolique* (Paris: Albin Michel, 1997), p. 23.

77   Conte, *L'héritage païen*, p. 23.

78   Conte, *L'héritage païen*, p. 23.

79   But also used differently by Kliuchevskii, see later. Conte explores the concept in his earlier article 'Paganism and Christianity in Russia: "double" or "triple" faith?', in Y. Hamant (ed.), *The Christianization of Ancient Russia: a millennium: 988–1988* (Paris: UNESCO, 1992), pp. 207–15.

80   Robert Mann identifies the dragon in the *bylini* as representing paganism, in *Lances Sing: a study of the Igor tale* (Columbus, OH: Slavica Publishers, 1990), chapter one. However, it is far from certain that the peasant in this anecdote would have perceived him in this way.

81   J. Haney, *Introduction to the Russian Folktale* (Armonk, NY and London: M. E. Sharpe, 1999), p. 47.

82   N. I. Tolstoi, 'Religioznye veronvaniia drevnikh slavian', in V. K. Volkov (ed.), *Ocherki istorii kul'tury slavian* (Moscow: Indrik, 1996), pp. 147–8.

83 V. O. Kliuchevsky, *A Course in Russian History: the seventeenth century*, tr. N. Duddington (Chicago: Quadrangle Books, 1968), pp. 307–8.
84 V. O. Kliuchevsky, *A History of Russia*, vol. 1, tr. C. J. Hogarth (London: J. M. Dent & Sons, 1911), p. 211.
85 Kliuchevsky, *A History of Russia* 1, p. 207.
86 Kliuchevsky, *A History of Russia* 1, pp. 214–15. The Russian is to be found in *Sochineniia, t. 1: Kurs russkoi istorii*, ch. 1 (Moscow: Gos. Izd. Politicheskoi Literatury, 1956), p. 307.
87 James C. Russell, *The Germanization of Early Medieval Christianity: a sociohistorical approach to religious transformation* (New York and Oxford: OUP, 1994), p. 4.
88 B. D. Grekov, *Kiev Rus*, tr. Y. Sdobnikov (Moscow: Foreign Languages Publishing House, 1959), p. 528.
89 Grekov, *Kiev Rus*, pp. 528–9.
90 G. P. Fedotov, *The Russian Religious Mind. Vol. 1: Kievan Christianity, the tenth to the thirteenth centuries* (New York, Evanston and London: Harper & Row, 1960), p. 8.
91 Fedotov, *Russian Religious Mind* 1, p. 346.
92 G. P. Fedotov, *The Russian Religious Mind. Vol. 2: The Middle Ages: the thirteenth to the fifteenth centuries* (Cambridge, MA: Harvard University Press, 1966), p. 138.
93 Fedotov, *Russian Religious Mind* 1, p. 3.
94 Simon Dixon, 'How holy was Holy Russia? Rediscovering Russian religion', in *Reinterpreting Russia*, edited by Geoffrey Hosking and Robert Service (London: Arnold, 1999), pp. 21–39.
95 D. S. Likhachev, 'Narodnoe poeticheskoe tvorchestvo v gody feodal'noi razdroblennosti Rusi – do tataro-mongol'skogo nashestviia (XII–nachalo XIII v.)', in V. P. Adrianova-Peretts (ed.), *Russkoe narodnoe poeticheskoe tvorchestvo*, t. 1 (Moscow and Leningrad: Akademii Nauk SSSR, 1953), pp. 237–8.
96 Likhachev, 'Narodnoe poeticheskoe tvorchestvo', p. 238.
97 D. S. Likhachev, 'Religion: Russian Orthodoxy', in N. Rzhevsky (ed.), *The Cambridge Companion to Modern Russian Culture* (Cambridge: CUP, 1998), pp. 38–56.
98 See for example Elizabeth Warner, *Russian Myths* (London: British Museum, 2002); *Religii narodov sovremennoi Rossii. Slovar'*, ed. M. P. Mchedlov et al. (2nd edn: Moscow: Respublika, 2003), pp. 82–5.
99 A. A. Turilov and A. V. Chernetsov, 'K kharakteristike narodnykh verovanii vostochykh slavian (po dannym pis'mennykh istochnikov)', in *Istoki russkoi kul'tury (arkheologiia i lingvistika)* (Moscow: Russkii Mir, 1997), pp. 99–110.
100 V. M. Zhivov, 'Dvoeverie i osobyi kharakter russkoi kulturnoi istorii', in V. N. Toporov (ed.), *Philologia slavica: k 70-letiiu akademika N.I. Tolstogo* (Moscow: Nauka, 1993), pp. 50–9.
101 V. Ia. Petrukhin, 'Drevnerusskoe dvoeverie: poniatie i fenomen', *Slavianovedenie* (1996), no. 1, 44–7.
102 A. M. Panchenko, 'Esteticheskie aspekti khristianizatsii Rusi', *Russkaia literatura* (1988), no. 1, p. 57.
103 A. E. Musin, 'K kharakteristike russkogo srednevekovogo mirovozzreniia (Problema "dvoeveriia": metodologicheskii aspekt)', in V. A. Khrshanovskii et al. (eds), *Rekonstruktsiia drevnikh verovanii: istochniki, metod, tsel'* (St Petersburg: GMIR, 1991), pp. 205–11.
104 Musin attributes words from the *Sermon of the Christlover* erroneously to the *Sermon of St Gregory* (which does not contain the term *dvoeverie*). Since the former sermon is often cited as a text preaching against double-belief, it is an understandable mistake.

105 A. V. Chernetsov, 'Dvoeverie: mirazh ili real'nost'?', *Zhivaia starina* (1994), no. 4, 16–19.
106 Chernetsov, 'Dvoeverie: mirazh ili real'nost'?', p. 16.
107 In an interview in Moscow, July 1998, Chernetsov acknowledged that his understanding of the word is not necessarily borne out by the medieval use of the term, but as an archaeologist he prefers it to the less specifically Russian 'syncretism'.
108 Chernetsov, 'Dvoeverie: mirazh ili real'nost'?', p. 16.
109 Turilov and Chernetsov, 'K kharakteristike narodnykh verovanii', p. 109.
110 V. P. Darkevich, 'K voprosu o "dvoeverii" v Drevnei Rusi', in V. T. Pashuto (ed.), *Vostochnaia Evropa v drevnosti i srednevekov'e: iazychestvo, khristianstvo, tserkov'* (Moscow: RAN, 1995), p. 12.
111 Darkevich, 'K voprosu o "dvoeverii"', pp. 12–13.
112 S. Franklin and J. Shepard, *The Emergence of Rus 750–1200* (London and New York: Longman, 1996), p. 352.
113 Musin, 'K kharakteristike', pp. 207–8.
114 Levin, '*Dvoeverie* and Popular Religion', p. 46.
115 Levin, '*Dvoeverie* and Popular Religion', p. 46.
116 In an interview June 1999, Levin confirmed that she suspected double-belief to be a 'scholarly construct'.
117 Levin, '*Dvoeverie* and Popular Religion', p. 43.
118 Levin gives a fuller exploration of the cult of St Paraskeva in 'Khristianskie istochniki kul'ta Paraskevy'.
119 Chernetsov, 'Dvoeverie: mirazh ili real'nost'?', p. 19.
120 Chris J. Chulos, 'Myths of the Pious or Pagan Peasant in Post-Emancipation Central Russia (Voronezh Province)', *Russian History/Histoire Russe* 22, no. 2 (1995), 181–216.
121 Chulos, 'Myths of the Pious or Pagan Peasant', p. 202.
122 J. E. Clay, 'Beyond Sectarianism and Dual-Faith [*Dvoeverie*]: A New Approach to Popular Religion'. This paper was presented to the AAASS convention in Washington, D.C., in 1990. It unfortunately remains unpublished and was kindly sent to me by the author.
123 Andreyev, 'Pagan and Christian Elements in Old Russia', p. 17.
124 Chernetsov, 'Dvoeverie: mirazh ili real'nost'?', p. 16.

4 How Russian is 'double-belief'?

1 Fray Diego Durán, *Books of the Gods and Rites and The Ancient Calendar*, trans and eds Fernando Horcasitas and Doris Heyden (The Civilization of the American Indian Series vol. 102; Norman, Oklahoma: University of Oklahoma Press, 1971) pp. 410–11.
2 See for example Golubinskii, discussed in Chapter 3 earlier.
3 M. Azbukin, 'Ocherk literaturnoi bor'by predstavitelei khristianstva s ostatkami iazychestva v russkom narode (XI–XIV veka)', *RFV* 35, no. 2 (1896), 222–72.
4 For a succinct discussion of these see pp. 9–12 of Richard Fletcher's *The Conversion of Europe: from paganism to Christianity 372–1386 AD* (London: HarperCollins, 1997).
5 J.-P. Migne (ed.), *Photiou, Patriarchou Konstantinoupoleos, Ta heuriskomena panta = Photii, Constantinopolitani patriarchae, Opera omnia*, vol. 2 (Patrologiae cursus completus. Series Graeca, t. 102; Paris: Migne, 1860; reprinted Turnhout: Brepols, 1967), cols 736–7. See also Vladimir Vodoff, *Naissance de la chrétienté russe : la conversion du prince Vladimir de Kiev (988) et ses conséquences (XIE–XIIIe siècles)* (Paris: Fayard, 1988).

6 Cited in Ihor Ševčenko, 'Religious missions seen from Byzantium', *HUS* 12/13 (1988/9), p. 24.

7 *The Russian Primary Chronicle: Laurentian text*, trs and eds S. H. Cross and O. P. Sherbowitz-Wetzor (Cambridge, MA: Mediaeval Academy of America, 1953), p. 77.

8 Cross, *Primary Chronicle*, pp. 95–6.

9 Cross, *Primary Chronicle*, p. 82.

10 The scholarly literature on the date and location of Olga's baptism is substantial. For a translation of the relevant *De ceremoniis* passages, a clear summary of sources – including Adalbert's contradictory record of her baptism in the reign of Romanus – and the various arguments for and against a mid-century baptism in Constantinople, see Jeffrey Featherstone, 'Ol'ga's Visit to Constantinople', *HUS* 14, nos. 3/4 (1990), 293–312; Dimitri Obolensky, 'Ol'ga's Conversion: the evidence reconsidered', *HUS* 12/13 (1988/1989), 145–58.

11 Adalbert, Archbishop of Magdeburg, 'Adalberts Fortsetzung der Chronik Reginos', in Albert Bauer and Reinhold Rau (eds), *Quellen zur Geschichte der sächsischen Kaiserzeit* (Ausgewählte Quellen zur deutschen Geschichte des Mittelalters. Bd. 8; Darmstadt: Wissenschaftliche Buchgesellschaft, 1971), pp. 185–231, especially pp. 218–19.

12 Obolensky, 'Ol'ga's conversion', pp. 157–8.

13 Thietmar von Merseburg, Bishop of Merseburg, *Ottonian Germany: The chronicon of Thietmar of Merseburg*, translated and annotated by David A. Warner (Manchester Medieval Source Series; Manchester and New York: Manchester University Press, 2001), p. 108.

14 Fletcher, *The Conversion of Europe*, p. 3.

15 Cross, *Primary Chronicle*, pp. 83–4.

16 Martine de Reu, 'The Missionaries: the first contact between paganism and Christianity', in L. J. R. Milis (ed.), *The Pagan Middle Ages*, trans. Tanis Guest (Woodbridge, Suffolk: Boydell Press, 1998), pp. 13–37, especially p. 18.

17 Bede, *A History of the English Church and People*, trans. Leo Sherley-Price (Harmondsworth, Middlesex: Penguin, 1955; reprinted 1964), pp. 124–6.

18 Bede, *A History*, p. 107.

19 Cross, *Primary Chronicle*, pp. 93–4.

20 See for example A. P. Vlasto, *The Entry of the Slavs into Christendom: an introduction to the medieval history of the Slavs* (Cambridge: CUP, 1970); A. Poppe, 'How the Conversion of Rus' was Understood in the Eleventh Century', *HUS* 11, nos. 3/4 (1987), 287–302; A. Poppe, 'Two Concepts of the Conversion of Rus' in Kievan Writings', *HUS* 12/13 (1988/9), 488–504; Miguel Arranz, S.J., 'The baptism of Prince Vladimir', in Yves Hamant (ed.), *The Christianization of Ancient Russia: a millennium: 988–1988* (Paris: UNESCO, 1992), pp. 75–93.

21 Arranz, 'The baptism of Prince Vladimir'; Petro Tolochko, 'Volodimer Svjatoslavič's Choice of Religion: Fact or Fiction?' *HUS* 12/13 (1988/9), 816–29.

22 Cross, *Primary Chronicle*, p. 93.

23 Cross, *Primary Chronicle*, p. 91.

24 Cross, *Primary Chronicle*, p. 88–90.

25 Gregory, Bishop of Tours, *The History of the Franks*, tr. Lewis Thorpe (Harmondsworth, Middlesex: Penguin, 1977), pp. 141–4; Carole M. Cusack, *The Rise of Christianity in Northern Europe, 300–1000* (London and New York: Cassell, 1998), pp. 70–1.

26 See Richard M. Price, 'The holy man and Christianization from the apocryphal apostles to St Stephen of Perm', in James Howard-Johnston and Paul Antony Hayward (eds), *The Cult of Saints in Late Antiquity and the Middle Ages: essays on the contribution of Peter Brown* (Oxford: OUP, 1999), pp. 215–38, for an interesting study of such tropes. See also Peter Brown, *Authority and the Sacred:*

aspects of the Christianisation of the Roman world (Cambridge: CUP, 1996), pp. 67–8.

27 Daniel T. Reff, *Plagues, Priests, and Demons: sacred narratives and the rise of Christianity in the Old World and the New* (Cambridge: CUP, 2005), pp. 37–8.

28 Tolochko, 'Volodimer Svjatoslavič's Choice of Religion'.

29 Cross, *Primary Chronicle*, pp. 116–17. See *The Povĕst' vremennykh lĕt: an interlinear collation and paradosis* (HLEUL Texts, vol. 10, pts 1–3; Cambridge, MA: Harvard University Press, 2003), pt. 2, pp. 911–24 for the various manuscript renditions of this passage.

30 The *Povest' vremennykh let* or *Tale of Bygone Years*, the 'Primary Chronicle' of medieval Russian historiography, has been tentatively identified as a compilation of earlier sources made in 1116 by the hegumen of a Kievan monastery. See the introduction by Donald Ostrowski to *The Povĕst' vremennykh lĕt*, HLEUL Texts, vol. 10, pt. 1 for a summary of manuscript history.

31 Richard E. Sullivan, 'Khan Boris and the Conversion of Bulgaria: a case study of the impact of Christianity on a barbarian society', in *Christian Missionary Activity in the Early Middle Ages* (Aldershot: Variorum, 1994), pp. 55–139, especially p. 80.

32 Mayke de Jong, *In Samuel's Image: child oblation in the early medieval West* (Leiden: E. J. Brill, 1996), p. 17.

33 R. Trexler, 'From the Mouths of Babes: Christianization by Children in 16th Century New Spain', in *Religious Organization and Religious Experience*, ed. J. Davis (London: Academic Press, 1982), pp. 115–35. See also Reff, *Plagues, Priests, and Demons*, pp. 193–5 on Jesuit boarding schools in New Mexico.

34 *The Hagiography of Kievan Rus'*, translated and with an introduction by Paul Hollingsworth (HLEUL 2; Cambirdge, MA: Harvard University Press, 1992), pp. 43–5.

35 See Paul A. Hollingsworth, 'Holy men and the transformation of political space in medieval Rus'', in Howard-Johnston and Hayward (eds), *The Cult of the Saints in Late Antiquity and the Middle Ages*, pp. 187–214 for an illuminating exploration of this process.

36 Cross, *Primary Chronicle*, pp. 150–3. This dualism may reflect Bogomil influence from the Balkans: see Yuri Stoyanov, *The Hidden Tradition in Europe: the secret history of medieval Christian heresy* (London: Penguin, 1995) on the Bogomil heresy.

37 *Novgorodskaia pervaia letopis' starshego i mladshego izvodov* (Moscow and Leningrad: Akademii Nauk SSSR, 1950), pp. 159–60. See also Henrik Birnbaum, 'When and How was Novgorod Converted to Christianity?', *HUS* 12/13 (1988/9), 505–30.

38 Adam Olearius, *The Travels of Olearius in Seventeenth Century Russia*, trans. and ed. by Samuel H. Baron (Stanford: Stanford University Press, California, 1967), p. 93.

39 See for example Gregory of Tours, *Glory of the Confessors*, translated and introduced by Raymond van Dam (Liverpool: Liverpool University Press, 1988), p. 19, who relates how the 'rustics' of Javols are persuaded to take the offerings they usually threw into a lake to the Church of St Hilary instead; for the reverse process see S. J. B. Barnish, '*Religio in stagno*: Nature, Divinity, and the Christianization of the Countryside in Late Antique Italy', *Journal of Early Christian Studies* 9, no. 3 (2001), 387–402.

40 Bede, *A History*, pp. 86–7.

41 See also Bede, *A History*, p. 89, for a contradictory instruction to King Ethelbert of Kent.

42 But see Petro P. Tolochko, 'Religious Sites in Kiev During the Reign of Volodimer Sviatoslavich', *HUS* 11, nos. 3/4 (1987), 317–22, for a discussion of the textual

and archaeological evidence for the temples of Perun and Veles in Kiev, and the location of the first Christian shrines.

43 Cross, *Primary Chronicle*, p. 116. See *Povĕst' vremennykh lĕt*, HLEUL Texts, vol. 10, pt. 2, pp. 905–8 for the various manuscript renditions of this passage.

44 Cross, *Primary Chronicle*, p. 117. See *Povĕst' vremennykh lĕt*, HLEUL Texts, vol. 10, pt. 2, pp. 921–3 for the various manuscript renditions of this passage.

45 See for example I. Ia. Froianov, A. Iu. Dvornichenko and Iu. V. Krivosheev, 'The Introduction of Christianity in Russia and the Pagan Traditions', in *Russian Traditional Culture: religion, gender and customary law*, ed. Marjorie Mandelstam Balzer (New York and London: M. E. Sharpe, 1992), pp. 3–15.

46 See also Robin Lane Fox, *Pagans and Christians in the Mediterranean world from the second century AD to the conversion of Constantine* (London: Penguin, 1988), pp. 137, 444, on the attribution of the 'indisputable' power of pagan gods to demons by early Christians.

47 Cited in Ruth Mazo Karras, 'Pagan Survivals and Syncretism in the Conversion of Saxony', *The Catholic Historical Review* 77, no. 4 (1986), p. 567.

48 Karras, 'Pagan Survivals and Syncretism', p. 566.

49 Ju. M. Lotman and B. A. Uspenskij, 'The Role of Dual Models in the Dynamics of Russian Culture (up to the end of the eighteenth century)', in Lotman and Uspenskij, *The Semiotics of Russian Culture*, ed. A. Shukman (Michigan Slavic Contributions, no. 11; Ann Arbor, MI: Ann Arbor, 1984), p. 8.

50 *Medieval Russia's Epics, Chronicles, and Tales* edited, translated and with an introduction by Serge A. Zenkovsky (New York: E. P. Dutton, 1964), p. 123.

51 Bede, *A History*, p. 128.

52 *Chronicon of Thietmar of Merseburg*, p. 364.

53 *The Laws of Rus – tenth to fifteenth centuries*, tr. and ed. Daniel H. Kaiser (Salt Lake City, UT: Charles Schlacks Jr, 1992), p. 5.

54 Kaiser, *The Laws*, pp. 15, 17.

55 Kaiser, *The Laws*, p. 20.

56 Sullivan, 'Khan Boris and the Conversion of Bulgaria', pp. 107–9.

57 *Chronicon of Thietmar of Merseburg*, p. 358.

58 *Chronicon of Thietmar of Merseburg*, p. 358.

59 Cross, *The Primary Chronicle*, p. 137.

60 See for example J. N. Hillgrath, *Christianity and Paganism, 350–750: the conversion of Western Europe* (Philadelphia: University of Pennsylvania Press, 1986), pp. 118–9; Peter Brown, *The Rise of Western Christendom: triumph and diversity, AD 200–1000* (Malden, MA and Oxford: Blackwell, 2003), pp. 330–5.

61 Sophia Senyk, *A History of the Church in Ukraine. Vol. 1: To the end of the thirteenth century* (Rome: Pontificio Istituto Orientale, 1993), p. 277.

62 See the appendix of monasteries founded between 988 and 1240 compiled by the contemporary editors of Makarii's *Istoriia russkoi tserkvi, kn. 2: Istoriia russki tserkvi v period sovershennoi zavisimosti ee ot konstantinopol'skogo patriarkha (988–1240)* (Moscow: Izd. Spaso-Preobrazhenskogo Valaamskogo monastyria, 1995), pp. 668–71.

63 Senyk's *A History of the Church in Ukraine. Vol. 1* contains an excellent survey of the Kievan Caves Monastery and monasticism in general in the early period; see also R. P. Casey, 'Early Russian Monasticism', *Orientalia Christiana Periodica* 19 (1953), 372–423.

64 S. Franklin, *Writing, Society and Culture in Early Rus, c. 950–1300* (Cambridge: CUP, 2002), pp. 123–5.

65 Michael Khordakovsky, '"Not by Word Alone": Missionary Policies and Religious Conversion in Early Modern Russia', *Comparative Studies in Society and History* 38 (1996), 267–93, especially pp. 268, 292.

66 N. Leskov, 'Na kraiu sveta', *Sobranie sochinenii* t.5 (Moscow: Gos. Izd-vo. Khudozhestvennoi Literatury, 1957), p. 460.

67 On missionary accounts about Altai neophytes' continued use of shamanism, and the development (and sometimes accommodation) of new religious beliefs and rituals, see Andrei A. Znamenski, *Shamanism and Christianity: native encounters with Russian Orthodox missions in Siberia and Alaska, 1820–1917* (Westport, CT and London: Greenwood Press, 1999), especially pp. 217–28.

68 See Khordakovsky, '"Not by Word Alone"' and Paul W. Werth, 'Orthodoxy as ascription (and beyond): religious identity on the edges of the Orthodox community, 1740–1917', in Valerie A. Kivelson and Robert H. Greene (eds), *Orthodox Russia: belief and practice under the tsars* (University Park, PA: Pennsylvania State University Press, 2003), pp. 239–51; Znamenski, *Shamanism and Christianity*, especially pp. 55–9.

69 Cross, *The Primary Chronicle*, p. 124.

70 William M. Daly suggests a more nuanced view of Clovis, following primary sources other than Gregory of Tours in his 'Clovis: How barbaric, how pagan?', *Speculum* 69, No. 3 (1994), 619–64.

71 Cusack, *The Rise of Christianity in Northern Europe*, p. 78.

72 Simon Franklin and Jonathan Shepard, *The Emergence of Rus 750–1200* (London and New York: Longman, 1996), p. 353.

73 V. G. Vlasov, 'The Christianization of the Russian Peasants', in Balzer, *Russian Traditional Culture*, pp. 18–19. Vlasov, however, based on calendar evidence, argues that most Western European peasantry did not adopt Christianity until the fifteenth century.

74 Senyk, *A History of the Church in Ukraine. Vol. 1*, p. 185.

75 Alain Dierkens, 'The Evidence of Archaeology', in Milis, *The Pagan Middle Ages*, pp. 39–64.

76 Television coverage a year after the massacre at Beslan showed Russian children pouring lemonade over the graves of their classmates – comparable behaviour is observable among the teenage friends of road accident victims in the UK; Christian parents commonly bury teddy bears in their children's graves; large 'new Russian' graves often come with integral tables and chairs for feasting alongside the dead.

77 See for example B. Filotas, *Pagan Survivals, Superstitions and Popular Cultures in Early Medieval Pastoral Literature* (Toronto: Pontifical Institute of Mediaeval Studies, 2005), especially pp. 12–18; Richard Kieckhefer, *Magic in the Middle Ages* (Cambridge: CUP, 1989; reprinted 1995); Richard Kieckhefer, 'The Specific Rationality of Medieval Magic', *The American Historical Review* 99, no. 3 (1994), 813–836; Valerie I. J. Flint, *The Rise of Magic in Early Medieval Europe* (Princeton, NJ: Princeton University Press, 1991).

78 Filotas, *Pagan Survivals, Superstitions and Popular Cultures*.

79 Peter Burke, *Popular Culture in Early Modern Europe* (London: Temple Smith, 1978; revised reprint Aldershot: Ashgate, 1996), p. 217.

80 Christophe Lebbe, 'The shadow realm between life and death', in Milis, *The Pagan Middle Ages*, pp. 65–82, especially p. 78.

81 With the exception of 'an insignificant, tiny excerpt . . . in the 1073 florilegium'; see F. J. Thomson, 'The Nature of the Reception of Christian Byzantine Culture in Russia in the Tenth to Thirteenth Centuries and its Implications for Russian Culture', *Slavica Gandensia* 5 (1978), p. 119.

82 An exception is St Gregory the Great, whose *Dialogues* were widely circulated. See Chapter 2, earlier.

83 Brown, *The Rise of Western Christendom*, p. 151.

84 See Reff, *Plagues, Priests, and Demons*.

85 *Caesarius of Arles: Life, Testament, Letters*, trans. with notes and introd. by William E. Klingshirn (Liverpool: Liverpool University Press, 1994), p. xiv.

86 *Caesarius of Arles: Life*, p. 37.
87 W. E. Klingshirn, *Caesarius of Arles: the making of a Christian community in late antique Gaul* (Cambridge: CUP, 1994), pp. 57–65.
88 *Saint Caesarius of Arles: Sermons. Vol. 1 (1–80)*, tr. Sister Mary Magdeleine Mueller, O.S.F. (Fathers of the Church vol. 31; Washington, DC: Catholic University of America Press, 1956), p. 263.
89 Klingshirn, *Caesarius of Arles: the making of a Christian community*, pp. 198–9.
90 Sermon 54: 'An admonition to those who not only pay attention to omens, but, what is worse, consult seers, soothsayers, and fortune-tellers in the manner of pagans', in *Saint Caesarius of Arles: Sermons* 1, p. 270.
91 Sermon 192: 'On the Calends of January', in *Saint Caesarius of Arles: Sermons. Vol. 3 (187–238)*, tr. Sister Mary Magdeleine Mueller, O.S.F. (Fathers of the Church vol. 66; Washington, DC: Catholic University of America Press, 1973), p. 30.
92 Brown, *The Rise of Western Christendom*, p. 161.
93 M. Azbukin, 'Ocherk literaturnoi bor'by', pp. 222–72.
94 Sermon 50: 'On seeking health of the soul rather than of body, and on avoiding soothsayers', in *Saint Caesarius of Arles: Sermons* 1, p. 254.
95 Brown, *The Rise of Western Christendom*, p. 154. See also Stephen McKenna, *Paganism and Pagan Survivals in Spain up to the Fall of the Visigothic Kingdom* (Washington, DC: Catholic University of America Press, 1938), p. 149.
96 E. K. Chambers publishes a useful appendix of Winter festival prohibitions from Tertullian to Burchard of Worms in *The Mediaeval Stage*, vol. II (Mineola, NY: Dover Publications, 1996), pp. 290–305.
97 Cited in R. A. Markus, 'From Caesarius to Boniface: Christianity and Paganism in Gaul', in Jaques Fontaine and J. N. Hillgarth (eds), *The Seventh Century: change and continuity: proceedings of a joint French and British Colloquium held at the Warburg Institute 8–9 July 1988* (London: Warburg Institute, 1992), p. 160.
98 Klingshirn, *Caesarius of Arles: the making of a Christian community*, pp. 216–18.
99 Hillgarth, *Christianity and Paganism, 350–750*, p. 108.
100 W. F. Ryan, *The Bathhouse at Midnight: an historical survey of magic and divination in Russia* (Thrupp, Stroud: Sutton Publishing, 1999), p. 47.
101 Ronald Hutton, *The Stations of the Sun: a history of the ritual year in Britain* (Oxford: OUP, 1996; reprinted 2001), chapter 30.
102 Ronald Hutton, *The Rise and Fall of Merry England: the ritual year 1400–1700* (Oxford: OUP, 1994), p. 38.
103 See also Bonnie Blackburn and Leofranc Holford-Strevens (eds), *The Oxford Book of Days* (Oxford: OUP, 2000), which suggests this is a thirteenth-century source, p. 259. Chambers has the monk of Winchelscombe as fifteenth century, with similar customs recorded in the twelfth century by Belethus. Chambers, *The Mediaeval Stage*, vol. 1, p. 126.
104 William of Auvergne, *De legibus* 1 (Paris: 1674), p. 82. I am grateful to Bernadette Filotas for this reference and translation.
105 And perhaps 'splashing' – see Chapter 1, earlier.
106 Sermon 33: 'On paying tithes: before the Nativity of St John the Baptist', in *Saint Caesarius of Arles: Sermons* 1, pp. 166–7. My thanks to Bernadette Filotas for this reference.
107 Atto of Vercelli, Sermon 13: 'On the annunciation of John the Baptist, the blessed precursor and martyr of Our Lord Jesus Christ', as cited by Filotas, *Pagan Survivals, Superstitions and Popular Cultures*, p. 176.
108 Alexander Kazhdan, 'The Peasantry', in *The Byzantines*, ed. Guglielmo Cavallo (Chicago and London: University of Chicago Press, 1992), pp. 43–73, especially p. 68.
109 Eve Levin, *Sex and Society in the World of the Orthodox Slavs, 900–1700* (Ithaca, NY and London: Cornell University Press, 1989; reprinted 1995), p. 29.

110 M. V. Korogodina, *Ispoved' v Rossii v XIV–XIX vekakh: Issledovanie i teksty* (St Petersburg: Dmitrii Bulanin, 2006), pp. 205–6; A. Almazov, *Tainaia ispoved' v Pravoslavnoi vostochnoi tserkvi, t. III: Prilozheniia* (Odessa: Tipo-litografiia Shtaba Odesskago Voennago Okruga, 1894; reprinted Moscow: Palomnik, 1995), p. 146.
111 Almazov, *Tainaia ispoved'*, t. III, p. 151. See also Levin, *Sex and Society*, p. 40, who suggests this is a fertility rite.
112 Almazov, *Tainaia ispoved'*, t. III, p. 152.
113 See Korogodina, *Ispoved' v Rossii*, pp. 211–12, 226–7, who suggests Balkan provenance for some of these questions.
114 Almazov, *Tainaia ispoved'*, t. III, p. 162; Korogodina, *Ispoved' v Rossii*, pp. 217–20.
115 Korogodina, *Ispoved' v Rossii*, pp. 213–14.
116 Almazov, *Tainaia ispoved'*, t. III, p. 167. See also Korogodina, *Ispoved' v Rossii*, p. 284 on questions about veneration of the created world.
117 Almazov, *Tainaia ispoved'*, t. III, p. 169.
118 See for example Kieckhefer, *Magic in the Middle Ages*, pp. 44–7; Flint, *The Rise of Magic*, especially p. 69; Keith Thomas, *Religion and the Decline of Magic* (London: Penguin, 1971, reprinted 1991), especially pp. 44–5.
119 Korogodina, *Ispoved' v Rossii*, p. 225.
120 Korogodina, *Ispoved' v Rossii*, p. 227.
121 *Medieval Handbooks of Penance: a translation of the principal* libri poenitentiales *and selections from related documents*, trans John T. McNeill and Helena M. Gamer (New York: Columbia University Press 1938; reprinted Octagon Books, 1965), p. 340.
122 This may mean either 'pagan' or 'kinsman', see *The Bishops' Synod (The First Synod of St Patrick): a symposium with text, translation and commentary*, ed. M. J. Faris (Liverpool: University of Liverpool, 1976) for arguments about why in this text it is likely to mean pagan, when *paganus* was the more common term in fifth- and sixth-century Europe, and for the text and translation of these examples.
123 'Kanonicheskie otvety mitropolita Ioanna II', *Russkaia istoricheskaia biblioteka VI: Pamiatniki drevne-russkogo kanonicheskogo prava, chast' 1 (Pamiatniki XI–XV v.)* (St Petersburg: Tip. Imp. Akademii Nauk, 1880), cols. 14, 15–16, 19 respectively. See also Franklin, *Writing, Society and Culture*, p. 150.
124 Filotas, *Pagan Survivals*, p. 45.
125 Yitzhak Hen, *Culture and Religion in Merovingian Gaul, A.D. 481–751* (Leiden, New York and Köln: E. J. Brill, 1995) pp. 163–4.
126 Hen, *Culture and Religion*, p. 167.
127 Aron Gurevich, *Medieval Popular Culture: problems of belief and perception*, trans. János M. Bak and Paul A. Hollingsworth (Cambridge Studies in Oral and Literate Culture, vol. 14; Cambridge: CUP, 1988), p. 37.
128 Hillgarth, *Christianity and Paganism*, p. xiii.
129 Ludo J. R. Milis, 'The Pagan Middle Ages – A Contradiction in Terms?', in Milis, *The Pagan Middle Ages*, p. 10.
130 Brown, *The Rise of Western Christendom*, p. 149.
131 Brown, *The Rise of Western Christendom*, p. 145.
132 Brown, *The Rise of Western Christendom*, p. 150.
133 R. Markus, *The End of Ancient Christianity* (Cambridge: CUP, 1990), p. 120.
134 F. R. Trombley, 'The Councils of Trullo (691–2): A Study of the Canons Relating to Paganism, Heresy, and the Invasions', *Comitatus* 9 (1978), p. 5.
135 Trombley, 'The Councils of Trullo', p. 3.
136 G. P. Fedotov, *The Russian Religious Mind. Vol. 1: Kievan Christianity, the tenth to the thirteenth centuries* (New York, Evanston and London: Harper & Row, 1960), p. 3.

137 Under 'Soviet studies' I am anachronistically including Heiki Valk, an Estonian
    historian who uses the term in his 'Christianisation in Estonia: A process of
    Dual-Faith and Syncretism', in *The Cross Goes North: processes of conversion
    in northern Europe, AD 300–1300*, ed. Martin Carver (Woodbridge, Suffolk: York
    Medieval Press, 2003), pp. 571–9. Since Tartu University was the home of Iurii
    Lotman (the founder of the Tartu school of semiotics), it is perhaps unsurprising
    that historiography of the Baltic peoples should continue to be influenced by the
    concept of *dvoeverie.*
138 Milis, 'The Pagan Middle Ages', p. 6.
139 See for example R. Martin Goodridge, '"The Ages of Faith" – Romance or Reality?',
    Sociological Review 23, no. 2 (1975), 381–96. See also Steve Bruce, 'The Pervasive
    World-View: Religion in Pre-Modern Britain' *The British Journal of Sociology* 48,
    no. 4 (1997), 667–80, for a different perspective.
140 See for example Anton Wessels, *Europe: was it ever really Christian? The inter-
    action between gospel and culture* (London: SMC Press Ltd., 1994), chapter 1,
    which addresses the call to 're-evangelize Europe'; Rodney Stark, 'Efforts
    to Christianize Europe, 400–2000', *Journal of Contemporary Religion* 16, no. 1
    (2001), 105–123.
141 John Van Engen, 'The Christian Middle Ages as an Historiographical Problem',
    American Historical Review 91, no. 3 (1986), 519–52. See also Gurevich's
    'Afterword' in *Medieval Popular Culture*, pp. 218–21.
142 Gabriel Le Bras, *Études de sociologie religieuse* (Paris: Presses Universitaires
    de France, 1955–6). See also Philip S. Gorski's 'Historicizing the Secularization
    Debate: Church, state, and society in late medieval and early modern Europe, ca.
    1300 to 1700', *American Sociological Review* 65, no. 1 (2000), 138–67, especially
    pp. 143–6 on the fall of the 'Golden Age' thesis.
143 Gabriel Le Bras, 'Déchristianisation: mot fallacieux', *Cahiers d'Histoire* 9, no. 1
    (1964), 92–7, especially, p. 93.
144 Jean Delumeau, *Catholicism between Luther and Voltaire: A new view of the
    Counter-Reformation*, trans. Jeremy Moiser (London: Burns and Oates, 1977).
145 Delumeau, *Catholicism*, p. 225.
146 Delumeau, *Catholicism*, p. 176.
147 Delumeau, *Catholicism*, p. 172.
148 Delumeau, *Catholicism*, pp. 166–7.
149 Delumeau, *Catholicism*, p. 231.
150 Thomas, *Religion and the Decline of Magic*, pp. 54–5.
151 Thomas, *Religion and the Decline of Magic*, p. 55.
152 See for example R. N. Swanson's *Religion and Devotion in Europe, c.1215–
    c. 1515* (Cambridge: CUP, 1995), p. 313.
153 Eamon Duffy, *The stripping of the altars: traditional religion in England, c.1400–
    c. 1580* (London and New Haven, CT: Yale University Press, 1992), p. 13.
154 See for example Jean-Claude Schmitt, 'Religion, Folklore and Society in the
    Medieval West', in Lester K. Little and Barbara H. Rosenwein (eds), *Debating the
    Middle Ages: issues and readings* (Oxford and Malden, MA: Blackwell Publishers,
    1998), pp. 376–87.
155 The classic argument for a spectrum of belief is made by John Van Engen, 'The
    Christian Middle Ages as an Historiographical Problem'. See also Schmitt's
    response, 'Religion, Folklore and Society in the Medieval West'.
156 Gurevich, *Medieval Popular Culture*, p. 5.
157 Gorski, 'Historicizing the Secularization Debate', p. 146.
158 See for example David Bachrach's 'Confession in the *Regnum Francorum*
    (742–900): The Sources Revisited', *The Journal of Ecclesiastical History* 54,
    no. 1 (2003), 3–22, which explores the issue of how 'Christian' the early Middle
    Ages were through a study of auricular confession among soldiers.

159 Chambers, *The Mediaeval Stage*, p. 94.
160 Chambers, *The Mediaeval Stage*, p. 98.
161 The Russian Orthodox Church has of course wrestled with the issue of what constitutes a legitimate miracle, as has the Catholic Church, and taken different approaches to the question at different times. See Eve Levin, 'False miracles and unattested dead bodies: Investigations into popular cults in early modern Russia', in James D. Tracy and Marguerite Ragnow (eds), *Religion and the early modern state: views from China, Russia and the West* (Cambridge: CUP, 2004), pp. 253–83, and P. Bushkovitch, *Religion and Society in Russia: the sixteenth and seventeenth centuries* (New York and Oxford: OUP, 1992), chapters 4 and 5.
162 Conyers Middleton, *A Letter from Rome, Shewing an Exact Conformity between Popery and Paganism: or, the religion of the present Romans to be derived entirely from that of their heathen ancestors* (2nd edition; London: W. Innys, 1729), pp. 13–4. Italics and capitalization as in the original.
163 Middleton, *A Letter from Rome*, p. 24.
164 Middleton, *A Letter from Rome*, p. 29.
165 Middleton, *A Letter from Rome*, p. 36.
166 Middleton, *A Letter from Rome*, p. 44.
167 Burke, *Popular Culture in Early Modern Europe*, pp. 209–10.
168 Erasmus, 'On praying to God', in *The Collected Works of Erasmus. Vol. 70: Spiritualia and pastoralia*, ed. John W. O'Malley (Toronto, Buffalo and London: University of Toronto Press, 1998), pp. 199–200.
169 David A. Lupher, *Romans in a New World: classical models in sixteenth-century Spanish America* (Ann Arbor, MI: University of Michigan Press, 2003), pp. 286–7.
170 Durán, *Books of the Gods*, pp. 410–11.
171 Lupher, *Romans in a New World*, pp. 274–5.
172 Lupher, *Romans in a New World*, pp. 276–7.
173 Lupher, *Romans in a New World*, pp. 280–1.
174 Polydore Vergil, *De Rerum Inventoribus*, trans. John Langley (New York: Agathynian Club, 1868), p. 149.
175 See for example Jonathan Z. Smith, *Drudgery Divine: on the comparison of early Christianities and the religions of late antiquity* (Jordan Lectures in Comparative Religion, XIV; Chicago: University of Chicago Press, 1990), especially pp. 20–5, 43–5.
176 Phillip Stubbes, *Anatomy of the Abuses in England in Shakespere's Youth. Part I*, ed. Frederick J. Furnivall (London: New Shakespere Society, 1877–9), p. 149.
177 Stubbes, *Anatomy of Abuses*, pp. 154, 168.
178 James Cracraft, *The Church Reform of Peter the Great* (London and Basingstoke: Macmillan, 1971), pp. 292–3.
179 See for example Walter Woodburn Hyde, *Greek Religion and its Survivals* (New York: Cooper Square Publishers, 1963), pp. 56–7 for similar accusations of paganism levelled at Greek Christians.
180 See for example Debra Coulter, 'Church Reform and the "White Clergy" in Seventeenth Century Russia', in Jarmo Kotilaine and Marshall Poe (eds), *Modernizing Muscovy: reform and social change in seventeenth-century Russia* (London and New York: Routledge, 2004), pp. 291–316; Georg Bernhard Michels, *At War with the Church: religious dissent in seventeenth-century Russia* (Stanford, CA: Stanford University Press, 1999); Bushkovitch, *Religion and Society in Russia*, especially pp. 54–8; Robert O Crummey, 'Ecclesiastical elites and popular belief and practice in seventeenth century Russia', in Tracy and Ragnow (eds), *Religion and the early modern state*, pp. 52–79.
181 *The Life of the Archpriest Avvakum by Himself*, trans. Jane Harrison and Hope Mirrlees (London: The Hogarth Press, 1963), pp. 47–8.
182 Michels, *At War with the Church*, p. 51.

183 Cited in Michels, *At War with the Church*, p. 153.
184 N. V. Rozhdestvenskii, 'Chelobitnaia Nizhegorodskikh' popov', v leto 7144', in *K istorii borby s tserkovnymi bezporiakami ot goloskami iazychestva i porokami v russkom bytu XVII v* (Moscow: Univ. Tip., 1902), pp. 18–31.
185 Cited in Michels, *At War with the Church*, p. 60.
186 *The canons and decrees of the sacred and oecumenical Council of Trent*, ed. and trans. J. Waterworth (London: Dolman, 1848), pp. 232–7.
187 Gregory L. Freeze, *The Russian Levites: parish clergy in the eighteenth century* (Cambridge, MA and London: Harvard University Press, 1977), p. 222.
188 Gregory L. Freeze, 'The Rechristianization of Russia: The Church and Popular Religion, 1750–1850', *Studia Slavica Finlandesia* 7 (1990), 101–36.
189 See for example the review article by Christine D. Worobec, 'Lived Orthodoxy in Imperial Russia', *Kritika: Explorations in Russian and Eurasian History* 7, no. 2 (2006), 329–50.
190 See for example Russell Zguta, 'Skomorokhi: The Russian Minstrel-Entertainers', *Slavic Review* 31, no. 2 (1972), 297–313; J. C. Roberti, 'Les elements paiens dans les ceremonies populaires Russes du XVIIe siecle: repetitivite et/ou creativite', *Slavica Gandensia* 7–8 (1980–1), 147–55.
191 'Tsarskaia gramota v Belgorod 1648 goda o ispravlenii nravov i unichtozhenii sueveriia', in *Opisanie Gosudarstvennago arkhiva starykh del*, ed. P. I. Ivanov (Moscow: Tip. S. Selivanovskago, 1850), pp. 296–9.
192 *The Spiritual Regulation of Peter the Great*, trans. and ed. Alexander V. Muller (Seattle: University of Washington Press, 1972), p. 15.
193 *The Spiritual Regulation*, pp. 13–15; *Zakonodatel'svto Petra I*, eds A. A. Preobrazhenskii and T. E. Novitskaia (Moscow: Izd. 'Iurodicheskaia literatura', 1997), pp. 547–9. See also Cracraft, *The Church Reform of Peter the Great*, especially pp. 290–3 and Lindsey Hughes, *Russia in the Age of Peter the Great* (New Haven and London: Yale University Press, 1998), pp. 348–51. Examining a local celebration involving rowan trees in 1612, Levin demonstrates the Christian nature of this apparently unorthodox act; *Dvoeverie i narodnaia religiia v istorii Rossii*, trans A. L. Toporkova and Z. N. Isidorovoi (Moscow: Indrik, 2004), pp. 149–51.
194 Eve Levin, 'Lay Religious Identity in Medieval Russia: the evidence of Novgorod birchbark documents', *General Linguistics* 35, nos. 1–4 (1997), 131–55.
195 See for example Daniel H. Kaiser, 'Quotidian Orthodoxy: domestic life in early modern Russia', in Valerie A. Kivelson and Robert H. Greene (eds), *Orthodox Russia: belief and practice under the tsars* (University Park, PA: Pennsylvania State University Press, 2003), pp. 179–92.
196 Simon Dixon, 'How holy was Holy Russia? Rediscovering Russian religion', in *Reinterpreting Russia*, eds Geoffrey Hosking and Robert Service (London: Arnold, 1999), pp. 21–39.
197 Vera Shevzov, *Russian Orthodoxy on the Eve of Revolution* (Oxford and New York: OUP, 2004), p. 8.
198 Gregory L. Freeze, 'Institutionalizing Piety: The Church and Popular Religion, 1750–1850', in Jane Burbank and David L. Ransel (eds), *Imperial Russia: new histories for the Empire* (Bloomington, IN: Indiana University Press, 1998), pp. 210–50, especially p. 215. See also the excellent regional study by Chris J. Chulos, *Converging Worlds: religion and community in peasant Russia, 1861–1917* (DeKalb, IL: Northern Illinois University Press, 2003).
199 Burke, *Popular Culture in Early Modern Europe*, p. 211.
200 Lotman and Uspenskij, 'The Role of Dual Models', p. 4.
201 Lotman and Uspenskij, 'The Role of Dual Models', p. 4.
202 Lotman and Uspenskij, 'The Role of Dual Models', p. 10. V. Ia Petrukhin, 'Drevnerusskoe dvoeverie: poniatie i fenomen', *Slavianovedenie* (1996), no. 1, 44–7.

203 See for example part I ('Destabilizing Dichotomies') of Kivelson and Greene (eds), *Orthodox Russia: belief and practice under the tsars*; Dixon, 'How holy was Holy Russia?', pp. 21–39.

204 M. Lewin, *The Making of the Soviet System: essays in the social history of interwar Russia* (New York: Methuen, 1994), p. 69.

205 See for example Brown, *The Rise of Western Christendom*, pp. 460–1.

206 Lotman and Uspenskij, 'The Role of Dual Models', p. 4.

207 Jacques Le Goff, *The Birth of Purgatory*, trans. Arthur Goldhammer (London: Scholar Press, 1984), p. 225.

208 Le Goff, *The Birth of Purgatory*, p. 227.

209 Bernard Hamilton, *Religion in the Medieval West* (second edition; London: Hodder Arnold, 2003), pp. 155–6.

210 Burke, *Popular Culture in Early Modern Europe*, p. 212.

211 Markus, *The End of Ancient Christianity*, p. 134.

212 Markus, *The End of Ancient Christianity*, p. 134.

213 Ramsay MacMullen, *Christianity and Paganism in the Fourth to Eighth Centuries* (New Haven, CT and London: Yale University Press, 1997), p. 91.

214 I Corinthians, 10:21.

215 See for example 'Conclusion: Remaking the State: The Limits of Fundamentalist Imagination', in Martin E. Marty and R. Scott Appleby, *Fundamentalisms and the State* (Chicago and London: University of Chicago, 1993).

216 V. M. Zhivov, 'Dvoeverie i osobyi kharakter russkoi kulturnoi istorii', in V. N. Toporov (ed.), *Philologia slavica: k 70-letiiu akademika N. I. Tolstogo* (Moscow: Nauka, 1993), p. 51.

217 Zhivov, 'Dvoeverie i osobyi kharakter', p. 54.

Conclusion

1 With the exception of Musin's erroneous quotation footnoted in Chapter 3.

2 G. P. Fedotov, *The Russian Religious Mind. Vol. 1: Kievan Christianity, the tenth to the thirteenth centuries* (New York, Evanston and London: Harper & Row, 1960), p. 346.

3 John Bossy, 'Some Elementary Forms of Durkheim', *Past and Present* 95 (1982), 3–18, especially pp. 17–18.

4 See for example Hildred Geertz's critique of Keith Thomas's work, 'An Anthropology of Religion and Magic, I', *Journal of Interdisciplinary History* 6, no. 1 (Summer, 1975), 71–89 (and Thomas's response in the same volume).

5 Markus' discussion of the sixteenth-century Dominican Durán's struggles to decide which local customs were acceptable and which should be uprooted among his flock in Spanish America is particularly enlightening. See R. A. Markus, *The End of Ancient Christianity* (Cambridge: CUP, 1990), pp. 1–3.

6 F. Conte, *L'héritage païen de la Russie: le paysan et son univers symbolique* (Paris: Albin Michel, 1997), p. 23.

7 I am grateful to Peter Burke for some thought-provoking comments on contemporary Brazilian religious 'pluralism' here.

Bibliography

Primary Sources

Unpublished

'Kniga sv[ia]t[a]go ap[o]s[to]la i evaggelis[ta] ivanna feloga. septiarbria.26 o zhitii, i o pre[d]stavlenii ego spisano prokhorom uch[en]ikom ego', *Sofiiskaia Biblioteka No. 1317, Velikaia Mineia Chet'ia na m. sentiabr'*, Ll.396a–415d (Archive of the State Public Library, St Petersburg).

Knigi Kirillovskoi Pechati, Izdannye v Moskve v XVI–XVII vekakh Film 281.947C685, reel No. 109 (the 'Kirillova kniga'), and No. 130 ('Kniga o Vere').

'M[esia]tsa maiia v 8 d~n' Prokhora v potrebakh samago sedmago postavlennago netiizh[e] stefanu prvomniku. Spisanii o zhitii v deanii ioanna b[og]oslovtsa i ev[an]g[a]lista'. *Fekula 16*, Ll.1r–120r (Fekula #15 in the Matejic Catalogue) (Hilandar Research Library, Ohio State University).

Paremeinik no. 4, Trinity-St Sergius Monastery (Moscow State Library Archive, Fond 304), l.71, available online at www.stsl.ru/manuscripts/book.php?manuscript=4.

'Pouchenie Feodosiia Pecherskago o kazniakh Bozhiikh "sviatyi ottsy ustavsha postnye dny"', *Paisievskii sbornik*, Kirillo-Belozerskii No. 4/1081 No. 230, Ll.95–99 (Archive of the State Public Library, St Petersburg).

'Rimskii Paterik', *Prolog GIM Sin* (*iz sobranii Mnshch.*) Fond No. 1668–1 (Archive of the State Historical Museum, Moscow).

Sermon no. 8: 'Slovo o nishcheliub'i', *GIM Sin No. 945*, Ll.92–108 (Archive of the State Historical Museum, Moscow).

Sermon no. 11: 'Slovo o makaveikh', *GIM Sin No. 945*, Ll.132–141 (Archive of the State Historical Museum, Moscow).

Sermon no. 12: 'Slov ~ nad'grobno o stem' vasil'i', *GIM Sin No. 945*, Ll.141–177 (Archive of the State Historical Museum, Moscow).

'Slovo o zhitii s[via]t[o]go ap[o]s[to]la i eva[n]g[e]lista ioanna bog[o]slova khozh[d]enie po vznesenii g[ospod]a nashego i[s]us kh[ristov]a s[via]t[o]go i ev[an]g[e]lista ioanna i uchenie i predstavlenie. spisano prokhorom uch[e]n[i]kom ego', *Sofiiskaia Biblioteka No. 1321, Velikaia Mineia Chet'ia na m. mai*, Ll.250a–270d (Archive of the State Public Library, St Petersburg).

'Ustav monastyrskii', *GIM Sin No. 330* (Archive of the State Historical Museum, Moscow).

'Zhitie i chudesa Antoniia Siiskago', RGADA, f.187, *Kollektsia rukopisnykh knig*, TsGALI, op. 1, No. 12 (transcript provided by Eve Levin).

'Zhitie i chudesa Antoniia Siiskago', *Soch. ieromonakha Iony*, 1578g, GBL f.310 (Und.) No. 284, XVIIv (Archive of the Lenin Library, Moscow).

Published

Adalbert, Archbishop of Magdeburg, 'Adalberts Fortsetzung der Chronik Reginos', in A. Bauer and R. Rau (eds), *Quellen zur Geschichte der sächsischen Kaiserzeit* (Ausgewählte Quellen zur deutschen Geschichte des Mittelalters. Bd. 8; Darmstadt: Wissenschaftliche Buchgesellschaft, 1971), pp. 185–231.

Adam von Bremen, *Adam von Bremen Hamburgische Kirchengeschichte* (Hannover and Leipzig: Hahnsche Buchhandlung, 1917; reprinted Hannover: Hahn, 1993).

Adam von Bremen, *A History of the Archbishops of Hamburg-Bremen*, tr., introd. and notes F. J. Tschan, with new introd. and bibliography by T. Reuter (Records of Western Civilization; New York: Columbia University Press, 2002).

Alexander, A. E., *Russian Folklore: an anthology in English translation* (Belmont, MA: Nordland Pub. Co., 1975).

Bede, *A History of the English Church and People*, tr. L. Sherley-Price (Harmondsworth, Middlesex: Penguin, 1955; reprinted 1964).

Beneshevich, V. N. (ed.), *Drevne-slavianskaia kormchaia XIV titulov bez tolkovanii*, t. 1, vyp. 1–3 (St Petersburg: Imperatorskoi Akademii Nauk, 1906–1907).

Beneshevich, V. N. (ed.), *Drevneslavianskaia kormchaia XIV titulov bez tolkovanii*, t. 2 (Sophia: Izd-vo Bolgarskoi Akademii Nauk, 1987).

Biblioteka literatury Drevnei Rusi, t. 1: XI–XII veka, eds D. S. Likhachev, L. A. Dmitriev, A. A. Alekseev and N. V. Ponyrko (St Petersburg: Nauka, 1997).

Biblioteka literatury Drevnei Rusi, t. 4: XII veka, eds D. S. Likhachev, L. A. Dmitriev, A. A. Alekseev and N. V. Ponyrko (St Petersburg: Nauka, 1997).

Biblioteka literatury Drevnei Rusi, t. 6: XIV – seredina XV veka, eds D. S. Likhachev, L. A. Dmitriev, A. A. Alekseev and N. V. Ponyrko (St Petersburg: Nauka, 1999).

Buslaev, F. I. (ed.), *Istoricheskaia khristomatiia: tserkovno-slavianskago i drevne-russkago iazykov* (Moscow: Universitetskoi tip., 1861).

Caesarius, of Arles, *Saint Caesarius of Arles: Sermons, vol. 1 (1–80)*, tr. Sr. M. M. Mueller (Fathers of the Church vol. 31; Washington, DC: Catholic University of America Press, 1956).

Caesarius, of Arles, *Saint Caesarius of Arles: Sermons, vol. 3 (187–238)*, tr. Sr. M. M. Mueller (Fathers of the Church vol. 66; Washington, DC: Catholic University of America Press, 1973).

Caesarius of Arles: Life, Testament, Letters, tr. with notes and introd. W. E. Klingshirn (Liverpool: Liverpool University Press, 1994).

Catalogus Codicum Astrologorum Graecorum 'Codicum Parisinorum', t. VIII, part 1 (Brussels: M. Lamertin, 1929).

The Chronicle of Novgorod: 1016–1471, trs R. Michell and N. Forbes (Camden Third Series, vol. XXV; London: Offices of the Society, 1914).

Die Chronik des Georgios Hamartolos: in altslavischer Übersetzung, Band 1, ed. V. M. Istrin (Munich: Wilhelm Fink Verlag, 1972).

Chteniia v Imperatorskom obshchestve istorii i drevnostei rossiiskikh pri Moskovskom universitet 1892g, kn. 2, cht. 2: Materialy istoriko-literaturnye pamiatniki prenii o vere, voznikshikh po delu korolevicha Val'demara i tsarevny Iriny Mikhailovny, ed. A. Golubtsov (Moscow: Universitetskaia tip., 1892).

Codex Canonum Ecclesiæ Universe: the canons of the first four general councils of the Church, and those of the early local Greek synods. In Greek, with Latin and revised English translations . . . with notes selected from Zonaras, Balsamon, Bishop Beveridge, &c., &c. by Rev. William Lambert (London: R. D. Dickinson, 1870).

Constantinescu, R. (ed. and tr.), *Nichita din Heracleea: comentarii la cele 16 cuvîntări ale lui Grigore din Nazianz – fragmente* (Bucharest: Direcţia Generală a Arhivelor Statului din Republica Socialistă România, 1977).

Costello, D. P. and Foote, I. P. (eds), *Russian Folk Literature: Skazki, Liricheskie pesni, Byliny, Istoricheskie pesni, Dukhovnye stikhi* (Oxford: Clarendon Press, 1967).

Darrouzès, J. (ed. and tr.), *Documents inédits d'ecclésiologie byzantine* (Archives de l'Orient chrétien no. 10; Paris: Institut français d'études byzantines, 1966).

Diddi, K., *Paterik Rimskii: Dialogi Grigoriia Velikogo v drevneslavianskom perevode* (Pamiatniki drevnei pis'mennosti. Issledovanie, teksty; Moscow: Indrik, 2001).

Dmitriev, L. A. and Likhachev, D. S. (eds), *Literatura Drevnei Rusi: khrestomatiia* (Moscow: Vysshaia shkola, 1990).

Dmytryshyn, B. (ed.), *Medieval Russia: a source book 900–1700* (2nd edn; Hinsdale, IL: Dryden Press, 1973).

Duichev, I. (ed.), *Kiril and Methodius: founders of Slavonic writing – a collection of sources and critical studies*, tr. S. Nikolov (Boulder, CO: East European Monographs, 1985).

Durán, F. D., *Book of the Gods and Rites and The Ancient Calendar*, ed. and tr. F. Horcasitas and D. Heyden (The Civilization of the American Indian Series, vol. 102; Norman, OK: University of Oklahoma Press, 1971).

Erasmus, 'On praying to God', in *The Collected Works of Erasmus, volume 70: Spiritualia and pastoralia*, ed. J. W. O'Malley (Toronto, Buffalo and London: University of Toronto Press, 1998), pp. 199–200.

Eremin, I. P., 'Literaturnoe nasledie Feodosiia Pecherskogo', *TODRL* 5 (1947), 159–84.

Faris, M. J. (ed.), *The Bishops' Synod (The First Synod of St Patrick): a symposium with text, translation and commentary* (ARCA Classical and Medieval Texts, Papers and Monographs 1; Liverpool: University of Liverpool, 1976).

Fletcher, G., *Of the Rus Commonwealth* (Ithaca, NY: Cornell University Press, 1966).

Franklin, S. (tr. and introd.), *Sermons and Rhetoric of Kievan Rus'* (HLEUL 5; Cambridge, MA: Harvard University Press, 1991).

Gal'kovskii, N., *Bor'ba khristianstva s ostatkami iazychestva v drevnei Rusi. T. 2: Drevne-russkiia slova i poucheniia, napravlennyia protiv ostatkov iazychestva v narode* (Moscow: A. I. Snegirev, 1913).

Geerard, M. (ed.), *Clavis Patrum Graecorum. Vol. 2: Ab Athanasio ad Chrysostomum* (Corpus Christianorum series; Turnhout: Brepols, 1974).

Georgii Monachi Chronicon, vol. II, ed. C. de Boor (Leipzig: Teubner, 1904).

Gregory, of Nazianzus, Saint, *A Panegyrick upon the Maccabees, by St Gregory Nazianzen: Of Unseasonable Diversions, by Salvian: A description of the manners of the pagan world; a consolatory discourse to the Christians of Carthage, visited by a mortality; of the advantage of patience; these three by St Cyprian*, tr. J. Collier (London: G. Strahan, 1716).

Gregory, of Nazianzus, Saint, 'Oration on the Holy Lights', in *A Select Library of Nicene and Post-Nicene Fathers of the Christian Church*, series II, vol. VII, eds P. Schaff and H. Wace, trs C. G. Browne and J. E. Swallow (Grand Rapids, MI: Wm. B. Eerdmans Publishing Company, 1894).

Gregory, of Nazianzus, Saint, *Tvoreniia izhe vo sviatykh ottsa nashego Grigoriia Bogoslova, Arkhiepiskopa Konstantinopol'skago*, t. 1 (St Petersburg: P. P. Soikina, 1912).

Gregory, of Nazianzus, Saint, *Funeral Orations by Saint Gregory Nazianzen and Saint Ambrose*, tr. L. P. McCauley et al. (Fathers of the Church vol. 22; Washington, DC: Catholic University of America Press, 1953).

Gregory, of Tours, Saint, *The History of the Franks*, tr. L. Thorpe (Harmondsworth, Middlesex: Penguin, 1977).

Gregory, of Tours, Saint, *Glory of the Confessors*, tr. and introd. R. Van Dam (Liverpool: Liverpool University Press, 1988).

Gregory, the Great, Saint, *Saint Gregory the Great: Dialogues*, tr. O. J. Zimmerman (Fathers of the Church vol. 39; New York: Fathers of the Church, Inc., 1959).

Gribble, C. E. (ed.), *Medieval Slavic Texts. Vol. 1: Old and Middle Russian texts* (Cambridge, MA: Slavica Publishers, 1973).

Die grossen Lesemenaen des Metropoliten Makarij: Uspenskij Spisok. Band 1: 1–11 Marz, ed. E. Weiher, S. O. Smidt and A. I. Skurko (Freiburg: Weiher Verlag, 1997).

Hellie, R. (tr. and ed.), *The Muscovite Law Code (Ulozhenie) of 1649. Part 1: text and translation* (Irvine, CA: Charles Schlacks Jr., 1988).

Heppell, M. (introd. and tr.), *The 'Paterik' of the Kievan Caves Monastery* (HLEUL 1; Cambridge, MA: Harvard University Press, 1989).

Herberstein, S. F. von, *Notes upon Russia: being a translation of the earliest account of that country entitled Rerum Moscoviticarum commentarii*, tr. R. H. Major, 2 vols (London: The Hakluyt Society, 1851–2; reprinted New York: Franklin, 1963).

Hollingsworth, P. (introd. and tr.), *The Hagiography of Kievan Rus'* (HLEUL 2; Cambridge, MA: Harvard University Press, 1992).

Howes, R. C. (tr. and ed.), *The Testaments of the Grand Princes of Moscow* (Ithaca, NY: Cornell University Press, 1967).

Istrin, V. M., *Knigy vremen'nyia i obraznyia Georgiia mnikha: khronika Georgiia Amartola v drevnem slavianorusskom perevode. T. 1: Tekst* (Petrograd: Izd. Otdeleniia Russkago iazyka i slovesnosti Rossiiskoi Akademii Nauk, 1920; reprinted Munich: Wilhelm Fink Verlag, 1972).

Ivanov, P. I. (ed.), 'Tsarskaia gramota v Belgorod 1648 goda o ispravlenii nravov i unichtozhenii sueveriia', in *Opisanie Gosudarstvennago arkhiva starykh del* (Moscow: Tip. S. Selivanovskago, 1850), pp. 296–9.

Izbornik Velikago kniazia Sviatoslava Iaroslavicha 1073 goda, ed. T. S. Morozov (St Petersburg, 1880; reprinted Wiesbaden: Otto Harrassowitz, 1965).

Jakobson, R. and Worth, D. S. (eds), *Sofonija's Tale of the Russian–Tatar Battle on the Kulikovo Field* (The Hague: Mouton, 1963).

John, of Damascus, Saint, *Saint John of Damascus: Writings*, tr. F. H. Chase, Jr (Fathers of the Church vol. 37; New York: Fathers of the Church, Inc., 1958).

John, of Damascus, Saint, *Des Hl. Johannes von Damaskus 'Ekthesis akribēs tēs Orthodoxou pisteōs' in der Übersetzung des Exarchen Johannes*, ed. L. Sadnik (Wiesbaden: Otto Harrassowitz, 1967).

Kaiser, D. H. (tr.), *The Laws of Rus – tenth to fifteenth centuries* (The Laws of Russia, Series 1, Medieval Russia, vol. 1; Salt Lake City, UT: C. Schlacks Jr, 1992).

Kaiser, D. H. and Marker, G. (eds), *Reinterpreting Russian History: Readings, 860–1860s* (Oxford and New York: OUP, 1994).

'Khozhdenie apostola Pavla po mukam', in N. Tikhonravov (ed.), *Pamiatniki otrechennoi russkoi literatury* (Moscow: Univer. tip., 1863).

Kostomarov, N. (ed.), *Pamiatniki starinnoi russkoi literatury, izdavaemye grafom Grigoriem Kushelevym-Bezborodko; skazaniia, legendy, povesti, skazki i pritchi*, vyp. 1 (St Petersburg: Tip. P. A. Kulisha, 1860).

Krasnorechie Drevnei Rusi: XI–XVII vv., ed. T. V. Chertoritskii (Moscow: Sov. Rossiia, 1987).

Leskov, N., 'Na kraiu sveta', in *Sobranie sochinenii*, t. 5 (Moscow: Gos. Izd-vo. Khudozhestvennoi Literatury, 1957), pp. 451–517.

The Life of the Archpriest Avvakum by Himself, tr. J. Harrison and H. Mirrlees (London: The Hogarth Press, 1963).

The Lives of the Holy Apostles, tr. I. E. Lambertsen (Buena Vista, CO: Holy Apostles Convent, 1988).

Loyn, H. R. and Percival, J. (eds), *The Reign of Charlemagne: documents on Carolingian government and administration* (Documents of Medieval History 2; London: Edward Arnold, 1975).

McNeill, J. T. and Gamer, H. M. (trs), *Medieval Handbooks of Penance: a translation of the principal* libri poenitentiales *and selections from related documents* (New York: Columbia University Press, 1938; reprinted Octagon Books Inc., 1965).

Migne, J.-P. (ed.), *Tou en hagiois patros hemon Theodorou tou Stouditou, Ta heuriskomena panta* = *Sancti Patris Nostri Theodori Studitae, Opera omnia* (Patrologiae cursus completus. Series Graeca, t. 99; Paris: Migne, 1860).

Migne, J.-P. (ed.), *Theophylaktou archiepiskopou Boulgarias, Ta heuriskomena panta* = *Theophylacti, Bulgariae archiepiscopus, Opera quae reperiri potuerunt omnia*, vol. 1 (Patrologiae cursus completus. Series Graeca, t. 123; Paris: Migne, 1864).

Migne, J.-P. (ed.), *Sancti Gregorii papae I, cognomento Magni, Opera omnia*, vol. 3 (Patrologiae cursus completus. Series Latina, t. 77; Paris: Garnier, 1896).

Migne, J.-P. (ed.), *Tou en hagiois patros hemon Gregorou tou theologou Archiepiskopou Konstantinoupoleos, Ta heuriskomena panta* = *Sancti Patris Nostri Gregorii Theologi, vulgo Nazianzeni, Archiepiscopi Constantinopolitani, Opera quae exstant omnia*, vol. 1 (Patrologiae cursus completus. Series Graeca, t. 35; Paris: Migne, 1857; reprinted Turnhout: Brepols, 1960).

Migne, J.-P. (ed.), *Chronikon syntomon ek diaphoron chronographon te kai exegeton syllegen kai syntethen hypo Georgiou Monachou tou epiklen hamartolou* = *Chronicon breve quod ex variis chronographis et expositorobus decerpsit concinnavitque Georgius Monachus cognomine Hamartolus* (Patrologiae cursus completus. Series Graeca, t. 110; Paris: Migne, 1863; reprinted Turnhout: Brepols, 1967).

Migne, J.-P. (ed.), *Photiou, Patriarchou Konstantinoupoleos, Ta heuriskomena panta* = *Photii, Constantinopolitani patriarchae, Opera omnia*, vol. 2 (Patrologiae cursus completus. Series Graeca, t. 102; Paris: Migne, 1860; reprinted Turnhout: Brepols, 1967).

Moskovskii letopisnyi svod kontsa XV veka (*PSRL* t. 25; Moscow: Akademii Nauk SSSR, 1949).

Muller, A. V. (tr. and ed.), *The Spiritual Regulation of Peter the Great* (Seattle: University of Washington Press, 1972).

Novgorodskaia pervaia letopis' starshego i mladshego izvodov (Moscow and Leningrad: Akademii Nauk SSSR, 1950).

Oelsch, R. (ed.), *Russian Folktales: Selections* (London: G. Bell, 1971).

Olearius, A., *The Travels of Olearius in Seventeenth Century Russia*, tr. and ed. S. H. Baron (Stanford: Stanford University Press, 1967).

Ottonian Germany: the chronicon of Thietmar of Merseburg, tr. D. A. Warner (Manchester Medieval Source Series; Manchester and New York: Manchester University Press, 2001).

Pamiatniki literatury Drevnei Rusi: Nachalo russkoi : XI – nachalo XII veka, eds L. A. Dmitriev and D. S. Likhachev (Moscow: Khudozhestvennaia literatura, 1978).

Pamiatniki literatury Drevnei Rusi: XII vek, eds L. A. Dmitriev and D. S. Likhachev (Moscow: Khudozhestvennaia literatura, 1980).

Pamiatniki literatury Drevnei Rusi: XIII vek, eds L. A. Dmitriev and D. S. Likhachev (Moscow: Khudozhestvennaia literatura, 1981).

Pamiatniki literatury Drevnei Rusi: XIV – seredina XV veka, eds L. A. Dmitriev and D. S. Likhachev (Moscow: Khudozhestvennaia literatura, 1981).

Pentkovskii, A. M., *Tipikon Patriarkha Aleksiia Studita v Vizantii i na Rusi* (Moscow: Izdatel'stvo Moskovskoi Patriarkhii, 2001).

Percival, H. R., *The Seven Ecumenical Councils of the Undivided Church: their canons and dogmatic decrees together with the canons of all the local synods which have received ecumenical acceptance* (Nicene and Post-Nicene Fathers of the Christian Church, Second Series, vol. 14; Oxford: James Parker and Company, 1900).

Petukhov, E. V., *Serapion Vladimirskii, russkii propovednik XIII veka* (St Petersburg: Tip. Imp. Akademii Nauk, 1888).

The Pilgrimage of the Russian Abbot Daniel in the Holy Land 1106–1107 A.D, ed. C. W. Wilson (London: Palestine Pilgrims' Text Society, 1895).

Ponomarev, A. I. (ed.), *Pamiatniki drevne-russkoi tserkovno-uchitel'noi literatury. Vyp. 2: slaviano-russkii prolog. Ch. 1: sentiabr'-dekabr'* (St Petersburg: Tip. Dobrodeeva, 1896).

Ponyrko, N. V. (ed.), *Epistoliarnoe nasledie Drevnei Rusi XI–XIII: issledovaniia, teksty, perevody* (St Petersburg: Nauka, 1992).

Pouncy, C. J. (ed. and tr.), *The 'Domostroi': rules for Russian households in the time of Ivan the Terrible* (Ithaca, NY: Cornell University Press, 1994).

The Povĕst' vremennykh lĕt: an interlinear collation and paradosis, ed. D. G. Ostrowski, associate ed. D. Birnbaum, senior consultant H. G. Lunt (HLEUL Texts, vol. 10, pts 1–3; Cambridge, MA: Harvard University Press, 2003).

Preobrazhenskii, A. A. and Novitskaia, T. E. (eds), *Zakonodatel'svto Petra I* (Moscow: Izd. 'Iurodicheskaia literatura', 1997).

Rozhdestvenskii, N. V., *K istorii bor'by s tserkovnymi bezporiadkami, otgoloskami iazychestva i porokami v russkom bytu XVII v. (Chelobitnaia nizhegorodskikh sviashchennikov 1636 goda v sviazi s pervonachal'noi deiatel'nost'iu Ivana Neronova)* (Moscow: Univ. tip., 1902).

The Rudder (Pedalion) of the metaphorical ship of the one holy catholic and apostolic church of the Orthodox Christians, or, All the sacred and divine canons . . . as embodied in the original Greek text / explained by Agapius and Nicodemus; tr. into English from the 5th ed. published in Athens 1908, tr. D. Cummings (Chicago: Orthodox Christian Educ. Soc., 1957).

The Russian Primary Chronicle: Laurentian text, trs and eds S. H. Cross and O. P. Sherbowitz-Wetzor (Cambridge, MA: Mediaeval Academy of America, 1953).

Russkaia istoricheskaia biblioteka, t. VI: Pamiatniki drevne-russkago kanonicheskago prava, chast' 1 (Pamiatniki XI–XV v.) (St Petersburg: Tip. Imp. Akademii Nauk, 1880).

Russkaia istoricheskaia khristomatiia (862–1850) s teoreticheskim ukazatelem, ed. K. Petrov (St Petersburg: Tip. Morskago ministerastva, 1866).

Sbornik otdeleniia russkago iazyka i slovesnosti, t. 65 (St Petersburg: Tip. Imperatorskoi Akademii Nauk, 1899).

The Septuagint version of the Old Testament and Apocrypha with an English translation and with various readings and critical notes (London: Samuel Bagster & Sons, 1956).

Smirnov, S. I., *Drevne-russkii dukhovnik: izsledovanie po istorii tserkovnago byta* (Moscow: Sinodal'naia tipografiia, 1914; reprinted Westmead: Gregg International Publishers, 1970).

Sreznevskii, I. I., *Svedeniia i zametki o maloizvestnykh i neizvestnykh pamiatnikakh I–XL* (St Petersburg: Tip. Imperatorskoi Akademii Nauk, 1867).

Sreznevskii, I. I., *Svedeniia i zametki o maloizvestnykh i neizvestnykh pamiatnikakh XLI–LXXX* (St Petersburg: Tip. Imperatorskoi Akademii Nauk, 1875).

Sreznevskii, I. I., *Drevnie pamiatniki russkago pis'ma i iazyka: X–XIV vekov: obshchee povremennoe obozrienie* (2nd edn; St Petersburg: Tip. Imp. Akademii Nauk, 1882).

Stoglav: issledovanie i tekst, ed. E. V. Emchenko, (Moscow: Izdatel'stvo 'Indrik', 2000).

Stubbes, P., *Anatomy of the Abuses in England in Shakspere's Youth*, Part I, ed. F. J. Furnivall (London: New Shakspere Society, 1877–9).

Theophylact, Archbishop of Ochrid and Bulgaria, *The Explanation by Blessed Theophylact, Archbishop of Ochrid and Bulgaria, of the Holy Gospel According to St Luke*, tr. Fr. C. Stade (Blessed Theophylact's Explanation of the New Testament, vol. 3; House Springs, MI: Chrysostom Press, 1997).

Thietmari Merseburgensis Episcopi Chronicon, ed. F. Kurze (Hannover: Impensis bibliopolii Hahniani, 1889).

Tikhonravov, N., 'Slova i poucheniia, napravlennyia protiv iazycheskikh verovanii i obriadov', in *Letopisi russkoi literatury i drevnostei*, t. 4, otd. 3 (Moscow: Tip. Gracheva, 1862), pp. 81–112.

Tikhon Zadonskii, Saint, Bishop of Voronezh, *Tvoreniia izhe vo sviatykh ottsa nashego Tikhona Zadonskago*, t. 1 (Moscow: Sinodal'naia Tipografiia, 1898).

Timofeev, I., *Vremennik Ivana Timofeeva*, ed. V. P. Adrianova-Peretts, tr. and commentary O. A. Derzhavina (Moscow and Leningrad: Akademii Nauk SSSR, 1951).

Veder, W. R. (introd. and tr.), *The Edificatory Prose of Kievan Rus'* (HLEUL 6; Cambridge, MA: Harvard University Press, 1994).

Velikiia Minei Chetii: sobrannyia vserossiiskim Mitropolitom Makariem: oktiabr' dni 4–18 (St Petersburg: Izd. Arkheograficheskoi Kommissii, 1874).

Velikiia Minei Chetii: sobrannyia vserossiiskim Mitropolitom Makariem: sentiabr' dni 25–30 (St Petersburg: Izd. Arkheograficheskoi Kommissii, 1883).

Vergil, P., *De Rerum Inventoribus*, tr. J. Langley (New York: Agathynian Club, 1868).

Vernadsky, G., et al. (eds), *A Source Book for Russian History from Early Times to 1917. Vol. 1: Early times to the late seventeenth century* (New Haven and London: Yale University Press, 1972).

The Vita of Constantine and the Vita of Methodius, tr. M. Kantor and R. S. White (Michigan Slavic Materials 13; Michigan: University of Michigan, 1976).

Waterworth, J. (ed. and tr.), *The canons and decrees of the sacred and oecumenical Council of Trent* (London: Dolman, 1848).

Wiener, L. (ed.), *Anthology of Russian Literature*, vol. 1 (New York and London: Putnam's Sons, 1902).

William, of Auvergne, *De legibus*, t. 1 (Paris: 1674).

Zahn, T. (ed.), *Acta Joannis unter Benutzung von C. v. Tischendorf's Nachlass* (Erlangen: Verlag von Andreas Deichert, 1880).

Zakonopravilo, ili, Nomokanon svetoga Save: ilovicki prepis 1262 godina: fototipija / priredio i priloge napisao Miodrag M. Petrovic (Gornji Milanovac: Decje novine, 1991).

Zenkovsky, S. A. (ed. and tr.), *Medieval Russia's Epics, Chronicles and Tales* (New York: Dutton, 1963).
Zhitie Antoniia Siiskogo: Tekst i slovoukazatel', ed. A. C. Gerd (St Petersburg: St Petersburg University Press, 2003).

Dictionaries and encyclopedias

Alekseev, P., *Tserkovnyi slovar'*, *ili istolkovanie rechenii slavenskikh drevnikh, takozh inoiazychnykh bez perevoda polozhennykh v sviashchennom pisanii i drugikh tserkovnykh knigakh*, chast 1 (St Petersburg: Ivan Glazunov, 1817).
Arndt, W. F and Gingrich, F. W. (trs), *A Greek-English Lexicon of the New Testament and Other Early Christian Literature* (2nd edn, revised and augmented by F. W. Gingrich and F. W. Danker from W. Bauer's German original, 5th edn, 1958; Chicago and London: University of Chicago Press, 1979).
Berezin, I. N., *Russkii entsiklopedicheskii slovar'* (St Petersburg, 1874).
Bolkhovitinov, Mitropolit Evgenii, *Slovar' istoricheskii o byvshikh v Rossii pisateliakh dukhovnogo china greko-rossiiskoi tserkvi* (St Petersburg: Ivan Glazunov, 1827; reprinted Moscow: Russkii dvor: Sviato-Troitskaia Sergieva Lavra, 1995).
Brokgauz, F. A. and Efron, I. A. (eds), *Entsiklopedicheskii slovar'* (St Petersburg: I. A. Efron, 1892).
Buck, C. D., *A Dictionary of Selected Synonyms in the Principal Indo-European Languages: a contribution to the history of ideas* (Chicago and London: University of Chicago Press, 1949).
Bulatov, D. A. (ed.), *Polnyi pravoslavnyi bogoslovskii entsiklopedicheskii slovar'* (St Petersburg: P. P. Soikina, 1913; reprinted Moscow: Vozrozhdenie, 1992).
Chalenko, O. T. (ed.), *Russko-angliiskii religioznyi slovar'* (Moscow: Nauka, 1998).
Cruden, A., *Cruden's Complete Concordance to the Old and New Testaments*, eds C. H. Irwin, A. D. Adams and S. A. Waters (London: Lutterworth Press, 1954).
Dal', V. I., *Tolkovyi slovar' zhivogo velikorusskogo iazyka* (2nd edn; St Petersburg and Moscow: Knigoprodavtsa-tipografa M. O. Vol'fa, 1880–2; reprinted Moscow: Gos. izd-vo inostrannykh i natsional'nykh slovarei, 1955).
Gil'tebrandt, P. A. (ed.), *Spravochnyi i obiasnitel'nyi slovar' k Novomu Zavetu*, t. 2 (Petrograd: Pechatnia A. M. Kotomina s tovarishchi, 1882–5; reprinted Munich: Verlag Otto Sagner, 1988).
Hatch, E. and Redpath, H. A., *A Concordance to the Septuagint and the other Greek versions of the Old Testament (including the Apocryphal books)*, vol. 1 (Graz, Austria: Akademische Druck- U. Verlagsanstalt, 1954).
Histarychny slounik belaruskai movy, vyp. 7 (Minsk: Navuka i Tekhnika, 1986).
Iuzhakov, S. N. (ed.), *Bol'shaia entsiklopediia: slovar' obshchedostupnykh sviedienii po vsiem otrasliam znaniia* (4th edn; St Petersburg: Prosvieshchenie, 1900–9).
Kazhdan, A. P. (ed.), *The Oxford Dictionary of Byzantium* (New York and Oxford: OUP, 1991).
Khristianstvo: entsiklopedicheskii slovar', t. 1–3 (Moscow: Nauch. izd-vo 'Bol'shaia rossiiskaia entsiklopediia', 1993–5).
Kniazev, E. A., *Rodnaia starina: slova terminy obrazy* (Moscow: Ostozh'e, 1996).
Kurz, J. (ed.), *Slovník jazyka staroslověnského* (Prague: Academia, 1966).
Lampe, G. W. H. (ed.), *A Patristic Greek Lexicon* (Oxford: Clarendon Press, 1961).
Liddell, H. G. and Scott, R. (eds), *A Greek-English Lexicon* (7th edn; Oxford: Clarendon Press, 1883).

Liddell, H. G. and Scott, R. (eds), *An Intermediate Greek-English Lexicon: founded upon the seventh edition of Liddell & Scott's Greek-English Lexicon* (Oxford: Clarendon Press, 1900).

Liddell, H. G. and Scott, R. (eds), *A Greek-English Lexicon*, rev. H. S. Jones and R. McKenzie, (9th edn; Oxford: Clarendon Press / New York: OUP, 1996).

Likhachev, D. S. (ed.), *Slovar' knizhnikov i knizhnosti Drevnei Rusi. Vyp. 1: XI-pervaya polovina XIV v.* (Leningrad: Nauka, 1987).

Likhachev, D. S. (ed.), *Slovar' knizhnikov i knizhnosti Drevnei Rusi. Vyp. 2: vtoraia polovina XIV–XVI v., chast' 1, A–K* (Leningrad: Nauka, 1988).

Likhachev, D. S. (ed.), *Slovar' knizhnikov i knizhnosti Drevnei Rusi. Vyp. 2: vtoraia polovina XIV–XVI v., chast' 2, L–Ia* (Leningrad: Nauka, 1989).

Miklosich, Fr. (ed.), *Lexicon Palaeoslovenico-Graeco-Latinum* (Vienna: Guilelmus Braumueller, 1862–5).

The Oxford Dictionary of the Christian Church, ed. F. L. Cross (London: OUP, 1957).

Oxford English Dictionary (2nd edn, Oxford: Clarendon Press, 1989).

Polnyj pravoslavnyj bogoslavskij enciklopedičeskij slovar' (St Petersburg: Izd-vo P. P. Soikina, 1913; reprinted London: Variorum Reprints, 1971).

Pravoslavnaia bogoslovskaia entsiklopediia ili Bogoslovskii Entsiklopedicheskii Slovar' (Petrograd: A. P. Lopukhin, 1903).

Preobrazhenskii, A. G. (ed.), *Etimologicheskii slovar' russkogo iazyka* (Moscow: Tip. G. Lissnera i D. Sovko, 1910–1949; reprinted Moscow: Gos. izd-vo inostrannykh i natsional'nykh slovarei, 1959).

Rahner, K. and Vorgrimler, H., *Theological Dictionary*, ed. C. Ernst, tr. R. Strachan (Herder & Herder, 1968).

Religii narodov sovremennoi Rossii. Slovar', ed. M. P. Mchedlov et al. (Moscow: Respublika, 1999; also 2nd edn, 2003).

Slovar' drevnerusskogo iazyka (XI–XIV vv), ed. R. I. Avanesov et al. (Moscow: Russkii Iazyk, 1988–).

Slovar' russkogo iazyka, ed. A. P. Evgen'eva (2nd edn; Moscow: Russkii Iazyk, 1984).

Slovar' russkogo iazyka XI–XVII vv, ed. S. G. Barkhudarov et al. (Moscow: Nauka, 1975–).

Slovar' russkogo iazyka XVIII veka, ed. S. G. Barkhudarov et al. (Leningrad: Nauka, 1984–).

Slovar' sovremennogo russkogo literaturnogo iazyka (Moscow and Leningrad: Akademii Nauk SSSR, 1954).

Slovnyk staroukraïns'koï movy XIV–XV st., ed. D. H. Hrynchyshyn et al. (Kiev: Naukova Dumka, 1977).

Sreznevskii, I. I., *Materialy dlia slovaria drevne-russkago iazyka po pis'mennym pamiatnikam*, 3 vols (St Petersburg: Tip. Imp. Akademii Nauk, 1893–1912; reprinted Moscow, 1958; also reprinted as *Slovar' drevnerusskogo iazyka*, Moscow: Kniga, 1989–90).

Starobulgarska literatura: entsiklopedichen rechnik, ed. D. Petkanova (Sophia: Petur Beron, 1992).

Staroslavianskii slovar' (po rukopisiam X–XI vekov), eds R. M. Tseitlin, R. Vecherka and E. Blagov (Moscow: Russkii Iazyk, 1994).

Steeves, P. D. (ed.), *The Modern Encyclopedia of Religions in Russia and Eurasia*, vol. 7 (Gulf Breeze, FL: Academic International Press, 1997).

Tvorogov, O. V. (ed.), *Literatura Drevnei Rusi: bibliograficheskii slovar'* (Moscow: Prosveshchenie: Uchebnaia literatura, 1996).

Vasmer, M., *Etimologicheskii slovar' russkogo iazyka*, tr. O. N. Trubachev, ed. B. A. Larin (Moscow: Progress, 1964; originally published Heidelberg, 1950–1958).
Wieczynski, J. L. (ed.), *The Modern Encyclopedia of Russian and Soviet History*, vols 10, 33, 37 (Gulf Breeze, FL: Academic International Press, 1979, 1983, 1984).

Secondary sources

Unpublished

Chulos, C., 'Peasant Religion in Post-Emancipation Russia: Voronezh Province 1880–1917', unpublished PhD thesis (University of Chicago, 1994).
Clay, J. E., 'Beyond Sectarianism and Dual-Faith [*Dvoeverie*]: A New Approach to Popular Religion' (unpublished paper presented at the National Convention of the American Association for the Advancement of Slavic Studies, Washington, DC, 19 October 1990).
Kollmann, J. E., 'The Moscow Stoglav (hundred chapters) Church Council of 1551', unpublished PhD thesis (University of Michigan, 1978).
Lee Anderson, J., 'Gender Role Construction, Morality and Social Norms in Early Modern Russia', unpublished PhD thesis (Ohio State University, 2001).
Sedakova, O., 'The Slavonic Mythology of Death' (unpublished conference paper given to the Neo-Formalists Conference, 25 March 1994).

Published

Abramovich, D. I. (ed.), *Opisanie rukopisei S.-Peterburgskoi dukhovnoi akademii: Sofiiskaia biblioteka, vyp. II: Chet'i Minei. Prologi. Pateriki* (St Petersburg: Tip. Imp. Akademii Nauk, 1907).
Afanas'ev, A. N., *Poeticheskiia vozzreniia slavian na prirodu*, t. 3 (Moscow: Izd. K. Soldatenkova, 1869; reprinted Moscow: Izd. Indrik, 1994).
Almazov, A. I., *Tainaia ispoved' v Pravoslavnoi vostochnoi tserkvi*, 3 vols (Odessa: Tipo-lit. Shtaba Odesskago voennago okruga, 1894; reprinted Moscow: Palomnik, 1995).
Ambroz, A. K., 'On the Symbolism of Russian Peasant Embroidery of Archaic Type', *Soviet Anthropology and Archaeology* 6, no. 2 (1967), 22–37.
Andreyev, N., 'Pagan and Christian Elements in Old Russia', *Slavic Review* 21, no. 1 (1962), 16–23.
Anichkov, E. V., 'Old Russian Pagan Cults', in *Transactions of the Third International Congress for the History of Religions*, vol. 2 (Oxford: Clarendon Press, 1908).
Anichkov, E. V., *Iazychestvo i Drevniaia Rus'* (St Petersburg: Tip. M. M. Stasiulevicha, 1914; reprinted Munich: Verlag Otto Sagner, 1995).
Arrignon, J.-P., 'La création des diocèses russes des origines au milieu du XII siècle', in *Mille ans de christianisme russe, 988–1988. Actes du colloque international de l'Université Paris-Nanterre 20–23 janvier 1988* (Paris: YMCA, 1989), pp. 27–49.
Azbukin, M., 'Ocherk literaturnoi bor'by predstavitelei khristianstva s ostatkami iazychestva v russkom narode (XI–XIV veka)', part 1: *Russkii Filologicheskii Vestnik* 28, no. 3 (1892), 133–53; part 2: *RFV* 35, no. 2 (1896), 222–72; part 3: *RFV* 37, nos. 1–2 (1897), 229–73; part 4: *RFV* 38, nos. 3–4 (1897), 322–37; part 5: *RFV* 39, nos. 1–2 (1898), 246–78.

Bachrach, D., 'Confession in the *Regnum Francorum* (742–900): The Sources Revisited', *Journal of Ecclesiastical History* 54, no. 1 (2003), 3–22.

Badone, E. (ed.), *Religious Orthodoxy and Popular Faith in European Society* (Princeton, NJ: Princeton University Press, 1990).

Barnish, S. J. B., '*Religio in stagno*: Nature, Divinity, and the Christianization of the Countryside in Late Antique Italy', *Journal of Early Christian Studies* 9, no. 3 (2001), 387–402.

Baron, S. H. and Kollman, N. S. (eds), *Religion and Culture in Early Modern Russia and Ukraine* (DeKalb, IL: Northern Illinois University Press, 1997).

Barsukov, N. P., *Istochniki russkoi agiografii* (St Petersburg: Tip. M. M. Stasiulevicha, 1882; reprinted Leipzig: Zentralantiquariat der DDR, 1970).

Bel'chenko, G. P., *Pouchenie blazhennago Feodosiia, igumena Pecherskago, o kazniakh Bozhiikh* (Odessa, 1899).

Benko, S., *The Virgin Goddess: studies in the pagan and Christian roots of Mariology* (Leiden and New York: E. J. Brill, 1993).

Bercken, W. van den, *Holy Russia and Christian Europe: East and West in the religious ideology of Russia*, tr. J. Bowden (London: SCM Press, 1999).

Bernshtam, T. A., 'Russian Folk Culture and Folk Religion', in M. M. Balzer (ed.), *Russian Traditional Culture: religion, gender and customary law* (Armonk, NY and London: M. E. Sharpe, 1992), pp. 34–47.

Biller, P., 'Words and the Medieval Notion of "Religion"', *Journal of Ecclesiastical History* 36, no. 3 (1985), 351–69.

Birnbaum, H., 'When and How was Novgorod Converted to Christianity?', *HUS* 12/13 (1988/9), 505–30.

Birnbaum, H. and Flier, M. S. (eds), *Medieval Russian Culture*, vol. 1 (California Slavic Studies 12; Berkeley, CA: University of California Press, 1984).

Blackburn, B. and Holford-Strevens, L., *The Oxford Companion to the Year: An exploration of calendar customs and time-reckoning* (Oxford and New York: OUP, 1999).

Blackburn, B. and Holford-Strevens, L., *The Oxford Book of Days* (Oxford: OUP, 2000).

Blane, A. (ed.), *Russia and Orthodoxy: essays in honour of Georges Florovsky. Vol. 2: The religious world of Russian culture* (The Hague: Mouton, 1975).

Blankoff, J., 'Survivances du Paganisme en vielle Russie', *Problèmes d'histoire du christianisme* 8 (1979), 29–44.

Blankoff, J., 'Deux survivances du Paganisme en vielle Russie: 1. Les ornaments en croissants de lune, 2. Le culte de l'ours', *Slavica Gandensia* 7–8 (1980–81), 9–25.

Boldur, A., 'Iaroslavna i russkoe dvoeverie v "Slove o polku Igoreve"', *Russkaia literatura* 7, no. 1 (1964), 84–86.

Bossy, J., 'Some Elementary Forms of Durkheim', *Past and Present* 95 (1982), 3–18.

Brandes, S., 'Conclusion: Reflections on the Study of Religious Orthodoxy and Popular Faith in Europe', in E. Badone (ed.), *Religious Orthodoxy and Popular Faith in European Society* (Princeton, New Jersey: Princeton University Press, 1990), pp. 185–200.

Brisbane, M. A. (ed.), *The Archaeology of Novgorod, Russia: Recent results from the town and its hinterland* (The Society for Medieval Archaeology, Monograph Series 13; Lincoln: Society for Medieval Archaeology, 1992).

Brown, A. D., *Popular Piety in Late Medieval England: the Diocese of Salisbury, 1250–1550* (Oxford Historical Monographs Series; Oxford: Clarendon Press, 1995).

210   *Bibliography*

Brown, P., *Authority and the Sacred: aspects of the Christianisation of the Roman world* (Cambridge: CUP, 1996).

Brown, P., *The Rise of Western Christendom: triumph and diversity, AD 200–1000* (2nd edition; Malden, MA and Oxford: Blackwell, 2003).

Bruce, S., *Religion in the Modern World: from cathedrals to cults* (Oxford: OUP, 1996).

Brumfield, W. C. and Velimirovic, M. M. (eds), *Christianity and the Arts in Russia* (Cambridge: CUP, 1991).

Buckland, T. and Wood, J. (eds), *Aspects of British Calendar Customs* (The Folklore Society Mistletoe Series 22; Sheffield: Sheffield Academic Press, 1993).

Budovnits, I. U., *Monastyri na Rusi i bor'ba s nimi krest'ian v XIV–XVI vekakh: po 'zhitiiam sviatykh'* (Moscow: Nauka, 1966).

Bulanin, D. M., *Antichnye traditsii v drevnerusskoi literature XI–XVI vv.* (Munich: Verlag Otto Sagner, 1991).

Bulanin, D. M., 'Mifologicheskie siuzhety Slov Grigoriia Bogoslova v russkoi pis'mennosti XVI veka', *Zhivaia starina* (1994), no. 4, 2–5.

Burds, J., 'A Culture of Denunciation: Peasant Labor Migration and Religious Anathematization in Rural Russia, 1860–1905', *Journal of Modern History* 68, no. 4 (December 1996), 786–818.

Burke, P., *Popular Culture in Early Modern Europe* (London: Temple Smith, 1978; revised reprint, Aldershot: Ashgate, 1996).

Burke, P., *History and Historians in the Twentieth Century* (Oxford: OUP, 2002).

Bushkovitch, P., 'V. O. Kliuchevskii as Historian of Religion and the Church', *Canadian-American Slavic Studies* 20, nos. 3–4 (1986), 357–66.

Bushkovitch, P., *Religion and Society in Russia: the sixteenth and seventeenth centuries* (New York and Oxford: OUP, 1992).

Callmer, J., 'The Archaeology of Kiev ca A.D. 500–1000. A survey', in R. Zeitler (ed.), *Les pays du nord et Byzance (Scandinavie et Byzance), Actes du colloque nordique et international de byzantinologie tenu à Upsal 20–22 avril 1979* (Acta Universitatis Upsaliensis. Figura, nova series 19; Uppsala: Almqvist & Wiksell, 1981), pp. 29–52.

Callmer, J., 'The Archaeology of Kiev to the End of the Earliest Urban Phase', *HUS* 11, nos. 3/4 (1987), 323–64.

Casey, R. P., 'Early Russian Monasticism', *Orientalia Christiana Periodica* 19 (1953), 372–423.

Chadwick, N. K., *The Beginnings of Russian History: an enquiry into sources* (Cambridge: CUP, 1946).

Chambers, E. K., *The Mediaeval Stage* (Mineola, NY: Dover Publications, 1996).

Chekin, L., 'The godless Ishmaelites: the image of the steppe in eleventh–thirteenth century Rus', *Russian History* 19, nos. 1–4 (1992), 9–28.

Chernetsov, A. V., 'Medieval Russian pictorial materials on paganism and superstitions', *Slavica Gandensia* 7–8 (1980–81), 99–112.

Chernetsov, A. V., 'Dvoeverie: mirazh ili real'nost'?', *Zhivaia starina* (1994), no. 4, 16–19.

Chertoritskii, T. V., *Krasnorechie Drevnei Rusi: XI–XVII vv.* (Moscow: Sov. Rossiia, 1987).

Chicherov, V. I., *Zimnii period russkogo zemledel'cheskogo kalendaria XVI–XIX vekov: ocherki po istorii narodnykh verovanii* (Trudy Instituta etnografii im. N. N. Miklukho-Maklaia. Novaia seriia, t. 40; Moscow: Izd-vo Akademii Nauk SSSR, 1957).

Christianity and Russia (Religious Studies in the USSR: Series 3; Moscow: 'Social Sciences Today' editorial board, 1988).

Chulos, C. J., 'Myths of the Pious or Pagan Peasant in Post-Emancipation Central Russia (Voronezh Province)', *Russian History/Histoire Russe* 22, no. 2 (1995), 181–216.

Chulos, C. J., 'The End of Cultural Survivals (*perezhitki*): Remembering and Forgetting Russian Peasant Religious Traditions', *Studia Slavica Finlandensia* 17 (2000), 190–207.

Chulos, C. J., *Converging Worlds. Religion and Community in Peasant Russia, 1861–1917* (DeKalb, IL: Northern Illinois University Press, 2003).

Colucci, M., 'The Image of Western Christianity in the Culture of Kievan Rus', *HUS* 12/13 (1988/9), 576–86.

Conte, F., 'Paganism and Christianity in Russia: "double" or "triple" faith?', in Y. Hamant (ed.), *The Christianization of Ancient Russia: a millennium: 988–1988* (Paris: UNESCO, 1992), pp. 207–15.

Conte, F., *L'héritage païen de la Russie: le paysan et son univers symbolique* (Paris: Albin Michel, 1997).

Coulter, D., 'Church Reform and the "White Clergy" in Seventeenth Century Russia', in J. Kotilaine and M. Poe (eds), *Modernizing Muscovy: reform and social change in seventeenth-century Russia* (RoutledgeCurzon Studies on the History of Russia and Eastern Europe 1; London and New York: Routledge, 2004), pp. 291–316.

Cracraft, J., *The Church Reform of Peter the Great* (London and Basingstoke: Macmillan, 1971).

Crummey, R. O., *Aristocrats and Servitors: the boyar elite in Russia, 1613–1689* (Princeton, NJ: Princeton University Press, 1983).

Crummey, R. O., 'Ecclesiastical elites and popular belief and practice in seventeenth century Russia', in James D. Tracy and Marguerite Ragnow (eds), *Religion and the early modern state: views from China, Russia and the West* (Cambridge: CUP, 2004), pp. 52–79.

Cusack, C. M., *The Rise of Christianity in Northern Europe, 300–1000* (London and New York: Cassell Religious Studies, 1999).

Daley, B. E., S. J., *Gregory of Nazianzus* (London and New York: Routledge, 2006).

Daly, W. M., 'Clovis: How barbaric, how pagan?', *Speculum* 69, no. 3 (1994), 619–64.

Darkevich, V. P., 'K voprosu o "dvoeverii" v Drevnei Rusi', in V. T. Pashuto (ed.), *Vostochnaia Evropa v drevnosti i srednevekov'e: iazychestvo, khristianstvo, tserkov'* (Moscow: RAN, 1995), pp. 11–14.

Davey, C., *Pioneer for Unity: Metrophanes Kritopoulos (1589–1639) and relations between the Orthodox, Roman Catholic and Reformed Churches* (London: British Council of Churches, 1987).

Davidson, H. R. E., *The Viking Road to Byzantium* (London: Allen and Unwin, 1976).

Davis, N. Z., 'From "Popular Religion" to Religious Cultures', in S. Ozment (ed.), *Reformation Europe: a guide to research* (St. Louis: Center for Information Research, 1982), pp. 321–42.

De Jong, M., *In Samuel's Image: child oblation in the early medieval West* (Leiden: E. J. Brill, 1996).

Delumeau, J., *Catholicism between Luther and Voltaire: a new view of the Counter-Reformation*, tr. J. Moiser (French original published 1971; London: Burns and Oates, 1977).

Dierkens, A., 'The Evidence of Archaeology', in L. J. R. Milis (ed.), *The Pagan Middle Ages*, tr. T. Guest (Woodbridge, Suffolk: Boydell Press, 1998), pp. 39–64.

Dixon, S., 'How holy was Holy Russia? Rediscovering Russian religion', in G. Hosking and R. Service (eds), *Reinterpreting Russia* (London: Arnold, 1999), pp. 21–39.

Dvornik, F., 'The Kiev State and its Relations with Western Europe', in *Transactions of the Royal Historical Society*, Fourth Series, vol. XXIX (London: Offices of the Royal Historical Society, 1947), pp. 27–46.

Dvornik, F., *The Slavs: their early history and civilization* (Boston: American Academy of Arts and Sciences, 1956).

Dvornik, F., *Byzantine Missions Among the Slavs: SS. Constantine-Cyril and Methodius* (New Brunswick, NJ: Rutgers University Press, 1970).

Ellis, J., 'Religion and Orthodoxy', in C. Kelly and D. Shepherd (eds), *Russian Cultural Studies: an introduction* (Oxford: OUP, 1998), pp. 274–96.

Fält, E., *Compounds in Contact: a study in compound words with special reference to the Old Slavonic translation of Flavius Josephus' 'Peri tou Ioudaikou polemou'* (Uppsala: Uppsala University, 1990).

Farrell, D. E., 'Shamanic elements in some early eighteenth century Russian woodcuts', *Slavic Review* 52, no. 4 (1993), 725–44.

Featherstone, J., 'Ol'ga's Visit to Constantinople', *HUS* 14, nos. 3/4 (1990), 293–312.

Fedotov, G. P., *The Russian Religious Mind (vol. 1): Kievan Christianity, the tenth to the thirteenth centuries* (New York, Evanston and London: Harper & Row, 1960).

Fedotov, G. P., *The Russian Religious Mind (vol. 2): The Middle Ages: the thirteenth to the fifteenth centuries* (Cambridge, MA: Harvard University Press, 1966).

Fennell, J., *The Crisis of Medieval Russia 1200–1304* (London and New York: Longman, 1983).

Fennell, J., *A History of the Russian Church to 1448* (London and New York: Longman, 1995).

Fennell, J. and Stokes, A., *Early Russian Literature* (London: Faber, 1974).

Fennell, J. L. I., 'The Recent Controversy in the Soviet Union over the Authenticity of the Slovo', in L. H. Legters (ed.), *Russia: essays in history and literature* (Leiden: E. J. Brill, 1972), pp. 1–17.

Filaret (Gumilievskii), Archbishop of Chernigov, *Obzor' russkoi dukhovnoi literatury: kniga pervaia i vtoraia, 862–1863* (St Petersburg: Izd. I. L. Tuzova, 1884; 3rd edition reprinted Oxford: Meeuws, 1984).

Filotas, B., *Pagan Survivals, Superstitions and Popular Cultures in Early Medieval Pastoral Literature* (Toronto: Pontifical Institute of Mediaeval Studies, 2005).

Fletcher, R., *The Conversion of Europe: from paganism to Christianity 371–1386 AD* (London: HarperCollins, 1997).

Flier, M. S., 'Sunday in Medieval Russian Culture: *Nedelja* versus *Voskresenie*', in H. Birnbaum and M. S. Flier (eds), *Medieval Russian Culture*, vol. 1 (California Slavic Studies 12; Berkeley, CA: University of California Press, 1984), pp. 105–49.

Flier, M. S. and Rowland, D. (eds), *Medieval Russian Culture*, vol. 2 (California Slavic Studies 19; Berkeley, CA: University of California Press, 1994).

Flint, V. I. J., *The Rise of Magic in Early Medieval Europe* (Princeton, NJ: Princeton University Press, 1991).

Florenskii, P. A., 'O Sueverii', *Simvol* 20 (1988), 241–67.

Florovsky, G., *Ways of Russian Theology*, tr. R. L. Nichols (Belmont, MA: Nordland Publishing Company, 1979).

Frank, S. and Steinberg, M. (eds), *Cultures in Flux: lower-class values, practices and resistance in late Imperial Russia* (Princeton: Princeton University Press, 1994).

Frankfurter, D., 'Syncretism and the Holy Man in Late Antique Egypt', *Journal of Early Christian Studies* 11, no. 3 (2003), 339–85.

Franklin, S., 'Literacy and Documentation in Early Medieval Russia', *Speculum* 60 (1985), 1–38.

Franklin, S., 'Booklearning and Bookmen in Kievan Rus': A Survey of an idea', *HUS* 12/13 (1988/9), 830–48.

Franklin, S., 'Malalas in Slavonic', in E. Jeffreys et al. (eds), *Studies in John Malalas* (Sydney: Australian Association for Byzantine Studies, 1990), 276–90.

Franklin, S., *Byzantium – Rus – Russia: studies in the translation of Christian culture* (Aldershot: Ashgate Variorum, 2002).

Franklin, S., *Writing, Society and Culture in Early Rus, c. 950–1300* (Cambridge: CUP, 2002).

Franklin, S. and Shepard, J., *The Emergence of Rus 750–1200* (London and New York: Longman, 1996).

Freeze, G. L., *The Russian Levites: parish clergy in the eighteenth century* (Cambridge, MA and London: Harvard University Press, 1977).

Freeze, G. L., *The Parish Clergy in Nineteenth Century Russia: crisis, reform, counter-reform* (Princeton, NJ: Princeton University Press, 1983).

Freeze, G. L., 'Russian Orthodoxy in Prerevolutionary Historiography: the case of V. O. Kliuchevskii', *Canadian-American Slavic Studies* 20, nos. 3–4 (1986), 399–416.

Freeze, G. L., 'The Rechristianization of Russia: The Church and Popular Religion 1750–1850', *Studia Slavica Finlandensia* 7 (1990), 101–36.

Freeze, G. L., 'Institutionalizing Piety: The Church and Popular Religion, 1750–1850', in J. Burbank and D. L. Ransel (eds), *Imperial Russia: new histories for the Empire* (Bloomington, IN: Indiana University Press, 1998), pp. 210–50.

Froianov, I. Ia., Dvornichenko, A. Iu. and Krivosheev, Iu. V., 'The Introduction of Christianity in Russia and the Pagan Traditions', in M. M. Balzer (ed.), *Russian Traditional Culture: religion, gender and customary law* (Armonk, NY and London: M. E. Sharpe, 1992), pp. 3–15.

Gal'kovskii, N., *Bor'ba khristianstva s ostatkami iazychestva v drevnei Rusi*, t. 1 (Kharkov: Eparkhial'naia tip., 1916).

Gardner, A., *Theodore of Studium: his life and times* (London: Edward Arnold, 1905).

Gasparini, E., 'Studies in Old Slavic Religion: Ubrus', *History of Religions* 2, no. 1 (1962), 112–39.

Gasparov, B. and Raevsky-Hughes, O. (eds), *Christianity and the Eastern Slavs. Vol. 1: Slavic cultures in the Middle Ages* (California Slavic Studies 16; Berkeley, CA: University of California Press, 1993).

Geertz, H., 'An Anthropology of Religion and Magic, I', *Journal of Interdisciplinary History* 6, no. 1 (Summer 1975), 71–89.

Gimbutas, M., 'Ancient Slavic Religion: a synopsis', in *To honor Roman Jakobson: essays on the occasion of his seventieth birthday, 11 October 1966*, vol. 1 (Mouton: The Hague, 1967), pp. 738–59.

Gimbutas, M., *The Slavs* (London: Thames & Hudson, 1971).

Ginzburg, C., *The night battles: witchcraft and agrarian cults in the 16th and 17th centuries* (London: Routledge, 1983).

Golubinskii, E. E., *Istoriia russkoi tserkvi*, t. 1.1 (Moscow: Lissner, 1880); t. 1.2 (Moscow: Univ. tip., 1904; 2nd edn reprinted The Hague and Paris: Mouton, 1969).

Goodridge, R. M., '"The Ages of Faith" – Romance or Reality?', *Sociological Review* 23, no. 2, (1975), 381–96.

Gorkii, A. V. and Novostruev, K. I., *Opisanie slavianskikh rukopisei Moskovskoi sinodal'noi biblioteki*, otd. I–III (Moscow: V Sinodal'noi tip., 1855–1917).

Gorski, P. S., 'Historicizing the Secularization Debate: Church, state, and society in late medieval and early modern Europe, ca. 1300 to 1700', *American Sociological Review* 65, no. 1 (2000), 138–67.

Grekov, B. D., *The Culture of Kiev Rus*, tr. P. Rose (Moscow: Foreign Languages Publishing House, 1947).

Grekov, B. D., *Kiev Rus*, tr. Y. Sdobnikov (Moscow: Foreign Languages Publishing House, 1959).

Grossman, J. D., 'Feminine Images in Old Russian Literature and Art', in *California Slavic Studies*, vol. 11 (Berkeley, CA: University of California Press, 1980), pp. 33–70.

Gurevich, A., *Medieval Popular Culture: problems of belief and perception*, tr. J. M. Bak and P. A. Hollingsworth (Cambridge Studies in Oral and Literate Culture, vol. 14; Cambridge: CUP, 1988).

Halperin, C. J., *Russia and the Golden Horde: the Mongol impact on medieval Russian history* (Bloomington, IN: Indiana University Press, 1987).

Hamant, Y. (ed.), *The Christianization of Ancient Russia: a millennium: 988–1988* (Paris: UNESCO, 1992).

Hamilton, B., *Religion in the Medieval West* (2nd edition; London: Hodder Arnold, 2003).

Haney, J. V., 'On the "Tale of Peter and Fevroniia, Wonderworkers of Murom"', *Canadian-American Slavic Studies* 13, nos. 1–2 (1979).

Haney, J. V., *Introduction to the Russian Folktale* (Armonk, NY and London: M. E. Sharpe, 1999).

Harmening, D., *Superstitio: überlieferungs- und theoriegeschic htliche Untersuchungen zur kirchlich-theologischen Aberglaubensliteratur des Mittelalters* (Berlin: E. Schmidt, 1979).

Harmening, D., 'The history of Western magic: some considerations', *Folklore* 17 (2001), 85–95.

Hebly, J. A., *Protestants in Russia*, tr. J. Pott (Belfast: Christian Journals, 1976).

Hen, Y., *Culture and Religion in Merovingian Gaul, A.D. 481–751* (Leiden, New York and Köln: E. J. Brill, 1995).

Hilton, A., *Russian Folk Art* (Bloomington, IN: Indiana University Press, 1995).

Hollingsworth, P. A., 'Holy men and the transformation of political space in medieval Rus', in J. Howard-Johnston and P. A. Hayward (eds), *The Cult of the Saints in Late Antiquity and the Middle Ages: essays on the contribution of Peter Brown* (Oxford: OUP, 1999), pp. 187–214.

Holmberg, U., *Mythology of All Races, vol. 4: Finno-Ugric Mythology*, eds J. A. MacCulloch and L. H. Gray (Boston: Marshall Jones, 1927; reprinted New York: Cooper Square, 1964).

Honigmann, E., 'Studies in Slavic Church History: the foundation of the Russian Metropolitan Church according to Greek sources', *Byzantion* 17 (1945), 128–62.

Hosking, G., *Russia: people and empire 1552–1917* (London: HarperCollins, 1997).

Hrushevsky, M., *History of Ukraine-Rus'. Vol. 1: from prehistory to the eleventh century*, tr. M. Skorupsky (Edmonton: Canadian Institute of Ukrainian Studies Press, 1997).

Hubbs, J., *Mother Russia: the feminine myth in Russian culture* (Bloomington, IN: Indiana University Press, 1993).

Hughes, L., *Russia in the Age of Peter the Great* (New Haven, CT and London: Yale University Press, 1998).

Hutton, R., *The Stations of the Sun: a history of the ritual year in Britain* (Oxford and New York: OUP, 1996).

Iakovlev, V. A., *K literaturnoi istorii drevne-russkikh sbornikov: opyt izsliedovaniia 'Izmaragda'* (Odessa: Tip. Sht. Voisk Odesskago voen. Okruga, 1893; reprinted Leipzig: Zentralantiquariat der DDR, 1974).

Ioann (Snychev), Metropolitan of Saint Petersburg and Ladoga (ed.), *Pravoslavnaia tserkov': Sovremennye eresi i sekty v Rossii* (St Petersburg: Izd. Pravoslavnaia Rus', 1995).

Ivakhnenko, E., 'Srednevekovoe dvoeverie i russkaia literaturno-filosofskaia mysl' novogo vremeni', *Rubezhi* (1996), no. 6; (1997), nos. 1–2.

Ivanits, L. J., *Russian Folk Belief* (New York and London: M. E. Sharpe, 1992).

Jakobson, R., 'Slavic Mythology', in M. Leach and J. Fried (eds), *Funk and Wagnalls Standard Dictionary of Folklore, Mythology and Legend* (New York: Funk & Wagnalls, 1949–50).

Johnson, M. A., 'Observations on the Hymnography of Certain Medieval Slavic Parimejniks', *Srpski jezik* 2, nos. 1/2 (1997), 363–76.

Kaiser, D. H., *The Growth of the Law in Medieval Russia* (Princeton, NJ: Princeton University Press, 1980).

Kaiser, D. H., 'Quotidian Orthodoxy: domestic life in early modern Russia', in V. A. Kivelson and R. H. Greene (eds), *Orthodox Russia: belief and practice under the tsars* (University Park, PA: Pennsylvania University Press, 2003), pp. 179–92.

Karras, R. M., 'Pagan Survivals and Syncretism in the Conversion of Saxony', *The Catholic Historical Review* 77, no. 4 (1986), 553–72.

Kartashev, A. V., *Ocherki po istorii russkoi tserkvi*, t. 1 (Paris: YMCA, 1959).

Keenan, E. L., *Josef Dobrovsky and the Origins of the Igor' Tale* (Cambridge, MA and London: Harvard University Press, 2004).

Kieckhefer, R., 'The Specific Rationality of Medieval Magic', *American Historical Review* 99, no. 3 (1994), 813–36.

Kieckhefer, R., *Magic in the Middle Ages* (Cambridge: CUP, 1995).

Kivelson, V. A. and Greene, R. H. (eds), *Orthodox Russia: belief and practice under the tsars* (University Park, PA: Pennsylvania University Press, 2003).

Klein, L. C., 'Pamiati iazycheskogo boga roda', in Dubov, I. V. (ed.), *Iazychestvo vostochnykh slavian: sbornik nauchnykh trudov* (Leningrad: Ministerstvo kul'tury SSSR, 1990), pp. 13–26.

Klingshirn, W. E., *Caesarius of Arles: the making of a Christian community in late antique Gaul* (Cambridge Studies in Medieval Life and Thought; Cambridge: CUP, 1994).

Kliuchevsky, V. O., *A History of Russia*, vol. 1, tr. C. J. Hogarth (London: J. M. Dent & Sons, 1911).

Kliuchevskii, V. O., *Sochineniia, t. 1: Kurs russkoi istorii*, chast 1 (Moscow: Gos. Izd. Politicheskoi Literatury, 1956).

Kliuchevsky, V. O., *A Course in Russian History: the seventeenth century*, tr. N. Duddington (Chicago: Quadrangle Books, 1968).

Koenigsberger, H. G., Mosse, G. L. and Bowler, G. Q., *Europe in the Sixteenth Century* (London: Longman, 1989).

Kollmann, J. E., 'The Stoglav Council and the Parish Priests', *Russian History* 7, nos. 1–2 (1980), 65–91.

Koncevičius, Rev. J. B., *Russia's Attitude towards Union with Rome (9th–16th centuries)* (2nd edn; Washington, DC: Catholic University of America Press, 1927).

Kondratieva, T., and Ingerflom, C.-S., '"Bez carja zemlja vdova": Syncrétisme dans le *Vremmenik* d'Ivan Timofeev', *Cahiers du Monde russe et soviétique* 34, nos. 1–2 (1993), 257–65.

Korogodina, M. V., *Ispoved' v Rossii v XIV–XIX vekakh: Issledovanie i teksty* (St Petersburg: Dmitrii Bulanin, 2006).

Kovalevsky, M., *Modern customs and ancient laws in Russia* (London: D. Nutt, 1891).

Kovaliv, P., *The Lexical Fund of the Literary Language of the Kievan Period X–XIV Centuries, vol. 1: Basic Fund* (New York: Shevchenko Scientific Society, 1962).

Kravchinsky, S. M., *The Russian Peasantry, Their Agrarian Condition, Social Life, and Religion* (New York: Harper, 1888; reprinted Westport, CT: Hyperion Press, 1977).

Kukushkin, Iu. S., Kniazevskaia, T. B., and Makarova, T. I. (eds), *Kul'tura slavian i Rus'* (Moscow: Nauka, 1998).

Kulikowski, M., *Bibliography of Slavic Mythology* (Columbus, OH: Slavica Publishers, 1989).

Lane Fox, R., *Pagans and Christians in the Mediterranean world from the second century AD to the conversion of Constantine* (Penguin: London, 1986; reprinted 1988).

Lazarev, V. N., *Old Russian murals and mosaics from the XI to the XVI century*, tr. B. Roniger (London: Phaidon, 1966).

Le Bras, G., *Études de sociologie religieuse* (Paris: Presses Universitaires de France, 1955–6).

Le Bras, G., 'Déchristianisation: mot fallacieux', *Cahiers d'Histoire* 9, no. 1 (1964), 92–7.

Le Goff, J., *The Birth of Purgatory*, tr. A. Goldhammer (London: Scholar Press, 1984).

Lea, H. C., *The History of Sacerdotal Celibacy in the Christian Church* (New York: Russell & Russell, 1957).

Lebbe, C., 'The shadow realm between life and death', in L. J. R. Milis (ed.), *The Pagan Middle Ages*, tr. T. Guest (Woodbridge, Suffolk: Boydell Press, 1998), pp. 65–82.

Levin, E., *Sex and Society in the World of the Orthodox Slavs, 900–1700* (Ithaca, NY and London: Cornell University Press, 1989).

Levin, E., 'Dvoeverie and Popular Religion', in S. K. Batalden (ed.), *Seeking God: the recovery of religious identity in Orthodox Russia, Ukraine, and Georgia* (DeKalb, IL: Northern Illinois University Press, 1993), pp. 31–52.

Levin, E., 'Lay Religious Identity in Medieval Russia: the evidence of Novgorod birch-bark documents', *General Linguistics* 35, nos. 1–4 (1997), 131–55.

Levin, E., 'Supplicatory Prayers as a Source for Popular Religious Culture in Muscovite Russia', in S. H. Baron and N. S. Kollmann (eds), *Religion and Culture in Early Modern Russia and Ukraine* (DeKalb, IL: Northern Illinois University Press, 1997), pp. 96–114.

Levin, E., 'From corpse to cult in early modern Russia', in V. A. Kivelson and R. H. Greene (eds), *Orthodox Russia: belief and practice under the tsars* (University Park, PA: Pennsylvania State University Press, 2003), pp. 81–103.

Levin, E., *Dvoeverie i narodnaia religiia v istorii Rossii*, trs A. L. Toporkova and Z. N. Isidorovoi (Moscow: Indrik, 2004).

Levinskaya, I., *The Book of Acts in Its Diaspora Setting* (Book of Acts in Its First Century Setting, 5; Grand Rapids, MI: Wm. B. Eerdmans, 1996), pp. 197–203.

Lewin, M., 'Popular Religion in Twentieth-Century Russia', in B. Eklof and S. P. Frank (eds), *The World of the Russian Peasant: post-emancipation culture and society* (Boston: Unwin Hyman, 1990), pp. 155–68.

Lewin, M., *The Making of the Soviet System: essays in the social history of interwar Russia* (New York: Methuen, 1994).

Lewis, D., 'Unbroken Pagan Traditions on the Edge of Europe', *Frontier* (2000), no. 1 (Oxford: Keston Institute), 6–7.

Likhachev, D. S., 'Narodnoe poeticheskoe tvorchestvo v gody feodal'noi razdroblennosti Rusi – do tataro-mongol'skogo nashestviia (XII–nachalo XIII v.)', in V. P. Adrianova-Peretts (ed.), *Russkoe narodnoe poeticheskoe tvorchestvo*, t. 1 (Moscow and Leningrad: Akademii Nauk SSSR, 1953), pp. 217–47.

Likhachev, D. S., 'The Type and Character of the Byzantine Influence on Old Russian Literature', *Oxford Slavonic Papers* 13 (1967), 14–32.

Likhachev, D. S., *The Great Heritage: the classical literature of Old Rus*, tr. D. Bradbury (Moscow: Progress, 1981).

Likhachev, D. S., 'Religion: Russian Orthodoxy', in N. Rzhevsky (ed.), *The Cambridge Companion to Modern Russian Culture* (Cambridge: CUP, 1998), pp. 38–56.

Lim, R., 'Converting the Un-Christianizable: the baptism of stage performers in late antiquity', in K. Mills and A. Grafton (eds), *Conversion in Late Antiquity and the Early Middle Ages: seeing and believing* (Studies in Comparative History; Rochester, NY: University of Rochester Press, 2003), pp. 84–126.

Limberis, V., *Divine Heiress: the Virgin Mary and the creation of Christian Constantinople* (London and New York: Routledge, 1994).

Litsas, F. K., 'Rousalia: the ritual worship of the dead', in A. Bharati (ed.), *The Realm of the Extra-Human: agents and audiences* (The Hague and Paris: Mouton, 1975), pp. 447–66.

Lomonosov, M. V., *Polnoe sobranie sochinenii. T. 6: Trudy po russkoi istorii, obshchestvenno-ekonomicheskim voprosam i geografii 1747–1765 gg.* (Moscow and Leningrad: Akademii Nauk SSSR, 1952).

Longworth, P., *Alexis, Tsar of All the Russias* (London: Secker, 1984).

Lotman, Ju. M., *Universe of the Mind: a semiotic theory of culture*, tr. A. Shukman (London: I. B. Tauris, 1990).

Lotman, Ju. M. and Uspenskij, B. A., 'New Aspects in the Study of Early Russian Culture', in Ju. M. Lotman and B. A. Uspenskij, *The Semiotics of Russian Culture*, ed. A. Shukman (Michigan Slavic Contributions, no. 11; Ann Arbor, MI: Ann Arbor, 1984), pp. 36–52.

Lotman, Ju. M. and Uspenskij, B. A., 'The Role of Dual Models in the Dynamics of Russian Culture (up to the end of the eighteenth century)', in Ju. M. Lotman and B. A. Uspenskij, *The Semiotics of Russian Culture*, ed. A. Shukman (Michigan Slavic Contributions, no. 11; Ann Arbor, MI: Ann Arbor, 1984), pp. 3–35.

Lotman, Ju. M., Ginzburg, L. I., Uspenskii, B. A. et al. (eds), *The Semiotics of Russian Cultural History: essays* (Ithaca, NY: Cornell University Press, 1985).

MacMullen, R., *Christianity and Paganism in the Fourth to Eighth Centuries* (New Haven, CT and London: Yale University Press, 1997).

Makarii (Bulgakov), Metropolitan, *Istoriia russkoi tserkvi* (Moscow: Izd. Spaso-Preobrazhenskogo Valaamskogo monastyria, 1995–6; originally published 1877–1889).

Makarii, Episkop Arkhangel'skii i Kholmogorskii (ed.), *Istoricheskiia svedeniia ob Antonievom Siiskom Monastyre* (Moscow: Universitetskoi Tip., 1878).

Malinin, V., *Starets Eleazarova monastyria Filofei i ego poslaniia: istoriko-literaturnoe izsledovanie* (Kiev: Tip. Kievo-Pecherskoi Uspenskoi lavry, 1901).

Mann, R., *Lances Sing: a study of the Igor tale* (Columbus, OH: Slavica Publishers, 1990).

Mansikka, V. J., *Die Religion der Ostslaven* (Folklore Fellows' Communications 43; Helsinki: Suomalainen Tiedeaktemia, 1922).

Markus, R. A., 'From Caesarius to Boniface: Christianity and Paganism in Gaul', in J. Fontaine and J. N. Hillgarth (eds), *The Seventh Century: change and continuity: proceedings of a joint French and British Colloquim held at the Warburg Institute 8–9 July 1988* (London: Warburg Institute, 1992), pp. 154–72.

Markus, R. A., *The End of Ancient Christianity* (Cambridge: CUP, 1990; paperback edition: Canto, 1998).

Markus, R. A., 'Gregory the Great's Pagans', in R. Gameson and H. Leyser (eds), *Belief and Culture in the Middle Ages: studies presented to Henry Mayr-Harting* (Oxford and New York: OUP, 2001), pp. 23–34.

Matejic, M., *Slavic Manuscripts from the Fekula Collection: a description* (Columbus, OH: Kosovo Publishing Co. / CIBAL, 1983).

Mazo, M., '"We Don't Summon Spring in the Summer": traditional music and beliefs of the contemporary Russian village', in W. C. Brumfield and M. M. Velimirovic (eds), *Christianity and the Arts in Russia* (Cambridge: CUP, 1991), pp. 73–94.

Metzger, B. M. and Coogan, M. D. (eds), *The Oxford Companion to the Bible* (New York and Oxford: OUP, 1993).

Meyendorff, J., *The Orthodox Church: its past and its role in the world today*, tr. J. Chapin (London: Darton, Longman & Todd, 1962).

Michels, G. B., *At War with the Church: religious dissent in seventeenth-century Russia* (Stanford, CA: Stanford University Press, 1999).

Middleton, C., *A Letter from Rome, Shewing an Exact Conformity between Popery and Paganism: or, The religion of the present Romans to be derived entirely from that of their heathen ancestors* (2nd edition; London: W. Innys, 1729).

Mikhailovskii, V. M., 'Shamanism in Siberia and European Russia, Being the second part of "Shamanstvo"', *Journal of the Royal Anthropological Institute of Great Britain and Ireland* 24 (1895), 126–58.

Milis, L. J. R., 'The Pagan Middle Ages – A Contradiction in Terms?', in L. J. R. Milis (ed.), *The Pagan Middle Ages*, tr. T. Guest (Woodbridge, Suffolk: Boydell Press, 1998), pp. 1–12.

Milner-Gulland, R. R., *The Russians* (Oxford and Malden, MA: Blackwell, 1997).

Murray, A., 'Missionaries and Magic in Dark-Age Europe', in L. K. Little and B. H. Rosenwein (eds), *Debating the Middle Ages: issues and readings* (Oxford and Malden, MA: Blackwell Publishers, 1998), pp. 92–104.

Musin, A. E., 'K kharakteristike russkogo srednevekovogo mirovozzreniia (Problema "dvoeveriia": metodologicheskii aspekt)', in V. A. Khrshanovskii et al. (eds), *Rekonstruktsiia drevnikh verovanii: istochniki, metod, tsel'* (St Petersburg: GMIR, 1991), pp. 205–11.

Netting, A., 'Images and Ideas in Russian Peasant Art', *Slavic Review* 35, no. 1 (1976), 48–68.

Nikol'skii, N. K., 'Materialy dlia istorii drevne-russkoi dukhovnoi pis'mennosti (I)', in *Izvestiia Otdeleniia russkago iazyka i slovesnosti*, t. 8, kn. 1 (St Petersburg: Tip. Imperatorskoi Akademii Nauk, 1903), pp. 212–21.

Nikol'skii, N. M., *Istoriia russkoi tserkvi* (3rd edn; Moscow: Izd-vo polit. lit-ry, 1983; 1st edition, 1930).

Nosova, G. A., 'Mapping of Russian Shrovetide Ritual (from materials of the nineteenth and early twentieth centuries)', *Soviet Anthropology and Archaeology* 14 (Summer–Fall 1975), 50–70.

Obolensky, D., *The Byzantine Commonwealth: Eastern Europe 500–1453* (London: Sphere, 1974).

Obolensky, D., 'Popular religion in medieval Russia', in A. Blane (ed.), *Russia and Orthodoxy: essays in honor of Georges Florovsky. Vol. 2: The religious world of Russian culture* (The Hague: Mouton, 1975), pp. 43–54.

Obolensky, D., *The Byzantine Inheritance of Eastern Europe* (London: Variorum Reprints, 1982).

Obolensky, D., 'Ol'ga's Conversion: the evidence reconsidered', *HUS* 12/13 (1988/9), 145–58.

Obolensky, D., 'Byzantium and the Slavic world', in A. E. Laiou and H. Maguire (eds), *Byzantium, a world civilization* (Washington, DC: Dumbarton Oaks, 1992), pp. 37–48.

Obolensky, D., *Byzantium and the Slavs* (Crestwood, NY: St Vladimir's Seminary Press, 1994).

Oinas, F., and Soudakoff, S. (eds and trs), *The Study of Russian Folklore* (The Hague: Mouton, 1975).

O'Neil, M. R., '*Sacerdote ovvero strione*: ecclesiastical and superstitious remedies in 16th century Italy', in S. L. Kaplan (ed.), *Understanding Popular Culture: Europe from the Middle Ages to the nineteenth century* (New Babylon Studies in the Social Sciences 40; Berlin and New York: Mouton Publishers, 1984), pp. 53–83.

Ostrovskaia, L. V., 'Khristianstvo v ponimanii russkikh krest'ian poreformennoi Sibiri (narodnyi variant pravoslaviia)', in L. M. Rusakova (ed.), *Obshchestvennyi byt i kul'tura russkogo naseleniia Sibiri: XVIII–nachalo XX v.* (Novosibirsk: Nauka, 1983), pp. 135–50.

Ostrowski, D., 'The Christianization of Rus' in Soviet Historiography: attitudes and interpretations (1920–1960)', *HUS* 11, nos. 3/4 (1987), 444–61.

Ostrowski, D., *Muscovy and the Mongols: cross-cultural influences on the steppe frontier, 1304–1589* (Cambridge: CUP, 1998).

Panchenko, A. M., 'Esteticheskie aspekty khristianizatsii Rusi', *Russkaia literatura* (1988), no. 1, 50–9.

Pascal, P., *The Religion of the Russian People*, tr. R. Williams (London and Oxford: Mowbrays, 1976).

Pavlov, A. S., *Kriticheskie opyty po istorii drevneishei greko-russkoi polemiki protiv latinian* (St Petersburg: Tip. Imp. Akademii Nauk, 1878).

Pavlov, A. S., *Mnimye sledy katolicheskogo vliiania v drevneishikh pamiatnikakh iugo-slavianskogo i russkogo tserkovnogo prava* (Moscow: Tip. A. I. Snegirevoi, 1892).

Petras, D. M., *The Typicon of the Patriarch Alexis the Studite: Novgorod-St Sophia 1136* (Cleveland, OH: Pontificium Institutum Orientale, 1991).

Petrukhin, V. Ia., 'Drevnerusskoe dvoeverie: poniatie i fenomen', *Slavianovedenie* (1996), no. 1, 44–7.

Petrukhin, V. Ia. (ed.), *Iz istorii russkoi kul'tury, t.1: Drevniaia Rus'* (Moscow: Iazyki Russkoi Kul'tury, 2000).

Picchio, R., 'The impact of ecclesiastical culture on old Russian literary techniques', in H. Birnbaum and M. S. Flier (eds), *Medieval Russian Culture*, vol. 1 (California Slavic Studies 12; Berkeley, CA: University of California Press, 1984), pp. 247–79.

Pluskowski, A. and Patrick, P. '"How do you pray to God?": Fragmentation and Variety in Early Medieval Christianity', in M. Carver (ed.), *The Cross Goes North: processes of conversion in northern Europe, AD 300–1300* (Woodbridge, Suffolk: York Medieval Press, 2003), pp. 29–57.

Podskalsky, G., 'Principal Aspects and Problems of Theology in Kievan Rus'', *HUS* 11, nos. 3/4 (1987), 270–86.

Podskalsky, G., *Khristianstvo i bogoslovskaia literatura v Kievskoi Rusi (988–1237 gg.): izdanie vtoroe, ispravlennoe i dopolnennoe dlia russkogo perevoda*, tr. A. V. Hazarenko (Subsidia Byzantinorossica, t. 1; St Petersburg: Bizantinorossika, 1996).

Popov, A., *Istoriko-literaturnyi obzor drevne-russkikh polemicheskikh sochinenii protiv latinian (XI–XV v.)* (Moscow: Tip. T. Ris, 1875; reprinted London: Variorum Reprints, 1972).

Poppe, A., *The Rise of Christian Russia* (London: Variorum Reprints, 1982).

Poppe, A., 'How the Conversion of Rus' was Understood in the Eleventh Century', *HUS* 11, nos. 3/4 (1987), 287–302.

Poppe, A., 'Two Concepts of the Conversion of Rus' in Kievan Writings', *HUS* 12/13 (1988/9), 488–504.

Porter, D., *Hallowe'en: Trick or Treat?* (Tunbridge Wells: Monarch, 1993).

Prestel, D. K., 'The Search for the Word: Echoes of the *Apophthegma* in the *Kievan Caves Patericon*', *Russian Review* 57 (1998), 568–82.

Price, R. M., 'The holy man and Christianization from the apocryphal apostles to St Stephen of Perm', in J. Howard-Johnston and P. A. Hayward (eds), *The Cult of Saints in Late Antiquity and the Middle Ages: essays on the contribution of Peter Brown* (Oxford: OUP, 1999), pp. 215–38.

Pronin, A. and Pronin, B., *Russian Folk Arts* (South Brunswick, NY and London: Barnes, 1975).

Propp, V. Ia., *Russkie agrarnye prazdniki: opyt istoriko-etnograficheskogo issledovaniia* (Leningrad: Leningradskogo universiteta, 1963).

Pushkareva, N. L., *Women in Russian history from the tenth to the twentieth century* (Armonk, NY: M. E. Sharpe, 1997).

Pypin, A. N., *Istoriia russkoi literatury*, t. 1 (St Petersburg: Tip. M. M. Stasiulevicha, 1907).

Quasten, J., *Patrology*, vols 1 and 3 (Utrecht/Antwerp: Spectrum, 1960/6).

Ralston, W. R. S., *The Songs of the Russian People, as illustrative of Slavonic mythology and Russian social life* (London: Ellis & Green, 1872).

Rapov, O. M., *Russkaia tserkov' v IX–pervoi treti XII v.: priniatie khristianstva* (2nd edn; Moscow: Russkaia Panorama, 1998).

Reff, D. T., *Plagues, Priests, and Demons: sacred narratives and the rise of Christianity in the Old World and the New* (Cambridge: CUP, 2005).

Reu, M. de, 'The Missionaries: the first contact between paganism and Christianity', in L. J. R. Milis (ed.), *The Pagan Middle Ages*, tr. T. Guest (Woodbridge, Suffolk: Boydell Press, 1998), pp. 13–37.

Riasanovsky, N. V., *A History of Russia* (5th edn; New York and Oxford: OUP, 1993; reprinted 2006).

Roberti, J. C., 'Les elements paiens dans les ceremonies populaires Russes du XVIIe siecle: repetitivite et/ou creativite', *Slavica Gandensia* 7–8 (1980–81), 147–55.

Rowell, S. C., *Lithuania Ascending: a pagan empire within east-central Europe, 1295–1345* (Cambridge: CUP, 1994).

Rowland, D., 'Towards an Understanding of the Political Ideas in Ivan Timofeyev's *Vremennik*', *Slavonic and East European Review* 62, no. 3 (1984), 371–99.

Rubin, M., 'The Middle Ages, or Getting Less Medieval with the Past', in P. Burke (ed.), *History and Historians in the Twentieth Century* (Oxford: OUP, 2002), pp. 11–36.

Ruether, R. R., *Gregory of Nazianzus: rhetor and philosopher* (Oxford: Clarendon Press, 1969).

Russell, J. C., *The Germanization of Early Medieval Christianity: a sociohistorical approach to religious transformation* (New York and Oxford: OUP, 1994).

Ryan, W. F., *The Bathhouse at Midnight: an historical survey of magic and divination in Russia* (Thrupp, Stroud: Sutton Publishing, 1999).

Ryan, W. F., 'Magic and Divination: Old Russian Sources', in B. G. Rosenthal (ed.), *The Occult in Russian and Soviet Culture* (Ithaca, NY and London: Cornell University Press, 1997), pp. 35–58.

Rybakov, B. A., 'Kalendar' IV veka iz zemli Polian', *Sovetskaia arkheologiia* (1962), no. 4, 66–89.

Rybakov, B. A., *Early Centuries of Russian History*, tr. J. Weir (Moscow: Progress Publishers, 1965).

Rybakov, B. A., 'Rusalii i bog Simargl-Pereplut', *Sovetskaia arkheologiia* (1967), no. 2, 91–116.

Rybakov, B. A., 'Paganism in Mediaeval Rus', *Social Science* 6, no. 1 (1975), 130–54.

Rybakov, B. A., *Iazychestvo drevnei Rusi* (Moscow: Nauka, 1988).

Rybakov, B. A., *Iazychestvo drevnikh slavian* (Moscow: Russkoe Slovo, 1997).

Sadnik, L., 'Ancient Slav Religion in the Light of Recent Research', *Eastern Review* 1, no. 1 (1948), 36–43.

Salzman, M. R., '"Superstitio" in the Codex Theodosianus and the persecution of pagans', *Vigiliae Christianae* 41 (1987), 172–88.

Savitsch, E. de, 'Religious Amulets of Early Russian Christendom', *Gazette des Beaux-Arts* 23 (1943), 111–6.

Schenker, A. M., *The Dawn of Slavic: an introduction to Slavic philology* (New Haven, CT and London: Yale University Press, 1995).

Schmitt, J.-C., 'Religion, Folklore and Society in the Medieval West', in L. K. Little and B. H. Rosenwein (eds), *Debating the Middle Ages: issues and readings* (Oxford and Malden, MA: Blackwell Publishers, 1998), pp. 376–87.

Scribner, R. W., 'Interpreting Religion in Early Modern Europe', *European Studies Review* 13 (1983), 89–105.

Sedov, V., 'Pagan sanctuaries and idols of the Eastern Slavs', *Slavica Gandensia* 7–8 (1980–81), 69–81.

Senyk, S., *A History of the Church in Ukraine. Vol. 1: To the end of the thirteenth century* (Orientalia Christiana Analecta, no. 243; Rome: Pontificio Istituto Orientale, 1993).

Ševčenko I., 'Religious missions seen from Byzantium', *HUS* 12/13 (1988/9), 7–27.

Ševčenko, I., *Ukraine Between East and West: essays on cultural history to the early eighteenth century* (Edmonton: Canadian Institute of Ukrainian Studies Press, 1996).

Shchapov, Ia. N., 'O sostave drevneslavianskoi kormchei efremovskoi redaktsii', in *Istochniki i istoriografiia slavianskogo srednevekov'ia: sbornik statei i materialov* (Moscow: Nauka, 1967), pp. 207–15.

Shchapov, Ia. N., *Vizantiiskoe i iuzhnoslavianskoe pravovoe nasledie na Rusi v XI–XIII vv.* (Moscow: Nauka, 1978).

Shchapov, Ia. N. (ed.), *Drevnerusskie pis'mennye istochniki X–XIII vv.* (Moscow: Krug, 1991).

Shchepkina, M. V. and Protas'eva, T. N., *Sokrovishcha drevnei pis'mennosti i staroi pechati; obzor rukopisei russkikh, slavianskikh, grecheskikh, a takzhe knig staroi pechati Gosudarstvennogo istoricheskogo muzeia*, ed. M. N. Tikhomirov (Pamiatniki kul'tury, vyp. 30; Moscow: Sovetskaia Rossiia, 1958).

Shevchenko, I., *Ideology, Letters and Culture in the Byzantine World* (London: Variorum Reprints, 1982).

Shevyrev, S. P., *Poezdka v Kirillo-Belozerskii monastyr': vakatsionnye dni professora S. Shevyreva v 1847 godu*, chast II (Moscow: Universitetskaia tipografiia, 1850).

Shevzov, V., 'Letting the people into Church: reflections on Orthodoxy and community in late Imperial Russia', in V. A. Kivelson and R. H. Greene (eds), *Orthodox Russia: belief and practice under the tsars* (University Park, PA: Pennsylvania State University Press, 2003), pp. 59–77.

Shevzov, V., *Russian Orthodoxy on the Eve of Revolution* (Oxford and New York: OUP, 2004).

Shnirelman, V. A., *Russian Neo-pagan Myths and Antisemitism* (Analysis of Current Trends in Antisemitism no. 13; Jerusalem: SICSA, 1998).

'Smes' khristianstva s iazychestvom i eresiami v drevne-russkikh narodnykh skazaniiakh o mire', in *Pravoslavnyi sobesednik*, chast 1 (Kazan: Kazanskaia Dukhovnaia Akademiia, 1861), pp. 249–83.

Smilianskaia, E. B., 'O kontsepte "sueverie" v Rossii veka Prosveshcheniia', in Zh. V. Kormina, A. A. Panchenko and S. A. Shtyrkov (eds), *Sny Bogoroditsy. Issledovaniia po antropologii religii* (St Petersburg: Evropeiskii universitete v S-Peterburg, 2006), pp. 19–31.

Smirnov, S., 'Baby bogomerzkiia', in Ia. L. Barskov (ed.), *Sbornik statei, posviashchennykh Vasiliiu Osipovichu Kliuchevskomu ego uchenikami, druz'iami i pochitateliami ko dniu tridtsatiletiia ego professorskoi dieiatel'nosti v Moskovskom Universitetie, 5 dekabria 1879 – 5 dekabria 1909 goda* (Moscow: Pechatnia S. P. Iakovleva, 1909).

Smith, G., 'Social Bases of Tradition: The Limitations and Implications of "the Search for Origins"', in *Language, Culture and Tradition: papers on language and folklore presented at the annual conference of the British Sociological Association, April 1978*, edited by A. E. Green and J. D. A. Widdowson (CECTAL Conference Papers Series, no. 2; Sheffield: Centre for English Cultural Tradition and Language, University of Sheffield, 1981), pp. 77–87.

Smith, J. Z., *Drudgery Divine: on the comparison of early Christianities and the religions of late antiquity* (Jordan Lectures in Comparative Religion, XIV; Chicago: University of Chicago Press, 1990).

Snegirev, I. M., *Ruskie prostonarodnye prazdniki i suevernye obriady*, vyp. 1 (Moscow: Univ. tip., 1837).

Sokolov, Y. M., *Russian Folklore*, tr. C. R. Smith (Detroit: Folklore Associates, 1971).

Solov'ev, S. M., *Istoriia Rossii s drevneishikh vremen* (Moscow: Izd-vo sotsial'no-ekonomicheskoi literatury, 1959–66).

Sreznevskii, I., 'Rozhenitsy u slavian i drugikh iazycheskikh narodov', in N. Kalachov (ed.), *Arkhiv istoriko-iuridicheskikh svedenii otnosiashchikhsia do rossii, kn. 2, polovina pervaia* (Moscow: Tip. A. Semen, 1855), pp. 99–121.

Stark, R., 'Efforts to Christianize Europe, 400–2000', *Journal of Contemporary Religion* 16, no. 1 (2001), 105–123.

Stavrou, T. G. (ed.), *Modern Greek Studies Yearbook*, vol. 6 (Minneapolis, MN: University of Minnesota, 1990).

Stewart, C., 'Syncretism and its synonyms. Reflections on cultural mixture', *Diacritics* 29, no. 3 (1999), 40–62.

Stewart, C. and Shaw, R. (eds), *Syncretism/anti-syncretism: the politics of religious synthesis* (London: Routledge, 1994).

Stokes, A., 'The Status of the Russian Church 988–1037', *Slavonic & East European Review* 37 (1959), 430–42.

Stoyanov, Yu., *The Hidden Tradition in Europe: the secret history of medieval Christian heresy* (London: Penguin, 1995).

Strakhov, A. B., 'Stanovlenie "dvoeveriia" na Rusi', *Cyrillomethodianum* 11 (1987), 33–44.

Sullivan, R. E., 'Khan Boris and the Conversion of Bulgaria: a case study of the impact of Christianity on a barbarian society', in *Christian Missionary Activity in the Early Middle Ages* (Aldershot: Variorum, 1994), pp. 55–139.

Svodnyi katalog slaviano-russkikh rukopisnykh knig, khraniashchikhsia v SSSR, XI–XIII vv., ed. S. O. Shmidt et al. (Moscow: Nauka, 1984).

Swanson, R. N., *Religion and Devotion in Europe, c.1215–c. 1515* (Cambridge: CUP, 1995).

Tachiaos, A.-E. N., *The Slavonic Manuscripts of Saint Panteleimon Monastery (Rossikon) on Mount Athos* (Thessaloniki: Hellenic Association for Slavic Studies / Los Angeles: Center for Russian and East European Studies, University of California, 1981).

Tachiaos, A.-E. N., 'The Greek Metropolitans of Kievan Rus': An Evaluation of Their Spiritual and Cultural Activity', in *HUS* 12/13 (1988/9), 430–45.

Tereshchenko, A. V., *Byt russkago naroda*, chast. 3–7 (St Petersburg: Tip. Ministerstva vnutrennikh diel, 1848).

Thomas, K., *Religion and the Decline of Magic: studies in popular beliefs in sixteenth- and seventeenth-century England* (London: Penguin, 1971; reprinted 1991).

Thompson, M. W., *Novgorod the Great: excavations at the medieval city directed by A. V. Artsikhovsky and B. A. Kolchin* (London: Evelyn, Adams & Mackay, 1967).

Thomson, F. J., 'The Nature of the Reception of Christian Byzantine Culture in Russia in the Tenth to Thirteenth Centuries and its Implications for Russian Culture', *Slavica Gandensia* 5 (1978), 107–39.

Thomson, F. J., 'Quotations of Patristic and Byzantine Works by Early Russian Authors as an Indication of the Cultural Level of Kievan Russia', *Slavica Gandensia* 10 (1982), 65–102.

Thomson, F. J., 'The Corpus of Slavonic Translations Available in Muscovy: The Cause of Old Russia's Intellectual Silence and a Contributory Factor to Muscovite Cultural Autarky', in B. Gasparov and O. Raevsky-Hughes (eds), *Christianity and the Eastern Slavs. Vol. 1: Slavic cultures in the Middle Ages* (California Slavic Studies 16; Berkeley, CA: University of California Press, 1993), pp. 179–214.

Thomson, F. J., 'On the Problems Involved in Translating Slavonic Texts into a Modern Language', *Byzantinoslavica* 55, no. 2 (1994), 360–75.

Thomson, F. J., *The Reception of Byzantine Culture in Mediaeval Russia* (Aldershot: Ashgate Variorum, 1999).

Tikhomirov, M. N., *The Towns of Ancient Rus*, tr. Y. Sdobnikov from 2nd Russian edn. (Moscow: Foreign Languages Publishing House, 1959).

Tolochko, P. P., *Drevniaia Rus': Ocherki sotsial'no-politicheskoi istorii* (Kiev: Nauka Dumka, 1987).

Tolochko, P. P., 'Religious Sites in Kiev During the Reign of Volodimer Sviatoslavich', *HUS* 11, nos. 3/4 (1987), 317–22.

Tolochko, P. P., 'Volodimer Svjatoslavič's Choice of Religion: Fact or Fiction?', *HUS* 12/13 (1988/9), 816–29.

Tolstoi, N. I., 'Religioznye veronvaniia drevnikh slavian', in V. K. Volkov (ed.), *Ocherki istorii kul'tury slavian* (Moscow: Indrik, 1996), pp. 145–95.

Trexler, R., 'From the Mouths of Babes: Christianization by Children in 16th Century New Spain', in J. Davis (ed.), *Religious Organization and Religious Experience* (London: Academic Press, 1982), pp. 115–35.

Trombley, F. R., 'The Councils of Trullo (691–692): A Study of the Canons Relating to Paganism, Heresy, and the Invasions', *Comitatus* 9 (1978), 1–18.

Turilov, A. A. and Chernetsov, A. V., 'K kharakteristike narodnykh verovanii vostochnykh slavian (po dannym pis'mennykh istochnikov)', in *Istoki russkoi kul'tury (arkheologiia i lingvistika)* (Moscow: Russkii Mir, 1997), pp. 99–110.

Uspenskij, B. A., 'On the Origin of Russian Obscenities', in Ju. M. Lotman and B. A. Uspenskij, *The Semiotics of Russian Culture*, ed. A. Shukman (Michigan Slavic Contributions, no. 11; Ann Arbor, MI: Ann Arbor, 1984), pp. 295–300.

Valk, H., 'Christianisation in Estonia: A process of Dual-Faith and Syncretism', in M. Carver (ed.), *The Cross Goes North: processes of conversion in northern Europe, AD 300–1300* (Woodbridge, Suffolk: York Medieval Press, 2003), pp. 571–9.

Van Engen, J., 'The Christian Middle Ages as an Historiographical Problem', *American Historical Review* 91, no. 3 (1986), 519–52.

Veder, W. R., 'Old Russia's "Intellectual Silence" Reconsidered', in M. S. Flier and D. Rowland (eds), *Medieval Russian Culture*, vol. 2 (California Slavic Studies 19; Berkeley, CA: University of California Press, 1994), pp. 18–28.

Veletskaia, N. N., *Iazycheskaia simvolika slavianskikh arkhaicheskikh ritualov* (Moscow: Nauka, 1978).

Vereshchagin, E. M., *Khristianskaia knizhnost' Drevnei Rusi* (Moscow: Nauka, 1996).

Vernadsky, G., 'The Status of the Russian Church during the first Half-Century Following Vladimir's Conversion', *Slavonic Yearbook. American Series* (1941), 294–314.

Vernadsky, G., *A History of Russia. Vol. 1: Ancient Russia* (New Haven, CT: Yale University Press, 1943).

Vernadsky, G., *A History of Russia. Vol. 2: Kievan Russia* (New Haven, CT and London: Yale University Press, 1948; paperback edition, 1976).

Vernadsky, G., *Origins of Russia* (Oxford: Clarendon Press, 1959).

Vernadsky, G., *A History of Russia. Vol. 5: The Tsardom of Moscow 1547–1682*, parts I and II (New Haven, CT: Yale University Press, 1969).

Vernadsky, G., *Russian Historiography: a history* (Belmont, MA: Nordland Publishing Company, 1978).

Vlasov, V. G., 'Russkii narodnyi kalendar'', *Sovetskaia etnografiia* (1985), no. 4, 22–36.

Vlasov, V. G., 'The Christianization of the Russian Peasants', in M. M. Balzer (ed.), *Russian Traditional Culture: religion, gender and customary law* (Armonk, NY and London: M. E. Sharpe, 1992), pp. 16–33.

Vlasova, Z. I., *Skomorokhi i fol'klor* (St Petersburg: Aleteiia, 2001).

Vlasto, A. P., *The Entry of the Slavs into Christendom: an introduction to the medieval history of the Slavs* (Cambridge: CUP, 1970).

Vodoff, V., *Naissance de la chrétienté russe: la conversion du prince Vladimir de Kiev (988) et ses conséquences (Xie–XIIIe siècles)* (Paris: Fayard, 1988).

Vostokov, A. Kh., *Opisanie russkikh i slovenskikh rukopisei Rumiantsovskago muzeuma* (St Petersburg: V Tip. Imp. Akademii Nauk, 1842).

Vucinich, W. (ed.), *The Peasant in Nineteenth Century Russia* (Stanford, CA: Stanford University Press, 1968).

Vytkovskaya, J., 'Slav Mythology', in C. Larrington (ed.), *The Feminist Companion to Mythology* (London: Pandora, 1992), pp. 102–17.

Walters, P., 'The Russian Orthodox Church and Foreign Christianity: The Legacy of the Past', in J. Witte Jr. and M. Bourdeaux (eds), *Proselytism and Orthodoxy in Russia: the new war for souls* (Maryknoll, NY: Orbis, 1999), pp. 31–50.

Ware, T., *The Orthodox Church* (London: Penguin, 1984; 2nd edn, 1993).

Warner, E., *Russian Myths* (London: British Museum Press, 2002).

Warner, M., *Alone of All Her Sex: the myth and the cult of the Virgin Mary* (London: Picador, 1985).

Werth, P. W., 'Orthodoxy as ascription (and beyond): religious identity on the edges of the Orthodox community, 1740–1917', in V. A. Kivelson and R. H. Greene (eds), *Orthodox Russia: belief and practice under the tsars* (University Park, PA: Pennsylvania University Press, 2003), pp. 239–51.

Wessels, A., *Europe: was it ever really Christian? The interaction between gospel and culture*, tr. J. Bowden (London: SMC Press, 1994).

Wigzell, F., *Reading Russian Fortunes: print culture, gender and divination in Russia from 1765* (Cambridge: CUP, 1998).

Worobec, C. D., 'Lived Orthodoxy in Imperial Russia', *Kritika: Explorations in Russian and Eurasian History* 7, no. 2 (2006), 329–50.

Yanin, V. L., 'The Archaeology of Novgorod', *Scientific American* 262, no. 2 (February 1990), 72–9.

Zabylin, M. (ed.), *Russkii narod: ego obychai, obriady, predaniia, sueveriia i poeziia* (Moscow: Izd. Knigoprodavtsa M. Berezina, 1880; reprinted Kniga Printshop, 1990).

Zelenin, D. K., *Vostochnoslavianskaia Etnografiia* (Moscow: Nauka, 1991).

Zernov, N., 'Vladimir and the Origin of the Russian Church', *Slavonic and East European Review* 28 (1949–50), 123–38 and 425–38.

Zernov, N., *The Russians and their Church* (London: SPCK, 1964).

Zguta, R., 'Skomorokhi: The Russian Minstrel-Entertainers', *Slavic Review* 31, no. 2 (1972), 297–313.

Zguta, R., 'The Pagan Priests of Early Russia: Some New Insights', *Slavic Review* 33, no. 2 (1974), 259–66.

Zguta, R., 'The Ordeal by Water (Swimming of Witches) in the East Slavic World', *Slavic Review* 36, no. 2 (1977), 220–30.

Zguta, R., *Russian Minstrels: a history of the skomorokhi* (Philadelphia: University of Pennsylvania Press, 1978).

Zhivov, V. M., 'Dvoeverie i osobyi kharakter russkoi kul'turnoi istorii', in V. N. Toporov (ed.), *Philologia slavica: k 70-letiiu akademika N. I. Tolstogo* (Moscow: Nauka, 1993), pp. 50–9.

Zimin, A. A., *Slovo o polku Igoreve* (St Petersburg: Dmitrii Bulanin, 2006).

Znamenski, A. A., *Shamanism and Christianity: native encounters with Russian Orthodox missions in Siberia and Alaska, 1820–1917* (Contributions to the Study of World History 70; Westport, CT and London: Greenwood Press, 1999).

Znamenskii, P., *Istoriia russkoi tserkvi: uchebnoe rukovodstvo* (Moscow and Paris: Krutitskoe Patriarshee Podvor'e/Bibliotheque slave de Paris, 1996).

Znayenko, M. T., *The Gods of the Ancient Slavs: Tatishchev and the beginnings of Slavic mythology* (Columbus, OH: Slavica, 1980).

Zubov, N. I., 'O periodizatsii slavianskogo iazychestva v drevnerusskikh spiskakh "Slovo sv. Grigoriia"', *Zhivaia starina* (1998), no. 1, 8–10.

Žužek, I., *Kormčaja Kniga: studies on the chief code of Russian canon law* (Orientalia Christiana Analecta, no. 168; Rome: Pont. Institutum Orientalium Studiorum, 1964).

Index

accommodation, assimilation of
paganism 24, 91, 96, 100, 107, 110,
123–4, 126–7, 144–5
Adalbert of Trier 121, 189n10
Adam of Bremen 9, 74
adultery 34, 138, 139
Aleksei Mikhailovich, Tsar 136, 149,
150–1
altar: placing objects on or under 11,
37–8
amulets 141; *see also zmeeviki*
ancestor-worship 3, 104; *Parentalia* 147;
see also dead, the
Anichkov, E. V. 19, 21, 26, 35, 91–2,
98–9, 113
animism 104, 131
Anna, Princess of Kiev 122–3
Antonii Siiskii, Saint 81–2
apocrypha 30, 89–90, 127
apostasy 7
archaeological evidence 8–9, 94, 96,
112, 113, 132, 190–1n42
Artemis 28, 32
ashes 29, 32
astrology 13, 38, 40; horoscope 28, 142;
see also zodiac
Augustine, Saint, Bishop of Hippo
133–4, 136, 140
Avvakum 149
Azbukin, M. 90–1, 128

Baal 18, 19, 20, 28
Bacchus *see* Dionysus
Balsamon 40, 135, 137
baptism: delayed 122, 162n19; forced
5, 9, 124; of houses, trees, grass 137;
as marker of identity 5–7, 131, 146;
of Olga 120–1, 189n10; rebaptism of
non-Orthodox Christians 64, 77–9;

of Rus 119–31; Saxon baptismal creed
127; of Vladimir 62, 121–4
Bartolome de Las Casas 147–8
Basil the Great, Saint 56; Feast of 39,
151; Kievan Church of 124, 127;
Sermon on Burial of 56
bathhouse 29, 30, 32, 170n83
bathing, washing *see* bathhouse, water
Bel 29
bereginy 28, 30, 32
Bible: Biblical references and themes
in sermons 18–21, 23–4, 28, 29–30,
31–2, 36, 40, 44, 102, 127, 133,
134–5, 167n16; clerics' poor
knowledge of 19–20; Corinthians
19, 20, 21, 127, 135, 156; Daniel
29–30, 36; Deuteronomy 127; Isaiah
23, 69, 169n54, 176n62; Jeremiah
22; Kings 18, 28, 128, 167n16;
Maccabees 49, 55; *Ostromir gospel*
130; Peter 36; Psalms 127; reading
as marker of Christian identity 143;
Romans 31, Slavonic translation of
48–9, 130
binary oppositions 97, 105, 118, 143,
145, 153–7, 180n148
birchbark documents 7
Blaise, Saint 96, 97
bogomils 190n36
Boris, Tsar of Bulgaria 52, 124, 125, 129
bread: -bin, -trough 31; offered in
church 31; offered to the Mother of
God 23; offered to *rozhanitsy* 23, 75;
unleavened, Eucharistic 7, 62, 64,
79–80
brides: bathwater given to husband 75;
going to water 30
Brown, P. 13, 134, 135, 141, 155
Brumalia 141–2